Alternate Assessment of Students with Disabilities in Inclusive Settings

Alternate Assessment of Students with Disabilities in Inclusive Settings

Sandra Alper
University of Northern Iowa

Diane Lea Ryndak
University of Florida

Cynthia N. Schloss
Bloomsburg University

Allyn and Bacon

Boston ▪ London ▪ Toronto ▪ Sydney ▪ Tokyo ▪ Singapore

Senior Series Editor: *Virginia Lanigan*
Vice President and Editor-in-Chief: *Paul A. Smith*
Series Editorial Assistant: *Jennifer Connors*
Senior Marketing Manager: *Brad Parkins*
Production Editor: *Christopher H. Rawlings*
Editorial-Production Service: *Omegatype Typography, Inc.*
Composition and Prepress Buyer: *Linda Cox*
Manufacturing Buyer: *Suzanne Lareau*
Cover Administrator: *Brian Gogolin*
Electronic Composition: *Omegatype Typography, Inc.*

A Pearson Education Company
160 Gould Street
Needham Heights, MA 02494

Internet: www.abacon.com

Library of Congress Cataloging-in-Publication Data

Alper, Sandra K.
Alternate assessment of students with disabilities in inclusive settings/Sandra Alper, Diane Ryndak, Cynthia Schloss.
p. cm
Includes index.
ISBN 0-205-30615-2 (alk.paper)
1. Handicapped children–Education–United States. 2. Educational tests and measurements–United States. 3. Inclusive education–United States. I. Ryndak, Diane Lea II. Schloss, Cynthia N. III. Title.

LC4031 .A58 2001
371.9'0973–dc21

00-030609

Printed in the United States of America

10 9 8 7 6 5 4 3 2 1 05 04 03 02 01 00

For Our Families:

To Seth and Cindy, for your love
To Michael Pagels, for your love and support
To Pat, Patrick, Rebecca, and Tarah, for your continued love and encouragement

CONTENTS

PREFACE

Alternate Assessment of Students With Disabilities in Inclusive Settings addresses a critical challenge faced by all teachers in inclusive settings. How do you consider the functional skill needs of students with disabilities in general education settings while providing access to the general education curriculum basic academic skills? One of the major concerns surrounding the inclusion of students with disabilities in general education settings is how to appropriately meet the IDEA 1997 mandate with its emphasis on *alternate assessments.*

The need to link functional skills with the general education curriculum within the context of inclusion is nowhere more apparent than in the area of assessment. An emerging literature addresses blending special and general education curricula for inclusive schools. This literature focuses on curriculum modification procedures for students with and without disabilities in the same instructional settings. However, textbooks in education assessment may be categorized into three basic types: (a) texts that focus on statistical concepts and norm-referenced assessment of basic cognitive and academic skills, (b) books that describe curriculum-based assessment strategies, and (c) those that describe assessing the functional skills needed in daily life by students with disabilities. This text is unique in that it addresses and, more importantly, links all three areas.

Alternate Assessment of Students With Disabilities in Inclusive Settings has several outstanding features. First, this unique text links assessment of relevant academic skills with assessment of functional skills as they are embedded in the general education curriculum. Second, each chapter includes learning objectives, key terms, and a summary review of the major concepts. These pedagogical elements result in a comprehensive, readable, and useful text. In addition, short vignettes and other practical boxed examples illustrate concepts and focus the reader's attention on key ideas. Tables and figures are used wherever appropriate. Perhaps the most unique feature of this text is the focus on assessment and its implications for general educators serving students with disabilities. Topics such as grading in the inclusive classroom, assessment and the IEP, and how to interpret test results for students with disabilities are covered. Profiles of students who vary in age and degree of disability and their sample assessments, as well as career planning forms, are also included. The text includes both subject and author indexes.

More and more states are revising teacher licensure regulations to reflect inclusion. In many states, for example, the majority of baccalaureate-level teachers are certified in both special and general education. Because of the critical shortage of educators fully certified to teach students with disabilities, large numbers of graduate students return to college to earn a special education licensure. Thus, the text is appropriate for a wide audience of both special and general education preservice and inservice educators. We have written the text for undergraduate- and graduate-level college and university courses that emphasize assessment. Students enrolled in educational and school psychology courses will also find this text useful.

Chapters 1–4 lay the technical foundation and outline basic concepts of assessment. The purpose and underlying assumptions of assessment are detailed along with particular considerations for assessment of students with disabilities in inclusive school settings. Basic statistical concepts commonly used in measurement and assessment are described and illustrated with functional applications. Standardized assessment and its use in inclusive classrooms is covered. Next, nonstandardized approaches are detailed and compared with more traditional forms of assessment. Alternate approaches to assessment (e.g., observation-based, curriculum-based, and portfolio assessment) are presented. This section of the text concludes with a chapter focusing on the unique roles and responsibilities of collaborative teams for assessment in inclusive schools.

Chapters 5–10 focus on the issues and techniques involved in the process of assessing students with disabilities in inclusive settings. First, the assessment of a student's need for special education services is addressed. Attention is given to how special services may be delivered within general education settings. Second, methods for determining what skills a particular student needs to learn are described. Both functional and general education curriculum content skills are covered. Third, assessment techniques useful during the acquisition, maintenance, and generalization of skills are covered. These chapters explain how to identify and assess relevant academic skills that are embedded in more functional tasks that students with disabilities need to perform in inclusive settings. Emphasis is placed on skills across subject areas of the general education curriculum as well as on approaches to modifying academic activities. This section concludes with a chapter that focuses on communicating information about student progress to empower students and families. Examples are drawn from practicing classroom teachers.

Chapters 11–14 allow us to give special consideration to four areas in which students with disabilities often present unique challenges for assessment. First, assessment of infants, toddlers, and young children with disabilities in inclusive settings is addressed. Emphasis is placed on assessment models and techniques based on behavioral and constructivist approaches to early childhood education. Second, assessing adolescents and young adults for the successful transition from school to adult life is described. Third, the functional analysis of challenging behaviors is detailed. Fourth, special considerations involved in the assessment of students with disabilities who have physical and health problems are addressed.

Appendixes 12.1 and 12.2 provide career planning details and a sample résumé. Appendix 5.1 includes student profiles of prereferral assessments conducted in inclusive settings. Each profile includes descriptions of the student, the area assessed, how the assessment was conducted, data collection and analysis, and recommendations.

Acknowledgments

We are indebted to a number of individuals whose assistance and support made completion of this text possible. Ray Short, recently retired as senior editor at Allyn and Bacon, provided invaluable support and insights that helped us frame this book. Virginia Lanigan, senior series editor; and Karin Huang and Jennifer Connors, series editorial assistants at Allyn and Bacon, gave us substantial assistance in the technical aspects of manuscript preparation. Katherine Coyle at Omegatype Typography, Inc. assisted us throughout the production phase of the book.

Delann Soenksen, Dan Scannell, Ryan Hartwig, and Jason Wrzeski, graduate students at the University of Northern Iowa, worked on the instructor's manual that accompanies this text. Marilyn Busch not only developed the indexes, but also typed and retyped the manuscript with expertise, patience, and good humor during our many revisions. Fred Lowrey assisted us in developing Tables 2.8, 2.9, and 3.1; and Figures 3.1 and 3.2.

We would also like to thank the reviewers of this text—Nancy Halmhuber, Eastern Michigan University; Sandy Lloyd, University of Texas at El Paso; Susan Miller, Northern Arizona University; and Beth L. Tulbert, University of Utah.

Finally, we are grateful to our contributing authors. Their outstanding work significantly shaped and enriched this project.

CHAPTER 1

Alternate Assessment of Students With Disabilities in Inclusive Settings

SANDRA ALPER
University of Northern Iowa

OBJECTIVES

After reading this chapter, you will be able to

1. Define inclusion
2. Describe practices that promote the process of inclusion
3. Describe traditional forms of assessment in special education
4. Describe reasons for the need for alternate forms of assessment for students with disabilities
5. Describe the major features of federal legislation with implications for alternate assessment

KEY TERMS

adaptive behavior (p. 6)
alternate assessment (p. 7)
authentic assessment (p. 7)
best practices (p. 2)
civil cases (p. 8)
criterion-referenced assessments (p. 4)
curriculum-based assessment (p. 7)
dual accommodations (p. 16)
due process (p. 12)
equal protection under the law (p. 9)
full inclusion (p. 2)
generalization (p. 3)
inclusion (p. 2)
portfolio assessment (p. 7)
standardized assessment (p. 3)

What Is Inclusion?

The trend toward including students with disabilities in general education classrooms has many implications for the field of assessment. Inclusion has provided much of the impetus for the search for alternate forms of assessment for students whose disabilities make traditional assessment options inappropriate. In this chapter, we define inclusion and review some of the practices that promote successful inclusion. Then we address concerns about traditional forms of assessment for students with disabilities. Finally, we provide the rationale for alternate assessment, including significant pieces of federal legislation.

Inclusion generally refers to the practice of educating students with disabilities alongside their chronological age peers in the same classrooms they would be in if they did not have disabilities (Ryndak & Alper, 1996; King-Sears, 1997). Sometimes the term **full inclusion** is used in the literature. This term has been interpreted to mean that all students with disabilities will be educated in general education settings all day, every day. Yet, as Brown and his colleagues (1991) pointed out, there is little support in the literature for the idea of educating all students with all types and degrees of disabilities only in the general education classroom. Some skill areas (e.g., vocational skills) can be learned only in the settings in which they naturally occur. Because of confusion, misconceptions, and controversy surrounding the term *full inclusion,* we will not address it in this text. Instead, we use the term *inclusion* to mean individualized education of students with disabilities in integrated settings for as much of the school day as is appropriate.

The term *integrated* is used to mean that opportunities will be provided to students with disabilities to learn functional activities and general education curriculum content as part of natural routines in general educational classes, the school building, and in the community. These opportunities for learning will be designed by a collaborative team. Members of the team include the student with disabilities and his or her family and friends, general and special education teachers, related services personnel, administrators, and paraprofessionals.

We assume that the purpose of instruction is to prepare each individual to function as independently as possible in a heterogeneous society of adults. This includes settings in which persons without disabilities live, work, engage in leisure activities and shared interests with their friends, and access the community at large. Further, we assume that skills targeted for instruction may be different for students with and without disabilities and for students with differing types and degrees of disabilities.

York, Doyle, and Kronberg (1992) argued that inclusion *is* interpreted as students with disabilities (a) attending the same schools as siblings and neighbors, (b) being in general education classrooms with chronological age-appropriate classmates, (c) having individualized and relevant learning objectives, and (d) being provided with the necessary supports and related services. According to the same authors, inclusion does *not* mean students with disabilities (a) must spend every minute of the school day in general education classes, (b) never receive small-group or individualized instruction, and (c) are in general education classes to learn only the core curriculum.

Inclusion as a Process

Ryndak and Alper (1996) pointed out that inclusion may be appropriately thought of as a process that includes certain **best practices,** or quality indicators. Inclusion typically evolves within a school building with different practices developed, modified, and refined over a period of time to meet the needs and demands of the staff and students in that particular school. While inclusion will not be implemented in exactly the same way in every school building, or even across different classrooms within the same building, there are several practices that are commonly found in inclusive schools. Williams, Fox, Thousand, and Fox (1990) identified several practices that support inclusion. These include

1. Age-appropriate placement in general education settings
2. Functional curriculum and materials
3. Instruction in natural settings in school and nonschool areas
4. Systematic data-based instruction
5. Integrated therapy in natural settings
6. Emphasis on developing social interactions and friendships between students with and without disabilities
7. Transition from school to adult life planning
8. Home-school partnerships
9. Follow-up evaluations

King-Sears (1997) described 10 practices that form a strong foundation for inclusion:

1. Heterogeneous cooperative learning groups
2. Learning strategy instruction
3. Differentiated curriculum content, level of difficulty, and performance expectations for students who vary in ability
4. Teaching students to become self-determined
5. An appropriate combination of student-centered and direct-instruction strategies
6. Curriculum-based assessment
7. Teaching for **generalization** of skills across settings
8. Collaboration
9. Proactive, preventative behavioral support methods
10. Activities that promote peer support and friendships

Assessment in the Field of Special Education

More than 80 years ago, Alfred Binet and Theodore Simon were asked by the Ministry of Education in France to develop a test that could be used to discriminate between persons with and without mental retardation. Their test was translated into English, revised in 1916 by Terman, and named the Stanford-Binet. Binet and Simon's test may be considered to have given birth to the field of formal assessment in special education. Attempts to measure a host of intellectual, personality, and emotional characteristics were popular during the 20s, 30s, 40s, and 50s, fueled primarily by the fields of psychology and psychiatry. Educators of the time were extremely interested in determining which students could or could not benefit from education.

Standardized assessment became particularly popular in the 1960s. It was during this same decade that the term *learning disabilities* was first used to describe students who (a) obtained measured levels of intelligence in the average to above-average range, (b) performed significantly below expectations in one or more of the academic areas, and (c) had no obvious visual, hearing, or physical impairment that would explain their low academic achievement. Great emphasis was placed on trying to explain learning disabilities from a medical or neurological model because these students were presumed to have some type of minimal brain damage. New tests were developed that went far beyond the measurement of intelligence, personality, and achievement. Efforts instead focused on measuring underlying psychological constructs or processes that were thought to explain the school difficulties experienced by students labeled as learning disabled. A great deal of emphasis was placed on how these students processed information and how their information processing abilities differed from students without learning disabilities.

Perceptual-motor theorists were very influential throughout the 60s. These theorists argued that the development of perceptual-motor skills, such as auditory and visual perception, were absolutely essential for acquisition of academic skills, such as reading and mathematics. The Illinois Test of Psycholinguistic Abilities (Kirk, McCarthy, & Kirk, 1968) and the Developmental Test of Visual Perception (Frostig, Lefever, & Whittlesey, 1966) are examples of two tests of perceptual-motor abilities that were very popular at the time.

Taylor (1997) explained how the great importance placed on perceptual-motor skills led to three movements in special education. First, perceptual-motor tests were used to predict academic achievement. Second, these tests were used to determine the modality preferences of children, or whether they were auditory or visual learners. Third, perceptual-motor remedial programs were developed. They were based on the assumption that improvements in a student's perceptual-motor skills would bring about improvement in academic skills such as reading and math. Taylor (1997) discusses each of these trends in detail. Research conducted throughout the 70s (e.g., Larsen & Hammil, 1975; Arter & Jenkins, 1977) yielded very little empirical support for any of these three trends.

Two important trends emerged during the 1970s that resulted in significant concerns about the use of standardized testing. First, the civil rights movement influenced special education. Educators argued that persons with disabilities, especially those from nonwhite, nonmiddle-class backgrounds, had been victims of discrimination. Data were published (cf. Mercer, 1973) revealing that special education classes for students labeled as mildly retarded were disproportionately comprised of poor, nonwhite children from cultural minority groups. Children who came from homes in which standard English was not the primary language were thought to have been erroneously diagnosed as mentally retarded and placed in self-contained special education classes. Charges of racial segregation and discriminatory testing were hurled. Standardized testing was cast in a negative light, and in some cases, legally halted (cf. *Larry P. v. Riles,* 1971).

A second major trend that occurred during the 70s was that the behavioral model, based largely on the early work of B. F. Skinner, had gained a strong foothold in U.S. education and particularly in the field of special education. Emphasis was placed on observable, directly measurable, and present behavior within this model. **Criterion-referenced assessments,** in which a child's performance was directly observed and compared only to his or her previous performance, rather than to some normative group, became more popular. Standardized test data on which only inferences about future behavior could be made were deemphasized.

The 1980s saw a call for the end of segregating students with disabilities, promotion of the mainstreaming movement, questioning of the validity of disability categories, and the reform of education. These movements were accompanied by trends in deinstitutionalization, the development of more community-based services for persons with disabilities, and the philosophy of normalization. Madeleine Will (1986), then the assistant secretary of the Office of Special Education and Rehabilitative Services in the U.S. Office of Education, argued persuasively for several fundamental changes in education. She advocated an end to the dual system of educating students with and without disabilities and an end to stigmatizing children with disability labels. Will also emphasized the prevention of problems rather than assuming the failure of children. She urged special and general educators to collaboratively develop more effective *prereferral* assessment and instructional programs.

Areas of Controversy

From its beginnings, rooted in psychological, and later neurological, testing, the assessment of students with disabilities has been plagued with criticism and controversy. Arguments have centered on the purpose of assessment, the validity of diagnostic categories, changes in the population referred for special education services, and alternate forms of assessment that can better document accountability of educational programs.

Concerns Over the Purpose of Assessment

There is a general consensus that educational assessment may be thought of as a process in which we collect data that are used to make educational decisions (Salvia & Ysseldyke, 1991; Sattler, 1988; Taylor, 1997; Witt, Elliott, Kramer & Gresham, 1994). Much more controversial, however, are questions related to the purpose and content of assessment, procedures, and types of decisions made based on assessment data.

Assessment is conducted for a variety of purposes: (a) initial screening, (b) formal diagnosis, (c) decisions about classification and placement, (d) assessment of specific strengths and weaknesses, (e) decisions about instructional programs and teaching strategies, (f) to evaluate short- and long-term goals of the Individualized Education Program (IEP), and (g) overall program evaluation. Obviously, the content, or what we assess and the process—that is, how we conduct educational assessments—will be dictated by the purpose of the assessment. Different stakeholders in education may place different degrees of relative importance on the various purposes of assessment, generating arguments about the content and process of assessment.

Parents and teachers have great concerns about the degree to which assessment data are fair to students who vary in cultural background and ability levels. They are also concerned with how accurately assessment data reflect actual individual student progress in the classroom. Administrators often have to be concerned about the degree to which student data reflect progress made on state- or districtwide standards and benchmarks for academic achievement. They are concerned with how students in their building or district compare with students in other areas. Legislators often focus on the degree of student progress relative to the level of financial support provided. Many educators are concerned that assessment often results in inappropriate categorization or sorting of students by ability level and subsequent segregation, rather than in the development of appropriate individualized instructional programs in integrated settings.

Concerns Over Diagnosis

One of the greatest debates in special education assessment relates to the definitions and procedures used to diagnose categories of disabilities. For example, controversy over the definition of learning disabilities has been raging for the past 20 years (cf. Lloyd, Sabatino, Miller, & Miller, 1977; McLoughlin & Netick, 1983; Yssledyke, Algozzine, Richey, & Graden, 1982). Educators have clashed over the validity of this category, etiological factors, and whether assessment should focus on underlying processes believed by some to be linked to academic performance or on direct observation of measurable skills in the academic content areas.

More recently, the definition of mental retardation has come under criticism (Greenspan, 1997; Smith, 1997; Switzky, 1997), particularly in reference to the definition and assessment of **adaptive behavior.** The current definition of mental retardation (Luckasson et al., 1992) adopted by the American Association on Mental Retardation uses deficits in intellectual functioning and adaptive skills as dual diagnostic criteria. Mental retardation is further characterized by the level of intensity of supports needed by the individual. This definition has been criticized, however, on the basis of placing too much emphasis on the Intelligence Quotient (IQ) score. In fact, many states use IQ scores as the sole criterion in defining eligibility for special education services for students with mental retardation.

A second criticism of the definition of mental retardation is that what is deemed "adaptive" behavior is too relative and changes across social contexts, time, and place. A particular behavior, such as not speaking, may be considered adaptive in one context and maladaptive in another. In addition, the determination of whether a particular individual is engaging in adaptive or maladaptive behavior is made by observers (e.g., teachers and parents) who may have different performance expectations and, therefore, disagree. These examples illustrate the problems inherent in the reliability and validity of measurement of adaptive behavior.

Some qualitative researchers (e.g., Biklen, 1988, 1992; Kliewer, 1998) have argued that disability categories in special education are not distinct and valid conditions at all, but rather normal variations along the continuum of human behavior. These authors hold that disability categories, as legally defined in the field of special education, are not really conditions that reside within individuals. Rather, they should be recognized as the products of social consensus or social construction and related to the cultural environment of the time and place in which they occur. Seymore Sarason observed,

> Mental retardation is never a thing or characteristic of an individual, but rather a social invention stemming from time-bound societal values and ideology that make diagnosis and management seem both necessary and socially desirable. (1985, p. 233)

Concerns Over Changing Population in Special Education

The population of students referred for special education services has changed dramatically since 1975 when Public Law (P.L.) 94-142 originally mandated a free and appropriate public education for all students with disabilities. No longer restricted to school-aged students, children between the ages of birth and 21 are now served. U.S. classrooms now reflect increasing cultural diversity, as more and more people from around the globe have moved to the United States. Problems in U.S. society related to poverty, unemployment, and drug and alcohol abuse have also brought about changes in the classroom. Children who have significant learning and behavioral challenges as a result of parental substance abuse and unsupportive home environments are in the classroom in increasing numbers. Developing assessment instruments that represent fair and valid reflections of the performance of these students is challenging.

Concerns Over Accountability

For well over a decade, reports from large-scale student assessments have been bleak. Students' achievement scores and their ability to think and reason have, purportedly, declined. U.S. students have been described as faring much worse than students of other industrialized countries. Whether these concerns are valid is debatable. Nevertheless, these charges have fed concerns over the United States' ability to produce a skilled workforce and maintain leadership in a global economy.

Educational accountability includes three factors: (a) expectations for learner outcomes or content standards, (b) some form of comparing these expectations with actual outcomes, and (c) positive and negative consequences of student outcomes for school systems (Erickson, Ysseldyke, Thurlow, & Elliott, 1998). For the past 15 years, state departments of education have attempted to develop assessments that match expected outcomes. Demands for accountability have fueled efforts to find better ways in which to monitor and measure not only student performance, but the competence of teachers as well. Forms of **alternate assessment** such as **curriculum-based assessment, authentic assessment,** and **portfolio assessment** have been developed and continue to be refined. These measures are designed to let teachers know when their programs are working and when they are not. Research is also being conducted on better ways to train teachers to translate the results of these measures into program modifications.

Special Education and the Law: Implications for Alternate Assessment

The following eloquent statement was written by Chief Justice Earl Warren in *Brown v. Board of Education:*

> In these days it is doubtful that any child may reasonably be expected to succeed in life if he is denied the opportunity of an education. Such an opportunity, where the state has undertaken to provide it, is a right that must be made available to all on equal terms. (1954, p. 493)

Students with disabilities are affected every day by litigation and legislation concerning their right to education. How and where we provide special education and support services to students with disabilities is a direct result of the legal framework with which we must comply. We now review some of the most significant historical events resulting in legislation related to students with disabilities. We will then look at several specific federal laws regarding persons with disabilities and their implications for alternate assessment in inclusive school settings.

When we think of special education and the legislation that guides the provision of educational services to students with disabilities, we often think only within the context of public schools. In fact, some of the legislation mandating a free and appropriate education to all students has been significantly shaped by litigation focused on persons without disabilities or originating in nonschool settings. Several major historical events have impacted the field of special education through related legislation. These are (a) institutionalization and the right to habilitation, (b) the civil rights movement and equal opportunity, (c) exclusion of students with disabilities from public schools, and (d) the growth of the advocacy movement.

Institutionalization

Although originally a well-intentioned humanitarian effort, public institutions for persons labeled with mental retardation and mental illness came to be characterized as little more than human warehouses. Institutions grew to the size of towns and small cities with, in some cases, thousands of residents. Individuals confined to institutions often lived in degrading circumstances with little or no meaningful activity, highly regimented lives, and almost no contact with the outside world. Trent (1994) chronicled the growth of institutions for persons with mental retardation in the United States. He documented the almost totalitarian control held over them by their superintendents and medical authorities.

Residents of institutions were often tied to chairs and beds, locked in isolation rooms, housed in rooms with wall-to-wall beds, ridiculed and physically abused by staff, and subjected to forced sterilization. So popular were the sterilization practices, thought at the time to be a cure for mental retardation, that in 1927 U.S. Supreme Court Justice Oliver Wendell Holmes upheld Virginia's forced sterilization laws in the famous case known as *Buck v. Bell.*

In 1966 Burton Blatt and Fred Kaplan published startling photographs of institutional conditions in *Look* magazine. *Christmas in Purgatory* (1966) was the title of their published photographic essay about life in institutions. Blatt (1969) lamented:

> There is a shame in America. Countless human beings are suffering needlessly. They are the unfortunate victims of society's irresponsibility. (p. 176)

Blatt and Kaplan's photographs led to more shocking accounts of abuse and neglect of persons with disabilities in U.S. institutions. Journalists uncovered and publicized repeated instances of the inhumane conditions within the walls of institutions. Parents and other human-service professionals united, and class action lawsuits were filed to end the horrid conditions. Two famous class action lawsuits were *Wyatt v. Stickney* (1971), filed against the Alabama Department of Mental Health, and *Halderman v. Pennhurst State School and Hospital,* filed in Pennsylvania in 1984. These two cases set the stage for nearly a decade of litigation focused on the right to treatment, the right to habilitation in the community, the right to education, and the closure of segregated programs. Although the *Wyatt* and *Halderman* cases were filed on behalf of persons with disabilities in institutions, they served as important precedents for lawsuits that extended into the arena of public education. **Civil cases** such as these also heightened awareness among the general public about the care and treatment of persons with disabilities.

The Civil Rights Movement and Equal Opportunity

One of the flash points for the civil rights movement in the United States was the separation of blacks and whites in residential areas, job opportunities, public facilities such as restaurants and hotels, public transportation, and education. While this racial segregation was calculated and deliberate, its proponents argued that because blacks had their own facilities that were "adequate," there was no need to integrate.

In *Brown v. the Board of Education* (1954), the U.S. Supreme Court, under the leadership of Chief Justice Earl Warren, unanimously declared that separate educational facilities are inherently unequal. *Brown* was not one case, but a group of four cases on appeal from Kansas, South Carolina, Virginia, and Delaware (Turnbull & Turnbull, 1998). These states operated a dual system of education that segregated blacks from whites. Black children were not allowed to enroll in schools attended by white children.

A key point in the Supreme Court decision was the Fourteenth Amendment constitutional right of **equal protection under the law.** The Fourteenth Amendment stipulates that no state may deny any person equal protection under the law. If states provide public education, they must do so for all persons. The Supreme Court declared that segregated education was damaging to the educational opportunities of those persons who were segregated, and, hence, separate schools could never be made equal.

Brown's landmark decision has had far-reaching implications for educational policy. Turnbull & Turnbull (1998) declared it the most significant educational law decision ever written. *Brown* was a class action lawsuit in that it extended equal protection under the law to an entire class of people—racial minorities. The principle that separate is not equal has since been used in relation to students with disabilities and as an argument against segregated classes and schools, particularly for students with severe disabilities (cf. Stainback, Stainback, & Forest, 1989). Equal opportunity, it has been argued, means that students with disabilities should have the same access to educational facilities and programs as their peers without disabilities.

Exclusion From Public Education

In the United States, we typically assume that public education is a constitutional right guaranteed to each and every citizen. In fact, the Tenth Amendment left the responsibility for public education up to the states. Compulsory education was first mandated by Rhode Island in 1840 and by all states by 1918 (Yell, 1998).

Despite the compulsory education laws, the exclusion of students with disabilities from public education was upheld in the courts, often based on the arguments of their inability to benefit from education and that their presence in the classroom would be detrimental to other students. In *Beattie v. the Board of Education* (1919), the Wisconsin Supreme Court banned a child with physical and speech disorders from the public schools because of his "nauseating effects" on teachers and other students and because he would require too much of the teacher's time. As late as 1969, North Carolina made it illegal for parents to continue to seek public education for a student with disabilities after the student had been excluded from school (Yell, 1998).

A landmark case that led to the end of excluding students with disabilities from public education was the *Pennsylvania Association for Retarded Citizens (PARC) v. Commonwealth of Pennsylvania* class action lawsuit, settled by a consent agreement in 1972. Prior to the *PARC* case, children with mental retardation could be legally excluded from public schools in Pennsylvania if school psychologists judged them to be unable to profit from education. *PARC* won the right to a public education for all children with mental retardation in Pennsylvania.

The *PARC* case was followed by *Mills v. Board of Education* in Washington, D.C. The *Mills* case secured the right to a public education for students in the District of Columbia with a wide array of disabilities, including mental retardation, emotional disorders, physical disabilities, hyperactivity, and epilepsy. Similar cases were filed all across the country, and, in 1976, President Ford signed into law the Education for All Handicapped Children Act, P.L. 94-142. This landmark federal law established the right to a free and appropriate education in the least restrictive environment for all school-age children with disabilities. In addition, the right to nondiscriminatory assessment was emphasized.

The Advocacy Movement

Parents of students with disabilities have long served as a driving force behind legislation and social policies that protect the rights of their children. The first White House Conference on Children was held in 1910. Yell (1998) described the social and political climate during the first third of the 20th century. Initially, great concern was placed on moving children with disabilities from isolated, segregated, congregate facilities into public schools. Some states established public school classes for children with disabilities, while others were privately staffed and supported by parents.

In part, because of the economic hardships of the Great Depression, many children with disabilities remained unserved or underserved by the schools. In 1933 the Cuyohoga County (Ohio) Council for the Retarded Child was formed by five parents in protest to the exclusion of their children from public schools (Turnbull & Turnbull, 1998). Grassroots groups of parents advocating on behalf of their children continued to develop throughout the 30s, 40s, and 50s. The National Association for Retarded Children (now known as the Association for Retarded Citizens, or ARC/USA) was formed in 1950. Roos (1975) described how the mission of parental advocacy groups changed from providing direct services to their loved ones to organized lobbying for legal, social, and economic changes on behalf of all persons with disabilities.

The Developmental Disabilities Assistance and Bill of Rights Act, originally passed in 1972 and since amended by P.L. 100-146 and P.L. 101-496, established a national system of advocacy. Under this legislation, every state must have a designated agency with primary responsibility for protecting the legal rights of three groups of citizens: (a) individuals with developmental disabilities, (b) persons who have been diagnosed with mental illness, and (c) those who qualify to receive services from vocational rehabilitation. Developmental disabilities was defined as a mental or physical impairment manifesting before the age of 22, that will be likely to persist for a long period of time, and that results in significant functional limitations in three or more areas of life activity (Administration on Developmental Disabilities, 1991).

The system of state protection and advocacy agencies established by the Developmental Disabilities Act has multiple functions. These agencies serve as a source of free information to direct consumers and their family members and provide referral services and technical assistance, legislative information, advocacy intervention, and legal representation (Schloss, 1994).

Influential Legislation With Implications for Assessment

We now review several major pieces of federal legislation with implications for assessment. These are Section 504 of the Rehabilitation Act of 1973, the Education for All Handicapped Children Act of 1975, the Education of the Handicapped Act Amendments of 1986, the Americans with Disabilities Act, the Individuals with Disabilities Education Act (IDEA), and the 1997 IDEA amendments. For an in-depth discussion of the law and students with disabilities, the reader is referred to Turnbull and Turnbull, 1998.

Section 504 of the Rehabilitation Act

Congress passed the Rehabilitation Act of 1973, P.L. 93-112. The primary purposes of this law were to provide (a) vocational rehabilitation services to persons with severe disabilities so that they could prepare and engage in gainful employment, and (b) rehabilitation services to those individuals for whom gainful employment may not be a viable option so that they may be enabled to live with greater independence. Section 504 of the Rehabilitation Act provides a significant civil rights statement in prohibiting discrimination on the basis of a physical, cognitive, or sensory disability in programs receiving federal funds. In both language and intent, Section 504 mirrors other civil rights legislation that prohibited discrimination on the basis of race or gender:

> No otherwise qualified handicapped individual in the United States, shall, solely by reason of his handicap, be excluded from the participation in, be denied the benefits of, or be subjected to discrimination under any program or activity receiving federal financial assistance. (Section 504, 29 U.S.C. 794)

The Rehabilitation Act was amended in 1986. The amendments required the provision of transitional services to students with severe disabilities. All students with disabilities are to have a written transition plan developed at least two years prior to graduation. Transition plans must stipulate goals that facilitate adult life in the community with as much independence as possible.

A major implication of the Rehabilitation Act and Section 504 is apparent in the area of vocational assessment and training. Prior to the late 70s, and the pioneer work of Mark Gold at the University of Illinois and Thomas Bellamy at the University of Oregon and their colleagues, many persons with disabilities, particularly intellectual disabilities, were automatically assumed to be incapable of learning job skills of any type. Many of these individuals were relegated to daily living programs that, in most instances, could be characterized as little more than adult day care. Today, due to legislation and our increased knowledge about the capabilities of persons with disabilities, persons with even severe disabilities are provided more appropriate vocational assessment and training services. The goal of these services is employment in competitive jobs.

The Education for All Handicapped Children Act of 1975

The Education for All Handicapped Children Act, P.L. 94-142, was signed into law after a long battle and signified a major victory of advocates for students with disabilities. This bill has been referred to as the most comprehensive piece of legislation on behalf of the rights of persons with disabilities. P.L. 94-142 provided funding provisions to assure all qualified students with disabilities between the ages of 3 and 18 years receive special education by September 1, 1978, and for all students with disabilities up to the age of 21 years by September 1, 1980. States not serving these students and found to be out of compliance with this law risked losing millions of dollars in federal financial aid.

P.L. 94-142 mandated the following rights for all students with disabilities: (a) a free and appropriate education; (b) nondiscriminatory testing, evaluation, and placement; (c) education in the least restrictive environment; (d) a written individualized education plan, or IEP; and (e) procedural **due process.**

In regard to assessment and evaluation, P.L. 94-142 mandates

1. Assessment outcomes reporting the student's current level of functioning be specified on the IEP
2. Annual goals developed on the basis of assessment data
3. Parental rights to obtain a comprehensive student evaluation from the school district that includes multiple measures and criteria
4. Right to reevaluation whenever indicated by a change in the student's condition, whenever requested by parents, and at minimum within every 3 years
5. Right to an independent evaluation of the student by nonschool district personnel
6. Right to reimbursement for the independent evaluation when it is determined that the school's evaluation was inaccurate or inappropriate

Education of the Handicapped Act Amendments of 1986

In 1986, P.L. 99-457 amended the Education for All Handicapped Children Act. The amendments extended the provisions of P.L. 94-142 to students between the ages of 3 and 5 years. Prior to these amendments, states had to serve 3,- 4,- and 5-year-olds with disabilities only if they provided services to their chronological age peers without disabilities. The 1986 amendments also replaced the IEP with the individualized family service plan, or IFSP.

The IFSP must contain a broad statement of services directed at not only the child, but also the family. In addition, a case manager responsible for coordinating services to the child with a disability and her family must be specified on this written document.

The Americans With Disabilities Act

Public Law 101-336, the Americans with Disabilities Act (ADA) of 1990, mandated a wide array of services and prohibited discrimination against adults with disabilities. The ADA extended equal opportunity and nondiscrimination protections of Section 504 to enterprises *not* receiving federal funds. This law requires all reasonable accommodations be made to ensure participation in public and private employment, housing, transportation, recreation, public libraries, health services, and telecommunication services. In writing this law, principally sponsored by Senator Tom Harkin of Iowa, Congress emphasized equality of opportunity, full participation, independent living, and economic self-sufficiency.

According to Yell (1998), the purposes of the Americans with Disabilities Act were to

1. Establish a national mandate against the discrimination of persons with disabilities
2. Set standards in regard to discrimination against individuals with disabilities that were consistent, clear, and enforceable
3. Use the power of Congress to enforce the Fourteenth Amendment and regulate commerce as a means of ending discrimination against individuals with disabilities in their day-to-day life
4. Make the federal government's role critical in enforcing the standards established by the ADA

The Individuals With Disabilities Education Act Amendments of 1990

Congress changed terminology in the federal right to education for students with disabilities legislation in 1990. The Education for All Handicapped Children Act was renamed the Individuals with Disabilities Education Act, IDEA. People first language was adopted, changing the term *handicap* to *disability* and *handicapped* or *disabled child* to *student with a disability* (Yell, 1998). The disability conditions of autism and traumatic brain injury were added to the law. Assistive technology and related services were addressed more specifically. Transition services and activities were emphasized in the 1990 amendments. These included functional vocational assessment and instruction and community experiences that facilitate the transition from school to living and working in the community.

The Individuals With Disabilities Education Act Amendments of 1997

The 1997 amendments extended several provisions of IDEA and restructured it. The original IDEA had nine subsections, and the 1997 amendments collapsed these into four. Part A includes general provisions of educational services to students with disabilities and includes definitions. Part B covers assistance to state departments of education and funding mechanisms. Part C addresses requirements for educational services to infants and toddlers with disabilities. Part D covers discretionary programs. These programs provide federal funding to improve or enhance educational services to students with disabilities. State departments of education, local school districts, institutions of higher education, and other entities have the discretion of applying for these competitive funds. The 1997 amendments authorize the availability of funding for personnel preparation, research and innovation, parent training, national assessment studies, technology development, and technical assistance and dissemination of information (IDEA, 1997; Turnbull, 1998).

The 1997 amendments expand the requirements for the Individualized Educational Program, or IEP. The IEP has to be developed by both general and special educators, as well as parents and other relevant team members. IEPs also must include statements of accurate measurements of progress toward short- and long-term goals. Students with disabilities are to be included in all state- and districtwide assessments. The amendments require that the IEP include what, if any, modifications are needed in order to ensure the student's participation in these assessments.

Discipline of students with disabilities was addressed in the 1997 IDEA amendments. Specifically, more emphasis was placed on developing positive behavioral supports for students identified with behavior disorders. A proactive behavior plan based on a functional analysis of the environment and its influence on student behavior must be included in the IEP. If a student's placement is changed as a result of inappropriate behavior in school and no behavioral intervention plan is contained on the IEP, a functional assessment and intervention plan must be developed within 10 days. The maximum amount of time that a student can be placed in an alternative setting or suspended from school as a result of behavioral problems is 10 days during any school year. The exception to this rule is applied to students who bring weapons to school or possess or use illegal drugs at school. In these cases, the school may place the student in an interim educational setting for up to 45 days.

In an attempt to resolve differences between parents and educators over the provision of appropriate educational services, Congress added a voluntary mediation process to IDEA. The states must offer mediation as an initial option for resolving conflicts. Mediators must be trained and cannot be employed by either the state or the school district.

Other provisions of the 1997 amendments address the rights adult prisoners have to special education services, conditions under which parents can recover attorneys' fees, review of the relationship between disability and misconduct in cases in which the school seeks to change placement or suspend a student for longer than 10 days, and the rights of students diagnosed with disabilities enrolled in charter schools to receive special education services and funds.

The 1997 IDEA Amendments and Assessment

Section 614 of IDEA maintains previous IDEA guarantees of nondiscriminatory testing and individualized education in the least restrictive environment. Section 614(b) specifically addresses the area of assessment and evaluation. The purposes of evaluation are to (a) make the initial determination of whether the student has a disability, and (b) specify educational supports necessary to meet the student's needs (Turnbull, 1998).

The amendments built in a link between evaluation, placement, and educational program by specifying that both a general educator and a special educator must serve on the evaluation (IEP) team. The team must also include one person who is knowledgeable about assessment and can interpret assessment data into implications for instruction.

The present safeguards for nondiscriminatory assessment are maintained. These include culturally fair tests and materials, tests administered in the student's native language, validated standardized tests and qualified examiners, and multiple measures and criteria during evaluation.

The 1997 amendments include a greater emphasis on parental participation in assessment and evaluation. Parents must receive a copy of all materials used to document student eligibility for special education. In addition, the parents may submit and require the other members of the evaluation team to consider information from evaluations they have initiated independently of school personnel.

According to Turnbull (1998), the 1997 IDEA amendments contain seven significant changes relative to assessment:

1. The rights of parents to participate in the evaluation process are strengthened
2. The educational team, including parents, general and special educators, the student, and other persons, is responsible not just for developing the IEP, but for evaluation, delivery of instruction, and monitoring student progress
3. Evaluation, the IEP, and instruction are linked
4. The evaluation process must consider and facilitate the student's participation in the general education curriculum
5. Classroom data must be gathered and used to monitor student performance as well as the staff's ability to provide both general and special educational services
6. Data from the cognitive, physical, behavioral, and developmental domains must be collected and used to make program decisions
7. The evaluation team must use strategies and tools to determine whether the school staff is meeting a student's needs

As mentioned earlier, the 1997 amendments require students with disabilities to participate in state- and district-wide assessments. IDEA of 1997 requires "alternate assessments" for students with disabilities who cannot be appropriately assessed with standard statewide academic achievement tests [P.L. 105-17, section 612(a)(17)]. Alternate assessments are specifically addressed in IDEA.

A. *In general.*—Children with disabilities are included in general State and district-wide assessment programs, with appropriate accommodations, where necessary. As appropriate, the state or local educational agency—
   i. develops guidelines for the participation of children with disabilities in alternate assessments for those children who cannot participate in State and district-wide assessment programs; and
   ii. develops and, beginning not later than July 1, 2000, conducts those alternate assessments.

B. *Reports.*—The State educational agency makes available to the public, and reports to the public with the same frequency and in the same detail as it reports on the assessment of nondisabled children, the following:
   i. The number of children with disabilities participating in regular assessments.
   ii. The number of those children participating in alternate assessments.

I. The performance of those children on regular assessments (beginning not later than July 1, 1998) and on alternate assessments (not later than July 1, 2000), if doing so would be statistically sound and would not result in the disclosure of performance results identifiable to individual children.

II. Data relating to the performance of children described under subclause I shall be disaggregated—

a.a. for assessments conducted after July 1, 1998; and

b.b. for assessments conducted before July 1, 1998, if the State is required to disaggregate such data prior to July 1, 1998. [PL 105-17, Section 612 (a)(17)]

Similarities Between the Laws

Laws such as IDEA and the Rehabilitation Act are entitlements. They make possible benefits for infants, toddlers, youth, and adults who are challenged by disabilities. Entitlements provide services and supports that assist the person with a disability to obtain an appropriate education and live, work, and play in the community alongside his or her peers without disabilities.

Turnbull and Turnbull (1998) distinguished between entitlements and laws that prohibit discrimination such as the ADA and Section 504. These laws require the nondisabled world to make reasonable accommodations for individuals with disabilities in schools, at home, in the workplace, and in public facilities in the community.

Turnbull and Turnbull (1998) used the term *principle of* ***dual accommodations*** to characterize the relatedness of the entitlements and the antidiscrimination laws. Together, these two sets of laws enable the person with a disability to accommodate to the world and require that the nondisabled world make reasonable accommodations to facilitate participation by the person with a disability.

There are other themes that are found repeatedly in the laws that affect persons with disabilities. IDEA, ADA, the Developmental Disabilities Act, and Section 504 are related by their emphasis on independence, productivity, and inclusion for persons with disabilities at home, in school, at work, and in the community at large. Terms such as *independent living, economic self-sufficiency,* and *full participation* are used in the law.

Empowerment is another theme relating the laws discussed in this chapter. Empowerment relates to the skills and knowledge one has. It is through skills and knowledge that we become more competent and independent human beings. We learn how to solve problems, make prudent choices, work harmoniously with others, cope with life's demands, and develop into responsible and self-sufficient adults. Empowerment also has to do with how we view ourselves. It relates to having hope, persistence, and a belief that we have some control over what happens to us. Clearly, the concepts of independence, productivity, inclusion, and empowerment embedded into our current laws are a far cry from the image of the "handicapped" beggar completely at the mercy of charity, or the poster children still featured in some national fund-raising campaigns.

Summary

We reviewed the process of inclusion in this chapter. A brief history of assessment in special education, including several points of controversy, was presented. We also reviewed historical trends and events resulting in significant legislation pertaining to persons with disabilities. We discussed the major pieces of federal legislation that provide the framework for the provision of special education services. The implications of legislation for assessment, particularly the IDEA 1997 amendments, were mentioned. Finally, the interrelated nature of the laws and concepts they share in common were addressed.

President George Bush, in signing the Americans with Disabilities Act on July 26, 1990, echoed a sentiment of Burton Blatt, who had referred to the abhorrent conditions in institutions for persons with mental retardation 21 years earlier:

> Let the shameful walls of exclusion finally come tumbling down. (*Weekly Compilation of Presidential Documents,* vol. 26, n. 30, p. 1165)

Basic statistical concepts and standardized testing are described in Chapter 2. Chapter 3 will address nonstandardized and alternate forms of assessment for students with disabilities. Chapter 4 focuses on the roles and responsibilities of collaborative teams in the assessment process.

REFERENCES

Administration on Developmental Disabilities. (1991). *Visions of: Independence—productivity—integration for people with developmental disabilities.* Washington, DC: Administration on Developmental Disabilities.

Americans with Disabilities Act of 1990, 42 U.S.C.A. § 12101 *et seq.*

Arter, J., & Jenkins, J. (1977). Examining the benefits and prevalences of modality considerations in special education. *Journal of Special Education, 11,* 281–298.

Beattie v. Board of Education, 172 N.W. 153 (Wis. 1919).

Biklen, D. (1988). The myth of clinical judgment. *Journal of Social Issues, 44*(1), 127–140.

Biklen, D. (1992). *Schooling without labels.* Philadelphia: Temple University Press.

Blatt, B. (1969). Recommendations for institutional reform. In R. Kugel & W. Wolfensberger (Eds.), *Changing patterns in residential services for the mentally retarded* (pp. 175–177). Washington, DC: President's Committee on Mental Retardation.

Blatt, B., & Kaplan, F. (1966). *Christmas in purgatory.* Boston: Allyn & Bacon.

Brown, L., Schwarz, P., Udvari-Solner, A., Kampschroer, E., Johnson, F., Jorgenson, J., & Gruenwald, L. (1991). How much time should students with severe intellectual disabilities spend in regular education classrooms and elsewhere? *Journal of the Association for Persons with Severe Handicaps, 16,* 39–47.

Brown v. Board of Education, 347 U.S. 483 (1954).

Buck v. Bell, 274 U.S. 200 (1927).

Developmental Disabilities Assistance and Bill of Rights Act, 42 U.S.C. § 6000–6083 (1996).

Education for All Handicapped Children Act of 1975, 20 U.S.C. § 1401 *et seq.*

Education of the Handicapped Act Amendments of 1986, 20 U.S.C. § 1401 *et seq.*

Erickson, R., Yssledyke, J., Thurlow, M., & Elliott, J. (1998). Inclusive assessments and accountability systems. *Teaching Exceptional Children, 31*(2), 4–9.

Federal Register. (1993). Washington, DC: U.S. Government Printing Office, July 30, 1993.

Federal Register. (1992). Washington, DC: U.S. Government Printing Office, September 29, 1992.

Federal Register. (1977). Washington, DC: U.S. Government Printing Office, August 23, 1977.

Frostig, M., Lefever, W., & Whittlesey, J. (1966). *Administration and scoring manual: Marianne Frostig Developmental Test of Visual Perception.* Palo Alto, CA: Consulting Psychologists Press.

Greenspan, S. (1997). Dead manual walking? Why the 1992 AAMR definition needs redoing. *Education and Training in Mental Retardation and Developmental Disabilities, 32,* 179–190.

Halderman v. Pennhurst State School and Hospital, 446 F. Supp. 1295 (E.D.Pa 1977), aff'd in part, rev'd in part, 612 F.2d 84 (3rd Cir. 1979), rev'd, 451 U.S. 1 (1981), on remand, 673 F.2d 647 (3rd Cir. 1982), rev'd, 465 U.S. 89 (1984).

IDEA '97. (1998, December/January). *The Association for Persons with Severe Handicaps (TASH) Newsletter, 23/24,* 13–17.

Individuals with Disabilities Education Act, 20 U.S.C. § 1415(e) (1986).

Individuals with Disabilities Education Act of 1990, 20 U.S.C. § 1401 *et seq.*

Individuals with Disabilities Education Act Amendments of 1997, P.L. 105-17, 105th Cong., 1st sess.

King-Sears, M. E. (1997). Best academic practices for inclusive classrooms. *Focus on Exceptional Children, 29*(7), 194–215.

Kirk, S., McCarthy, J., & Kirk, W. (1968). *Illinois Test of Psycholinguistic Abilities.* Urbana, IL: University of Illinois Press.

Kliewer, C. (1998). *Schooling children with Down syndrome: Toward an understanding of possibility.* New York: Teachers College Press.

Larry P. v. Riles, 343 F. Supp. 1306, aff'd., 502 F.2d 963, further proceedings, 495F. Supp. 926, aff'd., 502 F.2d 693 (9th Cir. 1984).

Larsen, S., & Hammill, D. (1975). The relationship of selected visual perceptual abilities to school learning. *Journal of Special Education, 9,* 281–291.

Lloyd, J., Sabatino, D., Miller, T., & Miller, S. (1977). Proposed federal guidelines: Some open questions. *Journal of Learning Disabilities, 10,* 69–71.

Luckasson, R., Coulter, D. L., Polloway, E. A., Reiss, S., Schalock, R. L., Snell, M. E., Spitalnik, D. M., & Stark, J. A. (1992). *Mental retardation: Definition, classification, and systems of support* (9th ed.). Washington, DC: American Association on Mental Retardation.

McLoughlin, J. A., & Netick, A. (1983). Defining learning disabilities: A new and cooperative direction. *Journal of Learning Disabilities, 16,* 21–23.

Mercer, J. (1973). *Labeling the mentally retarded: Clinical and social system perspectives on mental retardation.* Berkeley: University of California Press.

Mills v. Board of Education, 348 F. Supp. 866 (D.D.C. 1972).

Pennsylvania Association for Retarded Citizens v. Commonwealth of Pennsylvania, 343 F. Supp. 279 (E.D. Pa. 1972).

Rehabilitation Act of 1973, Section 504, 29 U.S.C. § 794.

Rehabilitation Act of 1973, Section 504 Regulations, 34 C.F.R. § 104.1 *et seq.*

Roos, P. (1975). Parents and families of the mentally retarded. In J. M. Kauffman & J. S. Payne (Eds.), *Mental retardation: Introduction and personal perspectives.* New York: Charles E. Merrill.

Ryndak, D. L., & Alper, S. (1996). *Curriculum content for students with moderate and severe disabilities in inclusive settings.* Boston: Allyn & Bacon.

Salvia, J., & Ysseldyke, J. E. (1991). *Assessment.* Boston: Houghton Mifflin.

Sarason, S. (1985). *Psychology and mental retardation: Perspectives in change.* Austin: Pro-Ed.

Sattler, J. (1988). *Assessment of children* (3rd ed.). San Diego: Author.

Schloss, C. N. (1994). Resources for the advocate. In S. Alper, P. J. Schloss, & C. N. Schloss, *Families of students with disabilities: Consultation and advocacy,* pp. 307–329. Boston: Allyn & Bacon.

Section 504 of the Rehabilitation Act of 1973, 29 U.S.C. § 794 *et seq.*

Section 505 of the Rehabilitation Act of 1973, 29 U.S.C. § 795a.

Smith, J. D. (1997). Mental retardation as an educational construct: Time for a new shared view? *Education and Training in Mental Retardation and Developmental Disabilities, 32,* 167–173.

Stainback, S., Stainback, W., & Forest M. (Eds.). (1989). *Educating all students in the mainstream of regular education.* Baltimore: Paul H. Brookes.

Switzky, H. N. (1997). Mental retardation and the neglected construct of motivation. *Education and Training in Mental Retardation and Developmental Disabilities, 32,* 194–196.

Taylor, R. L. (1997). *Assessment of exceptional students.* Boston: Allyn & Bacon.

Trent, J. W. (1994). *Inventing the feeble mind: A history of mental retardation in the United States.* Berkeley: University of California Press.

Turnbull, H. R. (1998). What does IDEA '97 say about evaluations, eligibility, IEPs, and placements? *TASH Newsletter, 23/24,* 19–22.

Turnbull, H. R., & Turnbull, A. P. (1998). *Free appropriate public education: The law and children with disabilities* (5th ed.). Denver, CO: Love Publishing Co.

Will, M. (1986). Educating children with learning problems: A shared responsibility. *Exceptional Children, 52,* 411–416.

Williams, W., Fox, T., Thousand, J., & Fox, W. (1990). Level of acceptance and implementation of best practices in the education of students with severe handicaps in Vermont. *Education and Training in Mental Retardation, 25*(2), 120–131.

Witt, J. C., Elliott, S. N., Kramer, J. J., & Gresham, F. M. (1994). *Assessment of children: Fundamental methods and practices.* Dubuque, IA: Brown and Benchmark.

Wyatt v. Stickney, 344 F. Supp. 373 (M.D. Ala. 1972), aff'd in part, rev'd in part sub nom.

Yell, M. L. (1998). *The law and special education.* Upper Saddle River, NJ: Merrill/Prentice-Hall.

York, J., Doyle, M. B., & Kronberg, R. (1992). A curriculum development process for inclusive classrooms. *Focus on Exceptional Children, 25*(4), 1–16.

Ysseldyke, J., Algozzine, B., Richey, L., & Graden, J. (1982). Declaring students eligible for learning disability services: Why bother with the data? *Learning Disability Quarterly, 5,* 37–44.

CHAPTER

2 Standardized Assessment in Inclusive Schools

CYNTHIA R. A. WATKINS
University of Northern Iowa

SANDRA ALPER
University of Northern Iowa

OBJECTIVES

After reading this chapter, you will be able to

1. Specify a use for each of the four measurement scales
2. Discuss the premises upon which the normal distribution is based
3. Compare and contrast among the basic characteristics of measures (objectivity, validity, reliability, and standard error of measures)
4. Describe the purposes of standardized assessment
5. Discuss how to interpret a score on a standardized test relative to the normative sample
6. Describe practical features in selecting a test
7. Discuss standardized assessment of intelligence
8. Describe the assessment of adaptive behavior using standardized tests
9. Discuss the assessment of academic achievement with standardized assessment batteries
10. Detail some of the issues and controversies involving standardized assessment
11. Delineate the implications of standardized assessment for professionals working in inclusive school settings

KEY TERMS

abscissa (p. 21)
achievement tests (p. 46)
adaptive behavior (p. 43)
concurrent validity (p. 35)
confidence interval (p. 33)
construct validity (p. 35)
content validity (p. 34)
correlation (p. 29)
correlation coefficients (p. 29)
criterion-related validity (p. 35)
descriptive statistics (p. 20)
equal-interval scale (p. 20)
equivalent-forms reliability (p. 31)
intelligence (p. 38)
intelligence quotient (IQ) (p. 38)
internal consistency reliability (p. 31)
interrater reliability (p. 32)
maladaptive behavior (p. 46)
mean (p. 23)

measure of relative position (p. 27)
measures of central tendency (p. 22)
measures of dispersion (p. 25)
measures of relationship (p. 29)
median (p. 23)
mode (p. 23)
nominal scale (p. 20)
norm groups (p. 34)
normal distribution (p. 25)
norm-referenced test (p. 36)
objectivity (p. 30)
ordinal scale (p. 20)
ordinate (p. 21)
percentile ranks (p. 28)
predictive validity (p. 35)
range (p. 25)
ratio scale (p. 20)
rational equivalence reliability (p. 31)
raw score (p. 21)
reliability (p. 30)
skewed (p. 27)
split-half reliability (p. 31)
stability of IQ (p. 41)
standard deviation (SD) (p. 25)
standard error of measurement (SEM) (p. 33)
standard score (p. 28)
standardized test (p. 36)
test bias (p. 41)
t scores (p. 28)
test-retest reliability (p. 30)
validity (p. 33)
variance (p. 25)
z scores (p. 28)

While the focus of this text is on alternate assessment, a review of standardized testing will be helpful. An overview of the basic statistical concepts and standardized tests commonly used in educational assessment will assist you in understanding the foundations on which standardized instruments should be developed and selected. Standardized tests in the areas of intelligence, academic achievement, and adaptive behavior are reviewed.

Descriptive Statistics

Teachers often must relate information to others about students' level of achievement, behavior, or aptitude. Information may be needed to describe an individual in a variety of settings or how a student performs as a member of a specific group. Information may be in the form of test scores or observational information sets. In either case, a method is needed that allows conveyance of the information to the recipient with maximum understanding, yet at the same time is concise. A method used to summarize or describe such data or information sets is known as **descriptive statistics.**

Types of Measurement Scales

How one begins the task of providing meaning to information sets will depend on characteristics of the data contained within the set. Data may be categorical, ordered, or quantified. The form of data will determine the type of measurement scale used. The type of scale in turn will determine the statistical procedures appropriate to summarize or describe the data set.

There are four types of measurement scales: **nominal, ordinal, equal-interval,** and **ratio.** Each scale provides us with a different form of data and uses a different set of mathematical procedures. The measurement scales are summarized in Table 2.1 and are arranged in hierarchical order from simplest to most elaborate.

TABLE 2.1 Characteristics of the Four Measurement Scales

Measurement Scale	Characteristics	Examples
Nominal	Measures by simple classification. Names, identifies, and categorizes without regard to order. Simply counts frequency of occurrence. No mathematical operations can be used with nominal scale.	Gender: Male vs. Female Area codes: 413 vs. 818 vs. 604
Ordinal	Measures by classifying or naming, then order ranking. Indicates best to worst or most to least. Does not indicate *how much* better, only better. Mathematical operation: ranking.	Letter grades: A, B, C, D, F Adjective: softest, softer, soft
Equal-interval	Measures by establishing equidistant units between scale points. Names categories, rank orders them, then ascribes an equal value to the intervals between the actual scores. Mathematical operations: addition or subtraction.	Thermometers, IQ
Ratio	Measures by establishing equidistant units between scale points. Utilizes *all* the elements of the preceding scales and has a definitive starting point (viz., absolute zero) that allows for true ratio comparisons. All mathematical operations can be used with ratio scale.	Weight, height, time

Distribution of Scores

To illustrate how statistics can help, a data set was constructed in Mr. Chi's class. For the set, a tally mark was made each time a student clearly said a word during a 20-minute period. Table 2.2 is the completed tally sheet.

The problem with the simple tally, or **raw score,** is that it is difficult to determine what is going on. A frequency table could be developed to assist in making sense of the scores. The frequency table is a listing of the occurrence rate (i.e., frequency count) in rank order. A commonly used convention to assist with interpretation is to group information into intervals. Table 2.3 depicts the frequency table for the data set from Mr. Chi's class in interval groupings.

A better understanding of what is going on can be gleaned from the frequency table. One can determine trends, locate high/low frequency occurrences, or determine jumps in the data (large gaps between scores). The old saying "A picture is worth a thousand words" is true for statistical data also.

Visual representations in statistics are usually portrayed with graphs. For most graphs, the **ordinate,** or vertical axis, displays the number of cases (frequency) receiving any given count or score. The **abscissa,** or horizontal axis, displays the continuum of what is being measured. For the data set in Mr. Chi's class, the abscissa is the numerical grouping for the count of words spoken in 20 minutes (e.g., 9–10, 11–12). The most commonly used graphs are the histogram, frequency polygon, and curve. Figure 2.1 demonstrates how Mr. Chi's class data set looks when graphed in all three forms.

TABLE 2.2 Tally Sheet for Number of Words Spoken in Class Within a 20-Minute Period

Student	Tally Marks	Total
Susie	𝍸 𝍸 𝍸 II	17
Mica	𝍸 𝍸 𝍸 I	16
JoJo	𝍸 𝍸 IIII	14
Juan	𝍸 𝍸 𝍸 𝍸 𝍸	25
Bobbie	𝍸 IIII	9
Hobie	𝍸 𝍸 𝍸	15
Toma	𝍸 𝍸 𝍸	15
TJ	𝍸 𝍸 𝍸 III	18
Jean	𝍸 𝍸 II	12
Bev	𝍸 𝍸 𝍸 I	16
Troy	𝍸 𝍸 II	12
Tina	𝍸 𝍸 𝍸 𝍸 I	21
Shasa	𝍸 𝍸 𝍸 IIII	19
Mike	𝍸 𝍸 𝍸 𝍸	20
El-lae	𝍸 𝍸 𝍸 II	17

TABLE 2.3 Frequency Table for Occurrence of Words Spoken in Class

Interval	Tally	Frequency
25–26	I	1
23–24	none	0
21–22	I	1
19–20	II	2
17–18	III	3
15–16	IIII	4
13–14	I	1
11–12	II	2
9–10	I	1

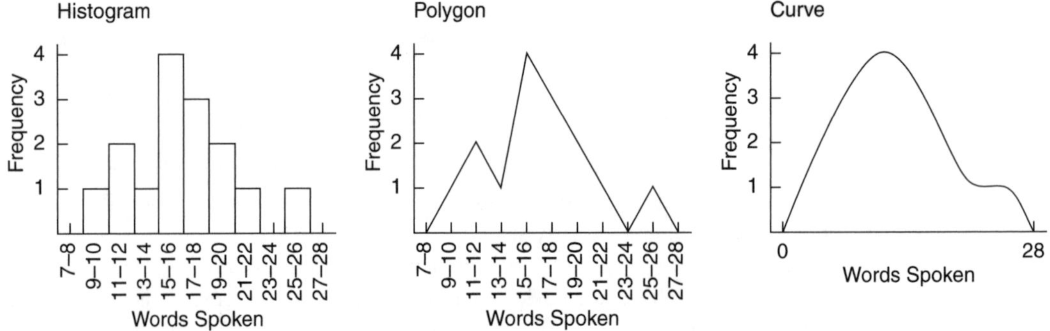

FIGURE 2.1 Visual representation of distribution of words spoken in class within a 20-minute period.

Describing a Distribution of Scores

To have a better understanding of data sets, one needs to examine how the scores relate to one another. This is typically done by examining the distribution of scores within the data set.

Measures of Central Tendency

Measures of central tendency provide a way to describe or look at how a group performs as a single unit. This can be accomplished by looking at the information that tends to cluster in the middle. One usually talks about this middle ground as the average of the group. The most commonly used averages are the mean, median, or mode.

To illustrate how to determine measures of central tendency, we'll use Miss Ray's class, which has 12 students. "Blurting out" has been targeted as the behavior of concern. To begin, Miss Ray specified in observable and measurable terms what was meant by blurting out. Next, she tallied each time a student displayed the target behavior. This simple count is called the raw score. She rank ordered the raw scores in Table 2.4. Now she is ready to describe the group data. Explanations of descriptive statistics, computational formulas, as well as examples for Miss Ray's class are found in Table 2.5.

Mean. The mean is the most commonly used measure of central tendency. Basically, the **mean** is the simple arithmetic average (see Equation 2.1 in Table 2.5). The mean is the measure of central tendency most often used to describe the group. In determining the mean, every case in the information set will contribute. Yet, the mean can be significantly affected by the magnitude of a single case in the group set. For Miss Ray's class, the mean is 9.

Median. The **median** is the midpoint in a set of data. The median specifies the position of a score with regard to rank. It divides the information set in half, with 50% of the scores or cases above and 50% below the midpoint. The magnitude of a single case will have little or no impact on the median. For our class, the midpoint falls halfway between Zin's score and Pat's score of 9. So, the median of Miss Ray's class is 9.

Mode. The **mode** is the score occurring with the highest frequency. A data set may have a single, multiple, or no mode. A single mode is said to have a unimodal distribution, a two-mode set is called a bimodal distribution, while a set with multiple modes is known as a multimodal distribution. Hence, for Miss Ray's class there is a unimodel distribution with a mode of 9.

TABLE 2.4 Rank Order of Blurting Out Behavior for 12 Students in Miss Ray's Class

Student	Raw Score (X)	$(X - \bar{X})$	$(X - \bar{X})^2$
Candy	15	$15 - 9 = 6$	$(15 - 9)^2 = 36$
Marion	13	4	16
Tom	12	3	9
SuLe	11	2	4
Lou	10	1	1
Zin	9	0	0
Pat	9	0	0
Jose	8	–1	1
Kim	7	–2	4
Chrila	6	–3	9
Sandy	5	–4	16
Cindy	3	–6	36
$N = 12$	$\Sigma = 108$	$\Sigma = 0$	$\Sigma = 132$

Note: N = number of cases, X = raw score, $\bar{X}$ = mean, and Σ = sum.

TABLE 2.5 Examples of Descriptive Statistics Using Miss Ray's Classroom Information Set

Statistical Measure	Explanation	Formula	Miss Ray's Class Example
Mean ($\bar{X}$)	Arithmetic average. Add raw scores, divide by number of scores.	Equation 2.1 $\bar{X} = \frac{\Sigma X}{N}$	$\frac{108}{12} = 9$
Median (Md)	Middle number in a ranked set. For odd number of scores, count half-way down. For even number of scores like ours, add the middle scores and divide by 2.		$\frac{9 + 9}{2} = 9$
Mode (Mo)	Score occurring with the highest frequency. Our list has only two reoccurring scores: Pat's and Zin's.		9
Range	Highest score minus the lowest score. Candy had the highest score (15). Cindy had the lowest score (3).		$15 - 3 = 12$
Variances (S^2)	Compute the difference from mean for each student	$(X - \bar{X})$	See Table 2.4
	Square difference from the mean for each student	$(X - \bar{X})^2$	See Table 2.4
	Find the sum of squared difference	$\Sigma(X - \bar{X})^2$	See Table 2.4
	Compute the variance	Equation 2.2 $S^2 = \frac{\Sigma(X - \bar{X})^2}{N}$	$\frac{132}{12} = 11$
Standard Deviation (SD)	Square root of the variance.	Equation 2.3 $SD = \sqrt{S^2}$	$\sqrt{11} = 3.32$
Percentile Rank (PR)	Compute percentile rank by counting up from the bottom to find the rank (R).	Equation 2.4 $PR = 100\frac{R - .5}{N}$	Percentile rank for SuLe: $100\frac{9 - .5}{12} = 71$st
z scores (*z*)	Standard score with mean equal to 0 and standard deviation of 1.	Equation 2.5 $z = \frac{X - \bar{X}}{SD}$	*z* score for Chrila: $\frac{6 - 9}{3.32} = -.9$
t scores (*t*)	Standard score with mean equal to 50 and standard deviation of 10. Avoids the use of negative values and extended decimals.	Equation 2.6 $t = 10z + 50$	*t* score for Chrila: $10(-.9) + 50 = 41$

A word of caution must be given when working with central tendency. Extremes may impact either the mode or mean by pulling the scores and provide an unrepresentative picture of the information set.

Measures of Dispersion

Although measures of central tendencies are used to see how information converges around an average score, they cannot provide the full picture. Two data sets can have identical means, medians, and modes, yet be very different. In one set, the data may be clustered very close together with all scores within a few counts of the mean, while the second set may spread across a wide range with a spread of many counts on either side of the mean. **Measures of dispersion** are used to describe how information is spread from the mean. Three measures of dispersion commonly used are range, variance, and standard deviation (SD).

Range. The **range** is the simplest measure of dispersion. The range is the difference between the highest and lowest score in the data set. Because the range only uses two pieces of data, it is considered a very crude measurement of dispersion. It depends on the number of cases within the sample. As the sample size increases, the less useful the range tends to be. An example of range is given in Table 2.5.

Variance. The **variance** is a numerical index used to describe the degree or amount of variability around the mean of a set of scores. The size of the variance indicates the spread of the scores. A large variance indicates the scores are widely spread, while a small variance indicates the scores are close together. The variance and range for our class indicate small variability. The size of the variance is not affected by the size of the mean or the number of cases in the set. The variance, by itself, is very useful in psychometric theory. For our use, computing the variance is the first step in computing the standard deviation (see Equation 2.2 in Table 2.5).

Standard Deviation. The **standard deviation** is the most frequently used and most stable index of variability (see Equation 2.3 in Table 2.5). Like the variance, the size of the standard deviation indicates the spread of scores from the mean. A small standard deviation indicates a small spread; a large standard deviation indicates a large spread.

Standard deviation is an important tool in interpreting individual case scores within the data set. The mean serves as a reference point from which determination of extremeness or significance of scores can be determined. Scores that fall 1 standard deviation above or below the mean are usually considered significant. Figure 2.2 illustrates the distribution of scores and the extremes for Miss Ray's class.

Normal Distribution

You have probably heard teachers say they are grading on the curve. What they are referring to is a grading system based on the concept of the **normal distribution.** A normal distribution is said to occur when four criterial assumptions are met:

1. Fifty percent of scores are above the mean and 50% of the scores are below the mean
2. The mean, median, and mode are the same

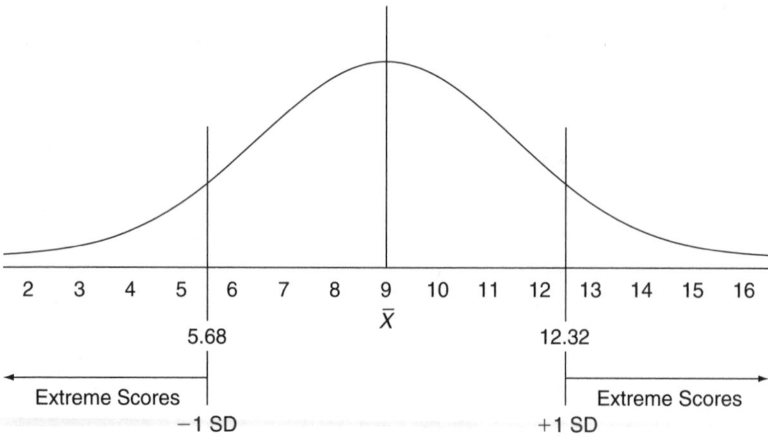

FIGURE 2.2 Distributions for Miss Ray's class set.

3. The majority of scores cluster around the mean, and the further from the mean a score is, the fewer number of scores that will be in that group
4. There is an equal number of scores from the mean to 1 standard deviation above the mean (i.e., +1 SD) as there are from the mean to 1 standard deviation below the mean (i.e., –1 SD)

A smooth curve graph meeting these four observations is called a normal distribution, normal, or bell curve. The important concept to remember is that the same four observations will hold true if you repeat the measurement again with a different group of individuals or if you look at most naturally occurring phenomena, such as height of cornstalks, academic achievement, or IQ.

For teachers, the importance of the normal distribution is in relation to the standard deviation. The standard deviation can be used as a unit of measurement. One can determine how far, or the number of standard deviations, from the mean a specific case may be. Because the distribution is normal, one can determine what percentage of the cases will fall between the mean and that specific standard deviation. This in turn allows teachers to determine what rate of behavior should be of concern. For Miss Ray's class, any score above +1 SD (approximately 84% of cases fall below +1 SD) or above 12.3 is of concern. Figure 2.3 depicts a normal distribution and the percentage of cases that fall between each standard deviation.

The significance of the standard deviation can be illustrated by examining one of the common uses of the normal distribution. Some states use absolute scores of 2 standard deviations above or below the mean on an intelligence test as the minimum criteria for consideration for placement in special programs. A score of 2 standard deviations above the mean is often used for consideration for gifted programs, while a score of 2 standard deviations below the mean may be used for diagnosis of mental retardation.

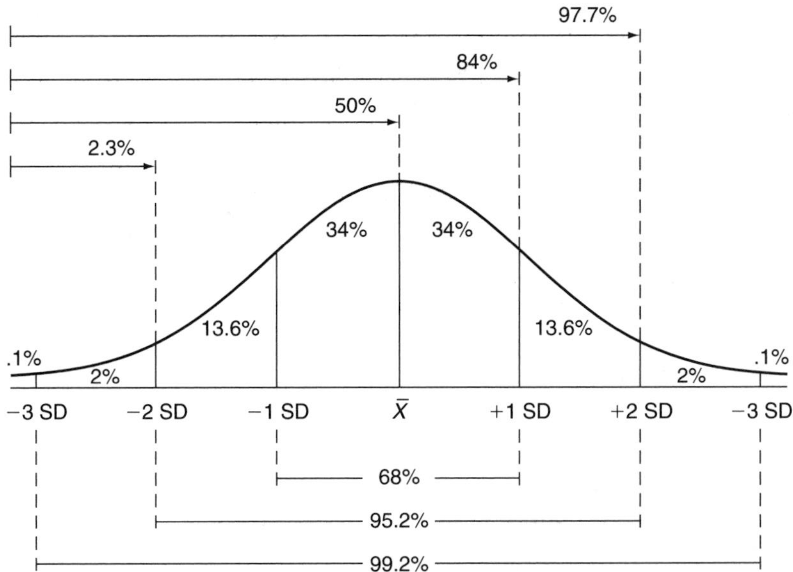

FIGURE 2.3 Characteristics of the normal distribution.

Skewed Distributions

Most naturally occurring phenomena (e.g., height, weight, aptitude, intelligence) form normal distributions if enough cases are involved in the information set. If the number of cases is very small, or if the nature of the participants comprising the cases are extremely similar, then the assumptions based on the distribution may or may not be valid. We have a **skewed** distribution when the assumptions are found to be invalid.

A skewed distribution is any distribution that does not meet the four basic criteria of a normal distribution. A typical skewed distribution has a large number of cases near one tail with a few extreme scores near the other tail. Skewedness also can be determined by simply computing the mean and median. The distribution is said to be negatively skewed when the mean is less than the median. The distribution is said to be positively skewed when the mean is greater than the median. If the mean and median are the same, or nearly the same, the distribution is symmetrical. We become concerned about skewedness when the mean and median are very far apart. Figure 2.4 depicts examples of skewedness for an easy and hard test.

Measures of Relative Position

Sometimes teachers need to determine how two or more scores relate to each other. They may want to see how a student compared to other students within the same data set. Or, they might need to know how one student has done comparatively on two tests. The teacher needs to determine the **measure of relative position.** The two most frequently used measures of relative position are the percentile rank and standard score.

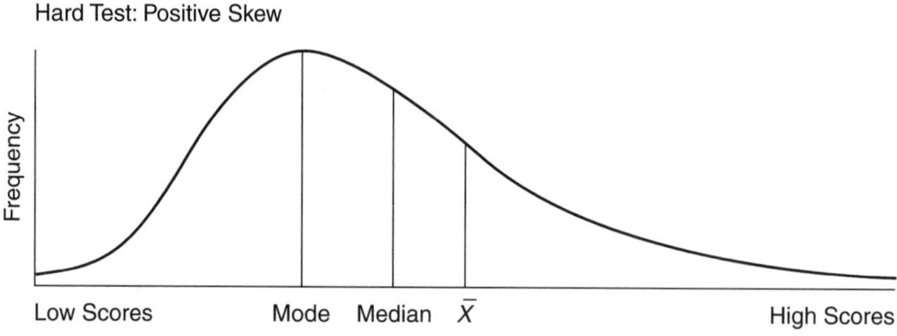

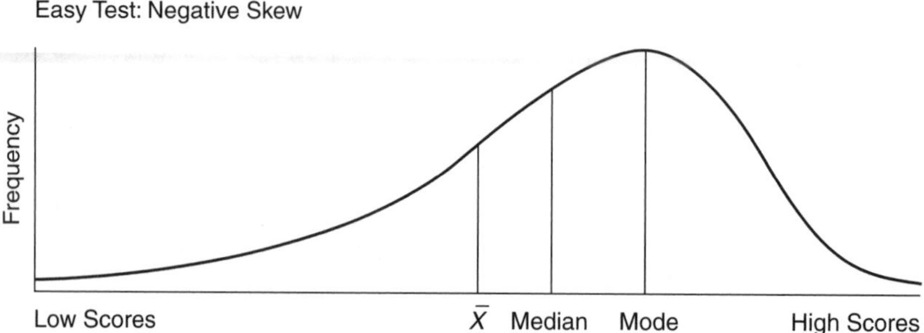

FIGURE 2.4 Two types of skewed test scores.

Percentile Rank. **Percentile ranks** are used to determine where an individual case falls in relationship to others in the same data set. A percentile rank expresses the percentage of cases that fall at or below a given score. If a student's score falls at the 68th percentile, it means the student scored better than 68 out of 100 other students on the same measure (see Equation 2.4 in Table 2.5).

Standard Scores. A **standard score** is a derived or transformed score that expresses the distance a given raw score is from some point of reference, usually the mean, in terms of standard deviation units. Standard scores are important to us for they allow for comparisons of scores from different tests or information sets. The most commonly used standard scores are the ***z* score, *t* score,** and deviation IQ. Computational examples for *z* score (see Equation 2.5) and *t* score (see Equation 2.6) are depicted in Table 2.5. A comparison of the most commonly used standard scores, as well as our class's scores, are provided in Table 2.6.

A word of caution must be given regarding comparing test scores. For information sets to be comparable, the population used to develop the distributions must be similar. If money were to be given to all persons over +1 SD in height, which distribution would you like to be compared with, the NBA players or a group of jockeys? In the same vein, to determine how well our student is doing, the population used to develop the distributions must also represent our student.

TABLE 2.6 Comparison of Commonly Used Standard Scores and the Scores for Miss Ray's Class

	Normal Curve Equivalents						
Standard Score Forms	−3 SD	−2 SD	−1 SD	$\bar{X}$	+1 SD	+2 SD	+3 SD
z scores ($\bar{X}$ = 0; SD = 1)	−3	−2	−1	0	+1	+2	+3
t scores ($\bar{X}$ = 50; SD = 10)	20	30	40	50	60	70	80
Deviation IQ							
WISC-III* ($\bar{X}$ = 100; SD = 15)	55	70	85	100	115	130	145
Miss Ray's Class ($\bar{X}$ = 9; SD = 3.32)	0	2.36	5.68	9	12.32	15.64	18.56

*Wechsler Intelligence Scale for Children-III

Measures of Relationship

Sometimes teachers need to know if two factors are related. They can find out by means of **measures of relationship.** If a relationship truly exists between two factors, one factor could be used to predict the second factor. While a relationship might exist, such a relationship does not necessarily indicate a causal relationship. Does a relationship between women and shopping at maternity stores indicate that shopping at maternity stores causes pregnancy?

In statistics, a relationship between variables is referred to as the **correlation.** Correlations that are represented by numerical indexes are referred to as **correlation coefficients.** Correlation coefficients provide an estimate or degree of how related the variables are. The correlation coefficient is represented by a decimal number between −1 and +1. Directionality is indicated by the sign of the coefficient (+ or −), while magnitude is indicated by the decimal number. The further away from 0, the more related the variables are considered to be. A correlation coefficient of .00 (read "point zero") would indicate no relationship exists, while a correlation coefficient of 1 (either positive or negative) indicates a perfect relationship. Coefficients with positive values indicate the relationship moves in the same direction (as one variable increases so will the other variable). For example, the more time you spend studying for a test, the more likely your grade will go up. Coefficients with negative values indicate the relationship moves in opposite directions (as one increases the other decreases). For example, the more days of school you miss, the lower your grade will be. The most frequently used correlation coefficients are the Spearman rho and Pearson *r.*

Characteristics of Measures

Teachers can get information from a variety of sources: observations, teacher-developed measures, or standardized measures. No matter the source, teachers want information that is truly representative of what the child or youth is doing. To ensure information is representative, one looks for three specific characteristics: (a) objectivity, (b) validity, and (c) reliability.

Objectivity

For a measure to be objective, the outcome should be the same or nearly the same regardless of who administers or scores the measure. The only way to ensure **objectivity** is to standardize the administration, scoring, and interpretation of the measure. This is done by spelling out exactly what is to occur in each area. For administration, directions should include instructions that are to be read to the taker, time limits, as well as the type and amount of communication permitted between the administrator and the taker of the measure. Specific criteria for scoring procedures should address what will be counted as appropriate, the number of points ascribed to a response or observation, and the procedures for calculating the total score. To standardize interpretation, clear guidelines should be given as to how to interpret the measure. This may address how to and if norming tables will be used. Interpretation examples may also be included.

Reliability

Reliability refers essentially to dependability or consistency: the dependability of a measure to yield the same results for the same individual if the measure is administered more than once. It also refers to the consistency with which the skill or trait being measured is treated across items in the measure. The more reliable a measure is, the more confident we are that the same score would be obtained if the measure were to be readministered. A measure that does not, on readministration, obtain the same score is considered to be unreliable and therefore worthless.

Reliability is usually expressed as a coefficient. The coefficient will range from 0 to +1.00, inclusive. A high coefficient indicates high reliability, while a low coefficient indicates low reliability. A perfect reliability has a coefficient of +1.00. But what does a coefficient of +.85 mean? Basically, it means that something is interfering with the obtainment of perfect reliability. That something is referred to as errors of measurement.

Errors of measurement that have impact on reliability are random errors. Some errors may increase the score while others may decrease the score. Errors may be caused by properties of the measure itself (an item may be ambiguous), by improper administration, by characteristics of the examinee (unmotivated, illness, and so forth), or by a combination of these factors. A high reliability indicates that these error sources were eliminated as much as possible.

There are four basic methods of measuring reliability: test-retest, equivalent-forms, internal consistency, and interrater. Each form of reliability addresses a different form of consistency.

Test-Retest Reliability. **Test-retest reliability** measures consistency over time. It is determined by readministering the same measure within a brief span of time, then correlating the outcomes. The assumption underlying this form of reliability is that the trait being measured will remain stable. A problem with this form of reliability is the length of time that should elapse between measures. If the span is too short, concerns with practice effect (i.e., remembering items or responses from one administration to the next) must be considered. If practice effect occurs, the estimate of reliability will be artificially high. If the span is too long, concerns with maturation effect (i.e., developmental or learning growth) must be considered. If maturation effect occurs, the estimate of reliability will be artificially low.

Equivalent-Forms Reliability. **Equivalent-forms reliability** measures consistency of two equivalent tests. Equivalent-forms reliability was developed to counter the problems with practice effect and maturation. Two matched forms of the measure are administered within a short period of time. The two measures should be identical in what is measured, the number of items, the level of difficulty, the administration; in fact, in every way possible. Outcomes from the two measures will result in a coefficient of equivalence. A primary problem associated with equivalent-forms reliability includes the difficulty of developing two forms that are truly equivalent. A secondary problem is the feasibility of administering two tests to the same group of individuals. Would you like to take a test twice? The length of the measure must also be considered. Some tests (e.g., GRE, ACT) take a great deal of time to administer, thus feasibility again comes into play.

Internal Consistency Reliability. **Internal consistency reliability** estimates consistency of content. As the terms *internal* and *consistency* indicate, one is looking for likeness within a single measure. One wants to determine if all the items actually measure the same skill or trait with the same consistency. Because the items in a single measure are what is being looked at, one needs only to administer the measure once. Several methods are used to determine the reliability of the items on a single measure using only one administration: split-half reliability, Kuder-Richardson 20, and Cronbach's coefficient alpha.

To determine **split-half reliability,** a single measure is administered, items are randomly divided into two comparable halves, the halves are scored independently, and finally the two halves are correlated. Split-half reliability establishes reliability between the two halves of the measure. Unfortunately, split-half reliability does not establish the reliability of the entire test. Split-half reliability is effective when the measure is long, when it is unfeasible to administer two forms of the same measure, or when it is unfeasible to administer the same measure twice.

A question that may arise is, Would a different combination of items in each half result in a different coefficient? The answer is possibly, but not necessarily. There are several ways to deal with this concern. One way would be to rank all the items from most to least difficult, then sort as odd-even. A second method would be to group items of like content together into item pools and then randomly assign each item to one of the halves of the measure. Or one could compute the correlation for all possible split-half divisions. Thankfully, rational equivalence reliability picks up where split-half reliability ends.

Rational equivalence reliability establishes the reliability of items within as well as to the entire measure. Rational equivalence reliability computes the average of all possible combinations of split-half correlations for a measure. Rational equivalence reliability is determined through application of the Kuder-Richardson 20 (KR-20) formula (Kuder & Richardson, 1937) or Cronbach's (1951) coefficient alpha rather than through correlation.

Internal consistency estimates have one very important drawback. This method cannot be used for untimed measures or for measures not completed by all examinees.

Interrater Reliability. The final form of reliability addresses not the measure, but the administrator or scorer of the measure. **Interrater reliability** (i.e., interscorer, interjudge, interobserver) refers to consistency of scorers to independently score a measure. Interrater reliability is determined by two scorers independently observing the same measure, each scoring the measure, and then comparing their final results. A common form of interrater reliability is point-by-point agreement (Kazdin, 1982). An example of interrater reliability is found in Table 2.7.

Factors Affecting Reliability. There are many factors that may impact a measure's reliability. Test length; time intervals between tests; makeup of the group; guessing; and environmental, psychological, or everyday factors must be considered. Test length is important in that longer measures tend to have greater reliability. Beware—measures that are very, very long may result in fatigue by the examinee, thus reducing reliability. We have already discussed time intervals and the potential for maturation effect as well as practice effect on reliability. The makeup of the group (as defined by age, grade level, demographics, and so on) in comparison to the general population needs to be considered. By stacking the group one can increase reliability. (Remember to examine the norm tables to determine if they are representative of whom you plan to evaluate.) Guessing impacts reliability by introducing error into the final score. (Maybe our student is a great guesser today; will he be tomorrow?)

TABLE 2.7 Examples of Reliability Measures

Statistical Measure	Explanation	Formula	Example
Point-by-Point Agreement	Each rater independently scores. Pair data points and examine to determine agreement (A) and disagreement (D) of the pairs. The reliability coefficient is r.	Equation 2.7 $r = \left(\frac{A}{A + D}\right)100$	Raters 1 and 2 had 10 pairs with the same score (A) and 4 pairs with different scores (D). $\left(\frac{10}{10 + 4}\right) 100 = 71$
Standard Error of Measure (SEM)	SD is the standard deviation of the test, and r is the reliability coefficient.	Equation 2.8 $SEM = SD\sqrt{1 - r}$	
Confidence Interval	Compute lower range of confidence interval by subtracting the SEM from the obtained score. Compute upper range of confidence interval by adding the SEM to the obtained score.		Student obtained score of 43. SEM was 2.6. Lower range: $43 - 2.6 = 40.4$ Upper range: $2.6 + 43 = 45.6$ Confidence range: 40.4 to 45.6 About 68% of the time.

Finally, environmental factors (e.g., excessive heat, noise), physiological factors (e.g., non-motivated, anxiety, daydreaming), or everyday factors (e.g., lose place on answer sheet, headache) will introduce error and reduce reliability.

Reliability Coefficients. By this point you may be asking, What is an acceptable level of reliability? The answer depends on the form of measure you are using as well as the use of the information obtained. A good rule of thumb is, if you are looking at group information to make decisions about the group as a whole, a minimum of .65 is recommended. On the other hand, if you are looking at an individual, much higher standards must be considered. If the measure is to be used for screening an individual, a minimum of .80 is desired. Placement or other important educational decisions about an individual would require a minimum of .90 (Gay, 1992; Salvia & Ysseldyke, 1998).

Standard Error of Measurement

In the discussion of reliability, we touched on the concept of error. We stated that errors of measurement impacting reliability are random errors. One can express statistically the concept of errors of measurement as it relates to reliability. This statistical concept is termed the **standard error of measurement (SEM).** Basically, the standard error of measurement is an estimate of how often errors of a given size in an individual's score can be expected. The SEM relates very closely to reliability. A small SEM indicates high reliability, and a large SEM indicates low reliability. In a perfect world where the reliability coefficient is 1.0 (perfect), the SEM would be 0 (perfect), and the score obtained would be the student's true score. We don't live in a perfect world, so an obtained score on any given measure is actually the true score plus any errors.

If you repeatedly gave a student the same measure, do you think the student would get the same exact score each time, or do you anticipate variability in the scores? Realistically, one would expect the scores to fluctuate, (once again we are talking about error of measurement). Because it would be inhumane to subject students to repeated measures simply to determine variance, a way is needed to estimate the amount of variation. Thus, the SEM provides us with a method to estimate the difference between the obtained and true score as it relates to the reliability of the measure (see Equation 2.8 in Table 2.7).

Confidence Intervals. A **confidence interval** is the range of scores in which a true score will fall with a given probability. A confidence interval of 68% is 1 SD. (Did you remember the percentage of the population that falls between –1 SD and +1 SD was 68%?) By knowing the SEM and the obtained score, one can establish a confidence interval. This can be done because the SEM is based on normal distribution theory (note the use of the standard deviation in the formula). This allows one to view the obtained score as the mean of a normal distribution and the SEM as the standard deviation of the distribution. An example of confidence interval is depicted in Table 2.7.

Validity

The most important characteristic of a measure is validity. **Validity** is defined as the ability and degree to which a measure successfully measures what it is supposed to be measuring.

If a measure is supposed to determine or measure an individual's ability to self-feed, we would expect to see observations of, or questions related to, self-feeding. In order to successfully measure what is intended to be measured, one must determine for whom and for what purpose the measure was developed (Gay, 1992). One would expect measures of algebraic competencies to provide a fairly accurate indication of the math achievement of tenth graders, but its usefulness for measuring attitudes related to art is probably rather limited. In addition, the usefulness of such measures for measuring the math achievements of third graders must also be questioned (Gay, 1992).

An important aspect of the "for whom" question relates to **norm groups.** Standardized measures traditionally provide information about the norm group. For a measure to be considered valid for a student, one needs to be sure that the norm group is representative of the student. Were individuals similar to the student included in the norming sample (i.e., age, gender, socioeconomic status, geographic representation, urban/rural, cultural group, and so forth)? Are the norms current? The question raised here is; Are the students of today like the students of 20 years ago?

Validity can be viewed as three basic types: content validity, criterion-related validity, or construct validity.

Content Validity. **Content validity** is the extent to which selected sample behaviors are representative of the domain being examined. To be representative, item validity, sampling validity, and appropriate presentation/response mode formats must be present. For item validity to be present, the items selected for inclusion in the measure must be taken from the content area of the domain. If we are measuring self-care skills, we would expect to see items related to toothbrushing, dressing, toileting, and so on. We would not expect to see items on money management or on letter writing.

Sampling validity is present when the items included in the measure are representative of the full array of the domain. In a measure of self-care skills, if the measure only sampled toothbrushing and did not include the other areas of the self-care domain (e.g., bathing, dressing), then the measure would have failed to sample adequately. One must be concerned not only with completeness of sampling, but also with balance of items in the sample. You would not want 20 items on bathing and only 2 items on hand washing. While one wants the sample to be complete and balanced, it must be remembered that a sample is only small pieces of the domain and does not include every item possible. If every item were included, it would result in a very long measure!

The final concern in content validity is the presentation/response mode format that addresses *how* content is measured. There are many teachers who use pencil-and-paper tests to measure if a student has learned the information presented in class. The test may be very well developed, using appropriately selected items that represent the full array of the domain under study. Yet, if the student can neither read nor write, the validity of the test comes into question. The question is, Does the test measure the ability to read and write (the presentation/response mode format), or does the test measure the student's knowledge of the information presented in class (the domain)? Presentation format is concerned with the use of appropriate methods to present items to the examinee. In the previous example, the presentation format concern would be giving a student with limited reading abilities a written test. Response mode format is concerned with the method required for an examinee to answer or respond to an item. If the student was able to read the test, had the knowledge being measured, but could not physically write a written response, then the response mode would interfere with the test's ability to measure the domain and would invalidate the test as given.

Criterion-Related Validity. **Criterion-related validity** is used to determine the extent of relationship between how an individual performs on one measure and some other measure of meaningful importance (e.g., criterion). The known criterion becomes the standard for validation to which the new measure is judged. This essentially means: we will compare the results of our measure with known criterion that have been determined to be indicators for the skill or trait we wish to measure to see how our measure stacks up.

The question must be raised as to why one would want to develop a measure if criteria already exist. Well, the answer is twofold. If it takes hours to determine the possession of the skill or trait of concern using the current criterion, but a measure can be developed that takes only minutes and is equally capable of determining the possession of the skill or trait of concern, which would you rather use? This type of validity is known as **concurrent validity.** Concurrent validity estimates current performance in relation to another criterion. As the term *concurrent* indicates, the measures are taken at or near the same time. The second answer, **predictive validity,** relates to the ability to predict the future. If you could develop a measure that could be given today that would allow you to estimate or predict future performance on some other measure or criterion of success at a later time, wouldn't you want the measure? You have probably been involved with many forms of predictive validity. Did you take a driving test in order to get a license? The state wanted an indicator of how safe you would be on the highways in the future. If you went to college, you probably took the American College Test (ACT). A strong correlation has been found with high scores on the ACT and successful completion of college.

Construct Validity. **Construct validity** is the degree to which one establishes how well outcomes can be explained in relation to some nonobservable hypothetical trait. Construct in this sense does not refer to the building of the measure. Rather, the term *construct* is used to describe nonobservable theoretical traits, characteristics, or attributes used to explain some phenomenon. A construct is an abstract concept to which we try to attach concrete measures based on presumed indicators. Examples of constructs would be intelligence, learning, or creativity. Tests of learning do not measure the amount of gray matter between your ears, nor do they measure what is in your brain (i.e., the number of neurons, synapses, blood vessels). Tests of learning measure changes in outcomes after a lesson is taught, not learning itself. One assumes learning has occurred because the outcome behavior has changed.

Validity is assessed as being logical, empirical, or a combination of both. The purpose of the measure will determine the method of assessing validity. Content validity is a form of logical validity. Expert judgment is used to assess if the selected samples truly represent the domain in substance, proportion, and presentation/response mode formats. Criterion-related validity is a form of empirical validity and is assessed by determining the magnitude of the relationship between the measure under study and an established criterion. Criterion-related validity uses a correlation coefficient, termed the *validity coefficient,* to measure the relationship. Construct validity is both a logical and empirical form of validity. Construct validity is logical due to the reliance on experts to determine if the theoretical factors are truly representative of the construct. Construct validity is empirical by virtue of the use of a variety of statistical procedures, including internal-structural analysis such as factor analysis or cross-structure analysis such as validity coefficients.

Often a single measure will be validated in a variety of ways. One might have an expert examine the measure to ensure content validity. In addition, one could compare the outcomes of the measure with existing criterion to ensure criterion-related validity.

After a discussion of reliability and validity, a few questions usually surface. Does reliability indicate validity? The answer is not necessarily. A high reliability indicates consistency, but we could be consistently measuring the wrong factors. Does validity indicate reliability? As Gay (1992) indicated, if a measure does not measure what it was designed to measure, then concerns about reliability are moot.

The remainder of this chapter will focus on standardized or norm-referenced assessment. Three widely used types of standardized assessment instruments will be described: tests of intelligence, measures of adaptive behavior, and achievement tests.

Introduction to Standardized Assessment

Standardized or **norm-referenced tests** constitute the most commonly used approach to assessment in public schools. Within this approach, a test score only has meaning in relation to how it compares to a particular representative group of scores. For example, a score of 110 may be meaningless in and of itself. But if we know that it is higher than 98% of the scores to which it is compared, we consider it to be a very high score. In standardized assessment, the performance of one person is compared and derives meaning only in comparison to the performance of some group of people.

In developing a standardized test, a large and representative group of people in the population of interest is tested. Thus, school children between 5 and 17 years of age who represent both genders, all major socioeconomic and cultural backgrounds, and geographic regions in the same proportions as they exist in the population as a whole might constitute the norm group. Then it can be determined how many children, or what percentage of the norm group, scored in different ranges of the test. We know, for example, that on the Wechsler Intelligence Scale for Children Revised-III (WISC-R), the norm group has an average score of 100. We also know what percent of the norm group falls within ranges above and below the mean. Less than 5% of the population score above 130 or below 70. Any individual child's score on the WISC-R can be interpreted accurately only by comparing it to the performance of a norm group whose members share characteristics similar to that child.

Norm-referenced tests are widely used in special and general education for several reasons. First, they are used to diagnose or categorize children as in need of special, remedial, or gifted education. Children are considered to be mentally retarded or gifted based, in part, by IQ scores. Second, they are commonly used to convey a great deal of information in an efficient manner. A parent may be told, for example, that her son scored higher than 99% of the population tested in math on the Iowa Test of Educational Development. Third, norm-referenced tests are used to determine eligibility for special educational services, programs for the gifted, college entrance, and admission to advanced graduate studies. Fourth, these tests are used in district- and statewide testing for comparative purposes with national norms. Fifth, standardized tests are sometimes used to determine public policy. Finally, standardized tests are frequently used in technical reports and research studies.

While standardized or norm-referenced tests may be quite helpful when used appropriately, as in the previous examples, there are several questions that they cannot answer. First, norm-referenced tests cannot yield information specific enough to develop individual student objectives. Second, these tests cannot measure a student's day-to-day progress on short-term objectives. Third, they cannot be used to compare an individual's test scores to students who vary in some primary characteristic such as age, physical condition, cultural background, or primary language spoken in the home.

Several questions or controversies continue to surround norm-referenced testing. First, is it possible to develop a test that is culturally fair to all individuals? Such a test would have to measure innate cognitive abilities alone and not be influenced by previous learning opportunities the student may or may not have had or the culture in which the child lives.

Second, norm-referenced tests, such as IQ tests, have sometimes been used to predict performance in areas other than school achievement. These tests have been used, for example, to predict vocational success, or whether a student with cognitive disabilities should be placed in competitive job training. Such instances involve overgeneralization of test scores. While there is a positive correlation between scores on standardized tests of intelligence and school achievement, these tests cannot predict an individual's performance in vocational, social, or physical skills.

Another difficulty is that the information yielded by norm-referenced tests is generally too broad to be used to plan daily instruction. They cannot tell the teacher what content or which instructional strategies might be appropriate for an individual student. Knowing that a particular student is 2.5 years behind her age peers in reading, for example, is insufficient information on which to prescribe reading content and instructional techniques for that student, or to determine which particular areas of reading challenge the student.

Standards for Selecting and Evaluating Standardized Tests

Many different standardized tests are available in many different areas of student performance. There are tests of intelligence, adaptive behavior, academic achievement, behavioral and emotional characteristics, aptitude, vocational potential, and perceptual-motor abilities. How do we know which test to select? How do we compare the merits of one test to those of other tests that purport to assess the same area? What are the features of a good test? What criteria should be used in evaluating a test? Standards used in selecting and evaluating standardized tests must include both technical and practical considerations. The technical standards of objectivity, validity, reliability, and norming were discussed in the statistical overview of this chapter.

When deciding what test is most appropriate for a given purpose, one should always consult the test manual. Information on reliability, validity, and norms should be available in detail. The most highly regarded source to consult when evaluating a test is, without question, the *Buros Mental Measurements Yearbook.* This publication contains critical reviews by experts of virtually every test marketed in English. Each test is reviewed in detail, and these reviews are painstakingly edited and checked for factual accuracy. The *Yearbook* also includes references of every published article investigating the technical merits of a particular test.

Practical Considerations in Selecting a Test

While the technical merits of a test should take priority in selecting one test over another, there are a number of practical considerations that enter into the decision. Among these are cost, time needed for administration, time required and ease of scoring, ease of interpretation, and whether multiple copies of test forms and other materials needed for administration are included with the basic test or have to be purchased separately. Publishing and marketing tests is profit motivated. Ultimately, which test will be selected should depend on the purpose for which it is to be used in a specific situation and reasoned and informed judgment about the relative technical merits and practical features of the test.

Now that we have described the basic characteristics of standardized tests and reviewed factors important in evaluating the technical merits of these tests, we will address three kinds of standardized tests commonly used in schools. It is beyond the scope and intent of this text to provide a comprehensive review of the field of standardized assessment. We will describe standardized assessment of intelligence, adaptive behavior, and achievement in the following sections.

Nature and Measurement of Intelligence

Although intelligence testing has been surrounded by several areas of controversy, the assessment of cognitive ability is mandated by the Individuals with Disabilities Education Act (IDEA) for the diagnosis and determination of eligibility for special education services for many disabilities. It is important to understand what tests of intelligence can and cannot measure. The **Intelligence Quotient (IQ),** obtained by a child's responses to a set of stimuli on a particular test, has often been misinterpreted and overgeneralized. Intelligence tests are relatively good predictors of academic achievement. Scores on intelligence tests correlate particularly well with achievement test scores. They are not good indicators of innate ability or potential to learn, however. Nor are they good predictors of performance in nonacademic areas such as social, domestic, or vocational skills. Above all, it is important to keep in mind that previous material learned and opportunities to learn that have been available to a child in his or her cultural background and experience significantly influence performance on the intelligence test.

Reaching a consensus on the definition of intelligence has long eluded psychologists and educators. Whether **intelligence** is a single ability or comprised of multiple factors or abilities has been the focus of controversy over the past 60 years. Binet and Wechsler, the authors of two of the most widely used standardized tests of intelligence, both conceived of intelligence as a polyfaceted and complex set of abilities. Yet, perhaps because their tests both yield a global score (the IQ), emphasis has often been placed on intelligence as a single, global capacity.

Early researchers such as Spearman (1927), Thurstone (1938), and Guilford (1967) all focused on theories of intelligence that involved more than a single factor. Spearman theorized a two-factor model of intelligence comprised of a general factor (g) and a group of specific factors or abilities. Spearman argued that the g factor was involved in problem solving and higher order thinking processes, while the group of more specific factors are unique to a specific test or task. He advocated the development of intelligence tests that could accurately measure the g factor, because it comes into play across all tasks.

Guilford (1967) developed a three-dimensional Structure of Intellect Model. Within this model, specific mental abilities are clustered into Operations (how information is processed), Products (e.g., classes, transformations, implications), and Content (e.g., symbolic, figural, behavioral, semantic). Guilford believed that any model of intelligence must be complex and multifaceted in order to account for the complexity of mental ability.

Intelligence tests fall into two categories: group tests and individualized tests. Examples of commonly used group tests are the California Test of Mental Maturity (Sullivan, Clark, & Tiegs, 1970) and the Cognitive Abilities Test (Thorndike & Hagan, 1994). It must be emphasized that group intelligence tests should be used only for general screening to determine which children may have a potential for significantly high or low intellectual functioning. Using the scores of these tests for any other purpose is not appropriate.

We will now briefly review three individualized tests of intelligence frequently used in schools. These are the Wechsler Intelligence Scale for Children–Third Edition (WISC-III), The Stanford-Binet Intelligence Scale–Fourth Edition, and the Kaufman Assessment Battery for Children (K-ABC). For the most comprehensive critical reviews of these tests, the reader is referred to the most recent edition of the *Buros Mental Measurements Yearbook.*

Wechsler Intelligence Scale for Children–Third Edition. The WISC-III (Wechsler, 1991), appropriate for children 6 through 16 years of age, is the most widely used of the three scales devised by David Wechsler. The other two scales are the Wechsler Preschool and Primary Scale of Intelligence–Revised, for use with children 3 to 7 years of age, and the Wechsler Adult Intelligence Scale–Revised, for individuals from age 16 years and older. The WISC-III has two separate parts, the verbal and the performance section. A Verbal IQ, a Performance IQ, and a Full Scale IQ score are obtained. These scores, as well as other information about a youngster, are considered by a multidisciplinary team in decisions about eligibility for special education services.

The verbal section has six subtests, each with multiple items: Information, Similarities, Arithmetic, Vocabulary, Comprehension, and Digit Span. The performance section of the WISC-III has seven subtests: Picture Completion, Picture Arrangement, Block Design, Object Assembly, Coding, Mazes, and Symbol Search.

Each subtest is timed and produces a raw score that is converted to a scaled score. Subtest scaled scores each have a mean of 10 with a standard deviation of 3. Subtest scores may be compared to each other, although this practice is not without criticism. The WISC-III Verbal, Performance, and Full Scale IQ scores each have a mean of 100 with a standard deviation of 15.

The WISC-III was developed with a national norm group consisting of 2200 children. The norm group had characteristics similar to those of the 1988 U.S. census in relation to geographic region, level of education of parents, and cultural background. There were an equal number of boys and girls in the norm group. In summary, the WISC-III is a well-standardized test and, based on the research conducted to date, may be used with confidence to determine a measured level of intelligence on an individual student.

Stanford-Binet Intelligence Scale–Fourth Edition. The SBIS-4 (Thorndike, Hagan, & Sattler, 1986) was developed for the following purposes, according to its authors: (a) to assist in differentiating between students with mental retardation and those with learning disabilities, (b) to shed information on why a student is having difficulty with academic work, (c) to help in the diagnosis of individuals who are gifted, and (d) to examine the development of cognitive abilities in persons from age 2 years to adulthood.

The SBIS-4 is based on a three-tiered hierarchical model of intelligence. First, there is a general intelligence level. The second level includes three broad factors, crystallized abilities, fluid-analytic abilities, and short-term memory. The third level of this test includes verbal reasoning, quantitative reasoning, and abstract-visual reasoning (Taylor, 1997; 2000).

The SBIS-4 has a total of 15 subtests. Individual subtest scores are standard with a mean of 50 and a standard deviation of 8. Standard scores with a mean of 100 and a standard deviation of 16 are also possible to obtain for Verbal Reasoning, Abstract-Visual Reasoning, Short-Term Memory, Quantitative Reasoning, and Total Test Composite.

The normative sample for the SBIS-4 was representative of the U.S. population relative to sex, community size, geographic region, and cultural background. More than 5000 individuals from all 50 states were included in the norm group.

Research on the SBIS-4 conducted to date indicates that the test is an adequate indicator of general intelligence. It is less reliable as a measure of more specific abilities, which it purports to measure. Interpretation of the composite score only is recommended at present. There is some research that indicates scores on the SBIS-4 differ from other traditional individualized tests of intelligence for gifted students. More research is needed before conclusions can be reached about the use of the SBIS-4 with very young children, particularly those who have mental retardation and those with different types of disabilities (cf. Glutting, 1989).

The Kaufman Assessment Battery for Children. The K-ABC, developed by Kaufman and Kaufman in 1983, is designed to provide information on both intellectual functioning and achievement of children from 2.5 to 12.5 years of age. This test, based on the theories of Luria and Das (Das, Kirby, & Jarman, 1979; Jarman & Das, 1977), divides intellectual functioning into two distinct styles of processing information, sequential and simultaneous. Sequential information processors organize and deal with stimuli in a one-at-a-time manner. Recalling one's telephone number or organizing and recalling words in a certain order are examples. Individuals who engage in problem solving and decision making in a simultaneous manner, on the other hand, process information in a holistic manner, considering a variety of stimuli at the same time. The basic question within this theoretical framework is not how much information has a child learned, but rather how that child learns. The K-ABC places great emphasis on how a child approaches problem solving (Witt, Elliott, Kramer, & Gresham, 1994). Two of the authors' goals for this test were to separate previously acquired factual knowledge from the ability to process information and solve unfamiliar problems and yield information that translates to educational interventions. The K-ABC has 16 subtests that are organized to yield 4 global scores: Sequential Processing, Simultaneous Processing, Mental Processing Composite (a combination of the first two areas), and Achievement. Each of the 4 global scores has a mean of 100 and a standard deviation of 15. National percentile ranks and percentile ranks for sociocultural groups represented in the norm group are available for each of the four areas as well. A child's scores may be compared to the national scores and to those of the ethnic and sociocultural group to which he or she belongs.

Two thousand children from 22 states were in the normative group of the K-ABC, including children with disabilities. The normative group was representative of 1980 census data.

Considerable research has been focused on the K-ABC since it was first put on the market. Although the psychometric features of the test are considered to be sound, the theoretical model on which the test was based remains in question. Much of the research on the K-ABC has examined the meaning and validity of the constructs of simultaneous and sequential processing. The results to date are unclear. The criterion-related validity of the test is considered good. Use of the test with very young children is questionable. The nondiscriminatory ability of the test has been questioned. Whether the information yielded from this test can be translated into appropriate educational interventions is also at issue (Witt et al., 1994). Clearly, more extensive research is needed.

Issues and Concerns in Assessing Intelligence

As we mentioned earlier, controversy over the definition of intelligence and how to measure it has been a part of the history of standardized assessment. Three issues, in particular, continue to be discussed in courts of law and in the professional literature: (a) the stability of the IQ, (b) nondiscriminatory assessment of cognitive ability, and (c) treatment validity (Witt et al., 1994). We will now consider each of these areas of continuing debate.

Stability of the IQ. Does intelligence, as measured by individualized, standardized tests, remain constant throughout one's lifetime? Or do we become more or less intelligent at various points in our lives? When we look at the test scores of large groups of people, it appears that most individuals would receive similar scores if retested. This generalization holds for the stability of IQ scores over shorter periods of time and for groups of individuals who are older children and adults. But what about the stability of IQ scores for individuals? Is it possible for an individual's IQ score to vary by 5, 10, or even 20 points or more from one time to another? The answer is yes.

The question of the **stability of IQ** is inextricably woven with the questions of what do intelligence tests test and what factors influence IQ scores. We know that a particular child's measured level of intelligence is largely due to previously acquired knowledge. And we also know that how much knowledge any one individual will learn depends on opportunity to learn new material. Exposure to new stimuli, quality of education, motivation to learn, encouragement and support for learning, physical health, and nutrition all can significantly affect how much one learns. These intra-individual differences mean that one's test score may fluctuate from one testing session to another. We may not safely assume that the score obtained on an intelligence test will always remain the same for an individual (Witt et al., 1994).

Nondiscriminatory Assessment. Perhaps no other issue has been debated as intensely as the question of whether IQ tests are biased against some groups of people. **Test bias** is said to occur when a test consistently differentiates members of particular groups of people on bases other than the characteristics being measured (Brown, 1983). When it was first noted that special education classes for students with mental retardation contained a disproportionate number of children from economically depressed, African American, and Hispanic backgrounds, charges of test bias were common.

Reschly (1980) described six kinds of test bias:

1. Mean differences between scores of various groups of people
2. Item or content bias in which portions of the test content differentially affect the performance of different groups
3. Factor analysis reveals that the factors being measured by a test (e.g., memory, verbal ability) are different for different cultural or economic groups
4. Predictive validity where scores predict with varying levels of confidence for different groups
5. Social consequences result when tests are misused to justify discriminatory social policy
6. Selection ratios result when tests are used in ways that underrepresent or overrepresent certain groups of people in diagnostic categories (such as mental retardation, gifted, schizophrenic)

Perhaps the most warranted conclusion at this time is that well-constructed tests of intelligence do not discriminate. Rather, it is the misuse or misinterpretation of tests that results in discriminatory practices. It is important to keep in mind that the primary purpose of intelligence tests is to predict academic achievement in school. Good tests accomplish that goal. When individual children and groups of children do not succeed in school, we must look for factors other than tests, such as discriminatory school policies or lack of opportunity to learn, to explain the reason.

Treatment Validity. The ability of a test to lead to effective and appropriate treatment has been referred to as treatment validity (Gresham, 1992). If, for example, we could translate a child's measured level of intelligence into appropriate educational objectives and instructional strategies, we could conclude that the IQ test had treatment validity.

In fact, there is no evidence to suggest that IQ tests may be used to design instructional programs. Nor have educators or psychologists been successful in establishing treatment by aptitude interactions, or the ability to use a child's educational diagnostic category to predict effective instructional programs.

To design effective and individualized instructional programs, more specific and directly observable information is needed. That type of information about a student's specific strengths and weaknesses and how to obtain it are emphasized throughout the remaining chapters.

Does this point out a flaw in intelligence tests? The answer is no. Once again we are reminded of the basic purpose for which intelligence tests were developed: that is to predict achievement in school. And well-designed tests do accomplish that purpose. Knowing that a particular youngster scored 70 on the WISC-III will not assist us in developing an appropriate IEP. But we may anticipate that the child will encounter difficulties and learn new information in school at a slower rate than a child who scores at a much higher level.

The use of intelligence testing remains controversial. This is largely because of the misuse and misinterpretations of the tests in the past. As test administrators and interpreters gain more knowledge and as the research on intelligence tests aids our understanding of their strengths and weaknesses, we hope to see fewer abuses of test scores in the future. The controversy surrounding intelligence testing should not be focused on the question of whether these tests are good. Rather, our efforts must be directed toward obtaining a better understanding of the characteristics, abilities, and limitations of the tests.

Nature and Measurement of Adaptive Behavior

The assessment of adaptive behavior is a relatively new practice in the field of education. In the early 70s, it was common practice to diagnose mental retardation primarily on the basis of intelligence tests that required good verbal proficiency in English. It became apparent that children whose primary language was not English were being labeled as mentally retarded at rates that were higher than their proportions in the general population. While these children did show delays in the acquisition of academic skills, their performance in nonacademic areas such as social skills and independent functioning, and their performance outside of the school setting, was normal. As a result of several court cases (e.g., *Guadalupe Organization v. Tempe Elementary School District,* 1972), evaluations of adaptive behavior became mandatory. Definitions of mental retardation were changed to include significant subaverage intellectual functioning and deficits in adaptive behavior.

Today, adaptive behavior is assessed for three specific reasons. First, adaptive behavior plays a significant role in classification decisions. The diagnosis of mental retardation should never be made without comprehensive assessment in the areas of intelligence and adaptive behavior. Second, adaptive behavior may be assessed for the purpose of developing instructional programs for functional, independent living skills. Taylor (1997) noted that a third purpose for the assessment of adaptive behavior is screening to identify individuals who may be in need of more thorough evaluations.

Most definitions of adaptive behavior include the concepts of age-appropriate independent functioning (i.e., dressing, eating, use of money) and social responsibility. Perhaps the most widely accepted definition of adaptive behavior was promoted by the American Association on Mental Retardation (AAMR) in 1992: **Adaptive behavior** is defined as the effectiveness or degree with which an individual meets the standards of personal independence and social responsibility expected for age and cultural group.

According to AAMR (1992), the diagnosis of mental retardation may be made only after documenting significantly subaverage intellectual functioning and related limitations in two or more of the following adaptive skill areas:

- Communication, or the ability to comprehend and express information through both symbolic and nonsymbolic behaviors
- Self-care skills such as eating, dressing, and toileting
- Home living skills such as housekeeping, clothing care, and food preparation
- Social skills including making friends, sharing, cooperating with others, and demonstrating honesty and trustworthiness
- Community use, including traveling, shopping, and making appropriate use of community resources
- Self-direction, or the ability to make appropriate choices
- Health and safety, or the ability to maintain one's own physical well being

- Functional academic skills, referring to practical academic skills that are related to independent functioning
- Leisure skills including the ability to select and appropriately engage in recreation and leisure time pursuits
- Work, or the ability to hold a part- or full-time job, job skill competence, and work-related skills

From this discussion, two points merit emphasis in regard to adaptive behavior. First, adaptive behavior is clearly a multidimensional concept. This approach allows for consideration of a person's change over time in relation to growth opportunities, environmental changes, and degree of support. Second, whether an individual's adaptive behavior is appropriate or inappropriate can be judged only against the standards for that person's age, cultural group, and environment(s).

Assessment of Adaptive Behavior

While there are several adaptive behavior scales available on the market, we will describe two of the most widely accepted and frequently used scales. These are the AAMR Adaptive Behavior Scales and the Vineland Adaptive Behavior Scales.

AAMR Adaptive Behavior Scale–Second Edition: Residential and Community Edition; School Edition. The AAMR Adaptive Behavior Scales (ABS) were revised in 1993 by Lambert, Leland, and Nihira. The Residential and Community Edition may be used with individuals between 6 and 79 years of age living in residential or community-based settings. The School Edition may be used with students from 6 to 21 years of age who attend public schools. Both scales are designed for use with individuals who have mental retardation, emotional disabilities, or both.

The ABS has two parts. Part One is designed to measure adaptive behaviors, while Part Two is designed for the assessment of maladaptive behaviors. Part One includes the areas of Independent Functioning, Physical Development, Economic Activity, Language, Numbers and Time, Domestic Activity, Prevocational/Vocational Activity, Self-Direction, Responsibility, and Socialization. There are 73 items on Part One of the Residential and Community Edition and 67 items on Part One of the School Edition.

Part Two of the ABS includes 8 domains of maladaptive behavior. These are Social Behavior, Conformity, Trustworthiness, Stereotyped and Hyperactive Behavior, Sexual Behavior, Self-Abusive Behavior, Social Engagement, and Disturbing Interpersonal Behavior. Specific behaviors on Part Two are scored as follows: 0 = behavior does not occur at all; 1 = behavior occasionally occurs; 2 = behavior frequently occurs.

On both parts of the ABS information may be obtained in one of two ways. The evaluator may observe and assess the individual directly if he or she is familiar with the person being assessed. Or, the information may be obtained by the evaluator from a third party (e.g., parent, teacher, attendant) who is very familiar with the individual being assessed.

The Residential and Community Edition was developed with more than 4000 individuals in the normative sample. Over 2000 students comprised the norm group for the School Edition. Part Two of the ABS, in particular, has been criticized on the basis that 40% to 50%

of the standardization group displayed no inappropriate behavior, and, therefore, were not representative. In addition, no consideration is given to the severity of the behaviors assessed by Part Two (Taylor, 1997). Clearly, much more research is needed on the technical properties of the 1993 Community and Residential and School Editions of the Adaptive Behavior Scales.

Vineland Adaptive Behavior Scales. The Vineland Adaptive Behavior Scales (VABS), developed by Sparrow, Balla, and Cicchetti (1984), is the most recent revision of Doll's (1965) Vineland Social Maturity Scale. The VABS can be used with individuals from birth to 18 years of age. This test has three separate editions: the classroom edition, the Interview Edition–Survey Form, and the Interview Edition–Expanded Form. These three forms may be used singly or in combination. Teachers may administer the classroom edition to gain assessment data about the student in school settings. The two Interview Editions are used to obtain information from the primary caregiver. The Expanded Form is more comprehensive and appropriate to assess individuals who have severe disabilities.

The classroom edition is presented in a checklist form. It is assumed that the teacher is very familiar with the student's behavior through direct observations of adaptive behavior in the classroom setting. This form may be used with children ages 3 through 13.

The interview editions each measure five domains of adaptive behavior: Communication, Daily Living Skills, Socialization, Motor Skills, and Maladaptive Behavior. Again, it is assumed that the primary caregiver providing the information is intimately familiar with the person assessed and has opportunities to directly observe all of the behaviors on the interview editions.

The VABS was normed with a national sample of more than 3000 individuals. Approximately 10% of this sample was receiving special education services. The VABS yields standard scores, percentile ranks, stanines, and age equivalents. There is also a summary report format for parents that has been designed to provide practical meaning to the numerical scores.

The VABS may be the most commonly used instrument with which to measure adaptive behavior. Its technical merits and theoretical basis are sound, according to Taylor's (1997) review of available research on the instrument. The VABS is most applicable for persons with mild to moderate levels of mental retardation.

Issues Related to the Assessment of Adaptive Behavior

The move to use more than a single IQ score cutoff point in the diagnosis and classification of mental retardation was well intentioned. Perhaps no other diagnostic label has such a negative stigma as does "mentally retarded." The attempt to define and assess adaptive behavior was intended to yield the most comprehensive information possible, based on many direct observations of an individual's behavior, before the diagnosis is made. The assessment of adaptive behavior is fraught, however, by at least two major concerns. The first concern relates to the degree of relativity and subjectivity inherent in decisions about what is and is not adaptive behavior. The second concern is the question of what happens to youngsters in school who score low on tests of intelligence but manifest no signs of maladaptive behavior.

Adaptive behavior is an elusive construct to define. One only has to watch vintage movies on TV to understand how standards for behavior change. Standards for adaptive behavior vary according to age, sex, cultural background, religious beliefs, time, and setting. The relative nature of the construct of adaptive behavior means that there is a very good possibility that two individuals will disagree as to whether a particular behavior is adaptive or **maladaptive** within a given context. Are behaviors such as masturbation, food hoarding, shyness and withdrawal, tattooing and piercing body parts, cohabitating intimately with a member of the same sex, refusal to eat certain foods, cutting off a person's hand as the penalty for stealing, or crying loudly adaptive or maladaptive? Obviously, the answer depends on the observer's own standards and the context (i.e., time period, place, setting) in which these behaviors are observed.

Another factor that adds to the relative and subjective nature of maladaptive behavior is the unit of measurement. Judgments of frequency of occurrence of maladaptive behaviors are used on tests of adaptive behavior. Yet, some behaviors, such as self-abuse or physical aggression, can be so disturbing to the beholder that judgments of frequency may be inaccurate. Parents frequently complain that their children never do homework or never clean their rooms or never pick up their toys. But almost all children engage in these activities at least some of the time. The relative nature of adaptive behavior has led some scholars to charge that it is much too subjective to be used as a diagnostic criterion for mental retardation.

The second issue concerning adaptive behavior is the question of what happens to students who score low on tests of intelligence but who demonstrate appropriate behavior in nonacademic areas outside of school. These youngsters would not be eligible for special education services in many states. Yet, we know that scores on IQ tests are good predictors of academic achievement and that these students are likely to experience significant difficulty in acquiring academic skills. Unfortunately, whether these at risk students receive any remedial supports depends, at present, on what school district they are enrolled in and the financial resources available to their families. The high dropout rates among public school students and the number of school graduates who do not qualify to enter the skilled workforce or postsecondary education are major problems confronting our society today. Witt et al. (1994) used the term *hardening of the categories,* to refer to the unavailability of educational supports to students who sorely need them because they do not meet the legally defined eligibility criteria for special education services.

Standardized Measures of Achievement

Achievement tests may be administered for a variety of reasons. First, achievement tests are often required for students who receive special education services under the Individuals with Disabilities Education Act. Second, group achievement tests may be used to identify individual students who may have academic difficulties and are then referred for more specific, individualized assessment. Third, group achievement tests may be used to compare how students in a particular building, district, or state compare to other local, state, or national groups of students. Fourth, achievement tests may be used to evaluate the effectiveness of teachers and the quality of the curriculum (Witt et al., 1994).

While achievement tests are conducted on a routine basis in schools across the country, there is a great deal of controversy and misunderstanding relative to their appropriate use and the valid application of data these tests yield. Interest in national standards or minimal competencies has grown because of calls for more accountability in education and increasing questions by legislators about how financial aid to schools is used and with what outcomes. Proponents of this trend have cited declining test scores among students in U.S. schools compared with those of other industrialized nations and the lack of a skilled labor force in the United States as rationale for minimal standards or competency testing. Critics of this viewpoint argue that human learning is far too complex to be able to measure the success of teachers and learning by the same production standards as used in the business world. Further, critics have charged that mass testing of students against some form of national standards or competencies unfairly penalizes students with disabilities, those who are at risk for significant learning difficulties, and students from nonwhite, nonmiddle-class backgrounds.

The situation is further compounded by the fact the 1997 amendments to IDEA mandate that whenever any school- or districtwide achievement testing is conducted, all students must participate, including those with disabilities. Previous to the 1997 IDEA amendments, schools had autonomy relative to including students with disabilities in mass testing.

As with any other type of technically sound standardized test, achievement tests are not inherently good or bad. Rather, they yield sound data when administered and interpreted as designed. They can result in inaccurate information when used inappropriately. In this section, we will examine the basis for achievement batteries and how data obtained from them may be used. We will review some of the more commonly used achievement tests.

Achievement Batteries

An integrated test that probes academic achievement across a number of skill areas is an achievement battery. As with any other test, it is important to specify the purpose of the assessment, the technical capabilities of tests available, and then to make an informed decision as to which achievement battery most closely matches the purpose of the assessment. In particular, it is important to consider the match between the curriculum content taught in the school and the academic content tested by the achievement battery (Taylor, 1997).

Achievement batteries are not to be confused with aptitude tests. Achievement batteries are designed to measure rather specific areas of the curriculum. They measure the results of previous instruction on a particular curriculum. Aptitude tests measure a broader domain of content. While they are influenced to some degree by the effects of prior learning, they are designed to indicate potential to benefit from future learning (Witt et al.,1994).

Achievement tests are categorized into survey or diagnostic tests. Survey tests assess very broad areas across several curriculum domains. They give a general indication of current levels of academic achievement across a wide cross section of the curriculum. Survey achievement batteries are most suited for use when the primary objective of assessment is screening.

Diagnostic batteries assess more specific skills within curriculum areas. For example, the area of math may be broken down into computation, number concepts, math facts, and so on. Reading may be subdivided into vocabulary, comprehension, word attack skills, and so on. A good number of items are then tested in each subdomain of math and reading. Diagnostic batteries are designed to identify more specific strengths and weaknesses of basic academic skills. They may be used in developing specific instructional programs.

Achievement tests may be administered either to groups or individuals. Group tests are more efficient in terms of time required to test large numbers of students. A second advantage is that they often require less training to administer. In addition, a well-constructed group achievement battery may be used to gauge a particular student's performance across several areas of the curriculum and across time, in cases where the same test is administered repeatedly on a regular basis (Witt et al., 1994).

Individual achievement batteries are better suited for individual classification decisions about students. It is possible to select a group of tests that are matched to a particular student's areas of difficulty, based on direct teacher observation. These tests are frequently used in the assessment of specific learning disabilities, in which a student of average or above average intelligence is significantly behind his or her chronological age peers in one or more areas of academic achievement.

While we will not provide an exhaustive review of group and individually administered achievement tests currently available, we will present some of the major characteristics of several frequently used tests of achievement. Some of the most commonly used group achievement tests are the Iowa Test of Educational Development, the California Achievement Tests, the Metropolitan Achievement Tests, and the SRA Achievement Series. Frequently administered individualized achievement tests include the Peabody Individual Achievement Tests–Revised, the Woodcock-Johnson Psycho-Educational Battery–Revised, the Wide-Range Achievement Tests–Revised, and the Kaufman Test of Educational Achievement. The primary features of each of these tests are highlighted in Tables 2.8 and 2.9.

Issues Related to Achievement Tests

Two issues merit attention in our discussion of the standardized assessment of achievement. The first issue pertains to the match between the curriculum taught in school and the content tapped on the test of achievement. From time to time, certain skill areas in U.S. school curricula are given greater or less emphasis. For example, throughout the 80s, less emphasis was placed on phonics and word attack skills and more emphasis was placed on the whole language approach to teaching reading. Currently, math educators debate the relative importance of basic computational math skills and more general math concepts. Achievement tests can only measure the academic content that students have had the opportunity to learn. It would be unfair to test students in phonics who had been taught reading solely by the whole language approach. It is imperative that the match between the curriculum of a school district and the achievement tests used in that district be carefully analyzed.

A second major issue relates to how data from achievement tests are used. We frequently read and hear in the public media that U.S. students are falling farther behind their counterparts in other industrialized nations, such as Japan. The usual result is that teachers, school administrators, and teacher trainers are blamed for incompetence and lack of high-quality programs. Politicians then often call for school reform, financial aid contingent on increased accountability, and national standards of minimal student competence.

Before we can conclude that U.S. students are ahead of, on a par with, or behind their peers in other nations, several questions must be answered. First, are the curricula studied by different groups of students really equivalent? Do fifth graders in the United States study the same academic content in math and reading as their age counterparts in Japan? Second, are the students compared across nations (or states or districts) similar? Japan has a much

TABLE 2.8 Frequently Used Group Achievement Tests

Test Name	Grade Level	Areas Tested	Special Considerations
California Achievement Tests	K–12	Reading: visual recognition, sound recognition, word analysis, vocabulary, comprehension; Spelling; Language: mechanics, expression; Math: computation concepts and application; Study Skills; Science; and Social Studies	Forms E and F available; adequately standardized; validity is limited in that items are placed in order of difficulty
Iowa Test of Basic Skills	K–9	Listening; Writing; Word Analysis; Vocabulary; Reading Comprehension; Language Skills; Work Study Skills; Mathematic Skills; Science; Social Studies; and Using Sources of Information	Test has adequate reliability; designed to provide comprehensive measurement of growth in functional skills
Iowa Test of Educational Development	K–12	Listening; Writing; Word Analysis; Vocabulary; Reading Comprehension; Language Skills; Math Skills; Using Sources of References; Social Studies; Work Study Skills; Science; and Listening Skills	Measures intellectual skills that are important to adult life and continual learning; no long-term stability
Metropolitan Achievement Tests	K–12	Reading; Reading Comprehension; Vocabulary; Word Recognition Skills; Mathematics; Math: concepts, problem solving, computation; Spelling; Language; Science; Social Studies; Research Skills	Judgment about validity must be made by users who consider the extent that the test covers subjects to be taught
SRA Achievement Series	K–12	Reading: visual discrimination, auditory discrimination, letters and sounds, listening comprehension, vocabulary, comprehension; Math: concepts, computation, problem solving; Language Arts: mechanics, usage, spelling; Reference Materials; Social Studies; Science	Both norm-referenced and criterion-referenced; adequate reliability, validity, and proper standardization

Source: Adapted from Witt, Elliott, Kramer, and Gresham (1994). *Assessment of Children.* Madison, WI: Brown & Benchmark.

more homogeneous culture than the United States. In many U.S. school districts, it is increasingly common for students representing many different cultural and socioeconomic groups to be enrolled. Third, is the structure of the school year similar across groups? Is the length of the school day, school week, and school year equivalent? Do the students being compared have the same opportunities and the same supportive resources to facilitate learning? If the answers to any of these questions is no, then we must be very cautious before making gross comparisons across groups of students.

TABLE 2.9 Frequently Used Individual Achievement Tests

Test Name	Grade Level	Areas Tested	Special Considerations
Kaufman Test of Educational Achievement	1–12	Math: application, computation; Reading: decoding, comprehension; Spelling	Short measure of global achievement to screen students for follow-up testing; comprehensive and brief forms available
Peabody Individual Achievement Tests–Revised	K–12	General Information; Reading: recognition, comprehension; Mathematics; Spelling; Written Expression	Arranged in order of difficulty; results help indicate students who may need more intense assessment; Level 2 has written expression tests
Wide-Range Achievement Tests–Revised	5–Adult	Spelling; Arithmetic; Reading	Limited by the short amount of time to present test and limited number of samples in test; limited for persons who have disabilities
Woodcock-Johnson Psycho-Educational Battery–Revised	K–Adult	Letter-word Recognition; Passage Comprehensions; Word Attack; Calculation; Applied Problems; Dictation; Writing Samples; Proofing; Science; Social Studies; Humanities	Tool kit for selective diagnostic disadvantage is more practical than technical; aptitude and achievement discrepancies can be calculated using actual norms

Source: Adapted from Witt, Elliott, Kramer, and Gresham (1994). *Assessment of Children.* Madison, WI: Brown & Benchmark.

Implications of Standardized Assessment for Inclusive Schools

We have placed great emphasis on the power of standardized tests in U.S. education. This has been true since the original work on developing an intelligence test that could, it was hoped, discriminate between students who could and could not benefit from schooling. Standardized testing continues to hold an elevated status today as policy makers, parents, teachers, school administrators, and teacher trainers are concerned about how to maintain high standards for learning outcomes while serving an increasingly diverse student body. What are the implications of standardized testing for inclusive schools? How much emphasis should be placed on standardized tests in schools attempting to include students of all ability levels?

Implications for Professional Development

It bears repeating that a technically sound standardized test can yield accurate information only if administered, scored, and interpreted appropriately. School and educational psychologists are required to take a great deal of coursework on tests and measurement. Teachers and school administrators, on the other hand, are usually required to take many fewer credit hours on this topic during the course of their training. Yet, in inclusive school settings, as required by IDEA, educational decisions for students with disabilities and IEPs must be developed by a multidisciplinary team.

Stiggins (1997) charged that it is a paradox that, although we place great faith in the precision and validity of standardized tests, and make significant decisions based on their results both for individual students and in educational policies affecting large groups of students, the majority of individuals in society and the schools are not well informed about these tests. Stiggins (1997) maintained that we have built the basis of school accountability on tests that are incapable of significantly contributing to school reform.

> Sadly, our general lack of understanding of these tests from classroom to boardroom to legislative chamber has prevented us from achieving the real accountability we all desire. (p. 353)

It is imperative that we do a better job of training professionals involved in making educational decisions on the basis of standardized test scores to be intimately familiar with what these tests can and cannot do. In addition, well-trained professional educators must help familiarize legislators, parents, and the general public about the appropriate uses of standardized tests.

Implications for Special and General Educators

Stiggins (1997) suggested that educators have the following responsibilities in regard to the appropriate use of standardized tests:

1. Request the resources necessary to become well informed on the match between the purpose of testing, the specific test selected, and how the test results are used
2. Participate in the selection of standardized tests
3. Make sure the curriculum matches the tests selected
4. Prepare students to participate comfortably in testing situations
5. Make sure prescribed test administration procedures are followed
6. Advocate for complete understanding, proper interpretation, and proper use of standardized test results

Implications for Parents and Advocates of Students With Disabilities

The majority of parents and other persons who serve as advocates for students with disabilities have varying degrees of familiarity with the technical strengths and weaknesses of standardized tests. In cases where they are not well versed in standardized tests, they can be good consumers of these instruments, nevertheless. Because these individuals often depend on others to translate the results of standardized testing to them, it is imperative that the following questions be asked:

- What is the purpose of this test?
- Why was it selected for use with my child?

- Whom will my child be tested by and under what conditions?
- Are other tests that accomplish the same purpose available?
- Are alternative forms of assessment more appropriate for my child?
- How do the standardized test results correlate with my child's performance in school?
- Where can I find further information on the technical merits of the tests administered (or to be administered) to my child?

Summary

In this chapter, we reviewed statistical concepts underlying standardized testing. We discussed how standardized tests are developed. Evaluating a test based on the technical features of reliability, validity, and norming was discussed. Standardized testing in the areas of intelligence, adaptive behavior, and academic achievement was covered, and brief reviews of some of the most commonly used tests in each area were presented. Finally, some implications of standardized tests for inclusive schools were addressed.

We have tried to maintain a balance in this chapter between presenting both the strengths of standardized tests and cautionary comments regarding their use. Standardized testing has been surrounded by controversy, and often emotion, almost since its inception with the development of the earliest tests of intelligence. This controversy has been generated not as much by bad tests as by improper uses of good tests.

It is important to maintain a proper perspective on what standardized tests can and cannot do. Their role in inclusive education will continue to be important, particularly for screening and classification. And yet standardized tests are only one component of the larger arena of educational assessment. The remaining chapters will address the many options for nonstandardized assessment in inclusive school settings.

REFERENCES

American Association on Mental Retardation (AAMR). (1992). *Mental retardation: Definition, classification, and systems of supports.* Washington, DC: Author.

Brown, F. G. (1983). *Principles of educational and psychological testing* (3rd ed.). New York: Holt, Rinehart, & Winston.

Buros, O. K. (1978). *Eighth mental measurements yearbook.* Highland Park, NJ: Gryphon Press.

Cronbach, L. J. (1951). Coefficient alpha and the internal structure of tests. *Psychometrika, 16,* 297–334.

CTB/McGraw-Hill. (1985). The California Achievement Tests. Monterey, CA: Author.

Das, J. P., Kirby, J. R., & Jarman, R. F. (1979). *Simultaneous and successive cognitive processes.* New York: Academic Press.

Doll, E. A. (1965). *Vineland Social Maturity Scale.* Circle Pines, MN: American Guidance Service.

Gay, L. R. (1992). *Educational research: Competencies for analysis and application* (4th ed.). New York: Macmillan.

Glutting, J. (1989). Introduction to the structure and approach of the Stanford-Binet intelligence scale–fourth edition. *Journal of School Psychology, 27,* 69–80.

Gresham, F. M. (1992). Misguided assumptions of DSM-III: Implications for school psychological practice. *School Psychology Quarterly, 7,* 79–95.

Guadalupe Organization v. Tempe Elementary School District, 71–435, District Court for Arizona, January 1972.

Guilford, J. P. (1967). *The nature of human intelligence.* New York: McGraw-Hill.

Hoover, H. D., Hieronymus, A. N., Frisbie, D. A., & Dunbar, S. B. (1993). *Iowa tests of basic skills.* Chicago: Riverside.

Jarman, R. F., & Das, J. P. (1977). Simultaneous and successive synthesis and intelligence. *Intelligence, 1,* 151–169.

Jastak, S., & Wilkinson, G. S. (1984). *Wide–range achievement test–revised.* Wilmington, DE: Jastak Associates.

Kaufman, A. S., & Kaufman, N. L. (1983). *Kaufman assessment battery for children.* Circle Pines, MN: American Guidance Service.

Kaufman, A. S., & Kaufman, N. L. (1985). *Kaufman test of educational achievement.* Circle Pines, MN: American Guidance Service.

Kazdin, A. E. (1982). *Single-case research designs: Methods for clinical and applied settings.* New York: Oxford University.

Kuder, G. F., & Richardson, M. W. (1937). The theory of the estimation of test reliability. *Psychometrika, 2,* 151–160.

Lambert, N., Leland, H., & Nihira, K. (1993). *AAMR adaptive behavior scale–school edition* (2nd ed.). Austin, TX: Pro-Ed.

Markwardt, F. C. (1989). *The Peabody individual achievement test–revised.* Circle Pines, MN: American Guidance Service.

Prescott, G. A., Balow, I. H., Hogan, T. P., & Farr, R. C. (1987). *Metropolitan achievement tests.* San Antonio, TX: Psychological Corporation.

Reschly, D. J. (1980). Concepts of bias in assessment and WISC-R research with minorities. In H. Vance & F. Wallbrown (Eds.), *WISC-R Research and Interpretation.* Washington, DC: National Association of School Psychologists.

Salvia, J., & Ysseldyke, J. (1998). *Assessment in special and remedial education* (4th ed.). Boston: Houghton Mifflin.

Science Research Associates. (1987). *SRA achievement series.* Monterey, CA: CTB Macmillan/McGraw Hill.

Sparrow, S. S., Balla, D. A., & Cicchetti, D. V. (1984). *Vineland adaptive behavior scales.* Circle Pines, MN: American Guidance Service.

Spearman, C. E. (1927). *The abilities of man.* New York: Macmillan.

Stiggins, R. J. (1997). *Student-centered classroom assessment* (2nd ed.). Upper Saddle River, NJ: Prentice-Hall.

Sullivan, E., Clark, W., & Tiegs, E. (1970). *California test of mental maturity.* New York: CTB/McGraw-Hill.

Taylor, R. L. (1997). *Assessment of exceptional students: Educational and psychological procedures* (4th ed.). Boston: Allyn & Bacon.

Taylor, R. L. (2000). *Assessment of exceptional students: Educational and psychological procedures* (5th ed.). Boston: Allyn & Bacon.

Thorndike, R., & Hagen, E. (1994). *Cognitive abilities test.* Boston: Houghton Mifflin.

Thorndike, R. L., Hagen, E. P., & Sattler, J. M. (1986). *Stanford-Binet intelligence scale* (4th ed.). Chicago: Riverside.

Thurstone, L. L. (1938). Primary mental abilities. *Psychometric Monographs* (Whole No. 1).

Wechsler, D. (1991). *Wechsler intelligence scale for children–III.* San Antonio, TX: Psychological Corporation.

Wechsler, E. (1974). *Wechsler intelligence scale for children Revised.* San Antonio: Psychological Corporation.

Witt, J. C., Elliott, S. N., Kramer, J. J., & Gresham, F. M. (1994). *Assessment of children.* Madison, WI: Brown & Benchmark.

Woodcock, R. W., & Johnson, M. B. (1989). *Woodcock-Johnson psycho-educational battery–revised.* Allen, TX: DLM.

CHAPTER 3

Nonstandardized Assessment in Inclusive School Settings

SANDRA ALPER
University of Northern Iowa

KAREN MILLS
University of Northern Iowa

OBJECTIVES

After reading this chapter, you will be able to

1. Discuss the term *alternate assessment*
2. Define and describe criterion-referenced assessment
3. Define and describe curriculum-based assessment
4. Discuss curriculum-based measurement
5. Describe observational assessment
6. Discuss portfolio assessment
7. Provide examples of performance assessment
8. Describe authentic assessment
9. Develop an example of portfolio assessment

KEY TERMS

accommodations (p. 55)
alternate assessment (p. 55)
authentic assessment (p. 70)
criterion-referenced assessment (p. 56)
curriculum-based assessment (CBA) (p. 60)
curriculum-based measurement (CBM) (p. 61)
interindividual differences (p. 56)
intra-individual differences (p. 56)
nonstandardized assessment (p. 55)
observational assessment (p. 66)
operational definition (p. 68)
performance assessment (p. 69)
portfolio assessment (p. 70)
target behavior (p. 68)
task analysis (p. 59)

We discussed the role of standardized assessment in the previous chapter. We reviewed some frequently used standardized tests in the areas of intelligence, adaptive behavior, and academic achievement. Standardized assessment is particularly important when decisions concerning diagnosis of disabilities, such as mental retardation and learning disabilities, or eligibility for special education services are considered. Standardized tests are not able to provide the degree of specificity required to design instructional programs, however.

Nonstandardized assessment is addressed in this chapter. Four types of assessment are commonly used: (a) criterion-referenced tests, (b) curriculum-based assessment, (c) observational assessment, and (d) alternate assessments including performance assessment and portfolios. These options for assessment are particularly useful in yielding information that can be used to develop instructional objectives for students. They are also helpful in the ongoing monitoring of student progress.

Alternate Assessment

The 1997 amendments to the Individuals with Disabilities Education Act (IDEA) is now referred to as P.L. 105-17, or IDEA 1997. As discussed in Chapter 1, IDEA requires students with disabilities to participate in district- and statewide academic achievement testing. Students with disabilities may (a) take part in the same standard testing procedures as students without disabilities, (b) participate in the same tests as other students with accommodations, or (c) be provided some alternate assessment if they cannot appropriately be tested by the standard testing format.

Testing **accommodations** refer to modifications in how a test is administered or how the student makes responses to test items. Accommodations are intended to correct for scoring distortions caused by a disability and, thus, increase the number of students with disabilities who can meaningfully participate in assessment.

Elliott, Kratochwill, and Schulte (1998) described an Assessment Accommodation Checklist (AAC). The AAC was developed to assist teachers in organizing, recording, and evaluating the effectiveness of assessment accommodations. The AAC consists of 74 accommodations organized into the following areas: (a) motivation, (b) assistance prior to testing, (c) timing of the assessment, (d) setting, (e) assessment directions, (f) assistance during assessment, (g) adaptive technology or equipment, and (h) changes in assessment format (Elliot, Kratochwill, & Schulte, 1998).

Erickson, Ysseldyke, Thurlow, and Elliott (1998) discussed *alternate* assessment. **Alternate assessment,** according to Erickson et al. (1998), is necessary for students with disabilities who cannot appropriately be assessed by traditional approaches, even with accommodations. These students may not be pursuing a regular high school diploma. Their curricula typically include functional life skills (e.g., vocational, daily living, recreation-leisure, community access skills) not routinely covered by the general education curriculum.

Ysseldyke and Olsen (1999) described three assumptions that characterize alternate assessment:

1. Alternate assessments are needed when students with disabilities cannot participate in standard procedures, even with accommodations
2. Alternate assessments are referenced to curricula that include functional life skills
3. Data obtained from alternate assessments may be used in place of information obtained by standard assessments as a measure of student progress

Criterion-Referenced Assessment

Unlike standardized assessment, which focuses on **interindividual differences,** or differences between students, **criterion-referenced assessment** emphasizes **intraindividual differences.** An individual student's performance is compared only to his or her previous performance relative to some standard or criterion. The number of yards Zach can hit a golf ball with a driver today might be compared to the distance he could drive the ball using the same club 6 months ago. A student's performance in arithmetic might be compared at the beginning, middle, and end of the semester to monitor that student's progress. If Pat needs to build a fence to keep her dog from roaming, she only needs to be concerned with how high her dog can jump. The average height at which other dogs can jump does not matter. We can develop criterion-referenced measures to assess a variety of skills, including academic, social, vocational, motor, and recreation-leisure skills.

Criterion-referenced assessment can be considered an alternate assessment if it is used with those students unable to participate in the general assessment system, even when they are provided with accommodations. These students typically have more significant disabilities. The percentage of such students is quite small: less than one half of 1% to no more than 2% of the student population. Most students with disabilities who participate in the alternate assessment will have IEPs that focus on broader goals than those students with disabilities in the general assessment system. An example of a criterion-referenced assessment for a high school student with severe disabilities is shown in Figure 3.1.

Criterion-referenced tests can also be used to assess students with mild disabilities. Here, criterion-referenced assessment would serve to augment the information gleaned from the standardized assessment. For example, criterion-referenced assessment can be very useful in determining which skills to teach. It allows for assessment of very specific skills against criteria determined by the teacher (e.g., John will correctly spell, define, and use in a sentence 95% of the vocabulary words on this week's list). Because criterion-referenced tests (CRTs) can identify both a student's strengths and weaknesses, they prevent reteaching skills that a student has already mastered. An example of criterion-referenced assessment for an elementary student with a mild disability is presented in Figure 3.2.

Although there are many criterion-referenced tests available on the market, these instruments may be designed by classroom teachers for individual students. Individually designed CRTs have the advantage of being locally referenced to the particular curriculum objectives taught in a specific school or classroom. They help assure that the goals and objectives assessed are relevant. Another advantage over commercial CRTs is that individually designed CRTs may be developed around goals and objectives that have been modified to meet the unique needs of a student with learning difficulties.

FIGURE 3.1 Criterion-referenced assessment for a high school student with severe disabilities.

Objective: The student will correctly complete 100% of the steps in making soup from a can.

Needs:

Utensils	**Ingredients**
medium saucepan	can of beef and vegetable soup
can opener	1 cup of instant potatoes
spatula/spoon	1 cup of mixed frozen vegetables
measuring spoons	¼ teaspoon salt
measuring cup	½ teaspoon pepper
serving ladle	¼ teaspoon dill weed
soup bowls	

Task analysis: The student will follow the steps in preparing a meal.

	Correct	*Incorrect*
1. Open can of soup	_____	_____
2. Empty contents in saucepan	_____	_____
3. Add salt, pepper, and dill weed	_____	_____
4. Put saucepan on stove at medium temperature	_____	_____
5. Continue to stir every minute	_____	_____
6. Add frozen vegetables	_____	_____
7. Bring contents to a boil	_____	_____
8. Reduce heat to low setting	_____	_____
9. Add instant potatoes	_____	_____
10. Stir ingredients	_____	_____
11. Serve in soup bowl	_____	_____

Steps:

1. Verbally cue before each step
2. Indicate performance of correct and incorrect responses
3. Allow student opportunity to perform each step in task analysis independently

Criterion-referenced assessment received much attention beginning in the late 70s for at least three reasons. First, as we have stated before, charges of discrimination against students of African American and Hispanic backgrounds were hurled at standardized tests, particularly individualized tests of intelligence. Second, attempts to measure and remediate underlying psycholinguistic and perceptual-motor abilities presumed to underlie the development of basic academic skills were disappointing (Ysseldyke and Salvia, 1974). Third, in the field of special education, great emphasis was placed on the behavioral model with its focus on direct observation of operationally defined behaviors.

FIGURE 3.2 Criterion-referenced assessment for an elementary student with a mild disability.

Objective: The student will correctly complete 100% of the 12 steps when ordering from a fast-food restaurant.

Task analysis: The student will follow the steps in ordering a meal.

	Correct	*Incorrect*
1. Check amount of cash in pocket	_____	_____
2. Choose item from menu	_____	_____
3. Subtract amount of menu item from cash	_____	_____
4. Decide if enough money is on hand for purchase	_____	_____
5. Make final choice	_____	_____
6. Get in line	_____	_____
7. Make order request to cashier	_____	_____
8. Make payment	_____	_____
9. Stand aside to wait for order	_____	_____
10. Count the change received from purchase	_____	_____
11. Thank worker	_____	_____
12. Select place to sit	_____	_____

Steps:

1. Verbally cue before each step
2. Indicate performance of correct and incorrect responses
3. Allow student opportunity to perform each step in task analysis independently
4. Analyze errors such as
   a. Choosing a menu item with not enough cash on hand to purchase
   b. Not correctly counting change received
   c. Holding up the line
5. Plan instruction to address skill deficiency areas

Developing a Criterion-Referenced Test

Criterion-referenced tests, even though they may be tailored to individual students and curriculum objectives, must be developed in a systematic manner (Taylor, 1997). The following steps are typically followed:

Step 1. Clearly define the specific set of instructional objectives to be assessed. A CRT may be developed that measures one instructional objective or a set of objectives within a given area of the curriculum. Make sure that a large enough sample of student behavior is assessed to accurately reflect each objective.

Step 2. Task analyze each objective into a sequence of teachable steps or skills. Break each objective into the sequence of steps that must be performed by the student in order to complete the objective. These teachable steps may be very small or broader, based on individual student ability.

Step 3. Operationally define each step in the task analysis. Each step in the **task analysis** should be an observable and measurable behavior. It helps to state each step in the task analysis in a verb/object format.

Step 4. Specify performance criteria for each skill assessed. Performance criteria may vary across teachers and individual students. Criteria must be measurable (e.g., percent correct, completion of a task within a given time frame, independent performance, and so on).

Step 5. Select items to be assessed based on their match with skills taught in the curriculum. In cases where understanding concepts, rather than performance of discrete skills, is emphasized, test items should reflect ways in which a student can demonstrate mastery of the concept.

Step 6. Develop a scoring and reporting system that efficiently and accurately describes student performance. Skills, performance criteria, and student performance need to be stated clearly. The results should be easy for teachers and parents to interpret.

Advantages and Disadvantages of Criterion-Referenced Tests

Criterion-referenced tests have several very positive features (Taylor, 2000). First, they allow for the assessment of specific objectives and skills. CRTs reveal strengths and weaknesses of an individual student in a particular area. Second, they do not require that a student's performance be compared to that of any other student. Third, they allow for ongoing monitoring of a student's progress. Fourth, CRTs reflect relevant and locally referenced curriculum objectives. Fifth, these assessment devices allow for assessment of objectives that have been modified based on the needs of an individual student. Finally, because the items selected for assessment and performance criteria are directly observable and measurable, validity and reliability are enhanced.

Criterion-referenced tests have at least two potential disadvantages. First, some areas of the curriculum are more difficult to operationally define and task analyze than others. CRTs that assess mastery of math facts, vocabulary, or performance of a concrete task are often easier to construct than those that assess complex and more abstract concepts such as cooperation, democracy, or ethical behavior. The second disadvantage of CRTs is that although they yield information useful in pinpointing what content to teach, they cannot prescribe how to teach that content.

Curriculum-Based Assessment

Several factors led to the development of curriculum-based assessment. Beginning in the 1970s and continuing today, the field of special education has moved away from disability categories toward a noncategorical approach. Some school districts and teacher preparation programs, for example, focus on mild and severe disabilities, with little or no additional categorization. Serving students with disabilities in general education classrooms also heightened the need for methods of assessment that focused on student progress through the curriculum rather than classification or labeling. Finally, there can be a mismatch between content assessed on standardized achievement tests and curriculum taught in a particular school. Curriculum-based assessment allows student progress to be measured based on the actual curriculum content to which students in a particular school have been exposed.

The term **curriculum-based assessment (CBA)** is generally understood to mean assessing a student's performance on the local curriculum. Items used in assessment are drawn from the school's curriculum. There are several types of CBA. CBAs may be formal or informal, standardized, or criterion-referenced (Fuchs & Fuchs, 1990; Taylor, Willets & Richards, 1988).

Taylor (1997) cited research by Shinn, Rosenfield, and Knutson (1989). These authors surveyed the research and organized CBA procedures into four groups: (a) CBA designed to determine instructional content based on a student's progress in the local curriculum, (b) curriculum-based evaluation developed to assess performance on components of curriculum objectives (this topic will be addressed in detail in Chapter 8), (c) criterion-referenced CBA, and (d) curriculum-based measurement. The latter two models are the most frequently used and researched, according to Taylor (1997), and are discussed next.

Criterion-Referenced CBA

Criterion-referenced CBA (CR-CBA) is based on two relatively simple assumptions: Students should be tested on material they are taught, and they should be assessed frequently. Typically, academic target behaviors, taken directly from the curriculum materials in use, are directly and frequently assessed. The steps in developing a CR-CBA are essentially the same as those for developing any criterion-referenced device. In this case, the local curriculum will dictate the skills to be assessed. If a child is not making satisfactory progress in a particular area, objectives may be modified or instructional techniques can be changed.

Criterion-referenced CBA has several advantages. Because of the emphasis on direct and frequent assessment, the child's progress on curriculum objectives can be pinpointed. In addition to student progress, instructional objectives and teaching strategies are also monitored. Information from CR-CBA may be used as the basis for program modification. In the case of lack of satisfactory student progress, it is not assumed that the problem is within the child. CR-CBA also permits specific and timely reporting of information for parents. This type of assessment provides a great deal of information that can be used to make educational decisions.

Two issues have been raised in relation to CR-CBA. First, although this type of assessment provides information directly related to the curriculum in place, it yields no information about how a child learns. Problem-solving strategies used by the student, analysis of errors, or why a child is not making satisfactory progress cannot be determined (Taylor, Willits, & Richards, 1988). Another potential concern is that CR-CBA is only as valid as the curriculum on which it is based. If the curriculum includes goals and objectives that are not relevant and useful for a particular child, assessment results may lead to irrelevant educational decisions.

Curriculum-Based Measurement

Curriculum-based measurement (CBM) was developed by Deno and his colleagues at the University of Minnesota (Deno, 1985; 1987; Deno & Fuchs, 1987; Fuchs, Fuchs, Hamlett, & Allinder, 1989; Fuchs & Fuchs, 1988; 1990). Deno and his colleagues wanted to develop a simple, effective, and easy-to-use form of student assessment. CBM is empirically derived and a well researched form of assessment.

CBM differs from CR-CBA in several ways. First, CBM focuses on long-term annual goals rather than on a series of short-term objectives. Items are drawn at random from an entire school year's curriculum content in a specific area. Second, the methodology used is prescribed. Behaviors measured are standard behaviors with documented reliability and validity. Third, CBM utilizes systematic procedures for summarizing and analyzing information on student progress (Fuchs & Fuchs, 1990).

One hallmark of CBM is the development of academic probes drawn from curriculum materials. Deno and his colleagues have developed the technology by which a series of academic probes from 1 to 3 minutes in duration can be developed and used reliably by teachers to accurately indicate student progress. Deno, Mirken, Lowry, and Kuehnle (1980) showed how simply counting the number of words orally read correctly from a basal reader once or twice weekly can reliably indicate a child's progress in reading. Measures such as number of letter sequences correct in spelling, number of digits calculated correctly in arithmetic, and number of words written can also be used as simple probes of academic progress. Examples of developing curriculum probes using CBM technology have been provided by Shinn (1989), Shapiro (1989), Taylor (1997), and Fuchs, Fuchs, Hamlett, and Allinder (1991). Fuchs, Hamlett, and Fuchs (1990) also developed a computer program for using CBM procedures to assess student progress in reading, spelling, and math. Examples of ways to construct and score curricular probes are shown in Figure 3.3.

An advantage of CBM is the emphasis placed on instructional decision making based on student progress in the curriculum. Taylor (1997; 2000) has provided excellent examples of how to graph student data points obtained from curriculum probes and identify trend or progress lines. Trend lines of student progress are then compared with the goals established for the student and instructional decisions are made accordingly. Steps for graphing student data are shown in Figure 3.4. Other advantages include the ability to accommodate any curricular paradigm and usefulness in training teachers how to assess students on an ongoing basis. (The latter is frequently cited as missing from teacher preparation programs.) Limitations of CBM include the inability of the technology to prescribe exactly how to modify curriculum (Frank & Gerken, 1990; Gable, 1990) and the focus on specific, isolated skills rather than on how students learn (Coleman, 1994).

FIGURE 3.3 Constructing and scoring CBM curriculum probes in spelling, math, reading, and written expression.

To construct a CBM spelling probe:

1. Choose three sets of 12 words from the student's spelling curriculum.
2. Dictate 1 word every 10 seconds (this is a 2-minute probe).
3. Give three probes.

To score the spelling CBM:

1. Count letter sequences (not correct words).
2. Count the first sequence as the space before the 1st letter and the 1st letter itself.
3. Count the last sequence as the space after the last letter and the last letter itself.

        1 2 3 4 5 6 7
        ^ ^ ^ ^ ^ ^ ^
    (space)BUTTER(space)

   The word *butter* has 7 possible letter sequences.
4. Divide the total number of correct letter sequences by 2 to get letter sequences per minute (LSPM). You may use the following cutoff levels to figure instructional grade levels in spelling. You may also use cutoff levels provided by the local school district.

	Grades 1–2	Grades 3–6
Frustrational	<20 LSPM	<40 LSPM
Instructional	20–39 LSPM	40–59 LSPM
Upper Instructional*	40–59 LSPM	60–79 LSPM
Mastery	more than 60 LSPM	more than 80 LSPM

*move on to next grade level

The important thing to remember is that cutoff levels may vary from school to school. You may raise or lower your own cutoffs. Doing an error pattern analysis on each CBM probe will further aid in selecting the types of skills to be taught.

To construct a written expression probe:

1. Select three story starters (one for each probe).
2. Give the student 1 minute to think about the story starter.
3. Give the student 3 minutes to write.

To score the written expression probe:

1. Count number of words written correctly (not counting spelling) during the 3 minutes. Include the story starter if it was repeated.
2. Divide by 3 to get correct words per minute.
3. If he or she stops before 3 minutes, number of words written ÷ number of seconds written × 60 = correct words per minute (WPM).

   You may use the following cutoff levels to figure instructional grade levels in written expression.

1 = 15 WPM	4 = 41 WPM
2 = 28	5 = 49
3 = 37	6 = 53

To construct a CBM reading probe you will need:

1. Three 1-minute probes at the student's instructional level (use graded reading passages).

Grades 1–3	Grades 4+
50–100 words	150–200 words

2. Two copies, one for the student and one for the teacher, to use for recording errors.
3. A set of comprehension questions (5–8) for each of the passages. The questions should reflect
   a. Vocabulary meaning
   b. Fact and detail
   c. Inference
   d. Sequence
   e. Main idea

To score the CBM reading probe:

1. Mark on the teacher's passage where the child is at the end of 1 minute, but allow him or her to finish.
2. Count the following as errors in the first minute:
   a. Omissions (redirect—count as an error)
   b. Student says wrong word (correct and count as an error unless it is due to his or her dialect or disorder)
   c. Student adds a word (count as an error)
   d. Student pauses for more than 5 seconds (supply and count as an error)

   Count correct words per minute for each of your three probes.

   Note: If the child is functioning at Frustration, Instructional, or Mastery level, you may use the following cutoff levels:

	Grades 1–3	Grades 4+
Frustrational	29 WPM	49 WPM
Instructional	30–49 WPM	50–99 WPM
Mastery	50+ WPM	100+ WPM

   Comprehension questions are scored by % correct: M = 90–100%, I = 80–89%, F = less than 80%.

To construct a CBM math probe:
You will need three 2-minute probes of no more than 65 correct digits each. (All digits below the line are counted.)

1. Determine the specific types of skills at instructional level.
2. Choose problems that represent these skills and mix the problems on each probe (2-minute probes, 2 or 3 samples of each type of skill, no more than 65 correct digits per probe).
3. Tell the student to move left to right and show his or her work. If the student does not know, move on.
4. At 2 minutes, stop the probe.

(continued)

FIGURE 3.3 Continued

To score the CBM math probe:

1. Score below the line.
2. Only count an error once.

```
                      45      Correct = 8 (7 plus the place holder)
                    × 28
                     350
                     800
(added correctly)   1150
```

3. In long division, count digits above and below the line.

```
  244 R1      Correct = 11 (count remainder once)
2)489
  4
  08
   8
   09
    8
    1
```

Math probe scoring criteria:

- To calculate digits per minute (DPM), divide number of digits correct on a 2-minute probe by 2.
- If the student completes the probe in less than 2 minutes, calculate DPM as follows:

  Number of correct digits ÷ number of seconds × 60

- To decide if the student is functioning at a frustrational, instructional, or mastery level, you may use the following cutoff levels:

	Grades 1–3	Grades 4+
Frustrational	0–9 DPM	0–19 DPM
Instructional	10–19 DPM	20–39 DPM
Mastery	20+ DPM	40+ DPM

Choosing the Most Appropriate Type of Assessment

In the area of reading, writing, math computation, and spelling, a CBM probe is helpful if you want to determine the following: (a) accuracy, (b) fluency, or (c) instructional level. These probes are quick and easily given two times per week to gauge the child's progress. A teacher must ask herself or himself if the child is capable of reading at least 50 words in context, spelling 20 letter sequences in context, writing 15 words in context, or computing 10 digits per minute. If the child is still reading or writing single words out of context or not computing problems or spelling words, the CBM may garner very little information on which to base instructional decisions. In that child's case, the CRT, which pulls skills out of context and tests them with enough samples to show mastery, may be what is needed. For

FIGURE 3.4 Graphing CBM assessment data.

To use CBM as a means to construct a goal, you must chart the results.

1. Plot the assessment probes on graph paper (this is the baseline).
2. Draw a line vertically through the second probe (probe #2).
3. Draw a line horizontally through the middle score (the score that falls numerically between the highest and lowest score).
4. Draw an X where these two lines intersect. This begins the goal line.
5. Count the number of weeks you will be teaching.
6. Multiply the number of weeks you will be teaching by 2. Add that number to your baseline number. (The number 2 is arbitrary, based on local district guidelines.)
7. Plot that point on the last day of teaching. This is your final goal.
8. Connect the beginning and end of the goal line.

- The goal line gives you an objective for correct words read per minute or correct digits completed per minute or correct letter sequences per minute or correct words written per minute.
- Skills to be taught would be ascertained by observing the types of errors made. The order in which these skills would be taught would depend on the teacher's skills analysis.
- The assessment probes should be repeated two times per week and charted so that the teacher and the child can see ongoing progress and goals achieved.

example, if the teacher wants to know if the child knows her initial consonant sounds, all of the consonant sounds could be assessed in a whole array CRT to see which ones she does not yet know (and are therefore instructional).

The choice between whole array CRT and samples of skills in the CRT is the difference in the types of skills. If all of the skills are homogeneous and are needed to master the group, they are considered whole array and all must be tested (alphabet letters, math facts, short vowel sounds are examples of these skills). Any assessment result below 100% tells the teacher to teach the skills. On the other hand, the sampled skills of the CRT may simply be testing the child's mastery of a concept. No more than 3–10 samples of that concept need be tested to see if the child is at mastery (90–100%), instructional (80–89%), or frustrational levels (below 80%). Examples of this type of skill would be time, money, reading comprehension, and so on.

The teacher does not need to settle for only one type of assessment. A combination of CBM, CRT (whole array and samples), and portfolio may be used. The variable factor is the type of data the teacher wants to collect. It is important to combine assessment types when necessary and continue to assess all through the child's instruction period so that decisions can be made and progress can be shown.

Figure 3.5 depicts an Assessment Option Chart. To use it, decide which core area is to be assessed and then find the desired skills to be assessed below the box. Choose any combination of assessment options to fulfill the needs of the child. Figure 3.6 shows examples of nonstandardized reading assessment options.

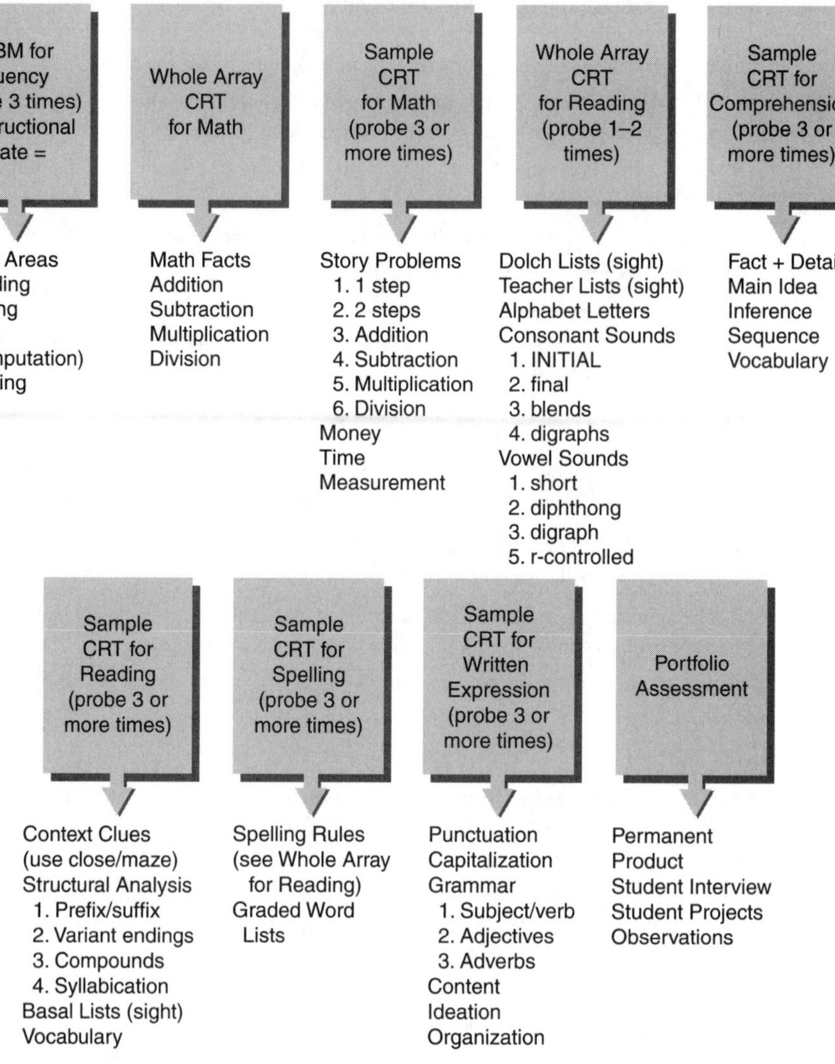

FIGURE 3.5 Assessment option chart.

Observational Assessment

The most direct form of assessment is observational assessment (see Chapter 9). **Observational assessment** refers to defining and systematically recording direct observations of an individual's behavior in a specific setting. Observational assessment can be used with any behavior that can be operationally defined and directly measured. We can use this type of assessment with a wide array of behaviors that occur in school and nonschool settings, in-

FIGURE 3.6 Example of combinations of assessment options (reading).

CBM probe (Grade 1 reading)

A Rat

A rat is an animal. It looks like a mouse. It is bigger than a	15
mouse. A rat can be white. A rat can be black. A rat can be	30
brown. Some rats are pets. Some rats are lab animals.	40
Some rats can even make a person sick.	48

CRT samples (comprehension)
Fact: What is a rat? (animal)
Fact: What color can a rat be? (white, black, brown)
Fact: Can a rat make a person sick? (yes)
Main idea: What is this story about?
Inference: Who should rats fear? (cats)

CRT whole array (sight words, list bedrock)

a	will	go	home
in	said	me	like
he	came	car	get
am	mother	and	have
the	it	dad	can
big	is	look	do

CBM
Fluency = ____ correct words per minute
- Substitutions =
- Omissions =
- Insertions =
- Reversals =
- Repetitions =

CRT samples
Word recognition = ____% accuracy
Comprehension = ____
- Main idea =
- Fact =
- Inference =

CRT whole array
Word recognition = ____% accuracy

cluding verbal and physical social interaction skills, basic academic skills, vocational skills, recreational-leisure skills, and functional skills.

Witt et al. (1994) clarified the distinction between indirect and direct assessment. Indirect assessment, according to these authors, refers to the measurement of responses that are indicative of a characteristic that cannot be directly observed or measured. A student's responses on an individualized test of intelligence, for example, can be directly observed but must be interpreted as an indirect measure of intelligence. Indirect assessment is also used when we are obtaining assessment data about behaviors that have already occurred. Instruments such as adaptive behavior scales require judgments about the frequency of behaviors that occurred prior to the time of testing.

Direct assessment is based on recording observations of behavior at the time and in the setting of actual occurrence. Direct assessment might involve a teacher observing how many words are correctly identified by a student during oral reading or a coach observing a youngster shoot free throws on the basketball court. No judgments or reports of past performance are involved.

A number of decisions have to be made by the teacher before conducting an observational assessment. The first decision is how to operationally define the behavior to be observed. According to Kazdin (1984), an **operational definition** must be clear, objective, and complete. The behavior to be observed, referred to as the **target behavior,** must be specified along with the conditions under which it occurs in enough detail so that different observers can consistently agree on when the behavior occurs. It would be difficult to observe and measure instances of good reading. We could, however, easily observe and record the number of words that are correctly read aloud during a specified passage within a given time. Similarly, compliance might be operationally defined in terms of appropriately responding to the teacher's verbal requests within 10 seconds.

The second decision to be made is how to measure the target behavior. We might measure and record the frequency of a behavior. If, however, the behavior occurs infrequently but lasts a long time when it does occur (e.g., temper tantrums), duration might be a better measure. In the case of compliance with the teacher's requests, latency, or amount of time elapsed between the verbal request and the behavior, would be an appropriate measure. We could also measure intensity, or force of a behavior, such as screaming. Or, we might measure permanent products, or the results of a behavior. Examples of permanent products are number of times a golfer sinks the putt on the first stroke on each green, number of arithmetic problems completed, or number of paragraphs written.

Third, we must decide how many behaviors to observe and over what period of time to ensure an adequate and representative sample of the target behavior. When observing some behaviors, such as arithmetic problems correctly completed or number of times a student verbally interrupts another person in the classroom, there may be many opportunities for the student to perform the behavior, and it may be observed and recorded over the course of a few days. In other cases, such as crossing the street safely or following safe driving rules, opportunities to perform the behavior may be limited because of safety or logistical concerns. These behaviors would have to be observed over a longer period of time.

How can a teacher decide the conditions or standards under which a particular behavior should be measured? Different teachers will have different performance expectations for behavior. One criterion might be standards for performing the response by most age peers. If the average three-year-old is able to sit still and listen to a story read by the teacher for 10 minutes, that might become the performance standard of a particular classroom. Another guide for determining performance standards to use during observational assessment can be parental expectations. Parents of a young child with severe disabilities may desire their child to eat appropriately in a fast-food restaurant without drawing negative attention. Whether the child learns to eat appropriately in a four-star restaurant may be of no concern.

Schloss and Smith (1997) provided some excellent examples of different types of data collection formats that have been used in school settings.

An essential requirement in observational assessment is that two or more observers will agree with a high degree of consistency on what they see. For example, a young child may be observed across home and school settings for behaviors such as toileting accidents or successfully transitioning from one activity to another. In these cases, the target behavior may be observed throughout the day by teachers, paraprofessionals, and family members. Kazdin (1977) identified three major threats to reliable observations of behavior: (a) observer drift, (b) reactivity, and (c) observer bias.

Observer drift refers to the tendency of the observer to change, or drift away from, the original operational definition of the target behavior. A student who is showing rapid improvement may not be observed as closely any longer. Observer reactivity means that observers tend to be more reliable when they know their observations are being checked by another person. Observer bias refers to how reliability may be affected by the expectations or bias of the observer. Does the observer expect high or low response rates? Does the observer have extremely low tolerance for certain behaviors and see them more frequently than they actually occur?

The degree of reliability between two or more observers can be calculated by a simple formula provided by Kazdin (1982). The number of agreements is divided by the number of disagreements and the resulting number multiplied by 100. For example, Mrs. Santos observed Connie getting out of her seat 10 times during a 35-minute class period, while Mr. Gray recorded the same behavior 12 times during the same period. The teachers' interobserver reliability would be calculated as $10 \div 12 = .83 \times 100 = 83\%$. The two teachers agreed on the occurrence of the target behavior 83% of the time. The two observers may now reconcile the differences in their observations by reviewing the definition of out-of-seat behavior to be used. Does out-of-seat behavior refer to any instance when the student's buttocks are not in contact with the chair or only when the student stands up and moves away from the desk?

Other Alternate Assessment Options

Taylor (1997; 2000) described three types of assessment typically included under alternate assessment: (a) performance assessment, (b) authentic assessment, and (c) portfolio assessment. We shall review each of these alternate types of assessment.

Performance Assessment

Performance assessment requires the student to perform a task. Student performance may be demonstrated in a number of ways such as building or constructing something, participating in creative arts, illustrating a task, or modeling the task for others to observe. Performance assessment requires the student to demonstrate in some way that he or she has mastered the competencies necessary to perform a certain task.

A junior high industrial technology class was studying building construction. In addition to reading materials and filmstrips about construction, students had to build a miniature model of a three-bedroom, one-story home using a blueprint supplied by the teacher. Students in a math class studying managing personal finances were required to develop a monthly budget that included housing, food, transportation, clothing, utilities, medical expenses, recreation, and savings not to exceed a specific amount of money. A class of young children first read a story and then produced a play based on the story. These illustrations are examples of some of the many forms performance assessment may take.

While seemingly more reflective of real-world tasks than items on a standardized test, performance assessment has received criticism. First, it may be possible for a student to demonstrate a particular task without thoroughly comprehending it. A teacher in training, for example, may demonstrate strategies for teaching reading consistent with the whole language philosophy without fully understanding this philosophy or why he uses it rather than a phonetics-based approach. Performance assessments have also been criticized because of the potential for subjectivity in their evaluation. What are the standards for judging a fine painting? Judging from the lack of support once given now renowned artists such as Vincent Van Gogh, the standards are somewhat relative. Practical concerns such as the time and expense required for performance assessments have also been raised.

Authentic Assessment

Could the students who built a scale model home succeed on the construction site of a real house? Attempts to more directly link performance assessment and real-world task requirements led to authentic assessment. The term **authentic assessment** has been used in the literature (e.g., Hughes, 1993; Witt et al., 1994; Erickson et al., 1998) to refer to assessment that occurs in real-life contexts with realistic performance demands.

Authentic assessment is not a new concept. Assessment of youth and adults with moderate to severe disabilities in job and daily living skills has emphasized assessment of real-world tasks under the conditions in which they actually occur for some time. Because the school setting is the primary real-world setting for many students during the daytime, the distinction between performance and authentic assessments can be blurred.

Portfolio Assessment

Paulson, Paulson, and Meyer (1991) described a portfolio as "a purposeful collection of student works that exhibits the students' efforts, progress, and achievement in one or more areas. The collection must include student participation in selecting contents, the criteria for selection, the criteria for judging merit and evidence of student self-reflection" (p. 60). **Portfolio assessment,** with its emphasis on products, student involvement and choice, and self-reflection on one's work, involves both the process and products of learning. Portfolio assessment is an attempt to link assessment to the learning process in a more holistic fashion than focusing on discreet skills.

Although individual portfolios will vary by student age, ability, and content area, several characteristics are typically present (Nolet, 1992). Portfolios can contain (a) behavior samples collected over a period of time, (b) learning products developed under a variety of settings and conditions, (c) products that reflect tasks frequently performed in natural contexts, (d) data consisting of student's products and teacher's summative information, and (e) student's choice of products. Typically, the portfolio includes a table of contents and a personal statement about the purpose and objectives of the portfolio.

The products included in three sample portfolios are illustrated in Table 3.1. These portfolios were developed by students of varying age and ability. Taylor (1997; 2000) pro-

TABLE 3.1 Three Samples of Portfolio Assessment Products

Science Portfolio for an Elementary Student Without Disabilities	**Language Arts Portfolio for a Junior High Student with a Mild Learning Disability**	**Transition Portfolio for a Secondary Student with a Mild Learning Disability**
Samples that represent the best of daily work, classroom projects, and exams	Poems about self as a character in the story	Copy of résumé
Drawings of processes such as the recycling process	Best of daily journal entries describing plot detail	Letter of application
Student-created dictionary of important science terms	Short story written by student if he or she was one of the characters.	Letter to postsecondary institutions introducing self
Transcript of student's speech that explains scientific theory, i.e., "The Planets' Rotation in our Solar System"	Short play written by student about characters' dialogue in the story	Letter requesting accommodation with specific needs to instructors
Play written by students of something that famous scientist may have dialogued about	Transcript of tribute speech about someone who influenced the student's life	Evaluations of work-site supervisors
Transcript of monologue presented by student about famous scientist explaining a theory or concept	List of "Things Important to Me and Why"	Student's preference for transition goals
Journal entries in which student dialogues with teacher about lecture material	Game created by student to help understand character development	Self-evaluation of on-site training
Examples of science game student creates in a small-group activity	Tests, quizzes, and daily work the student feels represents her or his best work	Transcript of mock interviews student creates in small-group work

vided an excellent discussion of portfolio development. According to Taylor, there are six steps to putting together a portfolio:

Step 1. Determine the conceptual content and physical format
Step 2. Determine the types of products to be included
Step 3. Determine which products to include
Step 4. Develop scoring criteria
Step 5. Specify evaluation procedures
Step 6. Decide how to utilize the portfolio

Portfolio assessment has received widespread attention in both general and special education. Some states (e.g., Kentucky, Vermont, and Rhode Island) have developed statewide student assessment systems that include portfolios of students' work. Portfolios are increasingly used to evaluate preservice teachers. How well the preservice teacher develops and implements instructional strategies and materials are emphasized rather than only scores on course examinations. Many institutions of higher education have also adopted portfolio assessment as part of the faculty tenure and promotion system. Faculty members are asked to submit examples of their work in teaching, research, and service with reflections on the impact of the work.

Kentucky students in grades 4, 8, and 12 are assessed using writing and math portfolios; on-demand tasks in math, social studies, and science; and transitional achievement tests. These achievement indicators, together with measures such as attendance, dropout rates, retention, and postschool outcomes, are used as indicators of accountability for each school. They are utilized in determining future resources available for the schools (Kleinert, Kearns, & Kennedy, 1997).

Students with mild disabilities in Kentucky fully participate in these assessments through the use of accommodations (e.g., calculators or word processors). The modifications used in testing must be consistent with those used during instruction. These accommodations must be specified on the IEP, and they may not interfere or alter the purpose of testing.

Students with severe cognitive disabilities may participate through the Kentucky Alternate Portfolio Assessment, the first statewide alternate assessment system implemented in 1992. The Alternate Portfolio includes the following components: (a) the student's primary mode of communication, (b) a description of how the student utilizes an individualized schedule to self-initiate daily activities, (c) a student letter to the reviewer, (d) student's projects that involve peers without disabilities and focus on learner outcomes, (e) a résumé of in-school and community work experience (for students in twelfth grade), and (f) a letter from the student's parent or legal guardian indicating level of satisfaction (Klienert, Kearns, & Kennedy, 1997; Kearns, Kleinert, Clayton, Burdge, & Williams, 1998). Students must demonstrate a common core of learner outcomes, but they may demonstrate these outcomes in different ways.

Recently, Gelfer and Perkins (1998) described the use of portfolios for teachers of early childhood and elementary-age children with disabilities. These authors also presented guidelines for planning new activities and improving instruction through portfolio-centered conferences.

The results to date of the effectiveness of portfolio assessment are mixed. Advantages include student input and choice on the products of their work to be assessed. Another advantage of portfolio assessment is tying the products assessed more directly to the curriculum and real-life contexts. Disadvantages include difficulties encountered in reporting clearly and efficiently to legislative and accreditation bodies based on portfolio assessments. Developing alternate assessments for students with severe disabilities poses many challenges. Concerns have been raised as to how well these assessments measure students' access to and progress through the general education curriculum, mandated by IDEA '97 (Kleinert & Kearns, 1999). One thing is clear. Both teachers and students should be trained in portfolio development and assessment before the practice is initiated.

Summary

In this chapter, we discussed alternate assessment mandated by the IDEA 1997 amendments. Several nonstandardized forms of assessment were described. Criterion-referenced testing, curriculum-based measurement, observational assessment, performance assessments, authentic assessment, and portfolios were all discussed. These measures were developed as options or supplements to standardized testing. They represent attempts to link assessment directly to the curriculum and student performance in natural contexts. Erickson et al. (1998) made an important distinction between assessment and accountability. Accountability does not mean that all students should be assessed in the same way. Rather, "What is important is that the ongoing progress and ultimate success of all students are consistently being accounted for" (p. 7).

While nonstandardized assessment of student performance has many positive attributes, several questions remain. First, educators need to clearly translate the results of these measures into accountability reports. Second, we must be sure that the curriculum on which nonstandardized assessment is based is matched to the unique needs of individual students. Therefore, all students will not be assessed on the same curricular objectives. Third, more work is needed in training teachers to change their behavior based on the results of student performance data. Using data for decision-making becomes an increasing challenge as today's teachers are faced with more and more diversity in the classroom.

REFERENCES

Coleman, L. J. (1994). Portfolio assessment: A key to identifying hidden talents and empowering teachers of young children. *Gifted Quarterly, 38,* 65–69.

Deno, S. (1985). Curriculum-based measurement: The emerging alternative. *Exceptional Children, 52,* 219–232.

Deno, S. L. (1987). Curriculum-based measurement. *Teaching Exceptional Children, 20,* 41.

Deno, S., & Fuchs, L. (1987). Developing curriculum-based measurement systems for data-based special education problem solving. *Focus on Exceptional Children, 19,* 1–16.

Deno, S. L., Mirken, P. K., Lowry, L., & Kuehnle, K. (1980). *Relationships among simple measures of reading and performance on standardized achievement tests* (Research Report No. 20). Minneapolis: University of Minnesota Institute for Research on Learning Disabilities.

Elliott, S. N., Kratochwill, T. R., & Schulte, A. G. (1998). The assessment accommodation checklist. *Teaching Exceptional Children, 31*(2), 10–14.

Erickson, R., Yssledyke, J., Thurlow, M., & Elliott, J. (1998). Inclusive assessments and accountability systems. *Teaching Exceptional Children, 31*(2), 4–9.

Frank, A., & Gerken, K. (1990). Case studies in curriculum-based measurement. *Education and Training in Mental Retardation, 25,* 113–119.

Fuchs, L., & Fuchs, D. (1988). Curriculum-based measurement: A methodology for evaluating and improving student programs. *Diagnostique, 14,* 3–13.

Fuchs, L., & Fuchs, D. (1990). Traditional academic assessment: An overview. In R. Gable & J. Hendrickson (Eds.), *Assessing students with special needs* (pp. 1–13). New York: Longman.

Fuchs, L., Fuchs, D., Hamlett, C., & Allinder, R. (1989). The reliability and validity of skills analysis within curriculum-based measurement. *Diagnostique, 14,* 203–221.

Fuchs, L., Fuchs, D., Hamlett, C., & Allinder, R. (1991). The contribution of skills analysis to curriculum-based measurement in spelling. *Exceptional Children, 57,* 443–452.

Fuchs, L. S., Hamlett, C., & Fuchs, D. (1990). *Monitoring basic skills progress* (computer program). Austin, TX: Pro-ed.

Gable, R. (1990). Curriculum-based measurement of oral reading: Linking assessment and instruction. *Preventing School Failure, 35,* 37–42.

Gelfer, J., & Perkins, P. (1998). Portfolios: Focus on young children. *Teaching Exceptional Children, 31*(2), 44–47.

Hughes, S. (1993). What is alternative/authentic assessment and how does it impact special education? *Horizons, 1993,* 28–35.

Kazdin, A. E. (1977). Assessing the clinical or applied importance of behavior change through social validation. *Behavior Modification, 1,* 427–451.

Kazdin, A. E. (1982). *Single case research design: Methods for clinical and applied settings.* New York: Oxford University Press.

Kazdin, A. (1984). *Behavior modification in applied settings* (3rd ed.). Homewood, IL: Dorsey Press.

Kearns, J., Kleinert, H., Clayton, J., Burdge, M., & Williams, R. (1998). Principal supports for inclusive assessment. *Teaching Exceptional Children, 31*(2), 16–23.

Klienert, H., & Kearns, J. F. (1999). A validation study of the performance indicators and learning outcomes of Kentucky's alternate assessment for students with significant disabilities. *Journal of the Association for Persons with Severe Handicaps, 24*(2), 100–110.

Klienert, H. L., Kearns, J. F., & Kennedy, S. (1997). Accountability for all students: Kentucky's alternate portfolio assessment for students with moderate and severe cognitive disabilities. *Journal of the Association for Persons with Severe Handicaps, 22* (2), 88–101.

Nolet, V. (1992). Classroom-based measurement and portfolio assessment. *Diagnostique, 18* (1), 5–26.

Paulson, F. L., Paulson, P. R., & Meyer, C. A. (1991). What makes a portfolio a portfolio? *Educational Leadership, 48*(5), 60–63.

Schloss, P. J., & Smith, M. A. (1997). *Applied behavior analysis in the classroom.* Boston: Allyn & Bacon.

Shapiro, E. S. (1989). *Academic skills problems: Direct assessment and intervention.* New York: Guilford Press.

Shinn, M. R. (Ed.). (1989). *Curriculum-based measurement: Assessing special children.* New York: Guilford Press.

Shinn, M. R., Rosenfield, S., & Knutson, N. (1989). Curriculum-based assessment: A comparison of models. *School Psychology Review, 18,* 299–316.

Taylor, R. L. (1997). *Assessment of exceptional students: Educational and psychological procedures* (4th ed.). Boston: Allyn & Bacon.

Taylor, R. L. (2000). *Assessment of exceptional students: Educational and psychological procedures* (5th ed.). Boston: Allyn & Bacon.

Taylor, R. L., Willets, P., & Richards, S. B. (1988). Curriculum-based assessment: Considerations and concerns. *Diagnostique, 14,* 14–21.

Witt, J. C., Elliott, S. N., Kramer, J. J., & Gresham, F. M. (1994). *Assessment of children: Fundamental methods and practices.* Dubuque, IA: William C. Brown.

Ysseldyke, J. E., & Salvia, J. A. (1974). Diagnostic-prescriptive teaching: Two models. *Exceptional Children, 41,* 181–186.

Yssledyke, J. & Olsen, K. (1999). Putting alternate assessments into practice: What to measure and possible sources of data. *Exceptional Children, 65*(2), 175–185.

CHAPTER

4 Collaborative Teaming in the Assessment Process

DONNA GILLES
University of Florida

DENISE CLARK
University of Florida

OBJECTIVES

After reading this chapter, you will be able to

1. Describe various educational teaming models
2. Describe the benefits of collaborative teaming
3. Discuss the benefits of collaborative teaming as they relate to alternate assessment
4. Describe potential team members and their roles
5. Discuss how collaborative teaming can be used in the assessment process

KEY TERMS

collaborative assessment process (p. 81)
collaborative team approach (p. 78)
integrated goals (p. 81)
interdisciplinary team approach (p. 76)
multidisciplinary team approach (p. 76)
role release (p. 78)
transdisciplinary team approach (p. 78)

Development of the Collaborative Teaming Model

The concept of teaming to maximize the effects of intervention or treatment in a variety of situations involving people with disabilities has existed for a long time. The following section traces the evolution of the teaming process from the widely used medical model to the current trend of using the collaborative team approach.

Early Models of Teaming

The need for the coordination of educational team members became more evident with the arrival of students with more severe disabilities in public schools. Although teams of professionals existed in programs serving students with mild and moderate disabilities, the numbers of professionals and the breadth of disciplines represented on those teams were minimal compared to teams serving students with more severe disabilities. As the Individuals with Disabilities Education Act (IDEA) has evolved through reauthorizations, however, the composition of educational teams has become more comprehensive regardless of the student's disability, adding such members as behavior specialists, counselors, recreation therapists, social workers, and transition coordinators. Table 4.1 provides descriptions of potential team members' areas of expertise. Though some or all of these members may be participants on teams for various students, they may function differently on each team, depending on the team approach used.

The Multidisciplinary Approach. The concept of teaming has evolved over time, exemplified by changes in team approaches (Orelove & Sobsey, 1996; Rainforth & York-Barr, 1997; Ryndak, 1996a). Each approach to teaming, however, continues to be used in schools. For example, when public schools began to serve students with more severe disabilities, the perceived medical nature of their needs resulted in the development of a **multidisciplinary team approach** that functioned similarly to the existing medical model of nonschool service delivery (Orelove & Sobsey, 1996; Ryndak, 1996a; Westling & Fox, 1995a). Professionals on multidisciplinary teams

- Evaluate a student in isolation of each other, on a variety of aspects of development
- Generate isolated, discipline-specific goals and objectives for that student, usually reflecting the "deficits" identified in the evaluation
- Deliver services designed to enable that student to reach those goals within isolated settings
- Evaluate the impact of the therapy or treatment
- Make recommendations for future therapy or treatment

The Interdisciplinary Approach. In an effort to shift from using a medical model to provide educational services, the **interdisciplinary team approach** emerged as having a more educational focus. Interdisciplinary teams include the same members and perform the same basic activities as multidisciplinary teams. Interdisciplinary team members, however, differ in that they share relevant information across the disciplines, particularly with educational personnel (Orelove & Sobsey, 1996; Ryndak, 1996a; Westling & Fox, 1995a). When utilizing the interdisciplinary model, teachers may have the opportunity to observe related service professionals as they provide services in the classroom, sometimes in the context of a classroom activity. Most often, however, related services are provided away from other students and outside of any functional context. Interdisciplinary team members typically work with each other to facilitate a better understanding of the multiple characteristics of the targeted student. IEP goals and objectives tend to be cross-discipline in nature. For example, classroom teachers may write communication goals as part of the IEP, separate from the communication goals written by a speech-language pathologist for the same IEP.

TABLE 4.1 Role Descriptions of Possible Team Members

Team Member	Role
Individual with Disabilities	Self-advocate who may need instruction in how to participate and have a strong voice in his or her educational experience.
General Education Teacher	Provides the classroom structure and age-appropriate curriculum and experiences to all students, including those with disabilities. Expertise includes grade- or subject-specific curriculum and assessment, and typical student development. Students may have more than one general education teacher, especially at the middle or high school level.
Special Education Teacher	Coordinates the support for a student with disabilities who is included in general education classrooms. Expertise includes instructional strategies, individualized assessment, adaptations and modifications that individualize general education activities, and life skills curriculum.
Family Members	Experience the closest relationship with the student and will have the longest commitment to the student's education. Family members can provide valuable information about the student's history, culture and family values, likes and dislikes, and goals and vision for the future. They can provide the most information about the student.
Behavior Specialist	Supports the student in mediating behavioral challenges, including conducting functional behavioral assessment and developing and monitoring positive behavioral support plans.
Reading Specialist	Expertise includes knowledge of theories of reading development and experience in reading and writing instruction.
School Psychologist	Administers and interprets standardized tests to determine eligibility for special education services. Assists school personnel in assessing classroom performance, including behavioral assessment.
Physical Therapist	Expertise includes knowledge of balance, coordination, and strength. Assesses the student and assists the team in developing programs in locomotion, maintaining appropriate body posture, and positioning. Assists with maintenance of adaptive equipment.
Occupational Therapist	Provides information and strategies on improving a student's participation in activities of daily living (e.g., dressing, feeding), manipulation of objects, manual dexterity, and use of writing implements.
Speech/Language Pathologist (and Related Professionals)	Assists teams in assessing and improving an individual's communication abilities, including verbal and nonverbal communication and written and oral language. Other levels of professionals trained in this area include speech therapists and speech clinicians.
Vision Specialist	Works with students who experience low vision or blindness. May provide orientation and mobility instruction, assist peers in using social prompts that help students who are blind, and provide braille instruction.
Audiology Specialist	Provides information, assessment, and intervention for students who are deaf or hard of hearing. Expertise includes monitoring hearing aides and providing sign language or lip reading instruction, to name a few.

(continued)

TABLE 4.1 Continued

Team Member	Role
Nurse	May provide medical services—dispense medication, assist with suctioning or gastronomy tube feedings, assess physical well-being.
Counselor	May conduct assessment, provide support, serve as a resource for student's behavior or emotional health, and provide direct counseling to the student.
Transition Specialist	Assists in the assessment of transition needs and in the development and implementation of the transition plan, including career development, postsecondary education, supported or independent living, self-advocacy, and natural networks of support.
Social Worker	Can provide a link between the school and parents, collect information about the student or the family, and provide a link to student or family support programs that are governed by local agencies. May also provide support for a student's behavioral issues.
Assistive Technology Specialist	May provide different types of support in areas ranging from the use of assistive writing programs and computerized instruction to computerized communication systems.
External Agency Supports	May include social services, parent support groups, technical assistance projects, or advocacy groups. Involvement of these personnel on the assessment team provides a broader perspective of the student's life beyond the school environment.
Other Individuals From Noneducational Settings	May include people who are important in the student's life but are not typically involved in a student's education: coaches, scout leaders, respite providers, family friends, or community businesspeople, and so on.

The Transdisciplinary Approach. Although the interdisciplinary approach results in team members being more informed about the services the student receives, it does not change the fact that students continue to receive services in isolation of others, a criticism of the multidisciplinary (medical model) approach. In order to change the focus of service delivery to be more integrated and less isolated, the **transdisciplinary team approach** emerged accompanied by an integrated model of service delivery (Orelove & Sobsey, 1996; Ryndak, 1996a; Westling & Fox, 1995a). Integrated therapy is accomplished through **role release,** which is the process of sharing discipline strategies (not just information) with those who are the primary service providers (e.g., teachers, early interventionists, other therapists, family members, paraprofessionals; Lyon & Lyon, 1980). Each team member monitors across personnel the use of the strategies they recommended in the context of the student's daily activities. Team members, in effect, serve as consultants to other team members, thus increasing the time that a student receives intervention toward meeting the goals for each discipline.

Collaborative Team Approach

Most recently, the **collaborative team approach** emerged as an alternative method to manage the sharing of information and the implementation of strategies generated by team members representing several disciplines (Rainforth & York-Barr, 1997). Ryndak (1996a) described six basic differences between collaborative teams and their predecessors:

1. The focus of the collaborative team is on the needs of the student rather than on the individual diagnosis and remediation paradigms of the professionals involved with the student.
2. Collaborative teams accept shared responsibility for the successes and failures of meeting the student's needs across environments.
3. Collaborative team members use role release but also make decisions as a group about what type of instruction is necessary and how it can be distributed across naturally occurring events and environments to meet the student's individual needs.
4. Services, including assessment procedures, are carried out in more natural locations where the demand will be the greatest for the student to use targeted skills.
5. Collaborative team members create schedules that afford each member the opportunity to observe and interact with the student across time, location, and personnel.
6. Collaborative team members assert and accept that all team members are equal in their level of knowledge about the various aspects, professional and personal, that affect educational outcomes of any given student.

Collaborative Team Membership. Collaborative teams comprise multiple members who have a common concern for a student's participation in his or her program, and who are willing to share their expertise (Downing, 1996). Each collaborative team member contributes to the development of a student's educational program, ensuring a well-rounded educational program and system of support for the student. Table 4.1 provides descriptions of potential team members' areas of expertise, however, anyone who has a relationship with the student or who can provide information that will be useful for the student's education, can serve as a team member. Conversely, Table 4.1 is not a list of specialists and team members who are required to be on every student's team. A team should consist of only those individuals who have a vested interest in the student's education or who can offer important insight into the student's educational program. Therefore, team membership can change often to meet the educational needs of the students it supports.

Benefits of Collaborative Teaming. There are several benefits to a collaborative team approach. First, students benefit from the person-centered nature of collaborative teaming because it addresses more of each student's needs in an integrated manner. Providing services in an integrated manner allows the team to work toward more meaningful student outcomes and can lead to more rapid acquisition and generalization of goals, because the student has more opportunities to practice skills across activities throughout the day. The benefit of the distribution of intervention is particularly important to justify providing related services to a given student. According to IDEA, the purpose of a related service is to assist a student with a disability to benefit from special education. In other words, though a student may benefit from receiving related services, deriving benefit alone is not enough to warrant providing those services. The IEP must establish that the related service(s) must assist the student in benefiting from special education. Ongoing collaboration among educators, paraprofessionals, family members, and related services personnel can lead to the establishment of discipline-free objectives, thereby producing a less fragmented, more cohesive delivery of services by integrating relevant goals and objectives into the daily education of the student (Giangreco, Cloninger, & Iverson, 1998). When a student makes progress on such discipline-free goals, it might be concluded that the provision of related services assisted the student in benefiting from special education services and experiences.

Second, the person-centered planning nature of collaborative teaming ensures the equal partnership of families (Orelove & Malatchie, 1998). This partnership is particularly important because family members have the most knowledge about the student and his or her performance in real-life situations, the ultimate environments in which acquired skills will be practiced.

Third, team members themselves benefit by practicing typical collaborative behaviors that lead to a supportive educational environment (Friend & Cook, 1996). In addition, team members increase their knowledge base through interacting with a diverse group of people with an interest in the focus student (Friend & Cook, 1996).

Finally, the school as a community with diverse membership benefits from collaborative teaming. Collaborative teams for students with disabilities employ effective problem-solving strategies that lead to the realization that every student plays an equally important role in supporting a school community.

Linking Collaborative Teaming With Alternate Assessment

The 1997 reauthorization of IDEA presents a challenge to the education community by mandating that all students participate in the state and local district assessment programs that measure student performance according to a predetermined set of educational standards or goals. States must decide whether students with severe disabilities (i.e., those who require alternate assessment) will be assessed using the same standards developed for children without disabilities, a modified version of those standards, or a separate set of standards reflecting a life skills orientation (Kleinert & Kearns, 1999). For many students with severe disabilities, the implementation of this mandate will mark the first time that school personnel will measure student progress toward acquiring skills that are deemed necessary for all children to learn prior to exiting the school system. Regardless of the nature of the standards on which students with severe disabilities are assessed, it is incumbent upon educational personnel to be thorough. A well-planned and executed assessment that results in each team member having a well-balanced understanding of a student's performance is one of the most important contributions to generating critical objectives, effective instruction, and meaningful outcomes. Conversely, the most useless material for a classroom teacher is an assessment that focuses on only one discipline and provides little information and few recommendations that are relevant to the total education of the student.

Ysseldyke and Olsen (1999) described the results of a focus group meeting of teachers of students with significant disabilities from five states. Three opinions were generated about alternate assessment: (a) assessment should address real skills in natural settings such as home, school, and community; (b) assessments should measure skills that are integrated across outcome domains; and (c) assessments should use multiple measures over time. We have provided a rationale for utilizing the collaborative team approach to designing meaningful educational programs for students with disabilities. It seems reasonable to assume that in order to facilitate better educational planning, implementation, and evaluation, professionals and families also must collaborate in the assessment process. By design, collaborative teaming during the assessment process can produce comprehensive information that can lead to **integrated goals** and objectives (i.e., those that embed multiple disciplines) that are specific to the student and that can be met in a variety of settings.

Completing the Collaborative Assessment

In the following section, we discuss four general phases of the assessment process and the role of collaborative team members in each phase. The **collaborative assessment process** includes (a) planning the assessment, (b) gathering and summarizing supportive information, (c) conducting direct assessment, and (d) making recommendations as a team.

Phase I: Planning the Collaborative Assessment

There are four steps in the planning phase of collaborative assessment: (a) identifying the assessment team membership, (b) determining what information will be gathered and what methods will be used, (c) determining the conditions under which the student will be assessed, and (d) determining who will conduct the various activities for the assessment.

Step 1: Identifying Assessment Team Membership. The first step of the planning phase of collaborative assessment is to identify the members of the assessment team (Rainforth & York-Barr, 1997). Although some assessments must be conducted by certified or licensed professionals (e.g., physical therapists), it does not preclude a team of people from collaborating for the duration of the assessment process. The first thing to determine when selecting team members is who can provide information that will satisfy the targeted outcome of the assessment. The collaborative assessment team may or may not include all of the members who work with the student. Membership will be driven more by what type of information is to be gathered.

To illustrate, consider the following: A team convenes to discuss the assessment procedures for evaluating the performance of a student with severe multiple disabilities over the last school year. The team will need to collect information, at minimum, on how the student moves in response to stimuli; how the student receives information through use of vision, hearing, tactile input; how the student provides information (e.g., with verbalizations, gestures, objects, two-dimensional representations); how the student reacts to environmental changes; and what types of medical problems interfere with optimal learning. During the planning phase for this example, the assessment team may include, but not be limited to, family members, a physical therapist, occupational therapist, speech-language pathologist, vision specialist, deaf/hard-of-hearing specialist, special education teacher, general education teacher, medical professional, and an assistive technology specialist. Once the team has been selected, members should designate a coordinator. Frequently, this position is filled by the teacher who sees the student on a more regular basis or who communicates with the family more often than other professionals on the team. This position can be filled, however, by any of the prospective team members. The team coordinator may need to set meeting times and facilitate future communication among the various team members.

Step 2: Determining Information to Be Gathered and Methods to Be Used. The second step for collaborative team members is to decide what information must be gathered and what data collection methods should be used in order to produce an educationally balanced assessment; that is, an assessment that provides a comprehensive characterization of a student's performance across areas assessed. This process will include making decisions as a team about the roles of tests (including standardized if appropriate), portfolio assessment, observations, record review, interviews, ecological inventories, classroom environment inventories, functional assessments for challenging behavior, play-based assessments, and person-centered planning in the overall assessment process. These methods are discussed in detail in other chapters.

Step 3: Determining Conditions for Direct Assessment. The third step of planning the collaborative assessment is to determine the conditions under which a student will be assessed based on three variables—first, the student's IEP goals and objectives; second, other experiences not reflected on the student's IEP (e.g., naturally occurring activities); and third, behaviors demonstrated by the student in various educational settings and activities. For instance, the planning phase for the assessment of the student who has autism may provide information related to (a) how long the student stays on task and under what conditions; (b) what setting events tend to affect the student's ability to perform skills for the desired length of time; (c) what signals the student exhibits when becoming frustrated or bored; (d) how the student behaves when frustrated or bored; (e) how the student initiates, maintains, and terminates favored activities; and (f) what types of activities result in success and in failure. Through collaboration the team could use this information to develop guidelines related to the presentation of assessment activities and materials to the child. The team then would determine the conditions under which the student will be assessed, possibly including (a) the environments where assessment will take place, (b) the accommodations that will be provided to honor the student's learning style and behavioral issues, (c) the length of time the assessment sessions will last, (d) the length of intervals between sessions, (e) the number of assessment activities that will be sufficient to reach valid conclusions, and (f) the period during which the entire assessment will be conducted. The conditions under which a student is evaluated should be flexible. If proposed assessment conditions create frustration, confusion, or failure for the student, then the assessment will not necessarily reflect the student's strengths and may inaccurately emphasize his or her perceived needs.

Step 4: Determining Who Will Conduct Various Collaborative Assessment Activities. Finally, regardless of the focus of the assessment and the level of intensity of need of the student, the assessment planning phase also should yield a list of individuals who will participate in gathering information for the assessment and who will conduct the direct assessment activities for a given student. With respect to students with severe disabilities, the list of participants could be fairly large, but how the assessments are conducted may limit the amount of time spent on assessing a child.

Collaborative assessment promotes more than one team member collecting assessment data in a given domain. For example, the National Center on Educational Outcomes identified five curricular domains to assess using alternate methods (Ysseldyke & Olsen, 1999). One of these domains is Personal and Social Adjustment. Collaborative team members who could be valuable in assessing this domain for a student with severe disabilities (e.g., autism or deaf–blindness) might include a speech/language pathologist, a family member, and a teacher. The rationale for this grouping is that social skills are linked directly to communication skills. A speech/language pathologist can assess across school, home, and community how the student's communication strengths and needs impact on the student's ability to initiate, maintain, and terminate social interactions. The family member in this instance can be instrumental in reporting how the student performs in natural settings, and the classroom teacher can provide information on similar behaviors at school using more quantitative measures.

Phase II: Gathering and Summarizing Supporting Information

For purposes of this phase of the assessment process, we will define information gathering as any means of gaining knowledge about the strengths, needs, and present levels of performance of a student prior to, or in conjunction with, conducting direct assessment. There are three general ways of obtaining this information: (a) through review of previous documentation, (b) through discussion with current and former team members, and (c) through completion of inventories and interviews. Traditionally, the person assigned to conduct the assessment for a particular discipline had been responsible for collecting previous documentation such as former assessments, past IEPs, videotaped performance, or products from a discipline-specific domain. In contrast to providing only information specific to each discipline represented on the team, collaborative team members also contribute to the assessment process by sharing their own knowledge about the student. This can include knowledge of the student's preferences, physical abilities, learning modalities, medical information pertinent to learning environments (including medication), communication abilities, and behavioral support needs (Westling & Fox, 1995b). When a student is newly assigned to the caseload of team members because of a recent transition between programs or settings, then the current team should invite members from the former team to discuss the student's former program and to report information about the student's strengths, needs, and present level of performance.

The use of inventories and interviews are a particularly good way of obtaining information about a student who, for any reason, is difficult to assess. In the assessment process, the information obtained from these processes can be used to determine the priorities of family members, school personnel, and the student. Ryndak (1996b) outlined a process for collecting information through the use of inventories. These inventories focus on the settings and activities with which a student potentially will interface using skills and knowledge across disciplines, rather than within a single discipline; and because of this cross-disciplinary focus, inventories are extremely useful to the collaborative assessment team in determining activities that warrant direct assessment.

According to Ryndak (1996b), two general categories of inventories are beneficial while assessing students with moderate to severe disabilities in inclusive settings. Inventories that provide information about performance levels and needs in functional curriculum include family inventories (Giangreco, Cloninger, & Iverson, 1998), peer inventories, community inventories (Brown, Branston-McLean, et al., 1979; Brown, Branston, et al., 1979), and related services assessments. Inventories that provide information about strengths and needs related to general education include an inventory of general education settings and an inventory of general education curriculum content. Another type of inventory that is beginning to emerge as a separate entity is the person-centered planning approach, which includes some components of family inventories. Haynes and Leatherby (1994); Mount and Zwernik (1988); Pearpoint, O'Brien, and Forest (1995); Turnbull and Turnbull (1997); and Vandercook, York, and Forest (1989) all have described some form of person-centered planning that includes both family members and other people who interact with a given student. The person-centered planning process is a critical feature of collaborative assessment because it generates information from all individuals involved with a student's life, for the purpose of establishing a direction and foundation for discipline-free goals, and for the corresponding assessment of discrepancies between desired and current performance.

Phase III: Conducting Direct Assessment

Among the assessment strategies to be described in later chapters, there are at least three types that are most effective when conducted using a collaborative team approach. First, transdisciplinary play-based assessment (Linder, 1993) involves representatives from a variety of disciplines who together observe a young student in play situations to collaboratively determine social and communicative developmental milestones. Second, functional assessment of challenging behaviors (Carr, et al., 1996; Koegel, Koegel, & Dunlap, 1996; O'Neill, Horner, Albin, Storey, & Sprague, 1990; Westling & Fox, 1995c) involves interviewing a variety of people, observing the student, and subsequently collaborating among individuals to generate assessment-based interventions that minimize a student's need to exhibit challenging behavior. Third, the use of discrepancy analyses during activities in the student's community involves professionals and family members determining priority educational targets. Later chapters specifically address direct assessment relative to a wide variety of individuals and areas of assessment.

As mentioned in the previous section, performance data for curricular domains can be assessed by several members of the collaborative team. Recall the previous example of the speech/language pathologist, parent, and classroom teacher working together to assess a social development domain. Concurrently, the speech/language pathologist can observe the student in settings other than school and use instruments that measure communication skills, members of the student's family can collect anecdotal data about how well the student exhibits communication and social skills in community settings, and the classroom teacher can collect data on social skills using event recording and a social skills inventory. Information from all three sources then can be viewed together by the team, providing a more holistic view of the student's communication abilities and instructional needs.

Another example of a collaborative effort to assess performance in a curricular domain might include a general education physical education teacher, a physical therapist, and a paraprofessional working together to assess the motor skills of a student with severe multiple disabilities across general education contexts (e.g., physical education class, recess, entering and exiting school). Concurrently, the physical education teacher may assess performance improvements in skills related to class activities (e.g., movement and mobility, strength, cooperative sports activities); the physical therapist might collect data on the changes in range of motion, improvements in balance, and increase in muscle strength; and the paraprofessional may collect data on the change in level of prompting required for the student to participate in physical activities. Although these team members collect different pieces of information, together they provide a comprehensive look at the student's overall improvement in the areas of motor and physical development and physical fitness.

Phase IV: Making Recommendations as a Team

Once the direct-assessment and information-gathering processes have been completed, then the assessment team should reconvene to generate an educationally relevant report on the student's progress during the designated assessment period, with recommendations for future instruction. This is particularly critical because education and related services should be delivered based on the results of an assessment report. The more easily an assessment report can be interpreted by all who are involved in the education of a student, the more likely that student will receive the adaptations and accommodations needed for effective instruction.

During this final phase of the assessment process, team members (a) share information about the assessment activities in which they participated and their findings, (b) make shared decisions about recommendations, (c) design the outline of the final report, and (d) assign duties related to the writing of the comprehensive report. At this time, all the information that has been gathered, including that which was collected through direct assessment procedures, is presented. When supporting students in inclusive settings, information gathered from inventories pertaining to the general education environments and curriculum should provide the context to which recommendations concerning instructional content and strategies should be referenced. Therefore, the collaborative team's goal is to report progress and make recommendations that are stated in a way that make it feasible for the student to receive effective instruction to meet his or her goals in general education settings. Only if specific recommendations cannot be carried out in a general education setting because of privacy or logistical issues should team members make suggestions as to how the recommendations can be followed with the least amount of disruption to the student's participation with nondisabled peers.

Giangreco (1996) described three methods of decision making by collaborative teams: autocratic, democratic, and consensus. Autocratic decision making usually accompanies a multidisciplinary approach by which professionals conduct their own assessments and make recommendations with little or no regard for the expertise of other professionals who interact with a given student. The recommendations more than likely would be carried out in an isolated setting because of the lack of collaboration and reference to general education. Democratic decision making, while incorporating team collaboration, uses voting to create a situation in which the majority rules and the minority fails. In situations where professionals outnumber family members and friends, the family's input into the assessment often is not given equal weight (Rowland, Schweigert, & Mar, 1999). In contrast, the consensus decision-making process is the most time consuming and requires more team effort than the other two methods. In theory, a team that makes decisions through consensus is more likely to understand the implications of the assessment report and follow the recommendations, because each team member has a vested interest in the recommendations being carried out. Giangreco (1996) points out that one drawback to the consensus decision-making process is the danger of false consensus. Occasionally, team members will overtly reach consensus on a matter, but in reality, some may defer to other team members' expertise or persuasiveness. In essence, a team member who defers to others is not participating in the true sense in the collaborative teaming process, the result of which may be similar to that of the autocratic or the democratic decision-making process.

Once decisions have been made about which recommendations are educationally relevant, the outline of the assessment report should be developed. Usually, comprehensive assessments are divided into sections for each discipline using the same reporting outline (e.g., background information, observations, assessment instruments, findings, recommendations). A report generated by a collaborative assessment team also can have these components, but the overall report may differ. For example, a collaborative team report may have separate sections for different disciplines, but one overall recommendation section written by the team as a whole. In contrast, a collaborative team report also may have each report section incorporate all of the discipline assessment results. In this case, a person must be designated to coordinate the writing of the report. Regardless of the design of the report, the critical issue is that the recommendations are reached by a team of professionals and family members, are educationally relevant, and are easily interpretable.

Summary

Our overall goal for this chapter was to present information about collaborative teams and how they can be used to produce a more comprehensive assessment. The evolution of the teaming process was discussed, with special emphasis on the structure, process, and benefits of a collaborative team approach. The phases of collaborative assessment include planning the assessment, gathering and summarizing information, conducting direct assessment, and making team recommendations. The chapter discussed these phases as they relate to alternate assessment in the general education environment.

Throughout the next chapters, the specific types of assessment are presented with collaborative teaming as a guiding principle. When any service or assessment is presented in isolation, the likelihood that the results will effect a positive change for the student that endures over time is minimized. Using collaborative teaming in the assessment process will result in a wealth of pertinent information rich with positive outcomes and easily leading to the next steps in a student's education.

REFERENCES

Brown, L., Branston-McLean, M. B., Baumgart, D., Vincent, L., Falvey, M., & Schroeder, J. (1979). Using the characteristics of current and future least restrictive environments in the development of curricular content for severely handicapped students. *AAESPH Review, 4,* 417–424.

Brown, L., Branston, M. B., Hamre-Nietupski, S., Pumpian, I., Certo, N., & Gruenewald, L. (1979). A strategy for developing chronological age appropriate and functional curricular content for severely handicapped adolescents and young adults. *Journal of Special Education, 13,* 81–90.

Carr, E. G., Levin, L., McConnachie, G., Carlson, J. I., Kemp, D. C., & Smith, C. E. (1994). *Communication-based intervention for problem behavior: A user's guide for producing positive change.* Baltimore: Paul H. Brookes.

Downing, J. E. (1996). Working cooperatively: The role of adults. In *Including students with severe and multiple disabilities in typical classrooms* (pp. 147–162). Baltimore: Paul H. Brookes.

Friend, M., & Cook, L. (1996). *Interactions: Collaboration skills for school professionals* (2nd ed.). White Plains, NY: Longman Publishers, USA.

Giangreco, M. (1996). *Vermont independent services team approach: A guide to coordinating educational support services.* Baltimore: Paul H. Brookes.

Giangreco, M. F., Cloninger, C. J., & Iverson, V. S. (1998). *Choosing outcomes and accommodations for children: A guide to educational planning for students with disabilities.* Baltimore: Paul H. Brookes.

Haynes, D., & Leatherby, J. (1994). Unpublished document.

Kleinert, H. L., & Kearns, J. F. (1999). A validation study of the performance indicators and learner outcomes of Kentucky's alternate assessment for students with significant disabilities. *JASH, 24,* 100–110.

Koegel, L. K., Koegel, R. L., & Dunlap, G. (1996). *Positive behavioral support: Including people with difficult behavior in the community.* Baltimore: Paul H. Brookes.

Linder, T. W. (1993). *Transdisciplinary play-based assessment.* Baltimore: Paul H. Brookes.

Lyon, S., & Lyon, G. (1980). Team functioning and staff development: A role release approach to providing integrated educational services for severely handicapped students. *JASH 5,* 250–263.

Mount, B., & Zwernik, K. (1988). *It's never too early it's never too late: A booklet about personal futures planning.* St. Paul, MN: Minnesota Governor's Planning Council on Developmental Disabilities.

O'Neill, R. E., Horner, R.H., Albin, R. W., Storey, K., Sprague, J. R. (1990). *Functional analysis of problem behavior.* Sycamore, IL: Sycamore Publishing Co.

Orelove, F., & Malatchie, A. (1998). *Creating collaborative IEPs: A handbook.* Virginia Commonwealth University: Virginia Institute for Developmental Disabilities.

Orelove, F. P., & Sobsey, D. (1996). Designing transdisciplinary services. In *Educating children with multiple disabilities* (pp. 1–34). Baltimore: Paul H. Brookes.

Pearpoint, J., O'Brien, J., & Forest, M. (1995). *Planning alternative tomorrows with hope* (2nd ed.). Toronto: Inclusion Press.

Rainforth, B., & York-Barr, J. (1997). *Collaborative teams for students with severe disabilities: Integrating therapy and educational services* (2nd ed.). Baltimore: Paul H. Brookes.

Rowland, C., Schweigert, P., & Mar, H. (1999). *Bringing it all home.* A presentation at the OSERS/OSEP Project Directors Meeting (State/Multi-State Projects in Deaf-Blindness). Washington, DC, October 1999.

Ryndak, D. L. (1996a). Education teams and collaborative teamwork in inclusive settings. In D. L. Ryndak & S. Alper, *Curriculum content for students with moderate and severe disabilities in inclusive settings* (pp. 77–96). Needham Heights, MA: Allyn & Bacon.

Ryndak, D. L. (1996b). The curriculum content identification process: Rationale and overview. In D. L. Ryndak & S. Alper, *Curriculum content for students with moderate and severe disabilities in inclusive settings* (pp. 33–60). Needham Heights, MA: Allyn & Bacon.

Turnbull, A. P., & Turnbull, H. R. (1997). *Families, professionals, and exceptionality: A special partnership* (3rd ed.). (pp. 251–272). Upper Saddle River, NJ: Merrill.

Vandercook, T., York, J., & Forest, M. (1989). The McGill action planning system (MAPS): A strategy for building the vision. *JASH, 4,* 205–215.

Westling, D. L., & Fox, L. (1995a). Collaborative teaming with parents, professionals, and paraprofessionals. In *Teaching students with severe disabilities* (pp. 56–82). Upper Saddle River, NJ: Prentice-Hall.

Westling, D. L., & Fox, L. (1995b). Conducting assessments to determine instructional needs. In *Teaching students with severe disabilities* (pp. 110–138). Upper Saddle River, NJ: Prentice-Hall.

Westling, D. L., & Fox, L. (1995c). Providing behavioral supports to improve challenging behavior. In *Teaching students with severe disabilities* (pp. 296–323). Upper Saddle River, NJ: Prentice-Hall.

Ysseldyke, J., & Olsen, K. (1999). Putting alternate assessments into practice: What to measure and possible sources of data. *Exceptional Children 65,* 175–186.

CHAPTER

5 Prereferral Assessment of Instruction

CYNTHIA N. SCHLOSS
Bloomsburg University

OBJECTIVES

After reading this chapter, you will be able to

1. Define prereferral intervention
2. Describe a prereferral team and the roles of individual members
3. Identify key targets for assessment and instruction for each of the disability categories
4. Assess a student's strengths and weaknesses based on identified targets for assessment
5. Describe the prereferral assessment model
6. Describe five key prereferral assessment strategies
7. Describe how implementation results can be easily documented

KEY TERMS

adversely affects (p. 98)
assistive devices (p. 104)
at risk (p. 102)
consultation and collaboration (p. 105)
cooperative learning (p. 105)
individualized instruction (p. 105)
prereferral assessment model (p. 99)
prereferral assessment strategy (p. 105)
prereferral intervention (p. 88)
referral (p. 88)
screenings (p. 90)
support team (p. 89)
targets for prereferral assessment (p. 91)
team roles (p. 89)

Prereferral intervention is the process through which professionals in the regular education setting exhaust all common methods of assessment and instruction prior to making a **referral** for special education services. Prereferral is described as a multistage process that

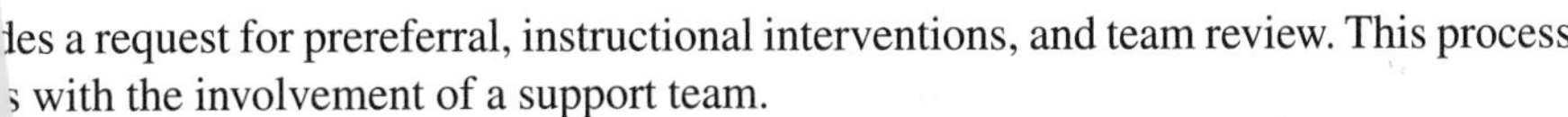
includes a request for prereferral, instructional interventions, and team review. This process begins with the involvement of a support team.

Support Teams

Prereferral intervention strategies may be designed and administered in collaboration with a **support team** (Smith, Polloway, Patton, & Dowdy, 1998). The prereferral process involves contacts between general and special education teachers. School personnel and family members need to collaborate in order to maximize educational efforts. A prereferral team is composed of stakeholders in a student's educational performance. Team members may include the regular educator, special educator, principal, school psychologist, school nurse, school counselor, consultant, and family members. This team may also be referred to as a multidisciplinary team, screening committee, child study committee, or an instructional support team.

Working With a Team

A multidisciplinary approach structures team interaction about the student with input from each team member (McLoughlin & Lewis, 1994; Wood, 1998). Team members represent various disciplines and interact with each other by promoting their particular discipline (Amlund & Kardash, 1994). The role of the team is to provide assistance to the teacher in addressing a student's key target area in the classroom. It will also define instructional strategies that address identified target areas.

Team Membership

Prereferral teams have common goals that define their existence. Focusing on their commonalties will assist in defining **team roles** and norms (Amlund & Kardash, 1994; Rosenfield & Gravois, 1996). Although team membership varies with each school, most will include the regular teacher, support teacher, and principal. Additional members will serve depending on the student's educational needs (Kovaleski, Tucker, & Stevens, 1996). Roles of key participants are described in the following sections.

Regular Educator. The regular educator provides the foundation for the team. When confronted with student difficulties or problem areas, it is the role of the regular education teacher to find effective solutions (Mamlin & Harris, 1998). Assessment data are collected by the classroom teacher and are shared with the prereferral team. This may include assessment data as referenced to the student's peers, anecdotal information, prereferral strategies, and student's current achievement level. The Individuals with Disabilities Education Act (IDEA, 1997) mandates that all students be provided a free and appropriate public education in the least restrictive environment (LRE). Placement in the regular education classroom is always to be considered. Appropriate justification is required when a student is not placed in the LRE. Inclusive practices should be incorporated in the regular education classroom promoting the inclusion of students with disabilities.

Special Educator. The special educator assists the regular education teacher during the prereferral phase (Kovaleski, Tucker, & Stevens, 1996). After observing a student in the classroom, strategies and adaptations are suggested. The student's progress is monitored and reported to the prereferral team. Based on prereferral assessment findings, the special educator is able to identify instructional strategies appropriate for the student. Goals and objectives are designed for the prereferral intervention stage, then implemented and monitored. Specially designed instruction is the focus of the special educator.

Principal. The principal serves on the prereferral team and is considered pivotal to the team's success (Mamlin & Harris, 1998). In this role he or she provides assistance by coordinating and monitoring the prereferral assessment and intervention. The principal's role focuses on scheduling, logistics, and resource issues. The principal has the same responsibilities for students with learning deficits as for other students.

School Psychologist. The school psychologist plays a key role on the prereferral team (Safran & Safran, 1996). This includes the coordination and administration of proposed **screenings** identified by team members. Interpretation of screening results is provided to the prereferral team and includes personal skill development and behavior management issues. Specific learning deficits are also identified and addressed by the team. The school psychologist may also provide guidance and counseling services to the student and family members.

School Nurse. A school nurse is able to identify health-related deficits through medical screenings and assessments. These activities include health, vision, and hearing checkups; obtaining and maintaining health histories; documentation of effects of medications; and noting any physical limitations. Interpretation of screenings and assessments can then be provided to the team for consideration in writing the prereferral evaluation report. Intervention strategies can then be included in the prereferral report. The school nurse is responsible for coordinating medical services to students with disabilities.

School Counselor. The school counselor's role is to provide screening and assessment information regarding a student's social history as a basis for providing educational services. This report will summarize educational, psychological, and medical records. Parent and student interviews are included. The school counselor, based on assessment findings, proposes intervention strategies. The school counselor may be responsible for coordinating educational services with community social service agencies and serving as a liaison between the school and the student's family. Services by the school counselor are based on the written goals and objectives and may be considered a related service.

Consultant. A consultant initiates the mutual interaction between two parties to prevent or solve a problem (Heron & Harris, 1993). Consultants are often identified by local education agencies in cases where expertise is not available regarding a disability, a characteristic, or both. Required assessments are conducted and interpretations of findings are provided. Consultants will participate as prereferral team members when necessary. Because there may be a lack of expertise within the local education agency, the consultant may also be involved in the student's prereferral intervention. Goals and objectives are designed, implemented, and carefully reviewed by the consultant depending on the need for the consultant's expertise.

Family Members. Another source to begin the prereferral process is a family member. Family members observe the student during nonschool hours and may have pertinent information regarding the student's progress and performance. Oftentimes they are considered the most important factor (Lian & Aloia, 1994; Turnbull, Turnbull, Shank, & Leal, 1999). As prescribed in IDEA (1997), parents are members of the multidisciplinary team. IDEA guarantees their right to participate in the decision-making process through procedural safeguards. Safeguards have been established to emphasize the importance of the parents' contribution in the process. The family serves many important functions including identification and referral, assessment and planning, intervention, and evaluation.

In conducting the prereferral process, specific targets for assessment must be reviewed by the support team. These are discussed in depth in the next section.

Targets for Prereferral Assessment of Instruction

Prereferral assessment of instruction is designed and conducted for students suspected of having a disability under P.L. 94-142 and subsequent reauthorizations of IDEA. Specific targets for prereferral interventions are considered in developing strategies in the assessment process. Targets vary depending on the area of disability that is being considered and are based on the nationally recognized definition of the disability. IDEA (1997) identifies 13 different definitions under the term *disability.* In this section, four disability categories are reviewed by definition and **targets for prereferral assessment** for each are provided. These were chosen due to their high incidence of occurrence in special education programs. A fifth group, composed of the remaining nine IDEA categories, are of low incidence. Figure 5.1 represents a modified version of Schloss and Sedlak's (1986) Characteristics of Specific Classification of Skills in identifying targets for prereferral assessment. Figures 5.2–5.5 identify a disability category noting specific targets for review. These are meant to be used in conjunction with the Performance Factors chart in Figure 5.1. A description of performance factors can be reviewed in Table 5.1. This system is an empirical approach to classifying an individual's characteristics. Strengths and weaknesses are described and provide adequate data for developing instructional goals and objectives.

Emotionally Disturbed

The current federal legislation (IDEA, 1997) refers to *emotionally disturbed* as a condition exhibiting one or more of the following characteristics over a long period of time and to a marked degree, which adversely affects educational performance:

- An inability to learn, which cannot be explained by intellectual, sensory or health factors
- An inability to build or maintain satisfactory relationships with peers and teachers
- Inappropriate types of behavior or feelings under normal circumstances
- A general pervasive mood of unhappiness or depression
- A tendency to develop physical symptoms or fears associated with personal or school problems

FIGURE 5.1 Emotionally disturbed.

Emotionally Disturbed *Targets for Prereferral Assessment*	**Performance Factors** — *Degree*: *Current Level*	*Expected Level*	*Nature*: *Skill Deficit*	*Motivational Deficit*	*Discrimination Deficit*	*Influencing Events*: *Antecedents*	*Consequences*
Inability to learn Inability to build or maintain relationships Inappropriate behavior or feelings under normal circumstances Pervasive mood of unhappiness or depression Physical symptoms or fears associated with personal or school problems							

The term includes children who are schizophrenic but does not apply to children who are socially maladjusted, unless it is determined that they have an emotional disturbance. (IDEA, 1997)

Students who are emotionally disturbed exhibit a wide range of characteristics (see Figure 5.1). These characteristics are grouped into five target areas and are described in the section that follows.

Inability to Learn. Students who are emotionally disturbed are generally at the low average level in intellectual ability (Turnbull, Turnbull, Shank, & Leal, 1999). Achievement is at or below grade level and is not explained by low intellectual levels, sensory deficits, or health problems. These students are frequently off task, have poor academic skills, are underachievers, and have poor language skills. Externalizing behaviors also tend to interfere with school achievement, which results in a deterioration from the elementary to secondary school levels.

Inability to Build or Maintain Relationships. Antisocial behavior is often exhibited by students with emotional disturbance (Heward, 1996). This behavior is described as those behaviors commonly displayed in the classroom but at an extreme rate: out of seat, disturbing peers, hitting, fighting, ignoring teachers or authority figures. Children with emotional disturbance appear to be in constant conflict with those around them. Their own aggressive behaviors cause others to strike back. Such students are rarely liked by others and have few friendships (Cartledge & Milburn, 1995).

TABLE 5.1 Classification of Skills Description

Performance Factors	
Degree of Severity	"The extent to which a learner's behavior deviates from social norms" (p. 30)
Nature of Deficiency	Deficits that "underlie the majority of educationally relevant exceptionality characteristics" (p. 31)
	Skill deficits: "absence of a response in the student's repertoire"; "determining whether the individual has ever performed the behavior" (p. 31)
	Motivational deficits: "failure to perform a behavior even though the prerequisite skills are present in his or her repertoire" (p. 32)
	Discrimination deficits: "possesses the skill and motivation necessary to engage in the desired behavior but is not aware of appropriate conditions for performing the behavior" (p. 33)
Influencing Events	"Cue conditions and motivational conditions that may influence the rate, duration, magnitude, or quality of the target behavior" (p. 33)

Source: From *Instructional methods for students with learning and behavior problems,* by P. J. Schloss & R. A. Sedlak, 1986, Boston: Allyn & Bacon.

Inappropriate Behavior or Feelings Under Normal Circumstances. Emotional disturbance is often categorized by the aggressiveness of the behavior exhibited. Two categories most commonly used are externalizing and internalizing behaviors (Achenbach, Howell, Quay, & Conners, 1991). Externalizing behaviors are those that are expressed outwardly, visible, and aggressive to others. Internalizing behaviors are those described as social withdrawal. While externalizing behaviors are described as striking out at others, internalizing behaviors involve mental or emotional conflicts with one's self. Behaviors exhibited may be considered normal but inappropriate when performed to a marked degree and for a long period of time. For example, a student might like to clean, but when it becomes a compulsion it is no longer appropriate. Other examples might include eating disorders and self-injurious behaviors.

Pervasive Mood of Unhappiness or Depression. Depression in children is often overlooked because its characteristics may be similar to those of another problem (Smith, 1998). For example, a student might be severely depressed and try to harm himself by swallowing a bottle of pills. An adult might not realize that the student was severely depressed and instead consider the child just being curious. Characteristics of depression might affect the student's emotions, motivation, physical well-being, and thoughts.

Physical Symptoms or Fears Associated With Personal or School Problems. Students with emotional disturbances often exhibit a wide range of behaviors that are both internalizing and externalizing. Both exhibit behaviors that might be considered inappropriate depending on their frequency and duration. Behaviors may become very intense, and the student may develop physical symptoms or fears associated with personal or school problems that he or she is experiencing. For example, a student internalizes fear of another student and becomes extremely nauseous to the degree of vomiting. Other examples might include heavy perspiration and grinding of teeth.

Specific Learning Disability

A specific learning disability is defined by the U.S. Department of Education in IDEA (1997) as a disorder in one or more of the basic psychological processes involved in understanding or in using language, spoken or written, which may manifest itself in imperfect ability to listen, think, speak, read, write, spell, or do mathematical calculations. This term includes such conditions as perceptual disabilities, brain injury, minimal brain dysfunction, dyslexia, and developmental aphasia. It does not include a learning problem that is primarily the result of visual, hearing, or motor disabilities; of mental retardation; of emotional disturbance; or of environmental, cultural, or economic disadvantage (IDEA, 1997).

Students who are eligible for special education services because of a specific learning disability must meet specific criteria (see Figure 5.2). These criteria are based on federal or professional definitions such as the definition stated in IDEA. Six key target areas for identification have been developed and are described in the following section.

Imperfect Ability to Listen. Children do not necessarily listen because they are told to do so. To be an effective listener, one must be able to initiate listening and then direct one's attention to the right source (Conte, 1991). Attention and listening are critical skills in learning. When children are not able to listen, they are not able to respond appropriately, answer questions, or take notes during class instruction.

Imperfect Ability to Think. Students who have the ability to think make good decisions with few errors (Hallahan, Kauffman, & Lloyd, 1996). Those who have difficulty lack initiative, respond verbally in a delayed manner, and need more follow-up and supervision. Concrete demonstrations are required, and teaching for generalization is necessary.

Imperfect Ability to Speak. Students with learning disabilities tend to have difficulty in the mechanical and social uses of speaking (Hallahan & Kauffman, 1997). Mechanics are the syntax, semantics, and phonology of spoken language, and social uses are described as the pragmatics. Long silences are typical of conversations because of the

FIGURE 5.2 Specific learning disability.

Specific Learning Disability

Targets for Prereferral Assessment

Imperfect ability to listen Imperfect ability to think Imperfect ability to speak Imperfect ability to read Imperfect ability to write Imperfect ability to do mathematical calculations

inability to use strategies to keep conversations going. Students tend to answer their own questions, make inappropriate comments, and make the person they are speaking with uncomfortable.

Imperfect Ability to Read. Reading is the key area of difficulty for students with learning disabilities. Word recognition, comprehension, and the inability to follow along cause problems and create their difficulty to read (Turnbull, Turnbull, Shank, & Leal, 1999). Word recognition errors may include omitting, inserting, or substituting words. Because students have limited time to recall or understand the meaning of what they read, comprehension may be limited.

Imperfect Ability to Write. Students with learning disabilities generally have problems in handwriting, spelling, and composition (Newcomer & Barenbaum, 1991). Students with learning disabilities experience difficulties more severe than the typical student. Slow writing, illegible handwriting, spelling, and noncreative aspects of composition are the most recognized areas of hardship.

Imperfect Ability to Do Mathematical Calculations. Math is second to reading as an area of difficulty. Computating math facts and solving math problems cause the most difficulties.

Mental Retardation

In IDEA (1997) mental retardation is defined as

> Significantly subaverage general intellectual functioning, existing concurrently with deficits in adaptive behavior and manifested during the developmental period, that adversely affects a child's educational performance.

The definition of mental retardation has changed numerous times over the years. The current AAMR (1992) definition represents a shift from mental retardation as a permanent state of being to an individual's present functioning and need for supports.

Three components are required to determine eligibility for supports: intellectual functioning, significant disabilities in two or more adaptive skill areas, and manifestation before age 18. Further clarification of the first two components is described in the following section (see Figure 5.3).

Subaverage General Intellectual Functioning. Intellectual functioning is the ability to solve problems in academic subject areas (Hallahan & Kauffman, 1997). Intelligence is estimated by an IQ test score of 70 to 75 or below. This is one of three criteria in determining mental retardation.

Adaptive Skills. Adaptive skills are the abilities needed to adapt to one's environment. Ability level is usually estimated by an adaptive behavior checklist or scale. By AAMR's (1992) definition, students with mental retardation have significant disabilities in two or more adaptive skill areas. Refer to Table 5.2 for a description of each of the skill areas.

FIGURE 5.3 Mental retardation.

Mental Retardation

Targets for Prereferral Assessment

Subaverage general intellectual functioning
Limitations in adaptive skills
- communication
- self-care
- home living
- social skills
- community use
- self-direction
- health and safety
- functional academics
- leisure
- work

TABLE 5.2 Adaptive Skill Areas

Adaptive Skill	Explanation	Examples
Communication	The ability to use the process in which speech and language occurs	Messages, conversations
Self-care	The ability to care for personal bodily needs	Bathing, eating
Home Living	To perform the skills necessary to live in a home independently	Cooking, budgeting
Social Skills	The ability to use the skills necessary to facilitate successful participation in a group	Giving compliments, asking questions
Community Use	The ability to use community resources in daily life activities	Shopping, banking
Self-direction	The ability to make one's own informed decisions and choices	Purchasing clothing, asking for assistance
Health & Safety	To perform skills necessary to meet personal health and safety needs	Exercising, fire drills
Functional Academics	To perform the skills necessary to function independently in the community	Reading a newspaper, using a calculator
Leisure	The ability to participate in recreational interests and activities	Community recreational program
Work	To perform skills necessary to seek competitive employment	On task behavior, basic math

Speech or Language Impairment

A speech or language impairment is defined by IDEA (1997) as a communication disorder, such as stuttering, impaired articulation, or a voice impairment, that adversely affects a child's educational performance. ASHA (1993) defines a speech disorder as "an impairment of the articulation of speech sounds, fluency, and/or voice." A language disorder is defined as "an impaired comprehension and/or use of spoken, written, and/or other symbol systems" (p. 40–41).

A child's speech or language impairment must have an adverse affect on his or her learning to be considered eligible for special education services (Data Research, 1998). Because these disorders vary, are difficult to identify, and generally occur in tandem with another disability, determining the prevalence is often difficult (Hallahan & Kauffman, 1997). Federal data indicate that approximately 5% of all children have a speech and language impairment serious enough to be eligible for special education services. Of the students receiving special education services, 21% receive speech and language services (U.S. Department of Education, 1996). Students with a speech or language impairment are the most highly included of all students with disabilities. Regular education teachers typically have students with a speech or language impairment in their classroom (Smith, Polloway, Patton, & Dowdy, 1998).

Speech and language impairments are generally distinguished from each other by most professionals in the field of communication disorders. Children with speech impairments have an imperfect production and use of oral language. Children with language impairments have difficulty in comprehending and using language for communication (see Figure 5.4). Refer to Table 5.3 for an explanation of the breakdown of speech and language impairments into target areas of intervention.

Other Disabilities

This section consists of the remaining nine IDEA categories, which are of low incidence. Smith (1998) defines low incidence as a "disability that occurs infrequently; the prevalence

FIGURE 5.4 Speech or language impairment.

Speech or Language Impairment

Targets for Prereferral Assessment

Impairment of speech
- voice
- articulation
- fluency

Impairment of language
- phonology
- morphology
- syntax
- semantics
- pragmatics

TABLE 5.3 Speech and Language Target Areas

Impairment	Explanation
Speech	Imperfect production and use of oral language
Voice	Absence or abnormal production of voice quality, pitch, loudness, resonance, or duration
Articulation	An abnormal production of speech sounds
Fluency	An abnormal flow of verbal expression
Language	Difficulty in comprehending and using language for communication
Phonology	Imperfect use of language and linguistic rules and the development of sound combinations
Morphology	Abnormal development of words and word forms
Syntax	Imperfect use of rules to form sentences
Semantics	Imperfect use of the psycholinguistics of meanings of words and sentences
Pragmatics	Imperfect use of sociolinguistics of meanings of words and sentences

and incidence are very low." (p. 566). The nine categories of low-incidence disabilities include

1. Autism
2. Deaf-blindness
3. Deafness
4. Hearing impairment
5. Multiple disability
6. Orthopedic impairment
7. Other health impairment
8. Traumatic brain injury
9. Visual impairment

IDEA defines each of these disabilities with specific criteria that includes the component "adversely affects a child's educational performance." Although not defined by IDEA, ***adversely affects*** will be defined by the answers to McLoughlin and Lewis's (1994) four questions in determining eligibility for special education services:

1. What is the level of academic achievement and strengths and weaknesses in school learning?
2. What is the level of intellectual performance and adaptive behavior?
3. What is the level of development of specific learning abilities and learning strategies?
4. What is the status of classroom behavior and social-emotional development? (p. 17)
   Figure 5.5 outlines the low incidence targets for prereferral assessment.

FIGURE 5.5 Low incidence.

Low Incidence

Targets for Prereferral Assessment

Limited academic achievement Limited intellectual functioning and adaptive behavior Limited learning abilities and strategies Limited classroom behavior

Academic Achievement. Academic achievement is determined by a student's school performance compared with other students (McLoughlin & Lewis, 1994). Formal and informal procedures can be used to determine a student's strengths and weaknesses. Data obtained might suggest additional assessment procedures and partially establish eligibility for special education services.

Intellectual Functioning and Adaptive Behavior. By combining both of these, classroom behavior can be predicted (McLoughlin & Lewis, 1994). Intellectual functioning is related to the student's ability to think, problem solve, and to his or her general academic aptitude. Adaptive behavior is determined by the student's ability to function in environments other than the classroom.

Learning Abilities and Strategies. These abilities and strategies are considered the foundation for readiness and success in school (McLoughlin & Lewis, 1994). Abilities include attention, perception, and memory. Organizational skills, time management, and study skills are examples of learning strategies.

Classroom Behavior. The student's ability to learn in a classroom setting is assessed. A severe deficit in one or more aspects of behavior is necessary for eligibility for services in behavior disorders (McLoughlin & Lewis, 1994). Assessment procedures predict the student's ability to successfully learn in a classroom environment.

Conceptual Model

Prereferral assessment and intervention strategies have been used successfully and considered quite effective in modifications to the instructional process (Kovaleski, Tucker, & Stevens, 1996; Safran & Safran, 1996; Sindelar, Griffin, Smith, & Watanabe, 1992). Graphic representations of instructional activities have also been reported effective in portraying instructional processes to the educational professional (Schloss & Sedlak, 1986; Schloss, Smith, & Schloss, 1995). It is for this purpose that a **prereferral assessment model** has been developed, highlighting each of the seven steps of the prereferral assessment process. Figure 5.6 illustrates the proposed model. Two scenarios highlighting each of the steps are provided in Appendix 5.1.

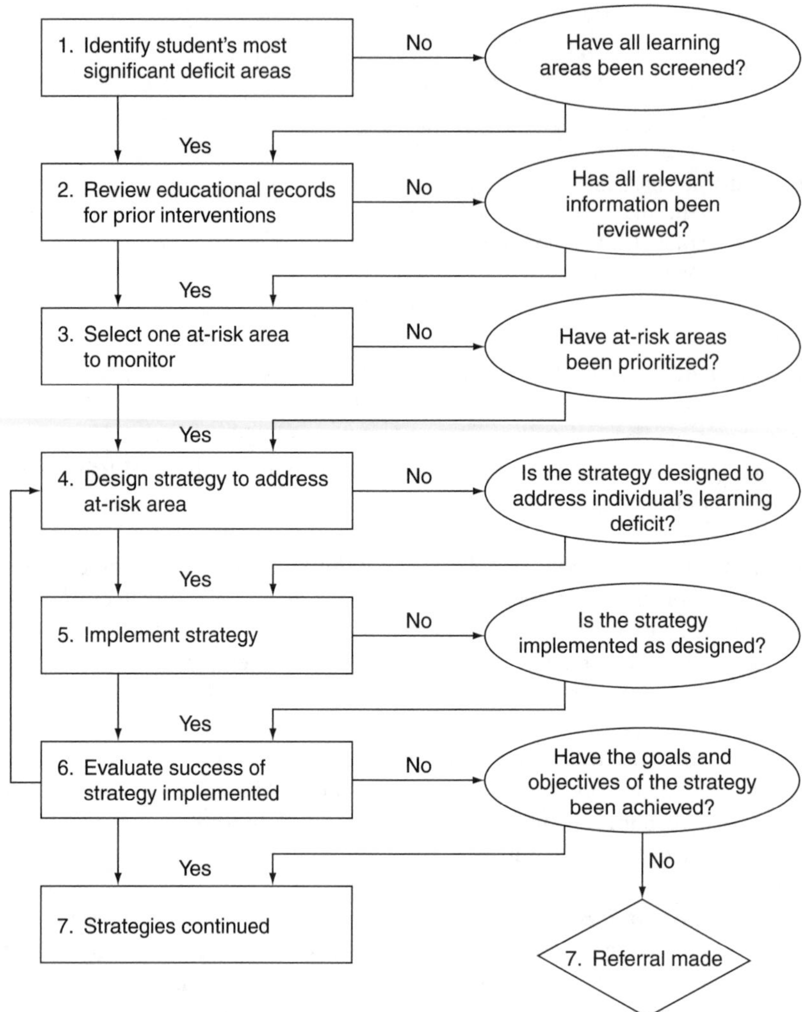

FIGURE 5.6 Prereferral intervention steps.

Rectangles one through seven on the left side of the figure refer to the steps that the teacher takes in providing prereferral intervention. Arrows connecting the rectangles indicate that the process is proceeding normally. When teachers experience difficulty, horizontal arrows direct the teacher to questions in the ovals on the right. The teacher focuses on how the intervention prereferral program can be modified. Arrows connecting the ovals to the rectangles illustrate that a modification was made and the teacher could then return to the process. Once the first six steps are completed, the process is repeated until all skills on the priority list are exhausted. If the goals and objectives of specific strategies are not achieved, a referral for special education services is made. If they are achieved, strategies are continued with no referral. Descriptions of each of the seven steps follow in the next sections.

Step 1. Identify Student's Most Significant Deficit Areas

The prereferral process involves collaborative teamwork among the regular education teacher, special education teacher, and family members (Smith, Polloway, Patton, & Dowdy, 1998). Additional persons may be involved with this prereferral team based on the student's learning needs (Kovaleski, Tucker, & Stevens, 1996). All learning areas are screened for strengths and weaknesses, highlighting those reported by the teacher as an area of need. These learning areas are compared to specific targets for assessment as identified by disability areas. Considered to be very effective in planning for prereferral assessment, these target areas assist the prereferral team in identifying the learning characteristics of students with disabilities.

Although prereferral strategies are considered to be very effective in the special education process, referrals for special education services continue to play an important role (Smith, Polloway, Patton, & Dowdy, 1998). Reasons for referral vary but include academic problems (Gottlieb, Gottlieb, & Trongone, 1991), misbehavior (Anderson, Cronin, & Miller, 1986), lack of teacher control (Gottlieb, Gottlieb, & Wishner, 1994), and gender/racial issues (Bahr, Fuchs, Stecker, & Fuchs, 1991; MacMillan, Gresham, Lopez, & Bocian, 1996). Lloyd, Kauffman, Landrum, and Roe (1991) report that academic problems are the key reason for referral for special education services. A review of other reasons is reported in Table 5.4. Figure 5.7 provides a sample form that may be used in identifying a student's various areas of deficit.

TABLE 5.4 Reasons for Referral

Reason	Description
General academic problems	Reading, writing, arithmetic
Behavioral and emotional problems	Aggressive, disruptive, delinquent behaviors; immaturity; inadequacy; emotional problems; anxious, fearful, withdrawn behaviors
Reading problems	Phonics, word recognition, decoding, comprehension
Attention problems	Attention deficits, hyperactivity
Writing problems	Writing skills, written expression
Arithmetic problems	Calculations, reasoning
Language problems	Oral expression, written expression, receptive
Sensory problems	Visual, auditory

FIGURE 5.7 Prereferral information form.

Student's Name ______________________________ Date ______________

Parent(s) Name ______________________________

Address ______________________________

____

Home Telephone ______________________________

Birthdate ______________________________ Grade ______________

Area(s) of Concern: Ability _______ Emotional _______

Achievement _______ Medical _______

Behavior _______ Motor _______

Other _______

Description of Concern(s) ______________________________

____

____

____

Please attach any available documentation.

Step 2. Review Educational Records for Prior Interventions

All available educational records should be reviewed by the team at this step. Records may include school histories, attendance reports, grade reports, medical screenings, testing results, and written reports by consultants. In reviewing the student's school record, duplication of screenings and interviews may be avoided if information is already available. Relevant and current available information may assist in determining your goals in selecting areas to assess. It may also provide feedback on strategies that have already been tried in the classroom or suggested strategies for the future. Refer to Figure 5.8 for a sample checklist that might be used in reviewing educational records.

Step 3. Select At-Risk Area to Monitor

Once the student's deficit areas are identified, the team needs to determine which area will be monitored first through the prereferral assessment process. After a careful review of the student's educational record, it is important for the team to gather all pertinent information regarding the student's performance in the classroom. The student's strengths are reviewed and noted, highlighting student's characteristics considered **at risk** (Smith, Polloway, Patton, & Dowdy, 1998). Characteristics considered at risk are reviewed and then prioritized in relationship to the extent that they adversely affect a student's educational performance. Remaining areas are saved for future strategy initiation.

FIGURE 5.8 Educational record checklist.

Student's Name ______________________ Date ____________ Grade ________

Information Needed

Last School Attended ______________________ _____

Attendance _____

- Excellent _______
- Above average _______
- Average _______
- Below average _______
- Poor _______

Grades (Average) _____

- Math _______
- Science _______
- Reading _______
- English _______
- Social Studies _______

Medical Screening _____

- Vision _______
- Hearing _______
- Speech/Lanugage _______
- Motor _______

Assessment _____

Area	*Test*	*Score*	*Date*
Ability			
Achievement			
Speech/Language			
Motor			
Statewide			
Other			

Consultation Reports _____

- Name
  Date:
  Area of Concern:
- Name:
  Date:
  Area of Concern:

Prior Strategies Conducted _____

- Strategy: Date:
  Result:
- Strategy: Date:
  Result:
- Strategy: Date:
  Result:

Step 4. Design Strategy to Address At-Risk Area

During the prereferral process, the team attempts to identify educational strategies that will address the most significant problems the student experiences in the classroom (Flugum & Reschly, 1994). Selection of the strategy is based on the goal(s) and objectives that have been designed by the prereferral team for the student. Goals are established by the team and reflect its informal findings regarding the problem area. The nature and number of goals are determined by the existing skills currently in the student's repertoire and his or her age (Schloss, Smith, & Schloss, 1995). Students at the elementary school level may have more flexibility in the design of their prereferral goal.

Goals designed by the prereferral team are restructured into assessment objectives that serve as a foundation for prereferral interventions. Each objective will include a description of the behavior to perform, a statement of the condition in which it will be performed, and the criteria for appropriate performance. A more thorough description of goals and objectives is provided in Chapter 7.

There are a number of effective intervention strategies that have been reported used for prereferral strategies (Brown, Gable, Hendrickson, & Algozzine, 1991; Rivera & Smith, 1997; Rosenfield & Gravois, 1996; Smith, Polloway, Patton, & Dowdy, 1998). Table 5.5 highlights those most used. The following sections review five key strategies.

Assistive Devices. Specific learning needs can often be overcome through the use of assistive devices (Chalmers, 1992; Chalmers & Wasson, 1993; Kovaleski, Tucker, & Stevens, 1996; Schloss & Sedlak, 1986). Calculators, coding, study guides, and word processors are examples of **assistive devices** that can be used to accommodate a student's learning. The extent that they are used can only be determined by the classroom teacher in consultation with the prereferral team. This is accomplished by weighing the benefits of the assistive device to the learning process. Data collection activities will aid in making this determination.

Classroom and Behavior Management. Students who are at risk often need to learn how to behave in the classroom (Chalmers & Wasson, 1993). Their failure to fit in is often the reason for referral to special education. Classroom social skills can be taught easily through direct instructional techniques in the regular education classroom, benefiting all students. Assessment of these skills is completed easily through direct observation techniques. Management of classroom behaviors will assist in promoting organization, consistency, and parameters for students (Rivera & Smith, 1997).

TABLE 5.5 Effective Intervention Strategies

Assistive Devices	Individualized Instruction
Behavior Management	Modified Classroom/Curriculum
Consultation/Collaboration	Parent Conferences
Cooperative Learning	Parent Volunteers
Graphic Organizers	Peer Tutoring

Consultation and Collaboration. With the movement toward teaching students with disabilities in the general education classroom, more school teachers and personnel are serving students through a consultation and collaborative approach (deBettencourt, 1999). In a study reported by Brown, Gable, Hendrickson, and Algozzine (1991), it was found that consultation was rated the most commonly used prereferral strategy among 355 participants. This inclusive approach requires special educators to work closely with general education teachers. **Consultation and collaboration** promotes the exchange of knowledge, skills, and expertise between the teachers of the prereferral team. Teachers work cooperatively in groups of two to five individuals, designing a **prereferral assessment strategy** that will provide information regarding a student's learning ability. Teachers share the responsibility in the development, implementation, and evaluation stages of instructional strategies in the general education setting.

Cooperative Learning. **Cooperative learning** is best described as an instructional strategy that promotes the use of small groups in maximizing a student's learning (Hoover & Patton, 1997) as well as another student's. Students work in pairs or a small group of three or more individuals. Cooperative learning is competitive, but it is achieved through group efforts. Goals are reached through shared work with a student's peers. There are five common elements (Roy, 1990) in implementing cooperative learning instruction: positive interdependence, individual accountability, opportunities for interactions, interpersonal training, and group processing. Once students are skilled in each of the elements, cooperative learning can take place. Cooperative learning is an effective prereferral strategy in that it supplements and enhances a teacher's instruction by giving students the opportunity to practice and discuss the information provided by the teacher. Cooperative learning differs from individualized instruction in its degree of competitiveness.

Individualized Instruction. **Individualized instruction** is best described as an instructional strategy where a student is expected to work independently to enhance information provided in a larger classroom environment. This strategy may be problematic for students with disabilities (Thousand, Villa, & Nevin, 1994) in that it is expected to be performed in a quiet, independent manner. One-to-one interaction provides instruction to individuals based on their specific behavior and learning needs (Rivera & Smith, 1997). This may include direct intervention, promoting self-initiation (i.e., prompts and reinforcement) in completing an assignment, or peer tutoring in learning specific content in an assignment. Students spend a great deal of time performing individualized instruction prior to receiving adequate group instruction. General guidelines (Chalmers, 1992) for use of individualized instruction with students suspected of having a disability are noted in Table 5.6.

Step 5. Implement Strategy

The prereferral assessment period is generally implemented for one grading period. This time frame should be flexible to meet the needs of the individual student (Smith, Polloway, Patton, & Dowdy, 1998). Results of each intervention implemented should be documented. Recorded data from each intervention will assist the prereferral team in making their recommendations for possible referral for special education services. Review Figure 5.9 for a sample form to use in documenting the results of strategies implemented.

TABLE 5.6 General Guidelines for Individualized Instruction

1. Preteach vocabulary
2. Preview major concepts
3. State a purpose for reading
4. Provide for repetition of instruction
5. Provide clear directions and examples
6. Make time adjustments
7. Provide feedback
8. Have students keep an assignment notebook
9. Provide an alternate assignment
10. Be sure the assignment is appropriate
11. Read material orally as much as possible
12. Allow manipulatives

Source: From *Modifying curriculum for the special needs student in the regular classroom* (pp. 8–10), by L. Chalmers, 1992, Moorhead, MN: Practical Press.

FIGURE 5.9 Documentation of implementation.

Student's Name ____________________ Date __________ Grade ______

Assessment Strategies	*No. of Days Attempted*	*Improved*	*No Change*	*Comments*
1.				
2.				
3.				
4.				
5.				
6.				
7.				
8.				
9.				
10.				

Step 6. Evaluate Success of Strategy Implemented

After a prereferral assessment strategy is implemented, it is important to determine if the strategy is effective. Have the goals and objectives of the strategy been achieved? If yes, then the strategy is continued. If not, the strategy's design, goals, and objectives are reviewed and possibly revised. The next deficit skill area is reviewed as previously described.

Step 7. Continue Strategies or Make a Referral

Up to this point in the model, prereferral assessment strategies have been conducted within the classroom environment. The focus has been on what can be achieved in the regular education classroom in lieu of a referral for special education services. If a referral is made, data from the prereferral assessment trials are provided as a basis for referring for further evaluation. If a referral is not made, continued use of the identified effective strategies is recommended. The referral process is discussed thoroughly in Chapter 6.

Summary

In this chapter, prereferral interventions were introduced. Support teams, assessment targets, and a conceptual model were highlighted. Prereferral intervention was described as the process of exhausting all common methods of assessment and instruction prior to referral for special education services.

Support teams are an intricate part of the prereferral process. Teams are composed of individuals who serve as a stakeholder in a student's educational performance. The team's role is to provide assistance to the classroom teacher regarding members' technical expertise. Members may include a regular educator, special educator, principal, school psychologist, school nurse, school counselor, consultant, and family members.

Prereferral intervention is designed for students who are being considered for referral to special education services. Specific targets for prereferral assessment are identified from the four high-incidence disability categories. These include emotional disturbance, specific learning disability, mental retardation, and speech or language impairments. A fifth category, other disabilities, is composed of the remaining low-incidence categories. Targets for assessment are described for each category, highlighting a student's characteristics. Through the prereferral assessment process, strengths and weaknesses are identified and provide adequate data for developing instructional goals and objectives.

A conceptual model for prereferral assessment is portrayed, graphically highlighting each of its seven steps. Collaborative teamwork is incorporated throughout the model. During the process, the team identifies various educational strategies that address the student's deficit skill areas. Five key strategies were described: classroom and behavior management, consultation and collaboration, cooperative learning, individualized instruction, and assistive devices. The prereferral assessment process will generally take one grading period to be implemented and evaluated. After all areas have been assessed, the prereferral team determines if a referral for further evaluation needs to be completed.

REFERENCES

Achenbach, T. M., Howell, C. T., Quay, H. C., & Conners, C. K. (1991). National survey of problems and competencies among four- to sixteen-year-olds: Parents' reports for normative and clinical samples. *Monographs of the Society for Research in Child Development, 56*(3), serial no. 225.

American Association on Mental Retardation (AAMR). (1992). *Mental retardation: Definition, classification, and systems of supports* (9th ed.). Washington, DC: Author.

American Speech-Language-Hearing Association (ASHA). (1993). Definitions of communication disorders and variations, *ASHA, 35* (Suppl. 10), 40–41.

Amlund, J. T., & Kardash, C. M. (1994). Group approaches to consultation and advocacy. In S. A. Alper, P. J. Schloss, and C. N. Schloss (Eds.), *Families of students with disabilities: Consultation and advocacy* (pp. 181–204). Boston: Allyn & Bacon.

Anderson, P. L., Cronin, M. E., & Miller, J. H. (1986). *Psychology in the Schools, 23,* 388–395.

Bahr, M. W., Fuchs, D., Stecker, P. M., & Fuchs, L. S. (1991). Are teachers' perceptions of difficult-to-teach students racially biased? *School Psychology Review, 20,* 599–608.

Brown, J., Gable, R. A., Hendrickson, J. M., & Algozzine, B. (1991). Prereferral intervention practices of regular classroom teachers: Implications for regular and special education preparation. *Teacher Education and Special Education, 14*(3), 192–197.

Cartledge, G., & Milburn, J. F. (1995). *Teaching social skills to children and youth: Innovative approaches.* Needham Heights, MA: Allyn & Bacon.

Chalmers, L. (1992). *Modifying curriculum for the special needs' student in the regular classroom.* Moorhead, MN: Practical Press.

Chalmers, L., & Wasson, B. (1993). *Successful inclusion: Assistance for teachers of adolescents with mild disabilities.* Moorhead, MN: Practical Press.

Conte, R. (1991). Attention disorders. In B. Y. L. Wong (Ed.), *Learning about learning disabilities* (pp. 55–101). New York: Academic Press.

Data Research, Inc. (1998). *Students with disabilities and special education* (15th ed.). Rosemount, MN: Author.

deBettencourt, L. U. (1999). General educator's attitudes toward students with mild disabilities and their use of instructional strategies: Implications for training. *Remedial and Special Education, 20*(1), 27–35.

Flugum, K. R., & Reschly, D. J. (1994). Prereferral interventions: Quality indices and outcomes. *Journal of School Psychology, 32*(1), 1–14.

Gottlieb, J., Gottlieb, B. W., & Trongone, S. (1991). Parent and teacher referrals for a psychoeducational evaluation. *The Journal of Special Education, 25,* 155–167.

Gottlieb, J., Gottlieb, B. W., & Wishner, J. (1994). Special education in urban America: It's not justifiable for many. *The Journal of Special Education, 27,* 453–465.

Hallahan, D. P., & Kauffman, J. M. (1997). *Exceptional learners: Introduction to special education* (7th ed.). Boston: Allyn & Bacon.

Hallahan, D. P., Kauffman, J. M., & Lloyd, J. W. (1996). *Instruction of learning disabilities.* Boston: Allyn & Bacon.

Heron, T. E., & Harris, K. C. (1993). *The educational consultant: Helping professionals, parents, and mainstreamed students.* Austin, TX: Pro-Ed.

Heward, W. L. (1996). *Exceptional children: An introduction to special education* (5th ed.). Englewood Cliffs, NJ: Merrill.

Hoover, J. J., & Patton, J. R. (1997). *Curriculum adaptations for students with learning and behavior problems: Principles and practices.* Austin, TX: Pro-Ed.

Individuals with Disabilities Education Act, 20 U.S.C., § 1400 *et seq.* (1997).

Kovaleski, J. F., Tucker, J. A., & Stevens, L. J. (1996). Bridging special regular education: The Pennsylvania initiative. *Educational Leadership, 53*(5), 44–47

Lian, M. J., & Aloia, G. F. (1994). Parental responses, roles, and responsibilities. In S. A. Alper, P. J. Schloss, and C. N. Schloss (Eds.), *Families of students with disabilities: Consultation and advocacy* (pp. 51–93). Boston: Allyn & Bacon.

Lloyd, J. W., Kaufman, J. M., Landrum, T. J., & Roe, D. L. (1991). Why do teachers refer pupils for special education? An analysis of referral records. *Exceptionality, 2,* 115–126.

MacMillian, D. L., Gresham, F. M., Lopez, M. F., & Bocian, K. M. (1996). Comparison of students nominated for prereferral interventions by ethnicity and gender. *The Journal of Special Education, 30,* 133–151.

Mamlin, N., & Harris, K. R. (1998). Elementary teachers' referral to special education in light of inclusion and prereferral: "Every child is here to learn . . . but some of these children are in real trouble." *Journal of Educational Psychology, 90*(3), 385–396.

McLoughlin, J. A., & Lewis, R. B. (1994). *Assessing special students* (4th ed.). Upper Saddle River, NJ: Merrill.

Newcomer, P. L., & Barenbaum, E. M. (1991). The written composing ability of children with learning disabilities: A review of the literature from 1980 to 1990. *Journal of Learning Disabilities, 24*(10), 578–593.

Rivera, D. P., & Smith, D. D. (1997). *Teaching students with learning and behavior problems* (3rd ed.). Boston: Allyn & Bacon.

Rosenfield, S. A., & Gravois, T. A. (1996). *Instructional consultation teams: Collaborating for change.* New York: Guilford Press.

Roy, P. A. (1990). *Cooperative learning: Students learn together.* Richfield, MN: Author.

Safran, S. P., & Safran, J. S. (1996). Intervention assistance programs and prereferral teams: Directions for the twenty-first century. *Remedial and Special Education, 17*(6), 363–369.

Schloss, P. J., & Sedlak, R. A. (1986). *Instructional methods for students with learning and behavior problems.* Boston: Allyn & Bacon.

Schloss, P. J., Smith, M. A., & Schloss, C. N. (1995). *Instructional methods for adolescents with learning and behavior problems* (2nd ed.). Boston: Allyn & Bacon.

Sindelar, P. T., Griffin, C. C., Smith, S. W., & Watanabe, A. K. (1992). Prereferral intervention: Encouraging notes on preliminary findings. *The Elementary School Journal, 92*(3), 245–259.

Smith, D. D. (1998). *Introduction to special education: Teaching in an age of challenge* (3rd ed.). Boston: Allyn & Bacon.

Smith, T. E., Polloway, E. A., Patton, J. R., & Dowdy, C. A. (1998). *Teaching students with special needs in inclusive settings.* Boston: Allyn & Bacon.

Thousand, J. S., Villa, R. A., & Nevin, A. I. (1994). *Creativity and collaborative learning: A practical guide to empowering students and teachers.* Baltimore: Paul H. Brookes.

Turnbull, A., Turnbull, R., Shank, M., & Leal, D. (1999). *Exceptional lives: Special education in today's schools* (2nd ed.). Upper Saddle River, NJ: Merrill.

U.S. Department of Education (1992). Assistance to states for the education of children with disabilities program and preschool grants for children with disabilities, final rule. *Federal Register,* 34 CRF Parts 300 and 301.

U.S. Department of Education (1996). *Eighteenth annual report to Congress on the implementation of the Individuals with Disabilities Education Act.* Washington, DC: Author.

Wood, J. W. (1998). *Adapting instruction to accommodate students in inclusive settings.* Columbus, OH: Merrill.

APPENDIX 5.1 PREREFERRAL INTERVENTION STEPS

Scenario 1: Jimmy, Grade 1

Significant Deficit Areas. Jimmy is extremely low in word attack, oral reading, comprehension, and sight word vocabulary. His spelling scores have been declining. He does not choose to read and appears very uninterested in school. On a recent test, he showed mild deficits in auditory memory, comprehension, and visual acuity. He rotates letters and reverses words in his writing.

Jimmy is extremely low in performing basic math operations and does not know his basic math facts. He needs manipulatives to do computations and is unsure what operation signs to use. When new concepts are introduced (i.e., addition) he experiences difficulty.

His teacher reports that he never participates in class, stays on task, or exhibits organized work habits. Absences are minimal. With prompting, he is able to complete class work and follow directions.

Review Educational Records. Jimmy was retained in kindergarten due to his inability to perform developmental milestones. He had significant difficulty in number and letter identification and understanding. Jimmy was referred to prereferral intervention for academic and social/emotional reasons. Jimmy's classroom teachers tried the following strategies:

Offered extra help and attention
Changed student's seat
Used clear and specific directions
Provided peer tutoring
Used limited directions
Conducted a parent conference by telephone

Select One At-Risk Area to Monitor. The prereferral intervention team identified three at-risk areas for consideration. The team rated these with 1 being highest and 3 being lowest.

1. Addition and subtraction facts to 10
2. Writing an understandable sentence
3. Completing 80% of class work

Design Strategy—Priority At-Risk Area 1. A prereferral team member worked with Jimmy individually. The team explored six intervention strategies designed to address Jimmy's needs.

1. Repetition
2. Manipulatives
3. Assistance from family
4. Manipulative flash cards as a craft project
5. Math game calculator
6. Math programs on computer

Implement Strategy. Jimmy met with his prereferral intervention teacher three times a week regarding addition and subtraction facts through 10. Interventions incorporating one-to-one help, manipulatives, and a number line were used as designed by the prereferral intervention team.

Evaluate Success. At the conclusion of the prereferral intervention, Jimmy's goal was achieved. He was able to add and subtract up to 12.

Design Strategy—Priority At-Risk Area 2. The prereferral team member designed strategies to address the at-risk area of writing an understandable sentence. Individual one-to-one intervention was conducted using illustrations, sentence modeling, story taping and transcription, and assistance from Jimmy's parents.

Implement Strategy. Jimmy met with his prereferral intervention teacher three times a week regarding writing an understandable sentence. Intervention was implemented as designed by the team, including idea illustrations, sentence modeling, story taping and transcribing, and assistance by Jimmy's parents.

Evaluate Success. Improvement was noted in Jimmy's goal of writing an understandable sentence. Independence completing this intervention was not obtained.

Design Strategy—Priority At-Risk Area 3. Prereferral intervention for homework completion was addressed. Behavior modification, direct instruction, and individual assistance were incorporated into a prereferral intervention strategy addressing homework completion.

Implement Strategy. Jimmy's teacher incorporated the strategy in his classroom instruction as designed by the prereferral team. An adult volunteer provided Jimmy individual assistance during the reading/writing class period.

Evaluate Success. At the conclusion of the prereferral intervention time period, Jimmy was completing 85% of his schoolwork. His success was higher than his prereferral intervention goal of 80%.

Continue Strategies. It was the opinion of the team that the strategies were successful and that referral for special education services was not necessary.

Scenario 2: Jenny, Grade 5

Significant Deficit Areas. Jenny is very good in math and science. She has difficulty when reading, but is able to comprehend after a period of time. She can do work when motivated, but it may take a while for the teacher to convince her to do something. Jenny will not ask for help. She avoids completing tasks and requires constant direction. Jenny disrupts others often for the effect it may have on the class. Her language is age appropriate. She appears very mature in what she says, but immature in her social behavior.

Review Educational Records. Testing data indicate that Jenny has good vocabulary development, word-usage abilities, and auditory comprehension. She tests lower in auditory memory, visual sequential memory, and written language. Grades of A and B were reported in all subjects except for language arts, where she has consistently received a grade of C. Jenny's behavior has been reported as inconsistent and impulsive. No alternative instructional strategies were reported.

Select One At-Risk Area to Monitor. The prereferral intervention team identified two at-risk areas and prioritized them.

1. Improve Jenny's written language
2. Improve Jenny's behavior patterns

Design Strategy. A prereferral team member worked with Jenny individually. The team explored one intervention strategy to meet her needs—use of a microcassette recorder for writing. Jenny's mother also requested that further testing be conducted at the end of the school year.

Implement Strategy. During the last month of school, Jenny met with the prereferral team teacher for instruction in using a microcassette recorder. Jenny then used the recorder for writing assignments in class.

Evaluate Success. At the conclusion of the school year, the classroom teacher reported some improvement in written language. The team recommended that the use of the recorder be continued in the fall term. No additional strategies were recommended by the team.

Make Referral. Jenny's second at-risk area identified was her behavior patterns. Since the time of identification, Jenny's mother and the school psychologist completed the district's ADD checklist. Follow-up is being conducted with Jenny's physician. The team did not design a prereferral intervention strategy.

Although a prereferral intervention strategy for written expression was reported to be somewhat effective, the team recommended referral for special education services to further investigate Jenny's ability level.

CHAPTER

6 Assessment in the Referral Process

CYNTHIA R. A. WATKINS
University of Northern Iowa

CYNTHIA N. SCHLOSS
Bloomsburg University

OBJECTIVES

After reading this chapter, you will be able to

1. Identify the four decision-making outcomes
2. List potential members of the multidisciplinary team and their respective roles
3. Describe the four areas for assessment to determine eligibility
4. Discuss the importance of collecting information from multiple sources using multiple strategies

KEY TERMS

academic achievement (p. 120)
assessment (p. 114)
attention deficit/hyperactivity disorder (ADHD) (p. 129)
checklist (p. 126)
curriculum-based measures (CBMs) (p. 121)
discrepancy analysis (p. 124)
functional assessments (p. 118)
informant (p. 120)
instructional decision (p. 116)
intellectual aptitude (p. 118)
interindividual differences (p. 124)
intra-individual differences (p. 124)
learning abilities or strategies (p. 122)
multidisciplinary team (MDT) (p. 116)
outcomes decisions (p. 116)
perceptual-motor skills (p. 123)
prereferral decisions (p. 114)
rating scale (p. 126)
referral decisions (p. 115)
sensory screenings (p. 122)
social-emotional behavior (p. 125)
sociogram (p. 127)

Assessment information is necessary to make appropriate referral decisions. Current federal law requires a comprehensive approach to assessment and evaluation for students referred for special education services. Yet, the specific assessment tools to be used are not stipulated by federal law. Rather, the assessment tools and procedures will change based on the information needed in relationship to the suspected disability area. For example, in the area of Learning Disabilities, the primary concerns are with Intellectual Aptitude and Academic Achievement, while in the area of Behavioral Disorders, the primary concerns are with Academic Achievement and Social/Behavioral Interaction. Assessment procedures for making appropriate referral decisions are addressed in this chapter.

Decision-Making Process

The Individuals with Disabilities Education Act (IDEA) mandates the development and approval of a process of decision making to ensure students are provided an appropriate education. Salvia & Ysseldyke (1998) suggested four decision types to be included in such a process: (a) prereferral classroom decisions, (b) entitlement decisions, (c) postentitlement classroom decisions, and (d) accountability or outcome decisions. While the specific guidelines and procedures of *how* evaluation and service/placement determination vary, the underlying decisions that are to be addressed are consistent (Osborne, 1996).

Assessment and evaluation are fundamental components of the decision-making process. **Assessment** is the fact-finding component and refers to how information is gathered. Assessment can consist of informal ways to gather information such as observations, work samples, or teacher-made tests (see Chapter 3 for an in-depth discussion of alternate assessments). Assessment can also consist of (as most of us traditionally think of it) formal or standardized tests (see Chapter 2 for an in-depth discussion of standardized tests). Once facts are collected, then interpretation of the facts can begin. This interpretation is referred to as evaluation (Turnbull, Turnbull, Shank, & Leal, 1995). Evaluation provides us with the framework for making decisions.

A model depicting the assessment and evaluation components of the decision-making process is presented in Figure 6.1. The model incorporates the four decision types suggested by Salvia & Ysseldyke (1998). Discussion of the model components follows in the ensuing sections.

Prereferral Classroom Decisions

Prereferral decisions are based on ongoing and episodic screenings. If the outcomes of the screenings indicate no problem exists, the student continues in the general education classroom and curriculum. If the outcomes of the screenings suggest the student is experiencing a problem, then prereferral or alternative intervention strategies are provided in the general education classroom to assist the student in effectively overcoming the problem. A detailed discussion of prereferral assessment is provided in Chapter 5.

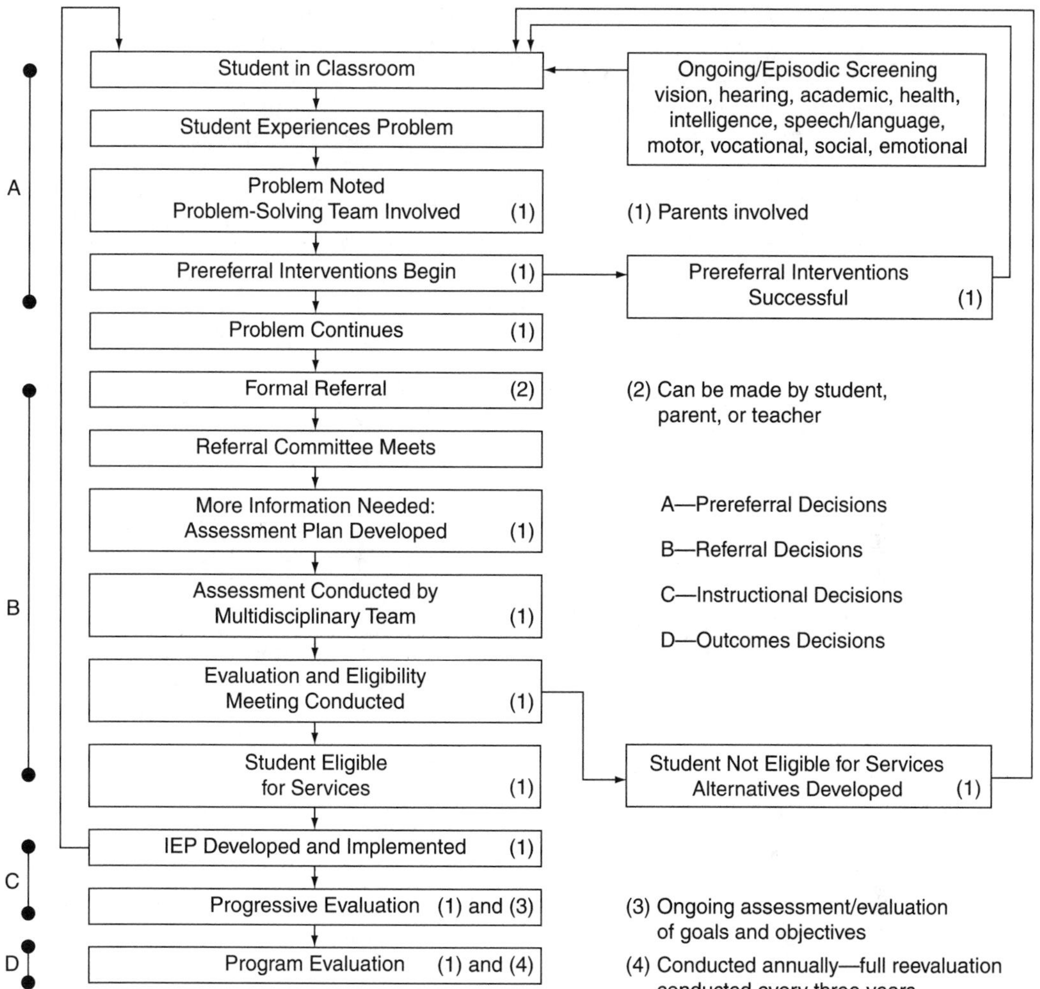

FIGURE 6.1 Decision-making process.

Referral Decisions

Referral decisions begin with the determination that the prereferral intervention strategies were unsuccessful and the problem continues. At this point, a formal referral is initiated. The referral committee meets and reviews the referral to determine if further assessment is warranted. If the committee concludes that additional information is needed, then an assessment plan that specifies how, what, and by whom the information will be collected is developed. A multidisciplinary team will conduct the assessment as outlined in the assessment plan.

The **multidisciplinary team (MDT)** is composed of those individuals who have a vested interest in the educational program of the student. Schools are required to "insure that the placement decision is made by a group of persons, including persons knowledgeable about the child, the meaning of the evaluation data, and the placement options" (IDEA Regulations, 34 C.F.R. section 300.533 (a)[3]). Potential MDT members and their roles are presented in Table 6.1.

The MDT is responsible for collecting information from a variety of sources, assessing "all areas related to the suspected disability" (IDEA Regulations, 34 C.F.R. section 300.533). Often this includes collecting and assessing information to rule out a possible disability. A case in point: Reana is a very bright fourth grader. She reads and spells on grade level, but the teacher has noticed she cannot copy information from the board. Does Reana have a visual-motor perception problem or a distance vision problem? The correct answer could be either. Only by collecting accurate information can it be ascertained if she needs glasses or curricular modification.

Once assessment has been completed by the MDT, then the evaluation and eligibility meeting is held (in most cases members of the assessment team and eligibility team are the same). The first consideration during the evaluation phase is to review all assessment findings. The assessment team develops an assessment summary, which details strengths, weaknesses, interests, and other pertinent information revealed through the assessment process. The second consideration is the determination of eligibility for services. The team considers all information, compares it to eligibility criteria, and decides if the student meets the eligibility criteria for special education services. The determination of eligibility is termed *entitlement.*

Instructional Decisions

The **instructional decision** component is enacted upon determination of entitlement. Once the student is found eligible, consideration of appropriate instructional interventions begins, and an individualized educational plan (IEP) is developed. The IEP details services to be provided, service delivery options, accommodations warranted, educational goals and objectives, as well as methods to evaluate effectiveness of the educational plan. Chapters 7 and 8 provide an in-depth discussion of assessment for the instructional decisions component.

Outcomes Decisions

The final component is concerned with program outcomes. **Outcomes decisions** are based on the extent of the benefits received by the student from the services that were provided. Was the curriculum and the system of delivery effective in meeting the needs of the student (Joint Committee on Standards for Educational Evaluation, 1994)?

Assessment Questions

Good decision making requires information gathered from multiple sources using a variety of fact-finding strategies. The information collected by the multidisciplinary team will aid in answering the question, Does the student have a disability that affects his or her

TABLE 6.1 Multidisciplinary Team Members and Their Roles

Team Member	Responsibilities
School nurse	Performs initial vision and hearing screens, checks medical records, refers health problems to other medical professionals
Special education teacher	Consultant to regular classroom teacher during prereferral process; administers educational tests, observes in other classrooms, helps with screening, and recommends IEP goals; writes objectives and suggests educational interventions
Special education supervisor	May advise all activities of special education teacher, may provide direct services, guides placement decisions, recommends services
Educational diagnostician	Administers norm-referenced and criterion-referenced tests, observes student in educational setting, makes suggestions for IEP goals and objectives
School psychologist	Administers individual intelligence tests, observes student in classroom, administers projective instruments and personality inventories; may be under supervision of a doctoral-level psychologist
Occupational therapist	Evaluates fine motor and self-help skills, recommends therapies, may provide direct services or consultant services, may help obtain equipment for student needs
Physical therapist	Evaluates gross motor functioning and self-help skills, living skills, and job-related skills necessary for optimum achievement of student; may provide direct services or consultant services
Behavioral consultant	Specialist in behavior management and crisis intervention; may provide direct services or consultant services
School counselor	May serve as objective observer in prereferral stage, may provide direct group or individual counseling, may schedule students and help with planning of student school schedules
Speech-language clinician	Evaluates speech-language development, may refer for hearing problems, may provide direct therapy or consultant services for classroom teachers
Audiologist	Evaluates hearing for possible impairments, may refer students for medical problems, may help obtain hearing aids
Physician's assistant	Evaluates physical condition of student and may provide physical exams for students of a local education agency, refers medical problems to physicians or appropriate therapists, school social worker, or visiting teacher
Home-school coordinator, school social worker, or visiting teacher	Works directly with family; may hold conferences, conduct interviews, and administer adaptive behavior scales based on parent interviews; may serve as case manager
Regular education teacher	Works with the special education team, student, and parents to develop an environment that is appropriate and as much like that of general education students as possible; implements prereferral intervention strategies
Parents	Active members of the special education team; provide input for IEP, work with home-school academic and behavioral programs

Source: Adapted from *Assessment in Special Education: An Applied Approach* (p. 39), by Terry Overton, 1992. Reprinted by permission of Prentice-Hall, Inc., Upper Saddle River, NJ.

performance to the extent that special education services are warranted? To determine eligibility of a student for special education services, questions arise in four areas: intellectual aptitude, academic achievement, learning abilities and strategies, and social-emotional behavior. An overview of the areas for assessment, sources of assessment, and strategies of assessing are provided in Figure 6.2.

Intellectual Aptitude

Intellectual aptitude refers to an individual's capacity for learning when presented with new information or experiences. As Wechsler stated, "intelligence is the overall capacity of an individual to understand and cope with the world around him" (Wechsler, 1974, p. 5). Thus, intellectual aptitude incorporates the concepts of retention and retrieval of learned information, and efficiency for learning new material, with problem solving (Sternberg & Grigorenko, 1997).

Information on a student's intellectual aptitude is gathered from a variety of sources in both formal and informal ways. From the student's school records, we look at past test results and school histories. We want to determine if there are patterns that indicate problems exist. Parents provide valuable information on the student's developmental history. Parents and teachers provide information through observations of the student's adaptive behavior. Interviews with the student provide insight into behaviors that influence test results. With each piece of information, we are trying to find out if there are patterns, discrepancies, or indicators of problems.

Strategies for collecting information include group tests, individual tests, and functional assessments. The purpose of the information, or why it is needed, will determine which strategy will be utilized.

Group Intelligence Tests. Group intelligence tests are administered to groups of students. They are primarily used as screening devices to identify which students deviate enough from the average to potentially need further testing. Typically, they are quick, teacher-administered pencil-and-paper tests.

Individual Intelligence Tests. Individual intelligence tests are used to assist in decision making about eligibility, classification, and placement. They are to be administered to a single student by a person prepared in administration and interpretation of that test (e.g., school psychologist, guidance counselor). See Chapter 2 for an in-depth discussion of group and individualized tests.

Functional Assessments. Functional assessments are used for screening as well as for diagnostic and eligibility purposes. **Functional assessments** provide information to determine how the student interacts or copes with various aspects of his or her world. Thus, information is gathered in the student's natural settings (viz., the school, community, and home) to determine if he or she can cope and adapt appropriately. Areas of interest often include knowledge, skills, and performance in response to differing physical environments (e.g., how to dress for climatic changes, how to avoid danger), social and cultural expectations

FIGURE 6.2 Assessment areas: Sources and strategies for collecting information.

Intellectual Aptitude

Sources	*Strategies*
School Records: test results, school histories	Group test
Student: test results, behavior	Individual tests
Teachers: observations, adaptive behavior	Functional assessments
Parents: developmental history, observation, adaptive behavior	

Academic Achievement

Sources	*Strategies*
School Records: grades, retentions, services, attendance, test results	Group tests
Student: tests, classroom performance, academic goals	Individual tests
Teachers: reason for referral, classroom performances, instructional modifications	Curriculum-based measures
Parents: reason for referral, past educational performance, performance at home and school	Functional assessments

Learning Abilities and Strategies

Sources	*Strategies*
School Records: readiness test scores, vision and hearing screening, aptitudes-achievement discrepancies	Sensory screenings
Student: individual measures, learning strategies, study skills	Perceptual-motor skills measures
Teachers: current abilities, strategies for learning, aptitudes-achievement discrepancies	Functional assessments
Parents: vision and hearing history, home observations	Readiness test
	Discrepancy analyses

Social-Emotional Behavior

Sources	*Strategies*
School Records: discipline and attendance records, observations, services	Direct observations
Student: classroom behaviors, attitudes, perceptions	Rating scales, checklists, questionnaires, and interviews
Teachers: observations, learning environment	Peer acceptance
Peers: acceptance, interactions	Learning environments
Parents: observations, home environment	Functional analysis
	Attention deficits and hyperactivity measures
	Interest, attitudes, and beliefs

(e.g., language usage for differing groups, role performance), and level of independence (e.g., self-care) (Salvia & Ysseldyke, 1998). Methodology for information collection for a functional assessment may involve informant, or indirect, assessment; direct observation; or experimental analysis (Lennox & Miltenberger, 1989).

To gather information for the indirect, or **informant,** assessment method, two general techniques are used. The first technique is the examination and review of school records, which has been discussed previously. In the second technique, teachers or parents are interviewed or are asked to complete questionnaires or checklists. Such information collection devices may or may not be standardized. An overview of the most commonly used standardized adaptive behavior measures are presented in Chapter 2.

The second method of information collection for functional assessments is direct observation. Observations may be made by parents, teachers, or teacher's assistants. Most observations occur in the student's natural environments. Direct observation provides information specific to what strategies the student uses to cope within environments, how the student develops or refines strategies, as well as the frequency with which he or she employs a specific strategy. As with all observations, two important aspects must be considered—the observer must be both objective and specific. Chapter 9 provides more detailed information on direct observation.

The final method of information collection for functional assessments is experimental analysis or manipulation of the environment. As the name implies, contrived situations are presented to the student to assess his or her ability to cope and adapt. The environment and skill may be one with which the student is readily familiar (e.g., preparing a breakfast of cereal and milk). A simple to complex variation is introduced (e.g., out of milk). During the assessment, parents or teachers note the student's coping response (or lack thereof) to the manipulated situation.

Academic Achievement

Academic achievement refers to an individual's current performance level in academic subject areas (e.g., math, science, reading, written expression). Academic achievement measures may concentrate on a specific area, such as reading, or may measure several areas, such as math, science, and social studies. Academic achievement measures provide information to determine strengths as well as weaknesses a student may be exhibiting. Such information is gathered from a variety of sources in both formal and informal ways.

The teacher first examines the student's school records to answer basic questions about the student's academic achievement. Are there patterns that might indicate a problem exists? Has the student had difficulty in a specific subject area as might be indicated by the student's grades? Have retentions occurred that might indicate overall academic concerns? Has the student received additional educational services in the past? In what area(s)? What was the outcome from these services? Was attendance a possible factor? Do past test results indicate areas of concern? With each piece of information, the teacher is trying to determine if there are patterns, discrepancies, or indicators of problems.

Students are an important and often overlooked source of information on academic achievement. Students can provide information on how they learn, their goals, how they view both specific and general academics skills areas, how these areas fit with their overall goals, as well as their motivation or lack thereof to learn specific skills. By interviewing the student, one may conclude that the reason for low achievement is not because the student *can't* learn the skills, but rather he or she sees no use for it, and *chooses not* to learn the skills. The issue may be motivation rather than disability. On the other hand, a student may hate (and thus avoid) a specific academic area due to a disability in that area. Students can also provide insight into behaviors that influence test results: Did they take the test seriously? Did they try?

Parents provide valuable information on the student's educational performance history. School records may not be complete, and parents often can fill in the gaps. Parents are also in the best position to relate how the student's performance in academic areas generalize to home and community. Parents may be the first to notice and refer for an academic problem due to the student's failure to perform an academic skill outside the school.

Teachers traditionally hold the role of primary referrer for academic achievement concerns. Teachers are often the first to suspect there is a problem based on the student's ongoing classroom performances. Teachers develop and implement instructional modifications based on the student's need. If the modifications are not enough, the teacher traditionally will refer the student. The entire process is documented by the teacher and this, too, provides us with insight into the student's academic performance.

Strategies for collecting information include group tests, individual tests, curriculum-based measures, and functional assessments. Each strategy provides specific information to determine the academic strengths and weaknesses of a student.

Group Achievement Tests. Like their counterparts in the intellectual aptitude area, group achievement tests are used as screening devices to identify which students would benefit from further academic testing. When we discuss group achievement tests, we traditionally talk about norm-referenced, multiple-skill pencil-and-paper tests administered by teachers to groups of students and used to estimate a student's current functioning level in comparison to age peers.

Curriculum-Based Measures. **Curriculum-based measures (CBMs)** are assessment tools that directly link assessment with the content of the curriculum the student is currently studying (Deno, 1985). CBMs are developed using actual items from the curriculum the student is currently using in the classroom. CBMs are standardized, empirically derived, teacher-developed, and teacher-administered assessments.

CBMs fulfill four basic functions in the decision-making process. First, CBMs are used for continuous assessment of the student's performance within the curriculum (progress monitoring). Second, CBMs assist teachers in developing appropriate goals (program planning). Third, CBMs are used for both screening and eligibility determination for special education services. Finally, CBMs are used for program evaluation (Marston & Magnusson, 1985). Chapter 3 provides more detailed information on curriculum-based measures.

Functional Assessments. Functional assessments for academic achievement are used to ascertain if and how well the student can generalize his or her skills within multiple environments. As with functional assessment for intellectual aptitude, we look at how the student uses his or her academic skills to cope and interact within his or her world. Information via functional assessments of academic achievement can be used for screening, eligibility determination, and goal development.

Functional assessments of the student's academic achievement are very important, yet often not conducted. The information obtained by functional assessments provides a much broader view of the student's ability to survive in the real world than more traditional tests. A prime example is the student that *can* count the correct amount of change to the teacher in the classroom but *can't* count change to make a simple purchase at McDonald's. Using this example from a first-person view, we can determine if the student can make change in a variety of settings by asking persons within those settings how the student functions (viz., informants). We could take the student to McDonald's and observe for ourselves (viz., direct observation). Lastly, we could contrive situations to determine how the student applies money knowledge (viz., experimental manipulation).

Learning Abilities and Strategies

The ability that refers to an individual's capacity to participate in certain aspects of a learning task is termed **learning abilities or strategies.** Attention, perception, memory, and processing are considered to be underlying aspects of a student's learning ability.

As with intellectual aptitude and academic achievement, information on the student's learning ability and strategies is gathered from a variety of formal and informal sources to assist with decision making. From the student's school records one can look at past test results and school histories to determine if aptitude-achievement discrepancies might exist. To determine if sensory problems might be a contributing factor, one looks at and conducts vision and hearing screenings. Parents provide additional information about the student's vision and hearing history, as well as family histories related to sensory impairments. The student could provide information about the learning strategies and study skills he or she uses. Teachers provide information about the student's current abilities, what strategies and the effectiveness of the strategies the student uses in learning, and possible aptitude-achievement discrepancies.

Strategies for collecting information include sensory screenings, perceptual-motor skills measures, functional assessments, readiness tests, and discrepancy analysis. Each strategy provides specific information on the student's learning abilities and strategies.

Sensory Screening. One of the first questions to be asked when a student is having educational problems is, What can be eliminated as a potential cause? **Sensory screenings** are conducted to eliminate vision or hearing problems by the school nurse or other trained school personnel (e.g., speech therapist, audiologist). Currently, most schools routinely conduct vision and hearing screenings for all students.

Ask most current or former public school students if they ever had their vision tested at school, and the answer is a resounding yes. The most commonly used test, and probably the one you experienced, was the Snellen Wall Chart Vision Test. The Snellen is a test of simple visual acuity (viz., clarity or sharpness with which an individual sees). The Snellen is administered by asking the student to stand at a specified spot usually 20 feet from a chart taped on the wall and to read the letters on a specific line on the chart. Each line of letters is smaller than the preceding line. Acuity is determined in relationship to what the average person reads at 20 feet, thus the concept of 20/20 vision. The Snellen measures only distance vision.

Two distance visual acuity tests similar to the Snellen, but requiring no reading skills, are the E Pointing Game (National Society to Prevent Blindness, 1991) and the New York

Lighthouse Symbol Flash Card Vision Test (Lighthouse Low Vision Services, 1970). Like the Snellen, both tests require positioning the student at a specified distance from the visual stimulus. In the E Pointing Game, the student looks at a specified row on a chart and with fingers indicates the direction the E points (e.g., up, down, left, or right). For the Lighthouse Symbol Test, the student identifies a picture on a flash card (viz., apple, house, umbrella). The pictures become progressively smaller in size as the test progresses.

Of concern to many educators is the failure to screen for other forms of vision problems (viz., near vision acuity, color blindness, peripheral vision, muscular balance). Screenings in these areas are often left to ophthalmologists and optometrists.

Hearing is also routinely screened in public schools. In 1990 the American Speech-Language-Hearing Association (ASHA) developed and recommended a three-step procedure for hearing screenings. The three steps include (a) review of hearing case history and visual inspection of the outer ear, ear channel, and ear drum; (b) pure tone audiometry; and (c) tympanometry (ASHA, 1990). The visual inspection is conducted to identify abnormalities within the ear that may impact hearing (e.g., wax buildup, rupture in eardrum, tympanic tubes). Pure tone audiometry is conducted by having the student raise a hand when he or she hears a series of tones from headphones. The audiometer is used to assess the type of hearing loss (e.g., sensorineural, conductive, or mixed), degree of loss, and frequency or pitch. A tympanometer is used to determine how well the ear transmits sound energy. Tympanometry failure signals a disorder of the middle ear. A failure in any of the three screening areas warrants a more in-depth evaluation by an audiologist.

Perceptual-Motor Skills Measures. Concerns with how a student perceives a given stimuli, discriminates between similar forms of stimuli, develops an understanding of a given stimuli, and retains that stimuli are all integral in the concept of **perceptual-motor skills.** Yet, the importance perceptual-motor skills play in the learning process is an area of controversy (Kavale & Forness, 1987; Mather & Kirk, 1985). Some educators view such skills as important prerequisites for academic skill development (Locher, 1988). Others view the concept of perceptual processing and modality instruction as unsubstantiated (Mather & Kirk, 1985). Regardless of the outcome of the controversy, perceptual-motor skill assessment is still a component of many psychoeducational assessments at this time.

Perceptual-motor skill measures come in a variety of formats and content and fit into one of three categories: (a) test of visual abilities (viz., perception, memory, and discrimination), (b) test of auditory abilities (viz., perception, memory, and discrimination), and (c) integration of responses (viz., visual-motor integration). Some instruments use a single format (e.g., copying geometric designs), while others use multiple subtests (e.g., copying, matching, figure-ground discrimination, memory). Such instruments are typically administered individually by school psychologists or psychometricians trained in their administration and interpretation.

Functional Assessments. Functional assessments in the area of learning abilities and strategies are used to ascertain if the abilities that are presumed to underlie this area (e.g., attention, perception, memory, and processing) are indeed developed. Educators want to determine the student's level of ability, strategies the student uses, frequency, and consistency of the application of strategies as they relate to the student's ability to function in various aspects of his or her world. As with all assessments, one wants to identify strengths and potential problem areas to determine if problematic discrepancies exist.

Functional assessment in the area of learning abilities and strategies consists of collecting information from school records; interviews with teachers, parents, and other knowledgeable informants; direct observations in a variety of environments; and experimental manipulation of environments. The information gathered can be used for screening, eligibility determination, and goal development.

Readiness Test. For many children, the Kindergarten Round-Up (i.e., preschool readiness test batteries) has become an important rite of passage into the world of formal schooling. The child comes to school in the spring prior to starting kindergarten and completes a series of activities used to measure potential school readiness. The series of screenings are used to predict which children are not ready for formal academic instruction and would benefit from remedial or compensatory programming. Many schools conduct the round-up as part of their child-find initiative.

The readiness battery customarily consists of measures of academic readiness (e.g., learning aptitude, perceptual-motor skills, language development, self-care), social skill development, physical development (e.g., height, weight), and sensory screenings.

Discrepancy Analyses. **Discrepancy analysis** describes two very distinct, yet related forms of evaluation. Both forms look to identify an incongruity that will have an impact on the individual student. One form looks at **intra-individual differences** (viz., differences within one individual), while the second looks at **interindividual differences** (viz., differences between individuals).

Intra-individual discrepancy analysis is required to determine eligibility of a specific learning disability under current federal regulations. A severe discrepancy must exist between the student's intellectual ability and achievement in one or more areas (IDEA Regulations, 34 C.F.R. Section 300.541). We can use Carla as an example of how the intra-individual discrepancy analysis would work. Carla has average intellectual abilities as measured by the WISC-III. Carla's most recent Iowa Test of Basic Skills score indicates that she is functioning on or near grade level in all academic areas except math. Classroom observations, teacher reports, review of her last six report cards, and a current test score which indicated she is three years below grade level on the KeyMath Test suggest that Carla has great difficulty in math. Using discrepancy analysis, determination was made that Carla was eligible for special education services (please note: the assumption is that all other required components of evaluation have been met).

Inter-individual discrepancy analysis is a four-step process. First, one identifies a skill content area or activity engaged in by students without disabilities (e.g., go to the show). Next, one task analyzes, or breaks down, the task into its component parts (e.g., wait in line, walk up to window, give cashier correct amount of money, use appropriate language and gestures, take ticket, and so forth). Then, one identifies discrepancies in performance between the targeted student and students without disabilities (e.g., James completed waiting in line independently, James walked up to window when prompted, James cannot give cashier correct amount of money, and so on). Finally, one analyzes the component parts the targeted student was unable to perform to determine if skill instruction, modification, or adaptation is needed to allow the targeted student to participate in the activity (e.g., teach walking up to the window; poor fine-motor coordination prevents James from removing individual dollar bills, adaptation needed). Historically, inter-individual discrepancy analysis has been used to provide educational programming for students with moderate to severe mental retardation. Today such analysis is being used with a broad variety of students (Turnbull, Turnbull, Shank, & Leal, 1995).

Social-Emotional Behavior

Social-emotional behavior is a broad term encompassing a range of nonacademic school behaviors. Such behaviors can interfere with academic performance just as academic performance can affect conduct in the classroom.

When education professionals discuss social-emotional behaviors, the discussion usually turns to those behaviors that are problematic. Problematic behaviors fall into three categories: behaviors directed at others (e.g., aggression, disruptiveness), behaviors directed at self (withdrawal, anxiousness), and academic-related behaviors (e.g., time on task, Bos & Vaughn, 1998). Problematic behaviors are assessed to determine if a disability exists.

When collecting information on the social-emotional behavior of students, one needs to examine a variety of sources using both formal and informal methods. As each source provides a unique glimpse of the student's behavior, the new information assists in determining how to best serve that student. Once again, the evaluator is trying to determine if there are patterns, discrepancies, or indicators of problems present.

Information collection begins by examining the student's school records to answer questions about the student's social-emotional development. Have problematic behaviors been noted? Is there a discipline problem? Do discipline records indicate a pattern of behavior? What discipline procedures were most or least effective? Do problem behaviors occur in a specific environment? Who is present when problem behaviors occur? Is a certain time of day more problematic? How is attendance? Is there a pattern of absences? Are health issues a factor? Has the student received additional services in the past? In what area(s)? What was the outcome from the services? The answers to these and similar questions assist in the decision-making process.

Because social-emotional interactions do not occur in a vacuum, it is important to get information from all impacted parties. The environment, how the student interacts within a specific environment, and how that behavior is perceived by others within that environment are also important issues. The targeted student, teachers, peers, and parents each can provide information from their particular perspective on the behaviors exhibited by the student.

Interviews with students often provide unique insight into their social-emotional behaviors. Students can explain how they perceive the world around them. Is it a caring, friendly place or a place to be fearful of? How does their behavior impact their environment, and how does their environment influence their behavior? What are their attitudes about school, peers, life in general? Often the only person able to provide this information is the student.

Teachers provide information about the learning environment itself, as well as observations of how the student responds within that environment. Details of class expectations, routines, structures, and instructional groupings are but a few of the classroom environmental factors that teachers can address. Teachers can provide information about chain of events in the classroom. What was occurring in the classroom prior to the behavior? What events followed the behavior? Because the learning environment is complex, the information provided by the classroom teacher also will be complex.

The role of peers in the information process is often overlooked. Yet peers are an important information source. One observes peers for social validation to determine what *is* normal within the targeted student's world. Through interviews with peers, the evaluator can determine the level of acceptance of the targeted student. Evaluators can observe peers' interactions with the targeted student, then interview the peers to obtain their perspective of the interaction.

Just as teachers provide information on the learning environment, parents provide information on the student's behavior in the community and home environments. Parents provide insight into what is considered appropriate behavior in the student's world (what is considered inappropriate behavior in school may be an important survival skill in the student's community). Observations by parents can provide information on consistency of behaviors. Does the problematic behavior occur at sites outside the school (e.g., is the student aggressive at home)? What is or has occurred in the student's world may be an important factor known only by the parents (e.g., student is on medication, 10 people living in a one-room apartment). Parents are a critical information source.

Strategies used for gathering information on social-emotional behaviors must be done by multiple informants using multiple methods from multiple sources (Clarizio & Higgins, 1989). Strategies should include interviews, observations, and standardized measures.

Direct Observations. Direct observation of the student's social-emotional behavior is one of the most frequently used and important behavior assessment strategies in the decision-making process. Observations may be conducted by parents, school personnel, or peers in a variety of settings to determine frequency, duration, and intensity of a given behavior. Observation may be informal and casual or formal and systematic. While both casual and systematic observations provide information, systematic observations tend to yield more accurate and less biased results. Chapter 9 provides more detailed information on direct observation.

Rating Scales, Checklists, Questionnaires, and Interviews. These four items are commonly used in assessing social-emotional behaviors. All four consist of a series of questions to which an informant knowledgeable about the student (e.g., parent, teacher, peer, or the student) is to respond. On a **checklist,** the respondent simply indicates the presence or absence of a series of behaviors. For example, the teacher checks all behaviors observed in class from a list of possible behaviors, or the parent checks yes or no to a list of behaviors. A **rating scale** differs in that the respondent rates the extent a specific behavior occurs. For example, the teacher is asked if a specific behavior occurs (a) never, (b) seldom, (c) occasionally, (d) frequently, (e) continually. On a questionnaire, the respondent is asked to describe a specific behavior or the conditions under which the behavior occurs, such as "How does the student react to praise?" The interview format differs from the questionnaire in that the respondent verbally answers the questions, and the evaluator has the opportunity to query in order to obtain more detailed and objective information. Figure 6.3 compares the four questioning formats.

Peer Acceptance. How a student responds to others is often a direct result of the student's social status in relationship to the group; therefore, information on a student's social status

FIGURE 6.3 Comparison of four questioning formats: Checklist, rating scale, questionnaire, and interview.

Checklist

Directions: Check the column that applies.	Yes	No
1. Student dislikes school	_____	_____
2. Student works well with others	_____	_____
3. Student is restless, unable to sit still	_____	_____

Rating Scale

Directions: Rate the following statements from 0 to 4 using the ranking scale.

0—never observed; 1—seldom observed; 2—occasionally observed;
3—often observed; 4—continuously observed.

1. Student indicates dislike for school _____
2. Student works well with others _____
3. Student is restless, unable to sit still _____

Questionnaires

Directions: Please answer the following questions fully:

1. How often does the student indicate a dislike for school?
2. Describe how the student works in group settings.
3. Describe the student's activity level in class.

Interviews

Directions to interviewer: Ask for response to the following probes. Query as needed.

1. Tell me how you feel about school. (student interview)
2. Describe Pat's behavior in a typical small group activity. (teacher interview)
3. What is a typical evening at home with Pat like? (parent interview)

and acceptance by peers is important. Indicators of how the student is perceived by his or her peers, how the student perceives himself or herself, and who peers view as leaders and outcasts all provide insight into the group dynamics of a specific classroom.

Sociometric techniques are used to assess a student's social status within a classroom. The sociometric method consists of a three-step process: peer-nomination, sociogram development, and data analysis. In the peer-nomination phase, all students in the class are asked to respond to probes that sample their peer preferences. Probes might include the following directives: (a) Name two classmates you would like to invite to a party, or (b) Name the person in our class who is most likely to get the job done. The **sociogram** is developed by representing the peer-nominations pictorially. Data analysis is conducted by visual inspection of the sociogram to determine who the class perceives as leaders, outcasts, members of cliques, and so forth. A sociogram is depicted in Figure 6.4.

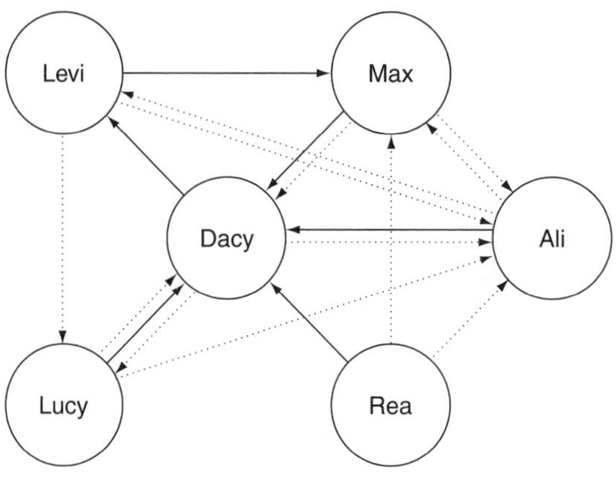

(a) Name two classmates you would like to invite to a party.

(b) Name the person in our class who is most likely to get the job done.

Class star: Ali—5 (a) hits Class isolate: Rea—0 hits Class worker: Dacy—4 (b) hits

FIGURE 6.4 A sociogram.

Learning Environment. The classroom environment and its impact on the social-emotional behavior of students has been discussed throughout. In reality, how important *is* the classroom environment? The best way to answer this question is to pose a personal question to you: Are there educational environments in which *you* have problems sitting still, focusing on the instruction? What is it about that classroom environment? Is it a straight lecture format or maybe a touchy-feely hands-on format? What level of student engagement is occurring? Are there noise distractions? Are you aware of rules and expectations? Is the heat level too high? Each of these factors contributes to the learning environment and how a particular student will respond.

Evaluations of learning environments should address three aspects: the physical, instructional, and social environments. In the physical environment, factors such as general layout and utilization of space, temperature, lighting, noise, seating, and so on are examined. The instructional environment consists of all factors directly related to instruction (e.g., curriculum, materials, methods, grouping, transitions, and so on). Factors to be addressed in the social environment would include teacher-student interactions, peer interactions, expectations, and the general classroom climate. Checklists, rating scales, and observations are the most commonly used methods to gather information on the learning environment.

Functional Analysis. A functional analysis is conducted to aid in understanding the relationship between problematic behaviors and the student's world (i.e., school, community, and home). The analysis involves the examination of the context of the behavior (viz., the events, environmental factors, physical and emotional dimensions) and the factors that support the behavior's occurrence to determine the purpose or function a specific behavior has for the student (i.e., to gain attention, to avoid or escape, to obtain; Green & Menscher, 1996).

This is accomplished by experimentally manipulating variables that occur prior to (antecedents) or after (consequences) the behavior and noting the outcomes.

Attention Deficits and Hyperactivity. A student's ability to attend to instruction is of great concern for teachers and parents. Attention deficits are viewed as extremely problematic behaviors. Attention problems typically fall into three types: (a) inattentive—trouble paying attention, forgetful, easily distracted; (b) hyperactive-impulsive—trouble sitting still, talks excessively, difficulty playing quietly, difficulty waiting; and (c) combined—characteristics of both inattentive and hyperactive-impulsive (American Psychiatric Association, 1993). The combined type is commonly referred to as **attention deficit/hyperactivity disorder (ADHD).** ADHD often occurs concomitant with other disabilities (Smith, Polloway, Patton, & Dowdy, 1999).

Information regarding problematic behaviors of attention deficits and hyperactivity should come from multiple sources. Observations provide detailed information on frequency, context, and the form of the ADHD behaviors. Medical personnel are often involved in the determination of ADHD through examination. School personnel often use rating scales and checklists to assess attention deficits and hyperactivity problems (Smith, Polloway, Patton, & Dowdy, 1999).

Interests, Attitudes, and Beliefs. An important and often overlooked determinant in assessing social-emotional behavior is the student's interests, attitudes, and beliefs. Students come to school having very different experiences. Each of these experiences is interpreted within the context of the student's prior knowledge. Thus, students will have developed personal views or beliefs and attitudes about how the world works for them. The student can provide information on his or her beliefs, dreams, likes, and dislikes via checklists, rating scales, open-ended questionnaires, interviews, and journals. Often this information provides great insight into why problematic behavior occurs.

An example of the importance of a student's views was Tom's belief system. Tom, a student with autism, had developed a set of rules he used to cope with his environment. One of Tom's rules was that he never ate green beans and corn at the same meal. After weeks of temper tantrums (Tom's coping mechanism for broken rules) and trying to determine why lunch was disrupted, a teacher had Tom journal about the lunch episode. In the entry, Tom wrote extensively about the evils of eating green beans and corn at the same meal. The staff replaced corn on Tom's tray with rice and the lunchtime tantrums ended.

Summary

Many students have difficulties that impact their learning. For some, the difficulties become so problematic that they interfere significantly with their ability to learn. When this occurs, one needs to determine what can be done to reduce the negative impact for that individual. Determination is made through a systematic decision-making process. Currently, the Individuals with Disabilities Education Act (IDEA) provides very detailed regulations on how this process is to be accomplished. Once eligibility is confirmed, programs for addressing the needs of the student are developed.

This chapter focused on assessment procedures in the referral process. A model for decision making, as well as sources and strategies used to gather information to assist in the decision-making process were presented. In Chapter 7, we will discuss establishing objectives to meet student's needs.

REFERENCES

American Psychiatric Association. (1993). *Diagnostic and statistical manual of mental disorders (DSM-IV).* Washington, DC: Author.

American Speech-Language-Hearing Association (ASHA). (1990). Guidelines for audiometric symbols. *American Speech-Language-Hearing Association Journal, 32(2),* 25–30.

Bos, C. S., & Vaughn, S. (1998). Strategies for teaching students with learning and behavior problems (4th ed.) Boston: Allyn & Bacon.

Clarizio, H. F., & Higgins, M. M. (1989). Assessment of severe emotional impairment: Practice and problems. *Psychology in the Schools, 26,* 154–162.

Deno, S. L. (1985). Curriculum-based measurement: The emerging alternative. *Exceptional Children, 52,* 219–232.

Green, J. C., & Menscher, S. L. (1996). Management of excessive behavior in inclusive settings. In D. L. Ryndak & S. Alper, *Curriculum content for students with moderate and severe disabilities in inclusive settings* (pp. 227–241). Boston: Allyn & Bacon.

Individuals with Disabilities Education Act (IDEA) of 1990 Regulations, 34 C.F.R. §300 *et seq.*

Joint Committee on Standards for Educational Evaluation. (1994). *The program evaluation standards* (2nd ed.). Thousand Oaks, CA: Sage Publications.

Kavale, K., & Forness, S. (1987). Substance over style: Assessing the efficacy of modality testing and teaching. *Exceptional Children, 54,* 228–239.

Lennox, D. B., & Miltenberger, R. G. (1989). Conducting a functional assessment of problem behavior in applied settings. *Journal of the Association for Persons with Severe Handicaps, 14,* 304–311.

Lighthouse Low Vision Services. (1970). *New York lighthouse symbol flash card vision test.* New York: Author.

Locher, P. (1988). The usefulness for psychoeducational evaluation of preassessment screening for sensory-motor and perceptual encoding deficits. *Psychology in the Schools, 25,* 244–251.

Marston, D., & Magnusson, D. (1985). Implementing curriculum-based measurement in special and regular education settings. *Exceptional Children, 52(3),* 266–276.

Mather, N., & Kirk, S. (1985).The type III error and other concerns in learning disability research. *Learning Disabilities Research, 1,* 56–64.

National Society to Prevent Blindness. (1991). *Home eye tests for preschoolers: E pointing game.* Schaumburg, IL: Author.

Osborne, A. G., Jr. (1996). *Legal issues in special education.* Boston: Allyn & Bacon.

Salvia, J., & Ysseldyke, J. (1998). *Assessment in special and remedial education* (4th ed.). Boston: Houghton Mifflin.

Senate Committee on Labor and Human Resources, *Individuals With Disabilities Education Act Amendments of 1997,* S. Rep. No. 17, 105th Cong., 1st Sess. 1–61 (1997).

Smith, T. E. C., Polloway, E. A., Patton, J. R., & Dowdy, C. A. (1999). *Teaching children with special needs in inclusive settings* (2nd ed.). Boston: Allyn & Bacon.

Sternberg, R. J., & Grigorenko, E. (1997). *Intelligence, heredity, and environment.* New York: Cambridge University Press.

Turnbull, A. P., Turnbull, H. R., Shank, M., & Leal, D. (1995). *Exceptional lives: Special education in today's schools.* Englewood Cliffs, NJ: Merrill.

Wechsler, D. (1974). *Manual for the Wechsler Intelligence Scale for Children–Revised.* Cleveland, OH: Psychological Corporation.

Ysseldyke, J. E., & Christenson, S. L. (1993). *The Instructional Environment System–II.* Longmont, CO: Sopris West.

CHAPTER

7 Writing Objectives for Assessment

MAUREEN A. SMITH
Buffalo State College

MICHAELENE MEGER
Buffalo State College

OBJECTIVES

After reading this chapter, you will be able to

1. Describe the link between conducting assessment and writing objectives
2. Provide a rationale for writing goals and objectives
3. Compare and contrast goal and objective
4. Discuss the relationship between goal selection and social validity
5. Write a goal statement
6. Differentiate between a short-term objective and a lesson plan objective
7. Identify four major components of objectives
8. Discuss different types of condition statements
9. Discuss how to use social comparison to determine a criterion level
10. Distinguish between verbs that do and don't describe measurable, observable behavior
11. Distinguish between checklists and rating scales
12. Develop a scoring rubric for cognitive, affective, and motor skills
13. Write measurable objectives containing the four major components
14. Identify and discuss criteria for evaluating objectives

KEY TERMS

behavioral (p. 139)
checklist (p. 145)
condition statements (p. 142)
criterion (p. 142)
goal (p. 134)
objective (p. 137)
performance criteria (p. 144)
scoring rubric (p. 146)
social comparison (p. 144)
social significance (p. 135)
social validity (p. 135)
subjective evaluation (p. 144)

Ample documentation shows that linking assessment and instruction improves learning (Black, 1993; Crooks, 1988). In fact, the relationship between planning for instruction and assessment of pupil performance is so close that it may be difficult to consider one without the other. Specifically, solid instructional planning is based on an assessment of students' current skill level. Additional assessment occurs after instruction to measure its effectiveness (Popham, Eisner, Sullivan, & Tyler, 1969).

This text is devoted to the selection, development, and use of appropriate alternate assessment techniques with students with special needs. We need these techniques to measure the success of instruction and learning, but if we select or develop instruments without regard to the teaching outcomes, then the information they yield will have no relationship to student success or failure. "Measurement must occur in a context . . . with respect to something. . . . Those elements that connect measurement to the classroom system are called objectives" (Tuckman, 1988, p. 14). Tuckman (1988) described the classroom as a small system in which a teacher and his or her students function. The mission of the system is that students learn and develop; to accomplish the mission, the teacher arranges the conditions of learning. A teacher's task is simplified when the goals of the mission are clearly identified, that is, when the objectives are spelled out. Writing or choosing goals and objectives provide the teacher with the targets at which to aim instruction.

Effective alternate assessment begins with a plan that clearly describes goals or instructional objectives, the content to be measured, and the relative emphasis to be given to each outcome. The only way that a teacher can ensure an assessment technique will serve its intended purpose is to identify the anticipated learning outcomes first. Next, he or she must select or construct an alternate assessment instrument that will provide students with the opportunities to perform in ways that reflect the anticipated learning outcomes. "Effective assessment depends as much on a clear description of what is to be assessed as on a determination of how to assess. Before we develop or select tests or other assessment instruments to measure student learning, we need to clearly specify the intended learning outcomes" (Linn & Gronlund, 1995, p. 26).

Tuckman (1988) defines a test as a "sample of student performance on items that have been designed to measure preselected objectives" (p. 31). As highlighted in this text, teachers have several alternate assessment options from which to choose. Regardless of testing format, however, the statement of goals and objectives in terms of anticipated student changes is one of the most important elements to be considered by teachers. For example, a teacher may decide that it is appropriate to use commercial instruments. In some cases, commercially available tests have explicitly stated goals and objectives; if not, they usually have a detailed content outline. Either format will help teachers select tests for use with their students and interpret the results in relation to the classroom goals and objectives. However, most classroom measurement is based on objectives-referenced or criterion-referenced approaches to testing. For example, Wortham (1995) identified five steps in criterion-referenced test design, and the determination of instructional objectives is the first step. To illustrate further, Cohen (1990) identified five steps for developing curriculum-based assessment, and developing test specifications or curriculum objectives is the second step on her list. Thus, whether developing a classroom test or selecting from commercial instruments, the roles of goals and objectives are obvious. Any alternate assessment that a teacher develops or selects will represent an attempt to measure student attainment of goals and objectives.

This discussion highlights the fact that the development of goals and objectives is the starting point for assessment. The purpose of this chapter is to define goals and objectives, discuss and illustrate essential components of objectives, and present suggestions for evaluating them.

Developing Goals and Objectives

As will become apparent in subsequent sections of this chapter, it is time consuming to develop goals and objectives, but several authors have noted excellent reasons for making the effort (Airasian, 1996; Howell & Nolet, 2000; Linn & Gronlund, 1995; Mager, 1984). These reasons are summarized in Table 7.1. Special education law requires that annual goals and short-term objectives be included on a child's individual education program (IEP). Only by having goals and objectives is it possible to determine if anticipated outcomes are being met and if the child's placement and services are appropriate for his or her needs. In addition to ensuring compliance with the law, written goals and objectives provide direction for the instructional process by clarifying the intended learning outcomes. It is up to classroom teachers to select instructional methods and materials to facilitate the achievement of goals and objectives, but it is essential to know in advance the direction in which such efforts are headed. To quote Mager (1984), "If you are not sure where you are going, you are liable to end up somewhere else" (p. v). Goals and objectives also allow teachers to communicate instructional intent to other interested parties, including students, parents, other school personnel, and the public. Goals and objectives are more likely to be achieved if the individuals most affected by them have a voice in their selection. Another advantage is that once written, goals and objectives help teachers select appropriate instructional methods and materials. An objective that requires the student to solve complex word problems should indicate that a calculator is required. An objective that focuses on vocational skills should highlight the importance of using authentic materials and having several hands-on demonstrations. Finally, as highlighted in the discussion at the beginning of this chapter, goals and objectives provide a basis for assessing student learning by specifying the performance to be measured.

TABLE 7.1 A Rationale for Goals and Objectives

Advantages to Developing Goals and Objectives
■ Compliance with federal and state mandates
■ Clarification of intended learning outcomes
■ Clear communication between the teacher, student, parents, and other school personnel
■ Selection of relevant materials and appropriate instructional methods
■ Establishment of a basis for assessing student learning by specifying the performance to be measured

Components of objectives, such as the condition and the criterion, help the teacher plan alternate assessments that indicate whether students have learned what was taught. The condition will clarify what instructions or materials need to be available during assessment. A comparison of performance during assessment to the criterion specified in the objective will determine if the student has demonstrated proficiency.

Goals

A **goal** may be defined as a broad statement of instructional intent that describes what will be accomplished in an academic year. It must be directly related to a student's present level of performance as documented by assessment data. The manner by which goals are selected for students receiving special education services is prescribed by law. After a child is referred and parental consent is obtained, professionals use a variety of assessment techniques to gather information in all areas related to the suspected disability. Results are shared at a meeting of the multidisciplinary team (MDT), which typically includes the parents, the student, a school psychologist, a general educator, a special educator, and a parent representative. Other members include those with expertise in the area of the suspected disability, such as a speech language pathologist, an occupational therapist, a physical therapist, an audiologist, a vision specialist, a counselor, a social worker, and medical personnel. After presenting the results of various assessment instruments, a decision is made as to the presence or absence of a disability. If it is determined that a student has a disability, the MDT identifies relevant goals that reflect the student's strengths and weaknesses to serve as the basis for the development of objectives that will be included on the IEP. Generally, the team will select several goals for the academic year. Together, these goals provide the overall framework within which the instructional program may be viewed (Payne, 1992). For example, for a kindergarten student with a visual impairment, the MDT may have as goals developing the ability to read and write letters in braille, increasing independent mobility at home and school, using self-help skills in dressing and eating, increasing recreational skills, and forming friendships. For an elementary student with emotional and behavioral problems, the MDT may select goals that address literacy skills, mathematical abilities, and the development of socially appropriate alternatives to aggression. For a middle school student who is moderately retarded, the MDT may establish goals that include the refinement of functional literacy skills, career exploration, and the development of social skills needed in community and vocational settings.

Selecting Socially Valid Goals

Careful analysis of assessment data will facilitate identification of a student's strengths and weaknesses and make obvious the goals that should be targeted by the MDT. A first grader who has cerebral palsy but no cognitive impairment may only need to improve articulation and fine and gross motor skills. A secondary student with a mild learning disability may need to develop better notetaking and study skills. The list of student weaknesses could be quite lengthy, as may be the case for youngsters with more severe disabilities. The more severely disabled a student is and the less time that remains in his or her academic career, the more important it is to choose goals that will make a difference in the quality of life. The team working with such a student is faced with the task of developing and prioritizing goals to address weaknesses. In such situations, the MDT can select among goals by examining their ability to contribute social validity. Howell and Nolet (2000) note that the purpose of education is to prepare people to be socially competent. A behavior should not be included in an objective simply because it makes professionals' lives easier. Behaviors should be considered for inclusion in objectives on the basis of their ability to contribute to the overall quality of the students' lives.

In a classic article, Wolf (1978) discussed the concept of social validity, explained its components, and described how it can be measured. **Social validity** refers to the social acceptability of the goals, objectives, instructional methods, criteria for performance, and student outcomes. There are three components to social validity: the social significance of goals and objectives, the social appropriateness of procedures, and the social importance of effects. Although we will discuss all three throughout this chapter, the first component is relevant to the present discussion. MDT members address the **social significance** of goals and objectives by ensuring these items reflect the desires of society and increase the overall quality of a student's life. The idea of selecting a goal of which society approves may sound very grand and, at the same time, very intimidating to team members. How will they find the time and resources to learn what society wants? In general, doesn't society value skills and accomplishments that contribute to the overall development of the human race, such as being able to prevent or treat a life-threatening disease? How will students live up to such high expectations? Actually, determining social significance of goals is not that difficult. Every member of the MDT represents society and as such has a feel for the skills society would value. While society does benefit from medical advances, it is important to note that it appreciates skills and achievements on a smaller, more individualized scale. Society benefits when all of its members can read and write; thus, goals that focus on the development of literacy skills are socially significant. Wolf (1978) recommends conducting subjective evaluation; that is, soliciting the opinion of informed others who know the student and who are affected daily by his or her performance. Two or three such individuals are already on the team: the parents and the student. We recall one MDT meeting for a student with a profound hearing impairment and severe behavior problems. After his teacher shared her ideas for goals and objectives, she asked his parents what skills they would like to have their son develop over the year. They lived eight hours away and their son's disability made ordinary phone conversations impossible. His parents wanted him to learn to use a telecommunication device for the deaf (TTD) and to write simple letters home. These goals were very important because they contributed to the quality of life enjoyed by the student and his family.

Stating Goals

As will be seen shortly, there is a clear format for stating instructional objectives; however, this is not the case for goal statements. In our work with students, we have found it useful to state goals so that they are most useful to the teachers who will have to translate them into instructional objectives. Toward that end, we recommend that a goal statement include four features. First, goals should be relevant in that they reflect the findings of the MDT. For example, a secondary student with learning disabilities may be at grade level for math and reading but may be experiencing difficulty with written language, organizing his or her work, studying, and taking tests. The MDT should target the development of written language skills and organizational, study, and test-taking strategies. Granted, data gathered by the MDT identified the student's strengths, but it is inefficient to select as goals those skills the student already performs proficiently. Instruction already available in the general education setting is strong enough to ensure continuing development in other curricular areas, and no additional supports are necessary. Second, the goal area should be identified clearly. The MDT has a great deal of data available to it, and these data should be used to target specific goal areas. For example, rather than just targeting the development of written language skills, goals can state that a student will develop the ability to plan written work and write for a variety of purposes. Rather than just increase math skills, the goals can state that the student will learn to use a calculator, basic facts, and manipulatives to engage in problem solving. On a related note, it is also helpful to link academic skills to curriculum or grade levels. For example, a goal that states the student will develop science concepts at the fourth-grade level tells the teacher which curriculum should be examined for exact content. Third, it is helpful to identify positive behaviors to be increased. Certainly, this task is easily accomplished when considering academic performance because, in general, teachers want students to improve their skills in areas such as literacy, mathematics, and science. The task is less clear in other areas such as behavior management. For example, MDT members want a child with behavior problems to be less aggressive. Rather than stating that the student will reduce aggressive outbursts, the team can select as its goal the development of prosocial alternatives to aggression. Fourth, it is acceptable to use terms such as *increase, develop,* and *improve.* These words have a positive orientation, yet they are global enough to keep the goals targeted by the MDT to a manageable number. Table 7.2 provides examples of goal statements that include these features. It is possible that high-quality instruction could be delivered without clear, formal statements of the goals of the educational program; however, assessment cannot be accomplished without a set of operational definitions of instruction. Goals are developed by the MDT after careful consideration of society's and individual needs, and it is up to the professionals working directly with the student daily to translate these goals into specific objectives that focus instruction (Payne, 1992).

TABLE 7.2 Sample Goal Statements

- The student will increase sixth-grade math abilities.
- The student will develop prosocial alternatives to aggressive behavior.
- The student will develop fifth-grade science concepts.
- The student will increase friendship-making skills among seventh grade peers.
- The student will increase study and test-taking skills.

Objectives

Objectives reflect a logical breakdown of annual goals. They are the intermediate steps between a child's current level of performance and the annual goals. An **objective** is defined as a clear, concise statement of the change in a student's behavior, knowledge, or affect that is expected upon completion of a unit of instruction (Kubiszyn & Borich, 1987; Popham, 1973). It is "an intended outcome stated in such a way that its attainment [or lack of it] can be observed or measured" (Tuckman, 1988, p. 15). It describes the intended result of instruction rather the process of instruction itself (Mager, 1984).

Actually, there are two types or levels of instructional objectives: a short-term objective (STO) and a lesson plan objective (LPO). Short-term objectives are broader in scope, describing student performance after the completion of a unit or several lesson plans. A lesson plan objective, on the other hand, describes student behavior after the delivery of a single lesson. As illustrated in Figure 7.1, one goal generates a few short-term objectives which in turn generate several lesson plan objectives. Despite this difference, STOs and LPOs have some features in common. First, both are essential to assessment. STOs are useful in developing summative assessment, and LPOs are useful during formative assessment. Second, they are identical in format, with both addressing specific content and including a condition, a student orientation, a behavior, and a criterion for successful performance.

Content of Objectives

The content refers to subject matter or the knowledge or skill to be learned. As discussed previously, the content of the objective should be socially valid in that it is responsive to the needs of the individual and society. Also, the objective should be real in that it addresses behaviors that the teacher actually intends to act on in the classroom (Payne, 1992). Specifically, the teacher should intend to plan and implement learning activities that will facilitate

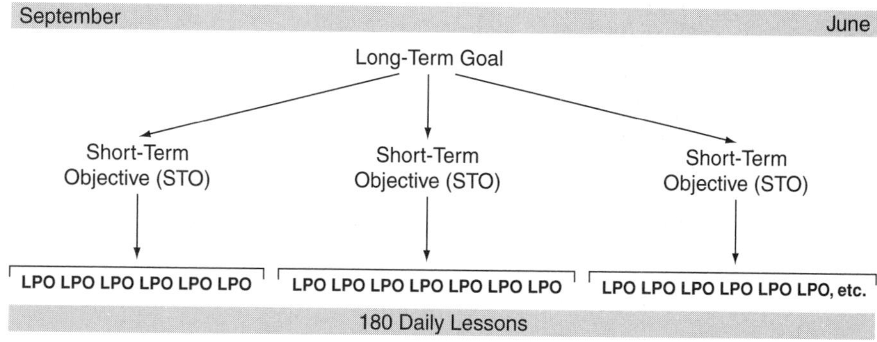

FIGURE 7.1 The relationship between goals, short-term objectives, and lesson plan objectives.

Source: From P. J. Schloss and M. A. Smith, *Applied Behavior Analysis in the Classroom,* 2nd ed. (p. 34). Copyright © 1998 by Allyn and Bacon. Reprinted by permission.

achievement of the objective. Content should be appropriate in that it builds on students' prior knowledge. Carefully sequencing instructional objectives so that they build on one another should enable students to move through instruction smoothly. Finally, the content included in the objective should be appropriate in terms of difficulty level.

Taxonomies

There are frameworks available to help teachers arrange objectives so that they build on prior knowledge and reflect an appropriate level of difficulty. The most well known of these frameworks is the Taxonomy of Educational Objectives (Bloom, 1956). The taxonomy is a hierarchical classification scheme, similar in form to the classification system used for chemicals and plants and animals. It offers teachers several advantages, including (a) definitions of vague terms such as *understand,* (b) enhanced communication among professionals, (c) the assurance that all types of learning are considered, (d) the identification of directions for instructional activities, (e) ease of planning learning experiences, and (f) preparation of measurement instruments (Bloom, 1956; Linn & Gronlund, 1995; Tuckman, 1988). In addition to helping teachers, the taxonomy also has the advantage of being widely accepted among educational testers and evaluators because it satisfies their need for explicit statements of objectives (Payne, 1992).

The taxonomy is divided into three domains: cognitive, affective, and psychomotor. Together, these domains address all different types of learning. The cognitive domain addresses knowledge outcomes and intellectual abilities and skills. The affective domain addresses attitudes, interests, and appreciation. The psychomotor domain addresses perceptual and motor skills. Each domain is subdivided into categories beginning with relatively simple knowledge outcomes and proceeding through increasingly complex ability. Originally, the lowest subcategories of behavior in each domain were believed to be prerequisite for achievement at higher, more complex subcategories. The results of recent research summarized by Linn and Gronlund (1995) challenges this assumption. Cognitive research disputes the idea that basic skills must be learned before the student can engage in higher-level thinking skills. Even the task of mastering basic skills requires students to be actively engaged in the construction of their own knowledge. Nonetheless, using the taxonomy can remind teachers of the importance of developing objectives that involve more than just simple recall and comprehension of information contained in the curricula. It also reminds teachers of the need to construct alternate assessments that tap student ability to demonstrate complex skills. Readers interested in additional information about Bloom's taxonomy are referred to Bloom (1956), Gronlund (1995), Harrow (1972), and Krathwohl, Bloom, and Masia (1964).

Components of Objectives

Although STOs and LPOs differ in their scope and purpose, they both require four components to be complete, including a condition, the name of the student, the behavior, and a criterion. In our work with preservice and in-service teachers, we have devoted a great deal of time to the rationale for writing objectives and their essential components. Our students would agree that it is not an easy task. Early drafts of their work support their feelings. We encourage readers who are just beginning to write objectives to give themselves several opportunities to practice and seek feedback from other knowledgeable individuals. Before continuing, we want to share a little tip. Of all the mistakes we see our students making, the most common is omitting a component. This mistake undermines the communicative purpose of an objective. Therefore, we encourage our students to think C-I-B-C (Condition-Individual-Behavior-Criterion) when writing objectives and reviewing their work. Despite the usefulness of this tip for writing objectives, we find it easier to explain the components by beginning with the individual.

Individual

In commercially produced materials, the objective is stated with teachers in mind. For example, the directives for a game may identify the objective as helping the teacher provide practice for basic math facts. No doubt the use of the game will make the teacher's responsibility for planning and implementing lessons more interesting, but it does little good if students' skill levels do not improve as a result of its use. We have also seen this mistake made by college students involved in early practicum experiences. Asked what the objective of a science activity is, they may respond, "For the teacher to show the students how electricity works." Just because the student teacher showed them, doesn't mean the students are now able to explain the principles of electricity. The point is that all objectives must be student oriented. This component ensures that the focus of assessment and subsequent instruction is on the learner's behaviors, not the teacher's actions. Although teachers are the primary producers of objectives, it is essential to remember that they are written for and about students. Objectives should describe what a student or group of students will do after instruction. STOs on an IEP are written for a single student with special needs; he or she will be referred to by name or as "the student." When writing objectives for a group of students, the teacher only needs to write "the students" or "the learners."

Behavior

An objective must describe what the students will do at the end of a unit of instruction to demonstrate that knowledge or a skill has been attained (Wortham, 1995). The focus here is not on the learning experiences but rather on the learning outcomes. Specifically, the teacher must describe what he or she is willing to accept as evidence that instruction has been successful (Linn & Gronlund, 1995). The **behavioral** component must be stated in unambiguous, measurable, observable terms that identify the skill the student should be able to demonstrate when assessed. Teachers should use what have come to be known as action words, that is, verbs that identify a specific response that can be observed and assessed by an outside observer. In other words, two people with a copy of the same objective should be able to observe the learner independently and agree on whether the behavior did or did not occur. Not only should the teacher and a second person agree on the meaning of the term; so too should there be an agreement on the meaning between the teacher and the students (Payne, 1992). For example, a teacher may intend for students to write an essay on topics of their own choosing. The teacher is looking for an organized essay with a clear purpose and a logical progression of thought. However, the students may think the teacher means correct spelling and punctuation. During assessment, the student whose primary concern is the mechanical aspects of the essay may receive a failing grade because he did not demonstrate the outcome the teacher had anticipated.

Lists of action verbs are available from many sources (cf. Alberto & Troutman, 1999; Gronlund, 1995). In Table 7.3, we included sample action words for Bloom's cognitive domain. Action verbs are far superior to vague terms such as *know, understand,* and *appreciate.* These verbs are not specific and do not convey what students are supposed to learn. They seriously undermine the usefulness of objectives during the assessment process. They cannot be directly measured; therefore, they must be inferred from some performance or behavioral act (Tuckman, 1988).

We offer a few suggestions to increase the usefulness of the behavioral component of an objective. First, the teacher needs to use terms that describe what the student will do, not what he or she won't do. A student with behavioral disorders may throw temper tantrums

TABLE 7.3 Action Words From Bloom's Cognitive Domain

	Example	Action Verbs
Knowledge The learner engages in simple recall or recognition of basic facts, principles, methods, patterns, structures, or settings.	The learner reads sight words or sound words out.	define, describe, identify, label, name
Comprehension The learner demonstrates understanding by paraphrasing, explaining, or summarizing content.	The learner reads a poem and identifies the main theme.	explain, give examples, predict, rewrite, summarize
Application The learner selects an idea, rule, procedure, or method, and applies it correctly to a new situation.	The learner writes a sonnet.	demonstrate, operate, produce
Analysis The learner breaks a concept down into its elements to illustrate how internal ideas are related.	The learner shows how a poem reflects a pattern.	break down, diagram, outline
Synthesis The learner arranges elements to create a new pattern or structure.	The learner writes an original poem.	categorize, compose, design, write
Evaluation The learner makes logical quantitative or qualitative judgments about a concept, method, or material.	The learner critiques poetry.	compare, criticize, justify, support

when her requests are denied or when she is criticized by others. Her teacher may address the behavior component of the objective by writing, "Patsy will not throw temper tantrums." It is an unfortunate possibility that the only response Patsy has under these circumstances is to throw a temper tantrum. Left to her own devices, it is very likely that a new response in these situations will be just as inappropriate; however, Patsy technically would have met the terms of the objective as long as she didn't have a tantrum. The behavior part of this objective would be vastly improved by describing what Patsy will do when criticized or denied a request. Her teacher could say "Patsy will continue working quietly in her assigned area."

Second, a teacher can clearly convey the meaning of the behavioral term by operationalizing the term. For example, what specifically does a teacher mean by terms such as *pay attention* or *stay in seat?* Teachers who use operational definitions develop lists of inclusionary behaviors and exclusionary behaviors. Inclusionary behaviors indicate the student is demonstrating the intent of the objective. Exclusionary behaviors indicate the student is demonstrating behaviors outside the scope of the objective. In Table 7.4, we have operationalized what is meant by cursing. This operational definition is based on the work of White and Koorland (1996). Third, we remind teachers of the importance of moving beyond simple recall and comprehension to include other more complex skills from the cognitive domain. Similarly, the majority of school work emphasizes skills from the cognitive domain. We encourage teachers to target skills from the affective and psychomotor areas to ensure adequate social, emotional, and physical development.

Finally, Payne (1992) and Linn and Gronlund (1995) advise that each objective should target the development of a single skill or piece of knowledge. Avoid developing objectives such as "The student should be able to recall, comprehend, and apply all equations

TABLE 7.4 An Operational Definition of Swearing

Objective: During independent, small-group, or large-group activities in the classroom or on school grounds, Charles will use only standard, polite English vocabulary to express himself all day.

Standard, Polite English Includes	Standard, Polite English Excludes
■ Proper names to refer people ■ Slang such as "darn," "shoot," heck," and so on.	■ Verbal assaults such as "F____ you," and "Go to h____" ■ Profanity using religion contemptuously, such as "Jes___ Chr___t!" ■ Epithets or outbursts of anger, such as "D____ it!" ■ Scatology or verbalization that refer to human excrement ■ Use of hand or finger gestures to convey any of the above ■ Use of words that criticize racial, ethnic, gender, or sexual orientation

Source: Adapted from "Curses! What Can We Do About Cursing?" by R. B. White and M. A. Koorland, 1996, *Teaching Exceptional Children, 28*(4), pp. 48–52.

for determining the perimeter and area of polygons." Incorporating more than one behavior into an objective complicates assessment. The teacher may have provided activities to facilitate student acquisition of all of these skills; however, the test based on such an objective may not reflect the diverse nature of his or her instruction. Any one of the three behaviors included in this objective may be measured but not in proportion to the emphasis given it in class. Actually, assessment items might focus exclusively on the student's ability to recall these formulas. More complex behaviors may be ignored altogether. It would be unfair to determine that a student has met the entire objective on the basis of responding to assessment items that are solely related to recall.

Condition

Each objective should begin with a very brief description of the circumstances under which the student is expected to demonstrate knowledge or skills. The condition component helps teachers during assessment and instruction because it clarifies the nature of the setting, material, and teacher support that should be available to students. **Condition statements** usually begin with the words such as *given, when,* or *during* and can be used to begin objectives representing all three domains specified in Bloom's taxonomy. Objectives from the cognitive domain can include, "Given a calculator, a bank statement, and a checkbook, . . ." and "Given laboratory equipment and an unknown chemical compound, . . .". Objectives from the affective domain can begin, "Given a warranted criticism about behavior from an authority figure at work, . . ." and "Given a situation in school that conflicts with personal values, . . .". Conditions for psychomotor skills can begin, "Given 40 hours of teacher instruction, a working vehicle, and a space between two parked cars, . . ." and "Given a keyboard and a document to type, . . .". Alberto and Troutman (1999) developed six categories of condition statements that are useful to teachers and test preparers. We present these categories in Table 7.5.

Criterion

The last component of an objective is the criterion or standard for acceptable performance. By including a criterion, the teacher makes public what is being judged and the standards for acceptable performance. A **criterion** is necessary because it helps teachers evaluate student performance in a reliable, fair, and valid manner. It should be shared with parents so that they will know what is expected and can support their child's efforts (Herman, Aschbacher, & Winters, 1992). The criterion can be set by the teacher, the school district, or the state department of education (Wortham, 1995).

Howell and Nolet (2000) described three levels of proficiency that teachers should consider when developing objectives and test items to measure them. The first level is frequency or accuracy, which is the most common criterion to document skill acquisition. Criterion levels included in LPOs can be low for initial skill acquisition but increase over time to the desired level identified in the STO. For example, students working on the Dolch list of basic sight vocabulary can have expectations for accuracy change over time. Early in the course of instruction, they can be 20% accurate, then 30%, 40%, and so on until they are reading the list aloud with 100% accuracy. The question may be raised regarding how high

TABLE 7.5 Six Categories of Condition Statements

	Example
1. Verbal requests or instruction The teacher provides the students with specific verbal directives.	When told to pay attention, . . . Given a request from any staff member, . . .
2. Written instructions or format The student receives directions in writing.	When instructed to diagram sentences, . . . When given a worksheet with T/F statements and the directions to cross out, . . .
3. Demonstration The teacher provides a demonstration of the skill before the student is expected to perform.	After watching the teacher change a tire and given appropriate tools, . . . After watching a demonstration of CPR and given a dummy, . . .
4. Materials The teacher includes a list of the materials the student will have access to while demonstrating knowledge or performing a skill.	Given a calculator and twenty word problems involving multiple steps, . . . Given a computer with a spell check program, a grammar check program, and a thesaurus, . . .
5. Environmental setting or timing The teacher describes the setting in which the student should perform the skill. (Appropriate for tasks that involve generalization and maintenance of skills acquired in the classroom.)	In the cafeteria, when given $3.00 and the task of purchasing lunch, . . . In the community, when approached by a stranger, . . .
6. Manner of assistance The teacher identifies the level of prompt that will be made available to a student as he or she is performing a skill.*	Given a graphic process prompt of the cursive alphabet, . . . Given only one teacher reminder to remain in her seat, . . .

*It is important to note that ultimately we are trying to enhance students' independent functioning. A prompt or some other level of assistance may represent an ongoing accommodation for a student's disability. However, the majority of other prompts should be faded over time. Assessment should verify the student's ability to perform unassisted.

Source: From *Applied Behavior Analysis for Teachers,* 5th ed., by P. Alberto and A. Troutman, 1999, Columbus, OH: Merrill.

a percentage must be. Sometimes, the answer is obvious. For very basic academic skills such as letter or number recognition and telling time to the hour or half hour, the level of accuracy must be very high, perhaps even 100%. For other academic skills, such as advanced long division or telling time to the exact minute, the accuracy level can be reasonably set at 80%. Students must also perform many functional life skills with a high level of proficiency. For example, it is essential that students distinguish correctly between the red and green lights at busy intersections all the time. A single error jeopardizes a student's safety. Proficiency levels for other skills may not be as obvious. For example, how often can a student be late for work before his or her job is at risk? For answers to questions such as these, we recommend using two of the techniques described by Wolf (1978) for ensuring social validation of goals and objectives. The first technique is called **social comparison,** which involves observations of others considered competent to determine how often they display the behavior in question. If observations or an examination of employment records indicate competent individuals are late for work no more than once every 60 days, then that should become the standard a teacher includes in the objective. Another technique recommended by Wolf (1995) is subjective evaluation. While social comparison requires teachers to gather objective data to make decisions about the criterion, **subjective evaluation** requires teachers to secure the opinion of informed others. Referring to the previous example, a teacher could ask several employers for their opinions on how often an employee can be late before jeopardizing continued employment. The criterion would then reflect the best judgment of these employers.

The second level of proficiency identified by Howell and Nolet (2000) is mastery, which refers to doing a task accurately and quickly so that it becomes functional in the individual's environment. Mastery is the difference between sounding out a word and decoding smoothly and quickly without hesitation. One student may still be learning the mechanics for decoding accurately, while another student has mastered these skills and can concentrate on comprehension (Haring & Eaton, 1978). A criterion level that addresses mastery may in fact be a combination of accuracy and time. For example, now that the student can read all the words from the Dolch list, she must now turn her attention to reading them without hesitation. Social comparison may assist the teacher in establishing the exact criterion. After observing how quickly students reading at grade level read these words aloud, the teacher may modify the original objective to read, "Given a list of Dolch words, Ellen will read each aloud with 100% accuracy within 3 seconds."

The third level of proficiency is automaticity, in which the student performs accurately, quickly, and in context (Howell & Nolet, 2000). This level suggests a change in the condition statement to include relevant aspects with real-world application. For example, the original objective developed in a learning center in the classroom may state, "When paying for items costing no more than $5.00, the student will count to make sure she has received the correct change each time." To ensure automaticity, the condition of the objective can be modified to state, "At the local convenience store when paying for items . . .". This change now has the learner in the community where stakes are a little higher and the pressure to perform acceptably has increased.

Performance Criteria. The recent shift to include alternate assessment or performance-based measures has resulted in the development of **performance criteria,** which are useful in judging the quality of a complex response and the process of arriving at it. "Performance criteria are the specific behaviors a pupil should perform to carry out a performance or produce a product" (Airasian, 1996, p. 140). As with all aspects of objectives, performance criteria need to be well conceived, clearly defined, and consistently applied. More time may be required to develop performance criteria, but it is worth the effort for two reasons. First, performance criteria help teachers be accurate, unbiased, and consistent in their scoring. Second, careful attention to performance criteria helps teachers define excellence and communicate it to their students. Such discussion can help students internalize the standards they need to become independent learners. Herman, Aschbacher, and Winters (1992) recommend that teachers discuss performance criteria with their students during instruction so that students can make improvements in the formative stages of their work. Waiting until the end of a unit of instruction may be too late for students to make important revisions that could affect the outcomes of assessment.

Airasian (1996) identified several steps for developing performance criteria. First, the teacher should look to see that performance criteria don't already exist for the process or product of interest. If they do and they meet the teacher's need, there is no need to proceed any further. Second, if performance criteria are unavailable, the teacher should decide if he or she will be observing a process or a product. For example, is the teacher interested in evaluating how students plan their written instruction, or is the teacher interested in evaluating the final draft of a student's work? For the former, criteria are needed to judge the student's actual performance while it is occurring. In the latter case, criteria are needed to judge the final product. It is also possible that the teacher is interested in both the process and the product. For example, a teacher may be interested in observing students as they write in cursive and in determining the legibility of the writing.

Third, the teacher needs to break the overall performance or product into its most important components or parts. To help with this step, the teacher can perform the task or imagine himself or herself performing it. Social comparison will also come in handy. The teacher can observe those who already demonstrate acceptable levels of competence, making note of what they do during the process. Similarly, the teacher can gather and examine work samples from these individuals. It helps if other teachers engage in these activities to ensure the sample is representative and that a complete list of process and product behaviors is obtained. The behaviors on this list should be emphasized during instruction and evaluated during assessment. Bear in mind that other teachers may identify different criteria for the same process or product. There is no one right answer. The teacher developing the criteria only needs to include and clearly describe items that are meaningful and important for students.

Next, the teacher needs to describe these components in behavioral terms so that he or she can focus on clearly defined characteristics of the performance or product. Descriptions need to be specific enough so that they can be explained to students, who will know what to do or what to produce. As is true for describing the behavioral component of an objective, the teacher should avoid using ambiguous words that cloud the meaning of the performance criteria. Airasian (1996) encouraged teachers to avoid using *good, appropriate,* and words that end in *ly.* Interpretation of these terms is often left up to the observer, reducing the fairness, consistency, and usefulness of the assessment.

Fifth, the teacher should arrange components in the order in which they are likely to be observed. The list should not be too long because the teacher probably won't have time to look for a large number of criteria for each child. Finally, a teacher probably won't get the performance criteria right the first time; thus, he or she will need to revise and clarify. A teacher can determine the acceptability of performance criteria if a second teacher can use the criteria without the first teacher being there to explain them.

Performance criteria can be displayed as checklists, rating scales, or scoring rubrics. A **checklist** is a written list of performance criteria. As the student performs or as the product is evaluated, the rater determines if the process or product reflects each item on the checklist.

FIGURE 7.2 A checklist for evaluating a social skill.

When asking for help, the student must

	Trials		
	1	*2*	*3*
1. Select a peer or authority figure in a position to help	____	____	____
2. Get the person's attention by using a name and saying, "Excuse me"	____	____	____
3. Identify the problem	____	____	____
4. Make a request for assistance that specifies what the helper will do	____	____	____
5. Say "Thank you" after the task is completed	____	____	____

If so, the rater places a check mark by that skill; if not, the rater omits a check mark. A sample process checklist for evaluating social skills is included in Figure 7.2. A sample checklist for evaluating a student's planning skills in written language is included in Figure 7.3. Checklists are diagnostic, reusable, and allow the teacher to chart student performance. They can be shared so that students know areas in which they need to make improvements. However, the teacher using a checklist only has two choices: either the characteristic is there or it isn't. To summarize a student's performance on the checklist, the teacher can convert to a percentage. For example, using the checklist in Figure 7.2, a student was supposed to demonstrate all five components over a three-day period for a total of 15 items. If she demonstrated 12, her performance rate is 80%.

Performance criteria can also be displayed as rating scales, which evaluate student performance over a continuum rather than as a dichotomy. The points on the continuum can be numbers such as 1 = never, 2 = seldom, 3 = usually, and 4 = always. The rater can also place an X on a line at or between two points to indicate the level of student performance. A rating scale is presented in Figure 7.4.

Finally, performance criteria can be presented as a descriptive rating scale, which is also called a **scoring rubric.** A rubric requires the rater to select from among different descriptions of actual performance the one that most closely matches what the student did. A rubric is presented in Figure 7.5.

For both rating scales and scoring rubrics, it is important to limit the number of rating categories. Few people can make reliable discriminations in student performance across more than five rating categories (Airasian, 1996). To summarize results, teachers can assign a point value to each category and sum points across the criteria. A teacher can determine what is the highest and lowest number of points possible, and develop categories in between these extremes. A teacher may also determine the number of points earned out of those possible and convert to a percentage.

Having read the information needed to write objectives, you may now want to see if you can recognize objectives that are written correctly and revise those in which there are errors. Figure 7.6 presents a self-test on objectives and Figure 7.7 presents the answers.

FIGURE 7.3 A checklist for evaluating a written product.

Prewriting Phase

1. Is the topic _____ teacher selected? _____ student selected?

Rate the student's	*Low*			*High*
prior knowledge	1	2	3	4
interest	1	2	3	4

2. Did the student spend time

_____ thinking about the topic?
_____ discussing the topic with a peer?
_____ making an outline, semantic map, or notes?
_____ in research outside of class?
_____ no observable planning

First Draft

3. Did the student refer to the plan? _____ Yes _____ No

4. The student drafted the text

_____ by handwriting _____ on a word processor _____ by dictating

Rate the mechanical demands	*Low*			*High*
Difficulty	1	2	3	4
Fluency	1	2	3	4

	Seldom			*Often*
5. How frequently did the student seek assistance?	1	2	3	4
6. How frequently did the student stop and reread?	1	2	3	4
7. Did rereadings result in changes?	1	2	3	4
8. Was the text shared as it was drafted?	1	2	3	4

9. The student received feedback on the finished draft from

_____ a friend
_____ peers in the response group
_____ a teacher
_____ no one

Final Draft

10. How many drafts were made before the final product? _____

11. Changes (from first to final draft) reflect

Surface concerns

_____ letter formation correction
_____ spelling corrections
_____ capitalization and punctuation rules
_____ margins and headings
_____ grammatical corrections
_____ word changes
_____ additions of adjectives, transition phrases
_____ syntax changes (rearranging sentences)

Content revisions

_____ elaboration (addition of detail sentences)
_____ reordering of information
_____ addition of topic sentences or summary statements
_____ improvement of style with respect to intended audience

12. The student shared his or her final product by

_____ reading orally to a large group
_____ reading orally to a small response group
_____ publishing (class anthology, school newspaper, and so on)

Source: From "Written Language" (pp. 200–224), by S. Isaacson, in P. J. Schloss, M. A. Smith, and C. N. Schloss, *Instructional Methods for Adolescents with Learning and Behavior Problems,* 2nd ed., 1995, Needham Heights, MA: Allyn and Bacon.

FIGURE 7.4 A rating scale suitable for evaluating an individual in entry-level employment.

Read each item carefully and rate the employee by circling one number. Use the following scale:

4 = Always 3 = Usually 2 = Seldom 1 = Never

1. The employee is on time.	1	2	3	4
2. The employee is dressed in a clean and neat uniform.	1	2	3	4
3. The employee demonstrates adequate personal hygiene.	1	2	3	4
4. The employee greets coworkers by name with "Hello."	1	2	3	4
5. The employee is polite to customers.	1	2	3	4
6. The employee works independently on assigned tasks.	1	2	3	4
7. The employee completes assigned tasks correctly.	1	2	3	4
8. The employee finds work to do when primary tasks are completed.	1	2	3	4
9. The employee leaves his or her locker area clean and neat.	1	2	3	4
10. The employee calls in if he or she will be late or absent.	1	2	3	4

Scoring

36–40 points = Excellent
32–35 points = Very good
28–31 points = Good
20–27 points = Weak
less than 20 points = Unsatisfactory

FIGURE 7.5 A scoring rubric to evaluate the content of a student's written language.

Content Scoring Guide

________ *1. Main Idea*

3 = The man idea is clearly stated.

2 = The main idea is implied in the paragraph or may be indicated in the title.

1 = The main idea is not discernible.

________ *2. Supporting Details*

3 = Two or more supporting details are evident or one supporting detail is evident and has been expanded.

2 = One supporting detail is evident but has not been expanded.

1 = One or more details are evident but are not related to the main idea.

________ *3. Unity*

4 = All sentences relate to the topic.

3 = More than half the sentences relate to the topic.

2 = At least one sentence relates to the topic.

1 = None of the sentences relates to the topic.

________ *4. Coherence*

3 = All sentences flow logically.

2 = There is some evidence of cohesiveness.

1 = There is no evidence of cohesiveness; sentences are disjointed.

FIGURE 7.6 Objective self-test.

Carefully review each objective below and place a check mark under each heading if that component* is present. If there is an error, rewrite the objective. Answers are located in Figure 7.7.

	C	I	B	C
1. During the lesson, the student will identify time to the minute with 100% accuracy.	____	____	____	____
Rewrite if necessary: ________________________________				
2. Given a recipe and all the necessary ingredients, the teacher follows the directions with 100% accuracy to make edible meals.	____	____	____	____
Rewrite if necessary: ________________________________				
3. The student will remain in his or her seat or other teacher-assigned areas the entire day.	____	____	____	____
Rewrite if necessary: ________________________________				
4. Given paper, a pencil, and a teacher directive, Bill will produce upper- and lower-case letters of the cursive alphabet with 100% legibility.	____	____	____	____
Rewrite if necessary: ________________________________				
5. At street corners with a traffic signal, Ann will cross at the red light with 80% accuracy.	____	____	____	____
Rewrite if necessary: ________________________________				
6. Given a computer with a writing program and the topic of his choice, Mark will write a paragraph that begins with a statement of the main idea followed by at least four supporting sentences.	____	____	____	____
Rewrite if necessary: ________________________________				
7. Given a book at her ability level, Mary will read with 90% accuracy.	____	____	____	____
Rewrite if necessary: ________________________________				
8. During the school day, Maureen will not swear ever.	____	____	____	____
Rewrite if necessary: ________________________________				

*Condition-Individual-Behavior-Criterion

FIGURE 7.7 Answers for the self-test in Figure 7.6.

How did you do? Check your answers against our recommendations.

1. The condition is inappropriate. It tells you nothing about what the student will have access to during instruction. The objective could be revised to say "Shown a clock with time to the minute, the student will orally identify the time with 100% accuracy."
2. The objective has a teacher orientation. It describes what the teacher will do, not the students. By substituting "students" for teacher, the objective is acceptable.
3. The condition has been omitted. The objective can be revised to say "During school hours, the student will remain in his or her seat or other teacher-assigned areas at all times."
4. Correct as stated.
5. The criterion is too low. As stated, it means that Ann could cross against the light 20% of the time. She is in danger of being injured. The objective can be revised to say, "At street corners with a traffic signal, Ann will cross the street when the light is red. She will do this 100% of the time."
6. Correct as stated.
7. "Read" is not a measurable, observable term. The objective can be revised to say "Given a book at her ability level, Mary will read silently then orally answer five comprehension questions with 80% accuracy."
8. This objective identifies what Maureen won't do. The objective can be revised to say "During school hours, Maureen will use standard English vocabulary 100% of the time. She will not swear ever."

Evaluating Objectives

Although we have discussed pitfalls to writing objectives throughout this chapter, Tuckman (1988) assembled a list of criteria against which teachers can evaluate their objectives.

1. Has the objective been written to reflect student performance? Is the focus on what the student will be able to do after the teacher has provided instruction?
2. Is the behavior measurable and observable? That is, can it be observed by one or more of the five senses?
3. Is the objective specific enough to be meaningful to the students? Remember, one of the purposes of writing objectives is to communicate instructional intent to the students. Using specific, behavioral terminology will help them understand how they will demonstrate knowledge or skill acquisition.
4. Is there a direct relationship between the goals and the objective? Are the short-term objectives a logical outgrowth of the goals established for the students?
5. Have the level of performance and the conditions under which the performance is to occur been clearly identified? Without sufficient attention to these two components, assessment is made more difficult.
6. Is there a sequence in relation to prior and subsequent objectives? That is, is there a relationship between two or more objectives derived from the same goal? Will achievement on one objective facilitate mastery of the next?
7. Is the objective relevant to the student's experience?
8. Is the objective attainable within the allotted time?

9. Is the objective challenging to each student? An analysis of assessment data from a variety of sources will help the teacher develop or select objectives that are within the student's reach, given sufficient instruction.
10. Is the objective acceptable in the society in which the student belongs? Is the objective a reflection of a goal that is valued by society? Will mastery of this objective enhance the quality of the student's life?

Summary

The purpose of this chapter was to establish a link between the assessment process and the act of writing objectives. If a clear description of the knowledge and skills students must acquire is absent, then precise, accurate, and meaningful assessment is not possible. Teachers must select goals and develop objectives that will contribute to their students' quality of life. In addition, objectives must be student-oriented and include a condition under which they will perform; a measurable, observable behavior; and a criterion for acceptable performance. With the completion of this chapter and mastery of the information it contains, the reader is prepared to move on to the next steps in the development and utilization of assessment techniques.

REFERENCES

Airasian, P. (1996). *Assessment in the classroom.* NY: McGraw Hill, Inc.

Alberto, P., & Troutman, A. (1999). *Applied behavior analysis for teachers* (5th ed.). Columbus, OH: Merrill.

Black, P. J. (1993). Formative and summative assessment by teachers. *Studies in Science Education, 21,* 49–97.

Bloom, B. S. (1956). *Taxonomy of educational objectives: The classification of educational goals: Handbook I, Cognitive domain.* New York: David McKay.

Cohen, L. G. (1990). Development of a curriculum-based assessment instrument. In L. G. Cohen & J. A. Spruill (Eds.), *A practical guide to curriculum-based assessment for special educators* (pp. 75–90). Springfield, IL: Charles C. Thomas.

Crooks, T. J. (1988). The impact of classroom evaluation practices on students. *Review of Educational Research, 58,* 438–481.

Gronlund, N. E. (1995). How to write and use instructional objectives (5th ed.). Englewood Cliffs, NJ: Merrill.

Haring, N. G., & Eaton, M. D. (1978). Systematic instructional procedures: An instructional hierarchy. In N. G. Haring, T. C. Lovitt, M. D. Eaton, & C. L. Hansen (Eds.), *The fourth R: Research in the classroom* (pp. 23–40). Columbus, OH: Charles E. Merrill.

Harrow, A. J. (1972). *A taxonomy of the psychomotor domain.* New York: David McKay.

Herman, J. L., Aschbacher, P. R., & Winters, L. (1992). *A practical guide to alternative assessment.* Alexandria, VA: Association for Supervision of Curriculum and Development.

Howell, K. W., & Nolet, V. (2000). *Curriculum-based evaluation: Teaching and decision making* (3rd ed.). Belmont, CA: Wadsworth-Thompson Learning.

Isaacson, S. (1995). Written language. In P. J. Schloss, M. A. Smith, & C. N. Schloss (Eds.), *Instructional methods for adolescents with learning and behavior problems* (2nd ed.), (pp. 200–224). Needham Heights, MA: Allyn & Bacon.

Krathwohl, D. R., Bloom, B. S., & Masia, B. B. (1964). *Taxonomy of educational objectives: Handbook II, Affective domain.* New York: David McKay.

Kubiszyn, T., & Borich, G. (1987). *Educational testing and measurement: Classroom applications and practice.* Glenville, IL: Scott, Foresman.

Linn, R. L., & Gronlund, N. E. (1995). *Measurement and assessment in teaching* (7th ed.). Englewood Cliffs, NJ: Merrill.

Mager, R. F. (1984). *Preparing instructional objectives* (2nd ed.). Belmont, CA: Pitman Learning.

Payne, D. A. (1992). *Measuring and evaluating educational outcomes.* New York: Merrill.

Popham, W. J. (1973). *Criterion-referenced instruction.* Belmont, CA: Fearon Publishers.

Popham, W. J., Eisner, E. W., Sullivan, H. J., & Tyler, L. L. (1969). *Instructional objectives.* Chicago: Rand McNally & Company.

Schloss, P. J., & Smith, M. A. (1998). *Applied behavior analysis in the classroom* (2nd ed.). Needham Heights, MA: Allyn & Bacon.

Tuckman, B. W. (1988). *Testing for teachers* (2nd ed.). San Diego, CA: Harcourt Brace Jovanovich.

White, R. B., & Koorland M. A. (1996). Curses! What can we do about cursing? *Teaching Exceptional Children, 28*(4), 48–52.

Wolf, M. M. (1978). Social validity: The case for subjective evaluation or how applied behavior analysis is finding its heart. *Journal of Applied Behavior Analysis, 11,* 204–214.

Wortham, S. C. (1995). *Measurement and evaluation in early childhood education* (2nd ed.). Englewood Cliffs, NJ: Merrill.

CHAPTER

8 Measuring Progress Against Objectives

LECH WISNIEWSKI

The Metropolitan State College of Denver

OBJECTIVES

After reading this chapter, you will be able to

1. State six types of instructional decisions that can be facilitated through the use of curriculum-based assessment
2. List four curriculum-based approaches to measuring student progress
3. For each curriculum-based approach, provide a short summary of the model, state at least two contributions of the model to curriculum-based assessment, state how the model assesses student performance, and describe how the model may facilitate instructional planning and instructional interactions
4. Define a probe and a baseline
5. Label and identify the following components of a performance graph: *x*- and *y*-axis, data points, goal and trend lines, data breaks, and phase change
6. State the steps needed to develop a goal and trend line
7. When comparing the trend line to the goal line, state the conditions under which acceptable progress toward the goal is being made; state the conditions under which a phase change is suggested

KEY TERMS

baseline (p. 164)
criterion-referenced (C-R) assessment (p. 155)
curriculum-based assessment (CBA) (p. 155)
curriculum-based assessment for instructional design (CBA-ID) (p. 156)
curriculum-based evaluation (CBE) (p. 157)
curriculum-based measurement (CBM) (p. 158)
data points (p. 164)
developmental curricula (p. 156)
goal line (p. 164)
phase (p. 163)
phase changes (p. 163)
probe (p. 162)
spiraling curricula (p. 156)
trend line (p. 166)
unestablished curricula (p. 156)
x-axis (abscissa) (p. 163)
y-axis (ordinate) (p. 163)

Curriculum-based approaches to assessment provide teachers with a variety of strategies and techniques to measure and evaluate student progress (Shinn, Rosenfield, & Knutson, 1989). Several curriculum-based approaches have been developed and were discussed in earlier chapters. These curriculum-based approaches differ on a number of important features: for example, philosophical assumptions, type of data collected, how specific test stimuli are linked to the curricula, psychometric technical adequacy, and focus of decision-making capability. These strategies and techniques do share a number of common features, however. They draw inferences on skill competencies from specific test stimuli, assess student progress through the use of repeated measurements, and index student learning as a function of instructional arrangements being invested.

Curriculum-based approaches to assessment, most importantly, provide teachers with a database from which to validate a number of instructional decisions. Curriculum-based approaches have been used to (a) determine the need for and evaluate prereferral and collaborative services, validating unrealized student performance expectations within the context of general education and vocational settings (Deno, Marston, & Tindal, 1986; Marston & Magnusson, 1985; Marston, Mirkin, & Deno, 1984; Ysseldyke & Thurlow, 1984); (b) determine program eligibility, assessing differences between a student's current performance and that of a referent group to which the student is being compared (Deno, 1986; Deno et al., 1986; Germann & Tindal, 1985; Marston, Tindal, & Deno, 1984; Shinn & Habedank, 1992; Shinn & Marston, 1985; Tindal, Wesson, Deno, Germann, & Mirkin, 1985); (c) evaluate program efficacy, permitting teachers to plan, develop, and compare the relative benefits of a variety of instructional arrangements (Deno, 1986; Fuchs, 1986; Fuchs, Fuchs, & Deno, 1982b); (d) monitor student progress, verifying student learning rates as a function of learning-time being invested (Fuchs, Fuchs, & Deno, 1982a; Germann & Tindal, 1985; Marston & Magnusson, 1985; Ysseldyke, Thurlow, Graden, Wesson, Algozzine, & Deno, 1983); and finally, (e) determine whether a student has mastered relevant instructional content, noting that the student has met basic skill competencies, that an instructional arrangement can be terminated, and that the student can be reintegrated into the mainstream (Fuchs et al., 1982a; Germann & Tindal, 1985; Shinn, Powell-Smith, Good, & Baker, 1993; Shinn, Powell-Smith, Good, & Baker, 1997; Marston & Magnusson, 1985).

In Chapter 7, curricular-based assessment strategies were linked to the development of instructional objectives. We continue that discussion, as we link objectives to a variety of performance measures that validate student progress. In this chapter, we focus on a number of curricular-based procedures to measure student progress against the objectives that students are working toward. We propose an integrated approach to curriculum-based assessment, permitting teachers to select performance measures that meet a teacher's curricular needs. We first briefly review a number of curriculum-based assessment approaches and focus on their contributions to measuring student progress. We identify relevant strategies and performance measures that permit a teacher to improve his or her instructional plan and monitor a student's progress through an instructional sequence. We next discuss the development of a performance database and the techniques to visually represent trends in student performance. Finally, we interpret the results in a manner that facilitates improved instructional planning and instructional interactions.

Models of Curriculum-Based Assessment to Measure Student Progress

Measuring student progress depends on selecting performance measures that produce relevant information from which valid judgments can be made. Various curriculum-based performance measures have been developed to evaluate student progress. Selecting any particular performance measure depends on one's focus, purpose, and instructional needs. For example, if the focus is to monitor and evaluate the rate of progress toward mastering short-term goals, to examine difficulties being experienced which may impede skill acquisition, or to analyze student errors, then one of several curriculum-based assessment (e.g., Blankenship, 1985; Blankenship & Lilly, 1981; Idol, Nevin, & Paolucci-Whitcomb, 1999; Gickling & Thompson, 1985; Howell & Morehead, 1987; Howell, 1986) approaches may be selected to meet one of these instructional needs. On the other hand, if a general measure of a student's academic health and progress toward a long-term goal is the focus, then curriculum-based measurement (Deno, 1992; Fuchs & Deno, 1991) may be better suited. Other distinctions also exist and are discussed.

Curriculum-based assessment (CBA) is not one unified approach or technique but rather several approaches (Shinn et al., 1989). CBA refers to any approach that uses direct and repeated observations to gather and record student progress. To measure student progress, CBA typically relies on a task analysis of the curriculum and on establishing objectives that are closely linked to relevant methods to measure student performance. CBA is also tied to the local curriculum (Deno, 1985; 1987). Several CBA models have been developed. These include two perspectives on criterion-referenced assessment (Blankenship, 1985; Idol et al., 1999), curriculum-based assessment for instructional design (Gickling & Thompson, 1985), and curriculum-based evaluation. Curriculum-based measurement will be discussed in the subsequent section.

Criterion-Referenced Models

Criterion-referenced (C-R) assessment models as exemplified by Blankenship (1985) and Idol et al. (1999) use the classroom curriculum to generate not only specific goal-level instructional objectives but also specific test stimuli that measure student performance. Accordingly, teachers carefully evaluate the scope and sequence outlined in the student's goal-level curriculum. Teachers develop a series of objectives, typically arranged hierarchically, and establish a criterion performance level for each objective. Table 8.1 outlines the sequence involved in developing and measuring student performance. Because the focus is on short-term progress and student mastery of instructional content, assessment of student progress focuses on repeated measurements (i.e., two to three times per week) to determine a student's progress as he or she moves through an instructional sequence, objective by objective. (Figure 8.2(a) provides an overview illustrating student progress on several objectives.) For each objective, students are tested with a representative number of test items. Performance measures typically rely on percentages, but the number of correct responses, instructional movements, and the like, could also be used. For example, the teacher may specify, as is illustrated in Figure 8.2(a), that the criterion performance (i.e., mastery level) is 85% correct. Other features of Figure 8.2(b) will be discussed later in this chapter.

TABLE 8.1 Procedure to Develop and Measure Student Progress Using Criterion-Referenced Performance Measures

- List the skills presented in the goal-level curriculum
- Examine the list and arrange in a logical order; ensure that important skills have been included
- Write an objective for each skill on the list
- Develop a pool of test items for each objective
- Draw a small random set and include on test
- Specify a criterion level for student performance (e.g., student will answer 85% correct); teachers may employ a number of sources to establish a criterion performance level; teachers could use guidelines established by Idol et al. (1999) or employ a normative comparison; teachers can compare a student's performance against that of a comparable peer-group on the same learning task
- Administer test and determine student's entry skill level
- Provide instruction and periodically assess progress toward established criterion
- After student has reached desired skill level, periodically readminister test to ensure long-term retention

Source: Adapted from "Using Curriculum-Based Assessment Data to Make Instructional Decisions," by C. Blankenship, 1985, *Exceptional Children, 52,* pp. 233–238, and *Models of Curriculum-based Assessment: A Blueprint for Learning,* 3rd ed., by L. Idol, A. Nevin, and P. Paolucci-Whitcomb, 1999, Austin, TX: Pro-Ed.

Criterion-referenced assessment models remain the standard, among curriculum-based approaches, to measure student performance. C-R approaches to CBA have been developed for a variety of curricula, including developmental, spiraling, and unestablished. In **developmental curricula,** the learning tasks are hierarchically arranged with performance expectations (i.e., mastery-level) set high (e.g., 95% or higher). To illustrate, reading, language arts, writing, and spelling often employ developmental curricular tasks sequentially arranged. **Spiraling curricula** are organized into levels with concepts repeating in subsequently higher levels. Performance expectations are set lower (e.g., mastery at 85%) than those in developmental curricula because concepts are repeated in subsequent lessons. Math, science, and, to some extent, social studies are examples of spiraling curricula. Finally, **unestablished curricula** are teacher-developed. Teachers, in establishing the curricula, define the developmental scope and learning sequence. Teachers then select relevant resources, which may include formally published materials, to use in their teaching. Performance expectations are comparable to those established in the spiraling curricula. Examples of unestablished curricula would include written language, handwriting, study skills, social studies, science, and transition curriculum. For an invaluable source of ready-made teacher resources and additional guidelines to develop additional C-R testing materials, see Idol et al. (1999).

Curriculum-Based Assessment for Instructional Design

Curriculum-based assessment for instructional design (CBA-ID) (Gickling & Thompson, 1985) is a curriculum-based approach to assessment designed to control and monitor the introduction of unfamiliar content within an instructional sequence. CBA-ID's premise is that by carefully controlling learning on a task-by-task basis, students will not only be more successful, but they will become less frustrated and better motivated. Teachers will also see fewer behavioral problems (Gickling & Armstrong, 1978).

Gickling and his associates (Gickling & Thompson, 1985) proposed a number of general guidelines to control the degree of instructional difficulty that a student may experience while still maintaining some degree of learning challenge. Teachers need to first identify content that a student may know, referred to as known materials. As a student enters an instructional sequence, teachers control the introduction of unfamiliar and more challenging materials (i.e., unknown materials) through a number of instructional techniques. Folding-in is one such technique that ensures the correct ratio between known and unfamiliar materials is maintained. To illustrate, in vocabulary drill and practice, the desired ratio is 70% known words to 30% unknown words. To maintain this 70:30 ratio, unknown words are interspersed with known words. By carefully controlling the ratio of known to unknown materials, learning can be controlled in predictable ways and skill acquisition facilitated. Several schedules (Gickling & Armstrong, 1978) have been proposed depending on the type of learning task that the student faces. For the task of oral reading, a ratio of 93%–97% known to 3%–7% unknown materials was recommended. The ratio for reading comprehension is specified as 75% known to 25% unknown material, while the recommended ratio for vocabulary drill and practice is 70%–85% known to 15%–30% unknown. In math, the following recommendations were made: for application tasks 85%–100% known and 0%–15% unknown, and in drill and practice of basic math facts 70%–85% known to 15%–30% unknown. General concepts of mastery learning (i.e., instructional, independent, or frustration levels of instruction) are also relevant as students move toward acquiring competency of basic skills. In our folding-in example, student mastery is achieved when the student has completed a predefined set of vocabulary words.

CBA-ID performance measures focus on a student's entering skill level, ensuring that the appropriate ratio of known to unknown materials is maintained (Gickling & Armstrong, 1978; Gickling & Thompson, 1985; Gickling, Shane, & Croskrery 1989; Shapiro, 1992). Accordingly, a student enters an instructional sequence at a relatively high success rate before new and more challenging materials are introduced. Consequently, CBA-ID assessment is more extensive prior to instruction. The teacher may devote 30 minutes or so to identifying known concepts, which becomes the baseline to control the introduction of more challenging content. To facilitate the desired ratio during instruction, ongoing assessment focuses on short-term progress being made through the skill sequence, while still maintaining that optimal level of difficulty. Because the expressed purpose of CBA-ID is to maintain a high rate of student success, measuring student progress becomes a near daily event repeated twice, prior to that day's lesson (pre-test) and upon its completion (post-test). Tests are of short duration, lasting 1 to 3 minutes.

Curriculum-Based Evaluation

Curriculum-based evaluation (CBE) (Howell & Morehead, 1987; Howell, 1986) is an assessment strategy better suited to monitoring student difficulties being experienced during instruction. This curriculum-based model of assessment, in considering a specific curricular task, employs procedures comparable to other task analysis models that assess component subskills that students must learn to perform. A curriculum's scope and sequence is task analyzed, appropriate student objectives are specified, and student progress is monitored as the student moves through that instructional sequence. The discussion here focuses on an interesting contribution to the overall CBA perspective; that is, the importance in understanding student errors.

Curriculum-based evaluation, in comparison to other CBA models, is unique because it considers errors and error patterns (Howell & Morehead, 1987; Howell, 1986). In developing a performance measure that reports on trends in learning, errors are a natural extension to correct responses. Errors indicate a lack of prerequisite knowledge, a misunderstanding of the rules or procedural skills students need to follow, or both. By analyzing student errors and error patterns, the reason or cause for their occurrence may become evident, and it is these component skills that are used to redesign the instructional plan and remediate the misconception (Fuchs, Allinder, Hamlett, & Fuchs, 1990; Gable, Enright, & Hendrickson, 1991). Howell and Morehead (1987) describe a general qualitative process for assessing student errors, regardless of the content area. They suggest that teachers survey student work, and identify and group errors. Next, teachers consider if there is a procedural fault or other basis for the error patterns. Simply put, is there a pattern among the errors? Finally, they test the hypothesis and verify the reason for the errors by constructing tests that reveal the underlying cause. For example, students may subtract

$$\begin{array}{r} 47 \\ \underline{-19} \\ 32 \end{array}$$

This error is often referred to as subtraction in the direction of least resistance. In the one's column, 9 cannot be subtracted from 7 (without getting into negative numbers), but 7 from 9 easily gives 2 as the difference in the one's column. Teachers can use this information and incorporate it within the instructional sequence to remediate the misunderstanding.

Measuring student progress is comparable to other CBA models (Howell & Morehead, 1987; Howell, 1986). After careful deliberation of the curriculum's scope and sequence, student objectives, and instructional task sequence, assessment focuses on observing short-term progress. In this way, CBE is like any other CBA task analysis model. However, there are some additional differences. In addition to the role of errors, CBE requires a closer match between the format used in instruction and the format used in testing. In other words, a teach-to-test perspective is employed. By ensuring that the testing format is closely aligned to the format used in instruction, students are more likely to be successful, and performance measures are viewed as being more valid. The contribution that CBE can make to CBA is a reduction of errors. Errors provide useful information about student difficulties and continue to remain an important source of information that can be measured and used to redesign the instructional plan and improve instructional interactions.

Curriculum-Based Measurement

The match between the curriculum and performance measures is the weakest for **curriculum-based measurement (CBM)** (Deno, 1985, 1986, 1987, 1992; Deno, Marston, & Tindal, 1986; Fuchs, 1986, 1987; Fuchs & Deno, 1991; Fuchs et al., 1982a, 1982b; Shinn & Hubbard, 1992). Surprisingly, CBM is not curriculum-based. CBM is not based on principles of task and subskill analysis, nor does it involve mastery learning on a task-by-task basis. CBM becomes curriculum-based, however, when it is applied against the curriculum to note student progress. This feature of CBM is unique among curriculum-based approaches. Table 8.2 highlights CBM performance measures used to assess reading, spelling, writing, and math skill development.

TABLE 8.2 Curriculum-Based Performance Measures

	Specify the Instructional Goal	Develop Test Materials	Measure Skill Performance
Reading	Goals are derived from current goal-level reading materials that the student is using. If the student is using a specific basal series, for example, then the goal is for the student to read 90 words per minute with no more than 14 errors. If the curriculum is a literature-based reading program, then the student will read 90 words per minute with no more than 14 errors from a graded passage.	Probes are developed by selecting at random a 200-word passage (shorter for younger readers) from the goal-level reading material that the student is using. Sufficient numbers of alternate probes are necessary to prevent a practice effect with the reading materials. Additional guidelines to consider: do not include extended lists, dialogues, and the like.	Student reads short passage orally for 1 minute, then the number of words read correctly and errors are counted.
Spelling	Goals are derived from current spelling curriculum that the student is using. The student will spell 12 words correctly (or 93 letter sequences) in 2 minutes.	Probes are developed by randomly selecting 20 spelling words from the student's goal-level spelling material. Spelling words may also come from the student's reading curriculum.	Student writes words that are dictated orally for 2 minutes. Count the number of words spelled correctly and count the errors. An optional performance measure is to count the number of letter sequences spelled correctly.
Written Expression	The student will write 27 words in 3 minutes.	Probes are developed by using common story starters. Or, have the student complete a topic sentence.	Student writes for 3 minutes (provide 1 minute to develop an outline). The number of words written, spelled correctly, or correct word sequences are counted.
Math	Develop a set of computational problems that are representative of the grade-level curriculum that the student is using. The student will answer 18 problems (or 40 instructional movements) correctly.	Probes are developed by drawing a select number (e.g., 25) of problems (i.e., addition, subtraction, fractions) that are proportionate to the curriculum being used. Alternate forms are necessary to prevent a practice effect. (Problems completed may vary—at the lower elementary level 25 problems, at the upper elementary level 40 problems.)	Student is given 3 to 5 minutes to complete problems. The number of correct problems or correct instructional movements are counted.

Source: Adapted from "Program Development," by L. Fuchs, 1987, *Teaching Exceptional Children, 20,* pp. 42–44.

In comparison to CBA, CBM is regarded as a more flexible and economical performance measure. CBM is more portable and can be readily applied to a wider number of reading, writing, spelling, and math programs (see Table 8.3). The potentially laborious procedures outlined in C-R models are avoided. To illustrate, two teachers in organizing their reading curriculum might identify a series of developmental tasks in word recognition, vocabulary development, phonics, and reading comprehension. To teach these skills, one teacher might select one of the many carefully sequenced basal reading series, available through numerous publishers. A second teacher might teach these skills through a literature-based approach to reading development. The second teacher could also identify a mixture of additional materials to teach those skills listed above. To measure skill development, both teachers would use the same performance measure—a 200-word reading passage to assess oral fluency—to judge not only the student's reading ability but to make a more general inference on the student's overall reading health. While CBM proponents have, in general, documented the appropriateness of these general performance measures to measure oral fluency and reading comprehension, the relation to other reading skills and higher order reading skills is unknown.

Relevant distinctions do exist between CBA and CBM (Shinn et al., 1989). On the one hand, CBA performance measures can be used to verify students' progress within a curriculum sequence that can be carefully task and subskill analyzed. Curriculum-based measurement, on the other hand, is better suited as a vital sign of growth. These subtle distinctions are relevant, because their selection will determine the utility of the data that one collects.

TABLE 8.3 Procedure to Develop and Measure Student Progress Using Curriculum-Based Measurement

Step 1: Determine Current Performance Level
- Select goal-level curriculum that student will be using over the next 3–9 month period.
- Create a pool of test items. Items are drawn from the student's goal-level curriculum (see Table 8.2 for specific performance measures in reading, spelling, writing, and math).

Step 2: Identify Long-Range Goal
- Establish baseline by administering approximately 3 tests and graph results.
- Determine goal at the end of the 3–9 month period and draw the goal line. (Steps 2 and 3 will be discussed later in this chapter.)

Step 3: Measure Performance
- Measure student performance two to three times per week.
- Plot data and note trend line periodically.

Step 4: Evaluate the Performance Database
- Compare trend line to goal line.

Sources: Adapted from "Using Curriculum-Based Assessment Data to Make Instructional Decisions," by C. Blankenship, 1985, *Exceptional Children, 52,* pp. 233–238; *Mainstreaming Students with Learning and Behavior Problems: Techniques for the Classroom Teacher,* by C. Blankenship and S. Lilly, 1981, New York: Holt, Rinehart, & Winston; and *Models of Curriculum-Based Assessment: A Blueprint for Learning,* 3rd ed., by L. Idol, A. Nevin, and P. Paolucci-Whitcomb, 1999, Austin, TX: Pro-Ed.

An Integrated Approach to Curriculum-Based Assessment

Curriculum-based approaches to assess performance can be used to facilitate a number of decisions. Teachers can use these data to determine prereferral services and program eligibility, evaluate program efficacy, monitor student progress, and determine skill mastery (Deno, 1986; Deno et al., 1986; Fuchs et al., 1982a, 1982b; Fuchs, 1986; Germann & Tindal, 1985; Marston & Magnusson, 1985; Marston et al., 1984; Marston, Tindal, & Deno, 1984; Shinn & Habedank, 1992; Shinn & Marston, 1985; Shinn et al., 1993, 1997; Tindal et al., 1985; Ysseldyke & Thurlow, 1984; Ysseldyke et al., 1983). What these decisions share in common are the failed expectations that teachers have for students to develop a number of essential skills to reach an expected performance level. An integrated approach to CBA assessment, which would include CBM, would provide teachers with a variety of strategies and techniques to measure student performance relative to these decisions. The specific strategies and techniques that a teacher would select would change as the instructional task, the nature of the instructional sequence, or teacher's planning needs changed.

In developing an integrated plan to CBA, teachers would first review the contributions that specific CBA models would provide to measure student performance at four instructional phases—prior to instruction, as a measure of ongoing student performance, as a student acquires the target skill, and long-term retention. While all models discussed in this chapter provide some degree of measure of student performance, there are relevant distinctions. CBA-ID, for example, places greater emphasis and effort prior to instruction, to establish the desired ratio of known to unknown materials. On the other hand, C-Rs and CBMs approaches' interest in entry skill level is limited to establishing baseline performance—a general index of entry-level skills prior to instruction. Additional distinctions between C-R and CBM also exist. Baseline in C-R assessment is used to note entry-level skill performance relative to student mastery on a short-term objective. CBM baseline is used to establish an entry-level performance relative to a long-term goal and to note performance trends. Finally in CBE (error analysis), entry-level performance is not relevant prior to instruction.

To measure ongoing student performance, skill acquisition, and long-term retention, relevant distinctions among CBA models are also evident. In CBA-ID, ongoing performance assessment is intended to control the introduction of new and unknown materials. Measuring student progress becomes a near daily event, repeated twice, prior to instruction (pretest) and after that day's lesson (post-test). This provides an index of daily growth as well as a measure of growth over a period of time. Ongoing assessment progresses incrementally toward the broader objective and student mastery.

Ongoing C-R and CBM assessment is frequent (two to three times per week) and evenly distributed across the week. However, ongoing C-R and CBM assessment serves different purposes. Ongoing C-R assessment is intended to monitor skill acquisition. A teacher becomes more vigilant as he or she views the student approaching skill mastery. Measuring student performance becomes better matched to anticipated performance mastery and the beginning of the next instructional objective. C-R's strength is its ability to provide information on short-term progress, but this comes at the expense of long-term progress. Ongoing CBM assessment is intended to develop a learning trend and compare this trend to the long-term goal. CBM's strength is to measure long-term progress, which comes at the expense of not being able to understand short-term progress. Finally, ongoing CBE (error analysis) focuses on identifying common errors, error patterns, and a qualitative understanding of the reason(s) for student errors.

Developing a Performance Database

An integrated approach to curriculum-based assessment needs to also consider the development of a performance database. A database ensures reliable measures of student performance are obtained as a student moves through an instructional sequence, validating student progress, skill mastery, and long-term retention. A database is the key to formative analysis (Deno, 1986), permitting teachers to note observable trends and providing the basis to make informed and valid decisions. A performance database also provides teachers with a practical method to improve their ability to plan instruction and monitor instructional interactions. To develop a performance database, teachers need to directly observe and repeatedly measure student performance, graph and visually inspect the data, establish goals, and interpret trends.

Direct and Repeated Measurements. Developing a performance database depends on probes, which are frequently repeated to directly assess student behaviors. Teachers develop specific testing materials using the procedures discussed earlier and select a performance index that provides a measure appropriate to the instructional decisions that need to be made. For example, teachers can measure the number of problems answered correctly; the number of letter sequences spelled correctly (spelling); and the number of instructional movements (math), percentages, or response rates (i.e., number of responses in *x* minutes). These can all be used to measure progress and determine trends.

Teachers will measure or probe student performance at various times. A **probe** is a measure of student performance specific at a point in time. Probes are repeatedly administered as a student moves through an instructional sequence and are also used to ensure long-term retention. The number of times student performance is probed depends on the specific CBA model selected. The amount of time necessary to administer a probe is typically 3 to 5 minutes. Teachers will probe student standing or progress according to the schedule suggested by the specific CBA model. For example, CBA-ID probes occur near daily and two times per day, C-R and CBM are two to three times per week, while CBE are conducted on an as needed basis. In order to prevent students from remembering a specific test item or to prevent a testing effect, teachers will need to develop a sufficiently large test pool to draw on at random. Probes are meant to be simple, efficient, and economical. The appeal of curriculum-based performance measures is self-evident. Probes also need to be administered under the same standard testing conditions to ensure reliability.

Graphing Student Performance. Unlike norm-referenced performance measures, curriculum-based performance measures provide teachers with numerical data that not only have greater fidelity to the curricular task being measured but are also more sensitive to changes in student growth. To depict these changes, graphs are often used to visually depict trends in the data (Fuchs, 1987; Gable, Arllen, Evans, & Whinnery, 1997; Gast & Tawney, 1984; Tindal, 1987; White & Harding, 1980). Visually graphing student performance presents several major advantages over typical tabular recording methods (Deno, 1992). The graph references not only one's learning history and current standing but can be used to determine a prevailing trend in the data, which is essential to evaluating whether a student will reach a desired goal within a predicted period of time. Visually representing data has additional benefits. Teachers can compare the relative benefits of one instructional paradigm versus another. Teachers can also compare a student's standing to his or her peers by integrating a normative comparison. Finally, graphs can be used by teachers to facilitate communication among teachers and parents or could be used to motivate students.

A number of guidelines and conventions have been developed to illustrate how to graph learning or performance trends (Fuchs, 1987; Gast & Tawney, 1984; Tindal, 1987; White & Harding, 1980). Typically, equal-interval graph paper is used to visually chart numerical data. Logarithmic graph paper can also be used. Logarithmic graphs are typically used to chart those behaviors that occur at extremely high or low frequencies (e.g., behavioral [social-behavioral] responses or vocational [assembly] skills) and when dramatic changes in response rates are anticipated.

Figure 8.1 highlights the various conventions used to graph student performance on equal-interval paper. On the ***x*-axis (abscissa),** tic marks are scaled to represent 35 weeks of instruction. On the ***y*-axis (ordinate),** tic marks are scaled to indicate growth. In this case, we are counting and plotting Number of Behaviors. Both the *x*- and *y*-axis are labeled with a short, self-descriptive label.

Within the field, a number of conventions are used to record probes and visually display performance data. These conventions permit easy and speedy interpretations of student performance trends. Notice the vertical lines, which represent **phase changes.** A **phase** refers to a period of time where a defined and consistent instructional arrangement or set of arrangements is being used to facilitate skill acquisition. After an initial brief baseline period, two intervention periods were recorded: Intervention A and B. It is during these periods that two

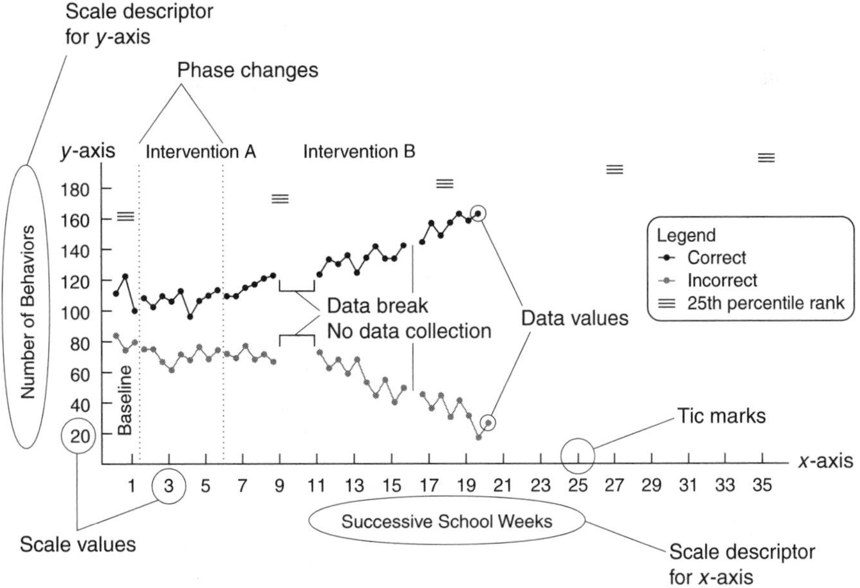

FIGURE 8.1 Components of a performance graph.

different instructional arrangements were compared to facilitate skill acquisition for our student. The relative performance of these interventions was also graphed. A legend provides the teacher with a key to visually note performance changes. Two types of behaviors were recorded: correct and incorrect responses. Over an approximate 20-week period, trends are noted in the database from which decisions can be made. The time-series data path, which changes as a function of time, is graphed across the field. Finally, the legend provides a normative comparison, referencing our student's progress against a comparison group of same grade-level peers. The legend also notes the bottom 25th percentile rank for that particular grade. This grade-level comparison provides a normative reference to compare our target student to a comparable group of same grade-level peers at the beginning of the academic year and at the end of each quarter throughout the remainder of the academic year.

All CBA models can visually display student performance (Fuchs, 1987; Idol et al., 1999; Tindal, 1987). However, only C-R, CBE, and CBM possess unique features whereby visually graphing student performance may better facilitate a teacher's ability to prepare an instructional plan and monitor instructional interactions. Figure 8.1 illustrates a performance chart incorporating CBE and CBM techniques, while Figure 8.2 incorporates many of the same visual and graphical conventions to illustrate C-R student mastery.

Making Data-Based Decisions. Frequent probes create the database and provide the basis for the decisions that follow. To develop that database, the focus is on establishing baseline performance, determining a starting point, and developing a reference from which future decisions can be made. As the database develops, other decisions can also be made.

Various guidelines have been proposed to establish baseline (Deno, 1986; Gable et al., 1997; Idol et al., 1999; Tindal, 1987; White & Harding, 1980). **Baseline** is a measure of student's prerequisite or entering knowledge. Various standards have been proposed as to the number of scores necessary to establish a baseline (Gable et al., 1997; White & Harding, 1980). However, this number will vary depending on the CBA model selected and other issues related to content domain being tested, fluctuations in the data, and the like. Task analysis models (e.g., C-R, CBA-ID, and CBE) typically rely on one probe (i.e., score) to establish baseline, while CBM typically employs three **data points.** Figures 8.2 and 8.3 illustrate this difference between CBA/task analysis models and CBM. In Figure 8.2, C-R baseline is used to establish an entry performance level relative to skill mastery, while in Figure 8.3 baseline is used to not only establish entry-level performance but also is, more importantly, used to establish long-term goals and note trends being observed to reach those goals. Regardless of which model is selected, all CBA models index a student's entering performance level against which to judge future academic progress.

In addition to establishing entry-level performance, the emerging performance database can also help establish goals and make judgments relative to student progress. All models of CBA establish a criterion goal-level (Deno, 1986; Gable et al., 1997; Idol et al., 1999; Tindal, 1987; White & Harding, 1980). The differences between CBA/task analysis models and CBM are also illustrated in Figures 8.2 and 8.4. Only CBM employs a goal line. A **goal line** is a visual representation of the rate of progress necessary between baseline and goal attainment. To draw the goal line (refer to Figure 8.4), first determine the median performance observed during baseline and mark an X on the performance graph at the next scheduled testing session. Next, determine the goal to be reached in the desired period of time and mark an X within the data field at the desired performance level, at the appropriate intersection of the x- and y-axes. By con-

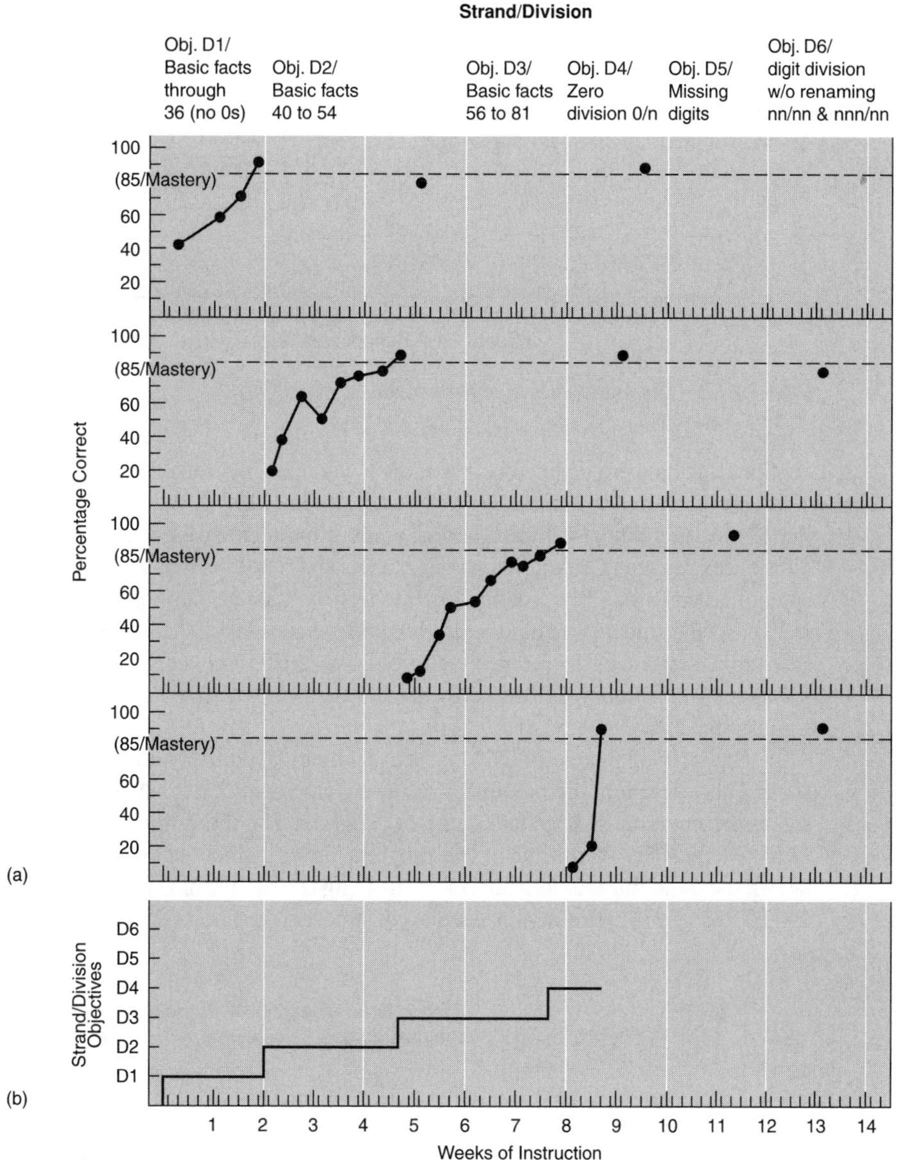

FIGURE 8.2 An example of a criterion-referenced performance graph.

necting the Xs with a straight line, a goal line is established—a visual representation of the rate of progress necessary to reach the target in the prescribed period of time. In Figure 8.4, our goal is to have our student reach the 25th percentile rank for words read correctly by the end of the academic year—a ranking comparable to low average relative to the student's grade-level peers.

After establishing baseline and determining either a criterion performance level (CBA/ task analysis models) or goal and goal line (CBM), instruction and ongoing data collection

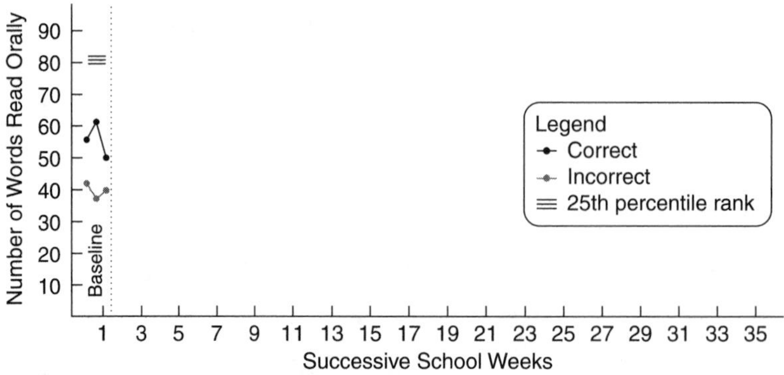

FIGURE 8.3 Illustrating baseline performance.

continue and data are graphed in accordance with the CBA model (Deno, 1986; Gable et al., 1997; Idol et al., 1999; Tindal, 1987; White & Harding, 1980). With direct, repeated, and continued measurements of student performance, a more extensive database is developed. The differences between CBA/task analysis models and CBM become more pronounced with the emerging database. CBA/task analysis models continue to monitor progress toward the objective. As the student reaches the desired performance level, the student moves on in the instructional sequence, from objective to objective. These concepts are illustrated in Figure 8.2(a) and (b). Similarly, CBM performance data also note ongoing student progress, which is illustrated in Figure 8.5.

One striking feature of CBM is its capacity to facilitate a number of instructional decisions. These decisions are possible with the development of a trend line. A **trend line** is a visual representation of a student's rate of progress. The trend line provides immediate and formative feedback on the rate of that progress. Several guidelines have been suggested to establish the trend line and to interpret its meaning (Deno, 1986; Gable et al., 1997; Idol et al., 1999; Tindal, 1987). The steps needed to construct a trend line are illustrated in Figure 8.6. The

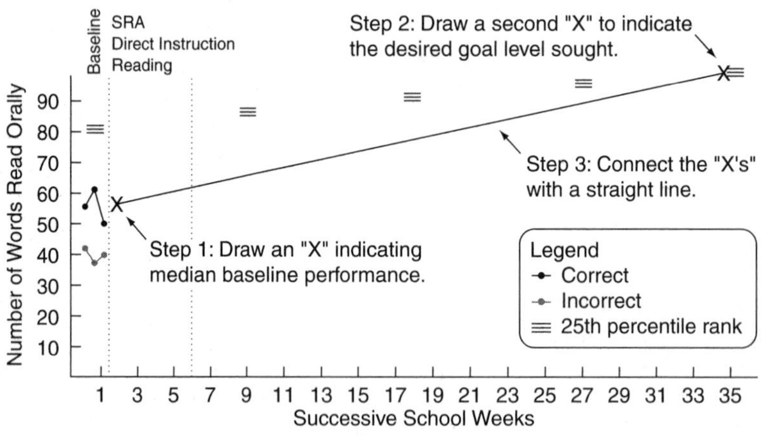

FIGURE 8.4 Developing a goal line.

Baseline
SRA
Direct Instruction
Reading
Number of Words Read Orally
90
80
70
60
50
40
30
20
10
Goal line
Legend
Correct
Incorrect
25th percentile rank
1 3 5 7 9 11 13 15 17 19 21 23 25 27 29 31 33 35
Successive School Weeks

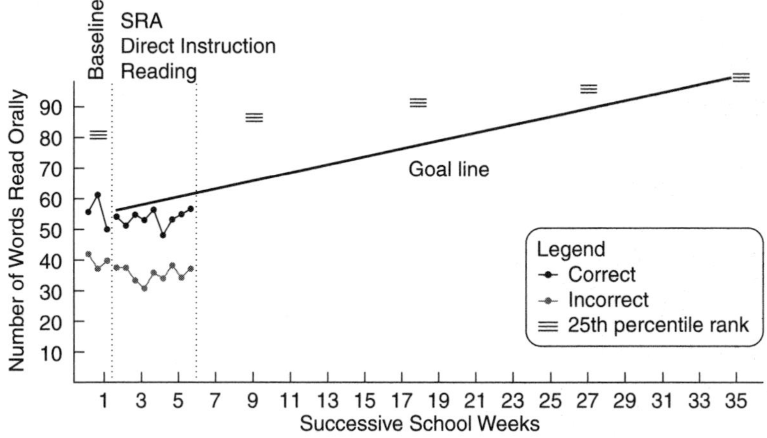

FIGURE 8.5 Developing a performance database.

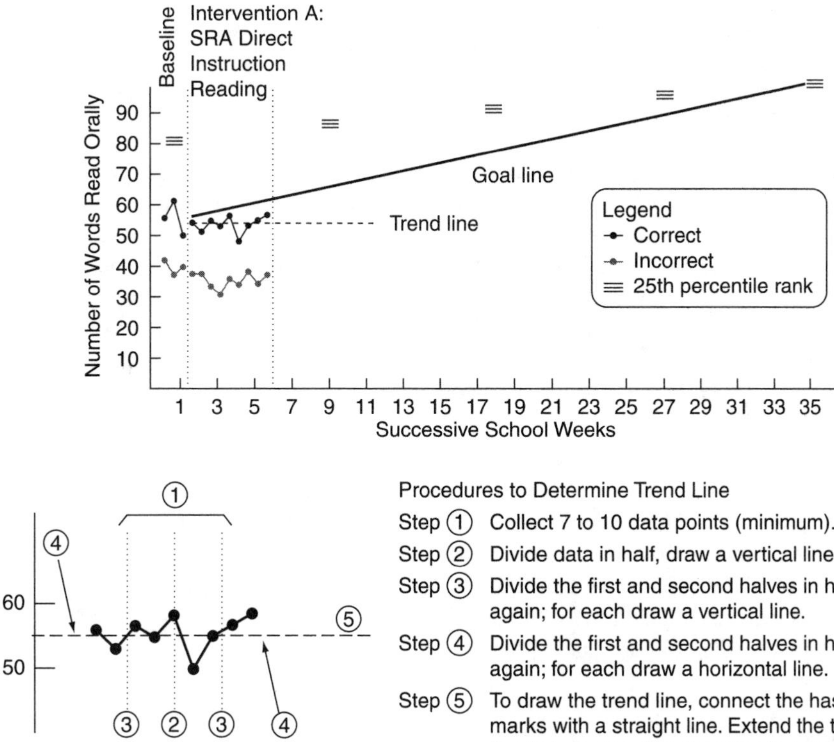

Baseline
Intervention A:
SRA Direct
Instruction
Reading
Number of Words Read Orally
90
80
70
60
50
40
30
20
10
Goal line
Trend line
Legend
Correct
Incorrect
25th percentile rank
1 3 5 7 9 11 13 15 17 19 21 23 25 27 29 31 33 35
Successive School Weeks
①
④
60
50
⑤
③ ② ③ ④

Procedures to Determine Trend Line

Step ① Collect 7 to 10 data points (minimum).

Step ② Divide data in half, draw a vertical line.

Step ③ Divide the first and second halves in half again; for each draw a vertical line.

Step ④ Divide the first and second halves in half again; for each draw a horizontal line.

Step ⑤ To draw the trend line, connect the hash marks with a straight line. Extend the trend line to help visualize the rate of progress.

Step ⑥ Note ascending, descending, or stable trend line. If trend is descending, a change in instruction is suggested. If stable trend is evident, then determine trend line for incorrect responses. If incorrect responses are ascending, then a change in instruction is suggested.

FIGURE 8.6 Developing a trend line.

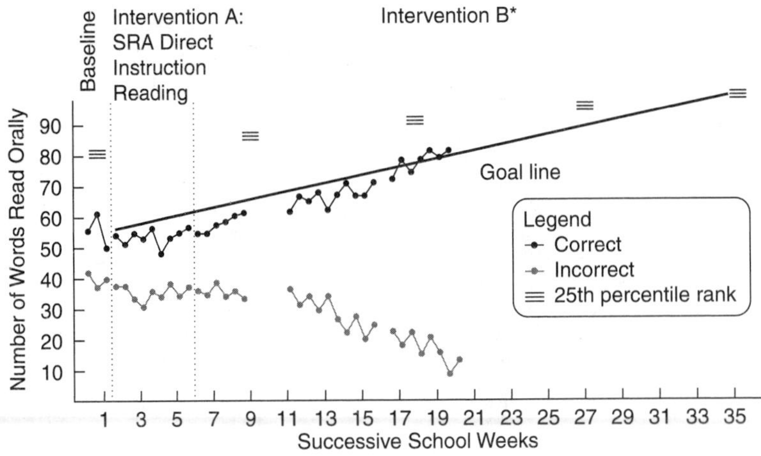

*Intervention A *plus* peer tutoring (unknown words, drill and practice of most frequent words, and common letter sequences missed based on error analysis) *and* parental-directed reading assignments (30 min./5 five times per week).

FIGURE 8.7 Curriculum-based measures as a dependent variable.

trend line can be used to verify that the rate of progress being made toward the instructional objective is sufficient to reach the desired goal within the prescribed time frame. If the slope of the trend line falls below the goal line, a change in teaching (i.e., phase change) is suggested.

With the development of a trend line, CBM introduces a new and unique performance index: a visual dependent variable that permits teachers not only to compare current rate of learning to the goal line but also to compare the relative benefits of one or more independent variables to one another. That is, the trend line permits teachers to compare the efficacy of one instructional arrangement with that of another. This concept is illustrated in Figure 8.7. We noted in Figure 8.6 and its related discussion that the trend line for our reading program, which is heavily based on SRA's Direct Instruction curriculum, was not sufficient to reach our desired goal. We introduce a phase change, where we modify the current instructional arrangement to include a number of additional strategies. In graphing the progress being made to reach our goal, we plot a new set of data to reflect the student's growth with the new intervention. From Figure 8.7, it is evident that the rate of learning will intersect and then cross the goal line. While it is premature, the rate of learning may lead us to reach our goal earlier than originally planned.

Summary

During the course of the academic year, teachers are faced with a number of decisions. Teachers may have to decide on the need for prereferral and consultative services. Teachers may have to decide whether a student is eligible for services. Teachers may have to evaluate both the efficacy of a particular program and the comparative benefits between one instructional program versus that of another. Teachers may have to monitor student progress within an instructional sequence. Finally, teachers may also have to determine that the student has reached a desired performance skill level. What teachers need are the tools to make these decisions. Teachers have traditionally relied on norm-referenced testing as the measure. Curriculum-based assessment, broadly defined, provides teachers with a set of tools that are more closely aligned to the school curriculum.

An integrated approach to curriculum-based assessment provides teachers with a variety of strategies and techniques that one can call on to meet specific instructional needs. Curriculum-based assessment provides teachers with the tools not only to measure and evaluate student progress but to improve our ability to plan effective instruction and monitor instructional interactions. Collectively, these techniques and strategies allow teachers to measure student performance, develop a performance database, and make decisions regarding student progress. Most importantly, the performance database empowers teachers to consider pedagogy as research. Teacher-directed research represents the next era in assessing student performance.

REFERENCES

Blankenship, C. (1985). Using curriculum-based assessment data to make instructional decisions. *Exceptional Children, 52,* 233–238.

Blankenship, C., & Lilly, S. (1981). *Mainstreaming students with learning and behavior problems: Techniques for the classroom teacher.* New York: Holt, Rinehart, & Winston.

Deno, S. (1985). Curriculum-based measurement. The emerging alternative. *Exceptional Children, 52,* 219–232.

Deno, S. (1986). Formative evaluation of individual student programs: A new role of school psychologist. *School Psychology Review, 15,* 358–374.

Deno, S. (1987). Curriculum-based measurement. *Teaching Exceptional Children, 20,* 41–42.

Deno, S. (1992). The nature and development of curriculum-based measurement. *Preventing School Failure, 36,* 5–10.

Deno, S., Marston, D., & Tindal, G. (1986). Direct and frequent curriculum-based measurement: An alternative for educational decision-making. *Special Services in the Schools, 2,* 5–27.

Fuchs, L. (1986). Monitoring progress among mildly handicapped pupils: Review of current practice and research. *Remedial and Special Education, 7,* 5–12.

Fuchs, L. (1987). Program development. *Teaching Exceptional Children, 20,* 42–44.

Fuchs, L., Allinder, R., Hamlett, C., & Fuchs, D. (1990). Analysis of spelling curricula and teacher's skills in identifying phonetic error types. *Remedial and Special Education, 11,* 42–52.

Fuchs, L., & Deno, S. (1991). Paradigmatic distinctions between instructionally relevant measurement models. *Exceptional Children, 58,* 488–499.

Fuchs, L., Fuchs, D., & Deno, S. (1982a). Linking assessment to instructional intervention: An overview. *School Psychology Review, 15,* 318–323.

Fuchs, L., Fuchs, D., & Deno, S. (1982b). Reliability and validity of curriculum-based informal reading inventories. *Reading Research Quarterly, 18,* 6–25.

Gable, R., Arllen, N., Evans, W., & Whinnery, K. (1997). Strategies for evaluating collaborative mainstream instruction: "Let the data be our guide." *Preventing School Failure, 41,* 153–158.

Gable, R., Enright, B., & Hendrickson, J. (1991). A practical model for curriculum-based assessment and instruction in arithmetic. *Teaching Exceptional Children, 24*(1), 6–9.

Gast, D., & Tawney, J. (1984). The visual analysis of graphic data. In J. Tawney and D. Gast (Eds.), *Single subject research in special education.* Columbus, OH: Merrill.

Germann, G., & Tindal, G. (1985). An application of curriculum-based assessment: The use of direct and repeated measurement. *Exceptional Children, 52,* 244–265.

Gickling, E., & Armstrong, D. (1978). Levels of instructional difficulty as related to on-task behavior, task completion, and comprehension. *Journal of Learning Disabilities, 11,* 559–566.

Gickling, E., Shane, R., & Croskrery, K. (1989). Developing mathematics skills in low-achieving high school students through curriculum-based assessment. *School Psychology Review, 18,* 344–355.

Gickling, E., & Thompson, V. (1985). A personal view of curriculum-based assessment. *Exceptional Children, 52,* 205–218.

Howell, K. (1986). Direct assessment of academic performance. *School Psychology Review,15,* 324–335.

Howell, K., & Morehead, M. (1987). *Curricular-based evaluation for special and remedial education.* Columbus, OH: Merrill.

Idol, L., Nevin, A., & Paolucci-Whitcomb, P. (1999). *Models of curriculum-based assessment: A blueprint for learning* (3rd ed.). Austin, TX: Pro-Ed.

Marston, D., & Magnusson, D. (1985). Implementing curriculum-based measurement in special and regular education settings. *Exceptional Children, 52,* 266–276.

Marston, D., Mirkin, P., & Deno, S. (1984). Curriculum-based measurement of academic skills: An alternative to traditional screening referral and identification of learning disabled students. *Journal of Special Education, 8,* 109–118.

Marston, D., Tindal, G., & Deno, S. (1984). Eligibility for learning disability services: A direct and repeated measurement approach. *Exceptional Children, 50,* 554–556.

Shapiro, E. (1992). Use of Gickling's model of curriculum-based assessment to improve reading in elementary age students. *School Psychology Review, 21,* 168–176.

Shinn, M., & Habedank, L. (1992). Curriculum-based measurement in special education problem identification and certification decisions. *Preventing School Failure, 36,* 11–15.

Shinn, M., & Hubbard, D. (1992). Curriculum-based measurement and problem-solving assessment: Basic procedures and outcomes. *Focus on Exceptional Children, 24,* 1–20.

Shinn, M., & Marston, D. (1985). Differentiating mildly handicapped, low achieving and regular education students: A curriculum-based approach. *Remedial and Special Education, 6,* 31–38.

Shinn, M., Powell-Smith, K., Good, R., & Baker, S. (1993). Using curriculum-based measurement to identify potential candidates for reintegration into general education. *Journal of Special Education, 27,* 202–221.

Shinn, M., Powell-Smith, K., Good, R., & Baker, S. (1997). The effects of reintegration into general education reading instruction for students with mild disabilities. *Exceptional Children, 64,* 59–79.

Shinn, M., Rosenfield, S., & Knutson, N. (1989). Curriculum-based assessment: A comparison of models. *School Psychology Review, 18,* 299–316.

Tindal, G. (1987). Graphing performance. *Teaching Exceptional Children, 20,* 44–46.

Tindal, G., Wesson, C., Deno, S., Germann, G., & Mirkin, P. (1985). The Pine County model for special education delivery: A data-based system. In T. Kratchowill (Ed.), *Advances in school psychology* (Vol. 4). Hillsdale, NJ: Lawrence Erlbaum.

White, O., & Harding, N. (1980). *Exceptional teaching.* Columbus, OH: Merrill.

Ysseldyke, J., & Thurlow, M. (1984). Assessment practices in special education: Adequacy and appropriateness. *Educational Psychologist, 9,* 132–136.

Ysseldyke, J., Thurlow, M., Graden, J., Wesson, C., Algozzine, B., & Deno, S. (1983). Generalizations from five years of research on assessment and decision making: The University of Minnesota Institute. *Exceptional Education Quarterly, 4,* 75–93.

CHAPTER

9 Measuring Responses Through Direct Observation

CYNTHIA N. SCHLOSS
Bloomsburg University

OBJECTIVES

After reading this chapter, you will be able to

1. Describe two standards in collecting samples of behavior
2. Describe the necessity for a strong relationship between the behavior being observed and the purpose for an assessment
3. Describe why the condition of an observation is important in the assessment process
4. Describe the difference between verbal behavior and actual practice
5. Describe the seven direct observation procedures
6. Describe the different procedures in determining interobserver reliability when conducting direct observations

KEY TERMS

ABCs (p. 175)
anecdotal recording (p. 174)
behavioral samples (p. 171)
chaining (p. 178)
conditions of observation (p. 172)
direct observation (p. 181)
duration (p. 179)
frequency (p. 175)
interobserver reliability (p. 180)
interval (p. 179)
latency (p. 179)
observational measures (p. 172)
observational recording (p. 174)
permanent product (p. 177)
rate (p. 175)
reliability (p. 180)
task analysis (p. 178)

Assessment is little more than the collection of **behavioral samples** under well-described or standardized conditions. Essential to the usefulness of the assessment is the manner in which the behavior is sampled and the conditions under which the sample is taken (McLoughlin & Lewis, 1994). Behavioral samples that are not related to the judgments being made do little to support the judgments. Samples that are closely related to the judgment but taken under unique circumstances are also ineffective in yielding valid conclusions. Prior to reviewing observational assessment methods, we will consider these two standards.

Behavioral Samples

An essential standard for developing valid **observational measures** involves the relationship between the behavior being observed and the purpose for the assessment. The closer the assessment procedure to real-life conditions about which one wishes to make a judgment, the more valid the procedure (Schloss & Smith, 1999). For example, National Football League (NFL) scouts use a number of tests to assess potential players. These include time in the 40-yard dash, vertical leap, bench press, squat, and reaction time. Though these measures form a general basis for subsequent decisions, they are minimally effective in predicting talent. Bruce Smith, the career sack leader in the NFL was not among the strongest players in the league, and his reaction time was not among the quickest. Walter Payton, the career rushing leader, was not even close to being the fastest man to play the game. Finally, Jerry Rice, the career pass reception leader, was overshadowed by a number of players in vertical leap and speed.

Why do these measures fail to predict performance? In part, because the sample of behavior is not directly matched to the objective. While quickness and strength are important for sacking quarterbacks, numerous attributes also contribute to performance: height, weight, motivation, conditioning, intelligence, balance, and so on. While additional speed would have helped Walter Payton, his desire, strength, knack for locating holes in the defense, and durability contributed to his record-setting ability. Finally, catching passes requires more than speed and vertical leaping ability. Concentration, quickness, communication, and so on all contribute to performance.

Given the complexity of the preceding skills and the number of attributes affecting performance, the most effective measure would be the direct observation of the behavior in question. The best prediction of sacking ability in the NFL may be the number of sacks at the collegiate level. The best measure of rushing ability may be the number of yards rushed during preseason games. The best measure of pass reception capability may be found in trials against a legitimate defense.

The same principle applies to children with disabilities in the regular education setting. The best measure of a child's ability to establish friendships is the number of young people with whom the child interacts. A valid test of a child's ability to follow class rules is to observe whether he or she complies with rules throughout the day. The test of whether an adolescent is able to read a manual is to record variations from the text as he or she reads orally.

Conditions of Observations

Astute readers may have questioned why, on occasion, the most capable collegiate players are not strong contributors to professional teams. The answer lies in the conditions under which observations are made. While the skills of sacking the quarterback, running with the football, and catching passes are the same at collegiate and professional levels, the **conditions of observation** change substantially. Professional players are all top athletes, and the teams are more uniformly strong in comparison to collegiate players and teams. Premier rushers in college may have been able to take advantage of slower and weaker defenses. When moving to the professional level, the consistent high quality of opposing teams may keep them from excelling. Conversely, collegiate passers are not all uniformly capable. An apparently less proficient pass receiver in college may excel as a professional because more passes are catchable as a consequence of playing with a better quarterback.

The same problem applies in assessing educational performance in schools. Judging that a child is free from tantrums at home may not reflect the likelihood of tantrums in school. At home, the child's mother or father may short-circuit disruptive social behavior by providing attention at key times. In school, the teacher may not be as astute. Also, the presence of a number of children competing for attention may make such interventions impractical. Similarly, a youth who consistently completes homework in high school may be less diligent in college. Again, the difference may be explained by conditions associated with college and high school life. In high school, the youth may be scheduled into mandatory study halls where teachers supervise homework. College generally includes open campuses void of adult supervision. College life also presents numerous temptations (parties) that may compete with study time.

Verbal Behavior Versus Actual Practice

One of the most frequently mistaken approaches is to make decisions based on verbal or written behavior that bears little relationship to the target skill or attribute (Schloss & Smith, 1998). In doing so we violate both the principles of similarity in behavioral samples and conditions discussed previously.

An example of how verbal behavior differs from actual performance can be observed when asking individuals about their slot machine winnings in casinos. Based on the laws of probability, it is extremely unlikely for a person who makes frequent wagers with a "one-armed bandit" to come out ahead. Casino operators precisely program the machines to pay out approximately 7% less money than is paid in. A customer may beat the odds and win over brief periods of time or on infrequent wagers. However, the more frequent the wagering, the more likely the return rate will approach 93% of all dollars wagered. Despite this assurance, rarely will you ever hear people talk about losing money. A survey of patrons would suggest that almost everyone is a winner. In fact, almost everyone is a loser, at least in the long run.

I once participated in a multidisciplinary staffing for an autistic adolescent who frequently engaged in echolalia, which is the rote repetition of the last phrase uttered by the last speaker in a conversation. For example, if I were to say "How was your vacation?," the young man would say "your vacation." If I said "Did you work hard at the bank?," he would say "work hard at the bank."

During the staffing, the school nurse reported that her assessment indicated that the young man had aggressive urges. This puzzled the family members and professionals at the meeting, as the young man was very gentle and never prone to incite conflict. Their puzzlement was resolved when one of the family members asked how the nurse was able to observe aggressive urges.

The school nurse indicated that she did not actually observe aggressive behavior. Also, because of his severely limited verbal ability, she was not able to discuss emotional reactions with him. In the absence of these direct approaches, she showed the youth a picture of a red-faced man with clenched fists. She asked, "Does this feel good?" to which he responded, "feel good."

As can be easily seen from this example, the nurse actually produced a sample of echolalia, not aggressive urges. She could have shown the youth a picture of a man walking on coals, sunning on the beach, kissing a girlfriend, or recovering from surgery and gotten the exact same response to the question, "Does this feel good?" Because the sample of behavior was verbal, she actually assessed echo speech. To assess aggression, she would have to observe the young man in a provoking situation and judge what he did, not what he said.

Assessments of individuals with disabilities should be consistent with the objectives being assessed (Schloss & Smith, 1998). Written behavior should be included in the assessment only when the objective of the assessment is to judge writing behavior or concepts that can be expressed directly in writing. Consistent with this principle, written or spoken assessments would be appropriate for objectives that include the following verbs:

write	select	describe
state	depict	discuss

Direct observation would be more appropriate for objectives that include actual performance. Verbs in an objective that suggest direct observation include

place	point to	assemble
circle	type	remove

Observational Recording

The preceding section provides a rationale for observing a student's behavior. It is appropriate for evaluating progress toward objectives that students will develop, perform, or demonstrate specific skills. Direct observation procedures must be consistent with the objective being evaluated. Seven **observational recording** procedures are described in the following sections and sample forms are provided.

Anecdotal Form

Anecdotal recording is a written narrative describing critical incidents focusing on entries limited to specific types of events (Schloss & Smith, 1998). Anecdotal records are used for four key reasons:

1. Confirm the existence of a problem
2. Reveal conditions that promote a behavior
3. Indicate events that affect the behavior
4. Identify positive behaviors that would substitute the problem behavior

The Anecdotal Recording Form (see Figure 9.1) is intended to facilitate anecdotal recording.

FIGURE 9.1 Anecdotal recording form.

Student's Name: ______________________ Date: ____________

Recorder's Name: ______________________ Time: ____________

Student Behavior	Setting	Individuals Present	Reaction

ABC Anecdotal Form

Another method of recording anecdotal information is to record the antecedents, behavior, and consequences **(ABCs)** of a student's behavior. ABCs can be used to explain behavior by its development and change (Cartwright, Cartwright, & Ward, 1995). Anecdotal information is entered on the ABC Anecdotal Form (see Figure 9.2) each time a student engages in a behavior. The objective event that immediately preceded the behavior is noted as the antecedent. Recording the event that immediately followed the behavior completes the consequence section. Individuals involved in the situation are also identified on the form.

Frequency Response

Frequency response can be easily recorded. It is a convenient and appropriate activity for observing repetitious behaviors. Simply making a mark on a piece of paper each time a specified behavior is performed within a specific time frame can identify levels of performance. Markings are totaled to determine the **frequency** of the specified behavior. Teachers can record these behaviors using a counter, plain paper, or a simple form (see Figure 9.3) that will accurately report findings in a logical fashion. Frequency response data are not always comparable if the observation times vary. They can be converted very easily into a rate of response (Schloss & Schloss, 1985) that will provide comparable data. The **rate** of response can be determined by dividing the reported frequency by the amount of time observed. For

FIGURE 9.2 ABC anecdotal form.

Student's Name: ______________________ Date: ______________

Recorder's Name: ______________________ Setting: ______________

Antecedent	Behavior	Consequence	Individuals Involved

FIGURE 9.3 Frequency response rate.

Student's Name: ______________________ Date: ______________

Recorder's Name: ______________________ Setting: ______________

Time			Behavior	Frequency	Rate
Beginning	Ending	Total			

example, a student taps his fingers 40 times in a 5-minute time period. This would yield a rate of 8 finger taps per minute:

$$\text{Rate} = \frac{\text{Frequency}}{\text{Time}} = \frac{40}{5} = 8.0$$

The time is determined by subtracting the ending time from the beginning time.

Permanent Product Analysis

A **permanent product** analysis is performed to determine the number of correct items a student can complete in a set amount of time. This is a fairly reliable method to observe a student's behavior (Schloss & Smith, 1998). Figure 9.4 illustrates a sample Permanent Product Analysis Form. There are four elements used in this analysis: the behavior or product, time necessary to complete the product, number correct, and the rate. In recording permanent products, it is important that the demands of the product be constant. For example, if a student is wiping tables in a cafeteria, the demands would be similar in size and comparable. If the student also wiped down kitchen counters, there would be a difference in the area to be wiped. It is important that the recorder define the expected outcome prior to the analysis in order to make appropriate comparisons.

FIGURE 9.4 Permanent product analysis.

Student's Name: ______________________ Date: ______________

Recorder's Name: ______________________ Academic Area: ______________

Outcome Defined: ______________________

____

Time			Product	Number Correct	Rate
Beginning	Ending	Total			

Task Analysis

Task analysis is a procedure for reducing complex tasks into smaller steps for the purpose of assessment and systematic instruction. Functional assessments can be conducted by observing a student performing a specific task and recording his or her behavior. A system of prompts is used to identify the support necessary for the student to achieve each step of the task. Instruction of the task can be introduced systematically to incorporate instruction into the assessment process (Snell & Brown, 2000). Each student is taught the next step contingent on the mastery of the prior step. This is called forward **chaining.** This is continued until all steps are mastered, and the student can accomplish the task without hesitation or error. Backward chaining is the same process in reverse order. You begin systematic instruction with the last step, move to the second to the last step, and then proceed to the final step without the student hesitating or experiencing error. Figure 9.5 illustrates a sample Task Analysis Form used for collecting task analysis data. The identified task, specific steps, and system of prompts used are key elements noted on the form.

FIGURE 9.5 Task analysis form.

Task: ______________________________

Student's Name: ______________________________

Recorder's Name: ______________________________

Date: ______________________________

I: Independent
IV: Indirect verbal
DV: Direct verbal
P: Physical
✓: Completed with prompt

Steps	Prompt Used					
	I	IV	DV	P		

Duration and Latency Analysis

When a teacher is concerned about the amount of time a student takes to perform a behavior, **duration** recording maybe of use. Analyzing the amount of time the student is engaged in a behavior may be of assistance when it is necessary to decrease or increase the duration of behavior. Often the amount of time it takes to begin the behavior is of concern. This time period is referred to as **latency.** For example, a student has difficulty in completing homework assignments. The teacher recorded the amount of time spent in doing the assignment and found that it was minimal. When recording the time spent in beginning the assignment from the time it was made, the teacher recorded a much larger time span. In this analysis, the teacher identified a latency problem in completing the assignment. Figure 9.6 illustrates a form that records both duration and latency data.

Interval Recording

Interval recording will note the occurrence of a behavior in a given time period (Choate, Enright, Miller, Poteet, & Rakes, 1995). Once the behavior is identified, the length of the **interval** needs to be determined. Frequency of the behavior is a key element in determining the length. Short intervals (seconds) are best used for frequently occurring behaviors. Longer intervals (minutes) are used with those that are infrequent. Recording of observed behavior can occur in one of three ways. The first method is to record if the behavior occurs during the interval. The second being that you record only if the behavior occurs for the full

FIGURE 9.6 Duration and latency data form.

Student's Name: ______________________ Date: ______________

Recorder's Name: ______________________ Behavior: ______________

Time		Duration	Latency
Beginning	Ending		

FIGURE 9.7 Interval recording form.

Student's Name: ______________________ Date: ______________

Recorder's Name: ______________________ Behavior: ______________

Sample: Partial ________ Interval Length ______________

Full ________ + = occurrence

Time ________ – = nonoccurrence

Interval										% Occurrence
1	2	3	4	5	6	7	8	9	10	

duration of the interval. The third method is to do a time sample. Unlike the first two methods, recording only occurs at the end of the interval. Because you are not required to continuously record during the interval, teachers can use this method while teaching students whom they are observing. For two of the three methods, observation is not required during the complete interval and can only be considered an estimate of occurrence of behavior. Figure 9.7 illustrates a sample Interval Recording Form for collecting data.

Reliability

The quality of any recording system depends on its **reliability** (Schloss & Smith, 1999). **Interobserver reliability** refers to the consistency among persons who record the behavior of an individual. It is important for two different professionals to record consistently when observing. To promote this consistency, reliability checks should be made prior to actual data recording and weekly throughout the collection of data. Two individuals tallying the same behavior over the same period of time determine reliability. **Direct observation** records are compared to analyze the number of agreements and disagreements. Calculations are then made to determine the reliability coefficient or the rate of agreement between observers. When calculating the reliability for frequency and permanent product recordings, the smaller frequency is divided by the larger frequency. For example, two teachers recorded the number of verbal outbursts displayed by a student in an elementary classroom in a 1-hour period. One identified 16 and the other identified 19. The reliability coefficient would be .84 (16 divided by 19).

$$\frac{\text{Smaller Frequency}}{\text{Larger Frequency}} = \frac{16}{19} = .84$$

Duration recording is similar in that the shorter duration is divided by the longer duration. For example, one teacher records the elementary student's verbal outbursts being 9 seconds in duration and the second records it at 10 seconds. The reliability coefficient would be .90 :

$$\frac{\text{Smaller Duration}}{\text{Larger Duration}} = \frac{9}{10} = .90$$

In calculating interval recording reliability, the number of intervals in which both scored an occurrence is divided by the number of intervals in which one or both observers recorded an observance. For example, two teachers conducted interval recording checks on the elementary school student with verbal outbursts for a 10-minute period. Intervals were 30 seconds in length. There were five intervals recorded by both observers and six intervals in which one or both recorded. The reliability coefficient would be .83:

$$\frac{\text{Intervals Scored by Both}}{\text{Intervals Scored by One or Both}} = \frac{5}{6} = .83$$

A minimum rate of agreement between observers is 80%. A high agreement rate may require fewer reliability checks in the collection process. A low agreement rate may indicate the need for a review of the response definition or recording protocol.

Summary

Collection of sample behavior under well-described or standardized conditions was discussed in this chapter. The necessity of real-life conditions was highlighted, promoting the validity of assessment procedures. Direct observation is quite useful in evaluating progress toward achieving assessment goals and objectives. Seven direct observation recording procedures were described: anecdotal, ABC anecdotal, frequency response, permanent product, task analysis, duration and latency, and interval. The importance of interobserver reliability was discussed, noting procedures to determine a reliability coefficient. A discussion on writing summative assessments and written reports on student progress follows in Chapter 10.

REFERENCES

Cartwright, G. P., Cartwright, C. A., & Ward, M. E. (1995). *Educating special learners* (4th ed.). Belmont, CA: Wadsworth.

Choate, J. S., Enright, B. E., Miller, L. J., Poteet, J. A., & Rakes, T. A. (1995). *Curriculum-based assessment and programming* (3rd ed.). Boston: Allyn & Bacon.

McLoughlin, J. A., & Lewis, R. B. (1994). *Assessing special students* (4th ed.). Upper Saddle River, NJ: Merrill.

Schloss, P. J., & Schloss, C. N. (1985). *Strategies for teaching handicapped adolescents: A handbook for secondary level educators.* Austin, TX: Pro-Ed.

Schloss, P. J., & Smith, M. A. (1998). *Applied behavior analysis in the classroom* (2nd ed.). Boston: Allyn & Bacon.

Schloss, P. J., & Smith, M. A. (1999). *Conducting research.* Upper Saddle River, NJ: Merrill.

Snell, M. E., & Brown, F. (2000). *Instruction of students with severe disabilities* (5th ed.). New York: Merrill.

CHAPTER 10

Summarizing and Communicating Assessment Information

Empowering Students and Families

LYNNE SOMMERSTEIN
Buffalo State College

JULIE SMITH
University of Florida

OBJECTIVES

After reading this chapter, you will be able to

1. Explain the importance of considering how assessment information is summarized and communicated to parents and students
2. Identify variables to consider when summarizing assessment information to parents and students
3. Identify variables to consider when communicating assessment information to parents and students

KEY TERMS

empowerment (p. 186)
family vision (p. 189)
holistic approach (p. 184)
person-centered planning process (p. 184)
self-advocacy (p. 187)
self-determination (p. 186)
strength-based approach (p. 194)

Effectively sharing the results from assessment activities with those invested in the decisions affecting the student's life (i.e., stakeholders) requires that school personnel recognize the importance of carefully considering how assessment information is summarized and communicated. Assessment information should be collected, interpreted, and communicated in a way that determines what students with disabilities need to learn and how effectively they are being taught. Assessment is most useful when it also facilitates empowerment, both for students with disabilities and for their parents; focuses on the development of functional skills in natural settings; and promotes the students' participation in school and community with nondisabled peers.

Linking Assessment Information to Functional Skills

Student-Centered Approach to Identifying Functional Skills

Summaries of assessment information should provide useful information to assist the development of individualized education programs (IEPs) that are meaningful to students' lives. One way to ensure meaningfulness is to use a **person-centered planning process.** Oriented to the student's own future, this type of planning process uses information from each stakeholder in the child's life as it has been, as it is now, and as it can be in the future. Stakeholders participate in person-centered planning by focusing on the student's hopes and dreams on an ongoing basis, rather than during one single event (Schaffner & Buswell, 1996). Particularly, the Personal Futures Planning process (Mount & Zwernik, 1990) uses a person-centered approach that does not focus on the child in just the school environment; rather, it includes all aspects of the child's life. Because school is not the only part of a student's life, this **holistic approach** also looks at the total student in all of the environments in which he or she functions (e.g., at home; in the community). To accomplish this, family members and friends can assist in identifying educational priorities that emphasize community participation. Other effective planning processes include Making Action Plans (MAP; Falvey, Forest, Pearpoint, & Rosenberg, 1994; formerly known as the McGill Action Planning System; Forest & Lusthaus, 1987), Choosing Options and Accommodations for Children (COACH; Giangreco, Cloninger, & Iverson, 1993), and Group Action Planning (Turnbull et al., 1996).

Person-centered planning processes help the team use a holistic approach because participants come from a variety of perspectives—from school, home, and the community. They work together voluntarily, collectively, and collaboratively to empower the student by emphasizing the student's strengths (Mount & Zwernik, 1990). Each stakeholder uses his or her experience with the student to share perspectives about the student's capabilities and the student's perceived wants and needs. Stakeholders also help identify potential obstacles for the student and assist in identifying ways to work around those obstacles. Assessment summaries should reflect this useful information from a variety of sources and help the student and parents make decisions about how best to achieve their goals.

Using a person-centered approach allows for the identification of desired functional skills that a student already demonstrates, as well as those skills still needed. It also identifies skills in a variety of the settings in which they will be used (Ryndak, 1996). When assessment reports provide information about skills that are meaningful and necessary for *that* student's life, it allows the team to develop an IEP that will help the child function in the settings in which he or she participates or wishes to participate. This allows the team to prioritize the skills that are most important for the student' s meaningful participation and provides the student frequent opportunities to practice these priority skills with family and friends. This, in turn, assists the student in generalizing the use of skills across settings and situations and developing a natural support network (Ryndak, 1996).

Family Involvement in Assessment

As indicated in Chapter 4, assessments should be a collaborative process in which parents and students are involved with educators from the beginning in planning what types of assessments are meaningful, where and how they will take place, and who will do them. Collaborative teams use parents as a valuable resource for important assessment information (Ulrich, 1991). Additionally, parents can respond to the cultural sensitivity of the planned assessment tools and give both valuable information about the various settings in which the child participates and feedback on priorities for skill attainment. Team members who desire meaningful parental participation explain the variety of assessment options (including both standardized tests and informal assessment methods) and discuss the purpose, the method of administration, and the strengths and weaknesses of each option. They then decide together the appropriateness of using any or all of the methods for the student at this point in time.

Standardized tests (e.g., intelligence tests, achievement tests, aptitude tests) have different value to different interpreters (Messick, 1995). Typically, these comparative tests are used by schools as (a) a gauge by which they compare their effectiveness with other schools, and (b) measures of accountability to school boards and state legislators (Messick, 1995). Standardized tests often present one of the greatest challenges for interpreting and communicating results to parents and students in a meaningful way (see Chapter 2).

While standardized tests may be useful for documenting a student's disability, they frequently fail to provide meaningful information about an individual student. For instance, standardized tests frequently fail to document students' adaptive skills, strengths, and needs in relation to life and goals for the future (Brown & Snell, 1991). This is evident more and more as the severity of a student's disability increases. Because standardized tests measure deficits in performance, comparing the performance of a student with disabilities to other students who do not have disabilities, they often document deficits without documenting current abilities. In contrast, parents of children with disabilities are far more concerned with the progress their own children are making in the classroom, in the community, and in society, than in comparison to students without disabilities (Shepard & Bliem, 1995). In addition, continued debate exists regarding whether standardized tests are sufficiently biased as to favor children from upper-middle-class Euro-American homes (Harry, 1992; Utley, 1995).

Standardized tests have other drawbacks for students with disabilities. For instance, they cannot be individualized to take into consideration a student's ability to communicate or to interact with his or her environment (Brown & Snell, 1991). Because skills are not measured in the contexts in which they naturally are used, standardized tests do not yield significant information that has application in the classroom or community for many students with disabilities (Brown & Snell, 1991; Rainforth, MacDonald, York, & Dunn, 1992). They provide little, if any, relevant information that is applicable to daily teaching and learning for many students with disabilities in the reality of daily classroom life, particularly for students with more significant disabilities (Falvey, Givner, & Kimm, 1996; Gaylord-Ross & Browder, 1991; Schuler & Perez, 1991). For instance, they fail to provide meaningful information about a student's use of functional skills in natural school and community participation. Further, the resulting documentation of deviance from the norm often produces low expectations for student achievement, especially for students with more significant disabilities (Linehan, Brady, & Hwang, 1991; Ryndak, Downing, Jacqueline, & Morrison, 1995; Ryndak, Morrison & Sommerstein, 1999; Schaffner & Buswell, 1996; Schuler & Perez, 1991).

Because the assessment process should be used to identify the tools to help each student function as independently as possible in his or her school and community, a useful alternative to formal testing is informal assessment strategies that incorporate information from the family. Informal assessment uses coordinated observations of the student in a variety of familiar settings as he or she performs meaningful daily activities (Brown & Snell, 1991; Gaylord-Ross & Browder, 1991; Rainforth et al., 1992; Ryndak, 1996). Although they are not standardized, informal assessments can provide reliable, useful information if they are planned, administered, and interpreted carefully (Falvey et al., 1996; Rainforth et al., 1992; Schuler & Perez, 1991). They focus on meaningful information that will suggest practical teaching and learning strategies to help the student develop functional skills that will enable him or her to live in the real world at home, at school, and in the community.

Parents and students have valuable information for determining some environments in which meaningful informal assessments could be conducted most effectively (Rainforth, York, & MacDonald, 1992). They know the settings in which the child is most successful, increasing the probability of documenting the student's strengths and interests. They also know the settings in which the student needs the most supports to be successful, allowing the team to glean useful information in areas for skill development and support strategies. Assessment in meaningful settings can identify areas of most and least interest to the student and assist the team in developing support strategies that promote participation in inclusive environments in the school and community. When assessments are not used as predictors of future success, but as ongoing measures of the child's learning requirements, parents and students can recognize more readily their importance in program planning.

Promoting Family and Student Empowerment

Rationale for Empowerment

Students and parents must have the central roles in making decisions that affect students' lives in school, in the community, and in society (Charlton, 1998). Team members need to allow for and encourage **empowerment** of students and families to fulfill these roles throughout the process of planning, conducting, interpreting, and making decisions from assessment activities.

Empowering parents and students is necessary to drive the mission of student-centered educational decisions, thus practices that facilitate empowerment should be used. Such practices include understanding self-determination of children with disabilities, using communication that is parent- and student-sensitive, maintaining an effective collaborative team process in assembling and interpreting assessment information, and producing meaningful verbal and written summaries of assessment information that are useful for all stakeholders.

Facilitating empowerment of students with disabilities results from the realization that each student's life belongs to that student. Therefore, students have not only a need but also a right to take control of the decisions that affect their lives. This is **self-determination:** a person with disabilities determining the future; setting personal goals; and making choices for self-direction, individuality, independence, and personal responsibility (Ferguson &

Meyer, 1993; Powers & Sowers, 1996; Ryndak & Alper, 1996; Turnbull, Turnbull, Shank, & Leal, 1999). No one better understands what is best for a person with a disability than that person with the disability (Charlton, 1998; Lovitt, 1990). Effectively summarizing and communicating assessment information with the parents and student can assist them in making informed decisions. Informed decisions, in turn, further empower students to advocate increasingly for themselves, resulting in lives in which they have more control and responsibility (Charlton, 1998).

For the National Information Center for Children and Youth with Disabilities (NICHCY), Kupper (NICHCY, 1995) identified six gains that students make as they participate in their own planning process:

1. Learn more about their strengths and skills and be able to communicate them to others
2. Learn more about their needs and disability, including how to talk about and explain them to others
3. Learn what types of accommodations might help them succeed in school, at work, and in the community
4. Learn how to speak for themselves
5. Learn to express their wants and needs for themselves
6. Develop the skills necessary for choice making and independent decision making, which result in self-determination (p. 1)

This is **self-advocacy,** the process that allows a student's own voice to make others aware of his or her abilities, needs, and concerns (Wood & Lazzari, 1997) and to guide the decisions that affect the future for that student. Participation as an equal member of the team allows a student to define goals for him- or herself and to take initiative for reaching those goals (Ward, 1988). If a student has empowered participation, "behavior that is detrimental to achieving those goals would decrease" (Field, 1996, p. 173), not only because the goals are more meaningful to the student, but also because of the student's greater commitment to achieving them.

Empowering Parents as Members of the Collaborative Team

The collaborative teaming approach to assessment (see Chapter 4) is effective in promoting empowerment of students and parents, as well as effectively allowing for gathering and using meaningful assessment information about functional skills in inclusive environments. Collaborative teams not only share information among all stakeholders (including parents and students), but they also take collective responsibility for planning and implementing an educational program that meets the student's varied needs in the context of life in natural settings (Ryndak, 1996). They develop programs that provide "instruction in naturally occurring settings, including general education classes, and . . . functional activities across the school and in the community" (p. 84). Assessment information is summarized and communicated by the collaborative team, using full and meaningful participation of all team members as the focus of its function. Information addresses the student's holistic strengths and needs and provides more meaningful information, promoting parent and student empowerment through active participation.

Empowering the Student as a Member of the Collaborative Team

When most educators and parents consider the composition of a collaborative team, they often think only of the *adults* who will be working together (Villa, Udis, & Thousand, 1994). Because students can provide information about all aspects of their lives, feelings, attitudes, goals, and aspirations (McLoughlin & Lewis, 1994; Turnbull et al., 1999), they must be members of their team as early as possible (Villa et al., 1994).

While the majority of special educators agree that self-determination is important for independence, many interventions focus on decisions and behaviors that professionals and parents believe are appropriate, rather than on choices determined by students (Powers & Sowers, 1996). Student participation in the entire assessment process, especially during summarizing and reporting of assessment information, is more likely to promote greater individualization and empowerment by ensuring that the information is most relevant to each student's life. Students can and should be an active agent in their own instruction (Gartner & Lipsky, 1990; Villa & Thousand, 1996).

Participating on a team could be challenging for any student, particularly for those students with more severe disabilities. It is the responsibility of the adults, therefore, to create an atmosphere that is supportive of student participation. The fact that students have disabilities should not be viewed as a barrier to participation; rather, during all team activities, supports and services needed for the student to be successful should be in place. For example, students should (a) have an idea of the purpose of the meeting, who will be there, and what will happen; (b) be offered the opportunity to prepare for their participation with an adult or peer they trust (e.g., develop a portfolio of work samples that demonstrates their abilities and needs, prepare a "presentation" of work that highlights accomplishments, create a collage representing how they see their strengths and needs); and (c) have assistance communicating their hopes and aspirations for the future (Field, Hoffman, & Spezia, 1998). Such active participation gives students a sense of equality and involvement and allows team members to observe the students demonstrating their strengths and abilities.

Communicating Assessment Information to Parents and Students

Working with parents and students in a collaborative team can be both challenging and highly rewarding (see Chapter 4), but working together effectively requires that people trust and value each other (Knackendoffel, Robinson, Deschler, & Schumaker, 1992; Pugach & Johnson, 1995; Thomas, Correa, & Morsink, 1995). When school personnel maintain positive and respectful relationships with parents and students, educators have access to information that traditionally is not readily accessible. For example, parents and students can share their knowledge of the student in areas of life not readily evident at school, including participation in family life, participation in the community, and information about the family's cultural context (Harry, 1992; Moll, Amanti, Neff, & Gonzalez, 1992). Keeping a focus on the family's and the student's wants, needs, and vision for the future facilitates developing and maintaining the trust necessary in a truly collaborative relationship.

Linking Assessment Summaries to Family and Student Vision

During the assessment process, collaborative team members invite parents and the student to communicate their vision for the future; that is, to identify the outcomes they want most based on their family values and opportunities (Mount & Zwernik, 1990). Such **family vision** should be based on expectations for nondisabled children of the same age, tailoring them to their own wants and needs. Assessment summaries, therefore, should reflect not only a student's current performance but also information about the family's vision and skills the student has or needs to achieve that vision. The assessment summary, after all, will be the formal report that explains and justifies the student's educational program. Without linking all decisions to the family's life and vision, a student's educational program would exist in a void and could appear to be arbitrary.

Limitations in envisioning the educational options that can be designed to support a child often produce an inability on the part of team members, including students and parents, to design a future that is inclusive, individualized, and age-appropriate. All team members must consider the *un*obvious options possible from which people with disabilities can choose, and they must be creative in pursuing these options before discarding possibilities that may become realities. This was true in the case of Michelle, a student with moderate developmental disabilities, and her family who wanted Michelle to have college experiences as part of her transition to adult living (see Box 10.1). While the school personnel privately thought that the parents were unrealistic about their daughter's capabilities, the family simply wanted to develop a creative form of community-based instruction.

Resolving Conflicting Information

Conflict can arise from many factors, including (a) the emotional need to blame someone for the disability or lack of student progress; (b) personal or professional stress; (c) societal

BOX 10.1
Michelle's Story

Going to college is what children do in our circle of family and friends. If we really believed and expected that Michelle could have the same life she would have had if she did not have a developmental disability, a college experience would have to be part of it. We knew that she needed to increase her independent living and social skills, and a high school class did not seem to be an age-appropriate place to do that. Fortunately, she had an older brother who reminded us that he had also needed those skills, and he developed them in college! It was a natural choice for him, but a controversial choice for his sister. We also knew that she would need more and different supports than her brother had needed. Some people thought we were "unrealistic" in wanting her to go to college, when all we wanted was a place away from home where she could learn and grow with nondisabled people her age. The independence she enjoys today is the direct result of her college experience away from home. Most important, she would not have the sense of belonging she feels in our circle of family and friends if she hadn't experienced the "gestalt" of college. (Sommerstein, 1995) stigma associated with disabilities; (d) lack of understanding among parents, students, and service providers; (e) lack of services; and (f) lack of knowledge about service options (Mayer, 1994). Being knowledgeable about potential sources of conflict can facilitate a proactive approach to preventing or ending conflicts. Sharing assessment information among the team members should occur in a manner that avoids or clarifies potential areas of conflict. For example, all verbal and written reports should be worded in ways that do not blame anyone for either a student's disability or a student's lack of progress and should avoid stigmatizing either the student or parents. Assessment information should be shared in a way that recognizes and appreciates the unique roles of all team members and the challenges that each experiences within the educational system. Additionally, assessment summaries can avoid conflict by describing how a recommended service would help a student or his or her team, and how those services can be accessed.

Sometimes assessment conclusions may conflict. Rainforth et al. (1992) identify team observation and subsequent team brainstorming as effective assessment strategies, but these same strategies could be used to resolve conflicting interpretations. For example, when conflicting interpretations are expressed, several team members could observe the student together and use brainstorming strategies to develop ideas for explaining the discrepancy between interpretations. Team members could generate a test hypothesis (Rainforth et al., 1992) to resolve conflicting information. Unresolved disagreements may be addressed by listing the concerns of the minority members as areas to be pursued in the future, so that all opinions are reflected in the assessment report. This process would validate the concerns of all team members and would ensure that the discrepancy in information will be pursued for the student's benefit.

When Parents Disagree

The real test of the collaborative team comes when parents disagree and conflict arises (Thomas et al., 1995). Sometimes that disagreement comes from parents' perceptions about their child's potential, about the results of assessment, or about the plan for educational services. The potential for conflict with parents increases when information is presented or discussed without parental or student involvement. There are situations in which parents and students need time to reflect on new information, discuss options, and reach their own conclusions before they are able to be collaborative team members. Just like school team members, parents and students need to see and review assessment information privately, or with someone they trust and perceive as supportive, before discussing it further in a team setting. Forced decisions invite discord. When this happens, team members may choose to describe the parents, students, or both as argumentative or unrealistic, perhaps even assuming that the conflict is a result of discord in the home. This puts parents and students in an impossible position and damages the relationship between home and school. Even parents who disagree with one another may disagree jointly with the school about their child.

Parents often report that educators have asserted their conclusions over those of the parent(s) by pointing to norm-referenced tests as hard data to refute parents' or other anecdotal evidence (see Ryndak et al., 1999). This situation can be avoided by collaboratively determining how and when assessment information will be gathered. Some team members may rationalize that parents disagree with them because the parents are being overprotective, angry, unrealistic in their expectations, or not accepting of their child's disability. Other team members may link parents' disagreement to assumed stages of grief (e.g., the death of the parents' dream of the perfect child; Moses, 1987), especially for parents of very young or newly diagnosed children (Moses, 1991). Maintaining and imposing a model of grief on parents equates the idea of disability with tragedy (Charlton, 1998), thereby perpetuating the stigma of disability. To explain parental disagreement by referring to denial in the grieving process will inhibit parental participation as an equal and valued member of the collaborative team. It negates the possibility that parents have valid perceptions and assumes the primacy of professional experts in the decision-making process (Charlton, 1998; Pugach & Johnson, 1995; Thomas et al., 1995; Vohs, 1989).

By contrast, collaborative team members are good listeners and use the parents' and student's opinions and supporting anecdotes as sources of valuable information to complete the picture of the child (Moll et al., 1992). Information from parents and students can be a catalyst for new ideas and inquiry into areas of strength or concern that may have been missed by other team members. Parental or student disagreement should be welcomed as an opportunity for further exploration of the student's abilities and needs. Team members who acknowledge their own fallibility and who value parents' and student's perceptions build bridges to a trusting relationship. Such an approach would have assisted in more meaningful programming in the following situation:

> Our daughter is 22 now. Those who used standardized tests as predictors of our daughter's future success (or lack of it), without listening to or valuing our stories that proved her abilities, were wrong. Those who relied on those tests to determine her educational program designed a program that would have been inappropriate for her if we had not intervened when she was 15 (see Ryndak et al., 1999). They were imposing their "professional judgement" on her and on us.
>
> We, her parents, have been right 100% of the time. Our daughter consistently has met OUR high expectations, instead of limiting herself to THEIR low predictions. Interestingly, no team member who sat around the table during team meetings and disagreed with us about our daughter is here now. Only us—her parents. (Sommerstein, 1995)

Empathy is an important part of building trusting relationships with families. Turnbull and Turnbull (1991) urge parents, educators, and advocates to make decisions as though they were the person being affected. This advice is particularly helpful for parents and students to remember when their decisions diverge from those recommended by other team members. While it smacks of pulling rank, the assessment team frequently *accepts* the judgment of the parents and student as long as safety issues are not involved or significant disruption does not occur in services for students without disabilities. After all, it is the parents and students who are involved for the long term; they will live with the results of the decisions. The ethical course of conduct is harmonious with the person whose life is affected most directly by the proposed action (Turnbull & Turnbull, 1991).

Despite efforts to avoid conflict, there may be times when parents or the student disagree with other team members about what is best for the student, and conflict may arise. IDEA mandates procedural safeguards for parents that range from mediation to federal court (Ordover & Boundy, 1991). Preventing or resolving conflict reduces the need for parents to exercise their due process rights and is in the best interest of the student, as well as other team members. When due process rights must be exercised, the situation is stressful, expensive, and emotionally and mentally exhausting for everyone involved, with the possible consequences of losing focus on the mission of the team and damaging relationships (Fiedler, 1991; Simpson, 1990).

Verbally Summarizing Assessment Information

Verbal reports of assessment information occur at team meetings, on the telephone with parents, and during informal encounters with parents at school. Effective verbal communication is a very complex activity—one that requires a great deal of skill. Communication is a dialogical or interactive process (Hybels & Weaver, 1986) that requires both a sender and a receiver. Our dialogue, however, consists of more than just the words we speak. For instance, we also communicate through body language, facial expressions, and our ability to actively listen. The combination of words, physical presence, and active listening projects our attitude both toward our conversation partner(s) and the student about whom we are speaking. For example, let's focus on effective listening skills. When team members effectively listen during conversations with parents, they communicate interest and trust. These are essential elements among educators, students, and parents when verbally reporting assessment information. Knackendoffel et al. (1992) stated that half of our interactions involve listening, but we are rarely taught how to listen effectively. They offered the following tips that can facilitate more effective listening:

1. *Assume a posture of involvement.* This includes facing the person with whom you are communicating, leaning slightly forward, using appropriate eye contact, using neutral or friendly facial expressions, and minimizing distractions (e.g., watching the clock, fumbling with papers) that might communicate to the receiver that complete attention is not being paid.
2. *Use nonverbal encouragers.* Nodding your head, smiling, touching the arm of the speaker, and taking occasional notes communicate interest on your part and encourage the speaker to continue.
3. *Use verbal encouragers.* Simple one- or two-word phrases (e.g., "I see," "uh, huh") indicate that you are "with" the speaker and without judgment.
4. *Note the speaker's tone and nonverbal behaviors.* This allows for a better match of listener's response to the speaker's needs.

These are simply guidelines and should not be interpreted to apply to all people of all cultures at all times. For example, certain cultures interpret eye contact as inappropriate under some circumstances, while other cultures would find touching offensive. It is important for team members to understand these variations on communication, traditions, and practices, and to be sensitive to the possible variations between and among different cultures. Appreciating cultural differences, values, class, family structure, and personal styles increases team members' ability to be helpful (Singer & Powers, 1993) in both verbal and written communication. Even within cultures, there is a very wide range of individuality. (See Grant and Gomez [1996] for in-depth information on multiculturalism.)

When all team members feel they are respected, valued, and safe in sharing (i.e., not judged), communicating assessment information with one another is more open. Establishing a genuinely caring climate in which team members bring out the best in one another, even when some team members are difficult to like, is essential to empowerment (Perl, 1995). Parents and students are more likely to trust other team members when they perceive the team members as positive, sensitive, honest, and committed to the student's goals (Simpson, 1990). Comments that reflect supportive communication (see Box 10.2) may seem obvious, but team members need to remind themselves to use them, especially in difficult situations.

BOX 10.2

Collaborative Communication of Assessment Information

- "Mr. and Mrs. Gonzalez, let's get together with Juan and the important people in his life to find out where he is now and where he wants to be in the future."
- "Ms. Fredericks, the team values your opinion. You are expert about Janet. Trust your instincts."
- "Juan, what are your dreams? What are you good at? What do you want to learn to do? What kind of job do you want to have? Where do you want to live as an adult?"
- "Is there anything that you are looking ahead to that we can help prepare Janet for? Is there anything that we can work on in school that will help you at home?"
- "Mr. and Mrs. Pfohl, what do you see as John's strengths? How does he spend his free time? What are his favorite things to do?"
- "Pete, as John's friend, tell us about some things John is smart about. What kinds of things do you think would help John achieve his goals?"
- "Mr. Kutlis, you've known John from the neighborhood for a while now. What kinds of things do you see he is interested in and good at?"
- "John, let's think about our team meeting next week and what information you would like to give to the team. How can we help you with that?"
- "Mr. Chang, the team is meeting to decide the types of assessment information we need to plan for Lin's program next year. When would be a convenient time and place to meet?"
- "We need to do some standardized testing in order to qualify Lin for services. However, we know that they do not give us an accurate picture of all Lin's abilities. Let's talk about other kinds of assessments and their purposes. Then we can decide which ones we will use, who will do them, and when."
- "Ms. Frederick, would you and Janet like to meet to discuss the assessment results before the team discusses them? I would like to hear your thoughts about them."
- "Let's schedule a team meeting to discuss the assessment results and decide which information is meaningful for Janet to achieve her goals."
- "We seem to have some assessment information that is not consistent. Let's observe Juan together to try to figure out what the problem is."
- "While the majority of us agree with the assessment results, there is some conflicting information that we haven't been able to resolve. Let's include it in the report as areas for further study."
- "Mr. and Mrs. Pfohl, I have a draft of the final assessment report. Would you like to meet to be sure that it is written in a way that is helpful to both you and the team?"

Written Summaries of Assessment Information

Parents more readily develop a trusting relationship with team members who precede written reports with face-to-face review of the information collected. As part of the assessment process, team members can choose to use either (a) a **strength-based approach** and document the student's capacity, talents, and interests (Ferguson & Meyer, 1993), or (b) a deficit-based approach and document weaknesses, deficits, and disinterests. The approach flavors not only the content of the report but also the image developed of the student, the services developed for the student, and the reader's emotional response to the report. One parent responded to written reports in the following way:

> When I received formal written reports from my daughter's psychologist, speech therapist, physician, neurologist, or whomever, I always considered them a draft. The first thing I did was sit down with a yellow highlighter and highlight every positive comment about her. If the report was not at least 50% yellow, I made additions about my daughter's strengths and talents, and asked that they be inserted in the report. (Sommerstein, 1994)

Despite norm-referenced test results, collaborative team members for students with disabilities should not be afraid to use the word *smart.* Everyone is smart in some way! Too often, written reports contain the comment N/A (Not Applicable) in response to areas in which the student has no documented deficit. These are areas of strength and should be described in as much detail as the student's needs were described. Informal assessments (e.g., interviews with the student, parents, or peers; observations during favorite activities) also can document the student's strengths and interests. Such positive information is essential not only in earning the trust of students and parents but also in developing self-esteem and skill development. Including it in written reports provides a balanced and holistic picture of the student. Remember that this is someone's child. Team members who demonstrate the ability to see the whole student by reporting on the whole student win parents' hearts and facilitate their active involvement in their child's education! In addition, a team member who harnesses a student's strengths in the learning process sets the stage for success.

Parents appreciate when team members keep in mind that written reports follow their child for years, even a lifetime. Unhappy experiences give parents baggage that team members know nothing about. That is why team members should be willing to review drafts of reports with parents before finalizing them—not to change the results, but to ensure that the language used and the information provided will be helpful, supportive, and useful for years to come, rather than harmful.

In addition to capturing a student's strengths, useful written reports identify effective adaptations and interventions for use at home, in school, and in the community; they describe successful settings and supports necessary for learning; they identify necessary accommodations to meet student's needs and facilitate success (Hahn, 1995). Such reports identify the priority skills on which a student needs instruction, the contexts in which the student needs to learn and demonstrate those skills, and the accommodations required for the student's success in learning environments.

If standardized test scores must be reported, the information can be expressed in such a way as to not become the child's defining characteristic (Charlton, 1998). Standardized test scores can be (a) put in paragraph form in the middle of the report, because people tend to flip to the back to get the IQ score without reading more useful parts of the report; (b) written in words rather than in numbers (i.e., "moderate mental retardation" rather than an IQ score); or (c) marked unreliable or invalid if the team feels the scores do not accurately reflect the student's ability. In addition, effective assessment summary reports avoid technical jargon and acronyms, making them easily read by a general audience. Student behavioral needs should be expressed in positive language (e.g., "Alex needs to increase ________" instead of "Alex needs to decrease ________"). They use precise, objective language that is nonjudgmental. Use of this positive, strength-based approach significantly affects the picture that is painted of the student (see Box 10.3).

BOX 10.3

Comparing a Traditional and a Strength-Based Written Report

Traditional Written Report

Jonathan is 11 years old with cerebral palsy. Results from the Wechsler Intelligence Scale for Children administered on 2–27–00 are

Verbal IQ	51
Performance IQ	71
Full Scale IQ	58

Verbal Scaled Scores:		*Performance Scaled Scores:*	
Information	1	Picture Completion	5
Similarities	5	Picture Arrangement	7
Arithmetic	3	Block Design	6
Vocabulary	1	Object Assembly	4
Comprehension	1	Coding	6

Jonathan has only minimal basic academic skills, which adversely affects his educational performance. He needs constant supervision in classroom settings because he is highly distractible with a low percentage of time on task and a low task completion rate. He is not able to complete simple classroom tasks without adult assistance, and because of hypertonia, he is significantly delayed in gross and fine motor coordination. Expressive and receptive language are at 5 years, 4 months, significantly discrepant with that of nondisabled peers. Written language and math are at a prekindergarten level.

Strength-Based Written Report

Jonathan is an active 11-year-old who enjoys looking at and learning about trains. He is very proud of having created himself a scrapbook of pictures, photographs, drawings, and articles about trains. He likes being with other children his age and making friends. While his expressive language is significantly delayed, he enjoys being part of a group of peers. He participates when he can and listens carefully, responding to comments by watching others' responses. He reads "body language" well and uses that awareness to correct his own behavior. He watches the behavior of others and attempts to imitate it. He has a good memory for people and events, noticing and remembering people he has met only once.

(continued)

BOX 10.3 Continued

Although Jonathan has significant delays on norm-referenced tests, they do not reflect his true potential. He is a visual learner, using it to compensate for an auditory processing disability. He benefits from visual cues to follow directions and stay on task. Because he likes to be independent, it is best to show him how to do something and then leave him alone to try it himself. He works well in small groups of peers, staying on task when they do.

Academically, Jonathan is working on increasing sight words and word attack skills. Phonics is very difficult for him because of his slow auditory processing and difficulty hearing all of the sounds in words. He reads best when words are in meaningful contexts or help him to "fit in" with other students. He uses a calculator for math facts but needs to work on identifying math operations. His handwriting is difficult to read and slow for him to form. He benefits from use of a computer and a word bank for written language.

Jonathan likes to please adults and peers but may say something inappropriate when he is frustrated, does not know what to do, or is overwhelmed by auditory stimuli. At these times, it is best to give him some silence and come back to him in a few minutes. He will need brief, emotionally neutral feedback if he is rude. He needs to practice the words he should have used to express his difficulty.

Reports that summarize assessment information should focus on activities that are meaningful to the student across natural settings. Effective written reports can become valuable resources for use, as a whole or in part, in both school and nonschool settings. Rather than describing the student's deficits or problems, written reports should provide information that prescribes in detail (a) modifications or accommodations necessary for the student to learn, communicate, or participate; (b) specific interventions for managing behavior; and (c) priority skills to be learned that will make a difference either in the student's participation with peers, participation in natural settings or activities, or independent functioning, either immediately or in the future.

Summary

This chapter has focused on variables to consider when summarizing and reporting assessment information in verbal and written form. The chapter supported a collaborative teaming approach that includes parents and students, and supported assessment as an ongoing and interactive process. Results from this assessment process are synthesized by team members to produce cohesive, consistent, and holistic results. These results should be useful to all team members in developing educational plans that identify priority functional skills that the student needs to participate in the settings in which he or she wants and needs to participate.

The assessment reporting process uses a person-centered approach to empower parents and students. It identifies useful strategies to help achieve the desired learner outcomes in inclusive environments in the school and community. This process emphasizes the meaningful participation of parents and students not only as receivers of information, but as equal partners in the planning and interpretation of assessment results. This approach uses assessment to develop an educational program that assists parents and students in reaching their goals for the student throughout and beyond life in school.

REFERENCES

Brown, F., & Snell, M. (1991). Meaningful assessment. In L. C. Meyer, C. Peck, & L. Brown (Eds.), *Critical issues in the lives of people with severe disabilities* (pp. 61–98). Baltimore: Paul H. Brookes.

Charlton, J. I. (1998). *Nothing about us without us: Disability, oppression, and empowerment.* Berkeley: University of California Press.

Falvey, M., Forest, M., Pearpoint, J., & Rosenberg, R. (1994). Building connections: All my life's a circle. In J. S. Thousand, R. A. Villa, & A. I. Nevin (Eds.), *Creativity and collaborative learning: A practical guide to empowering students and teachers* (pp. 347–368). Baltimore: Paul H. Brookes.

Falvey, M., Givner, C., & Kimm, D. (1996). What do I do Monday morning? In S. Stainback & W. Stainback (Eds.), *Inclusion: A guide for educators* (pp. 117–138). Baltimore: Paul H. Brookes.

Ferguson, D., & Meyer, G. (1993). The elementary/secondary system: Supportive education for students with disabilities (Module 1C). *Activity-based assessment.* Eugene, OR: University of Oregon.

Fiedler, C. R. (1991). Preparing parents to participate: Advocacy and education. In M. J. Fine (Ed.), *Collaboration with parents of exceptional children* (pp. 313–333). Brandon, VT: Clinical Psychology Publishing.

Field, S. (1996). A historical perspective on student involvement in the transition process: Toward a vision of self-determination for all students. *Career Development for Exceptional Individuals, 19,* 169–176.

Field, S., Hoffman, A., & Spezia, S. (1998). *Self-determination strategies for adolescents in transition.* Austin, TX: Pro-Ed.

Forest, M., & Lusthaus, E. (1987). The kaleidoscope: Challenge to the cascade. In M. Forest (Ed.), *More education/integration* (pp. 1–16). Downsview, Ontario: Allan Roeher Institute.

Gartner, A., & Lipsky, D. K. (1990). Students as instructional agents. In W. Stainback & S. Stainback (Eds.), *Support networks for inclusive schooling: Interdependent integrated education* (pp. 81–93). Baltimore: Paul H. Brookes.

Gaylord-Ross, R., & Browder, D. (1991). Functional assessment. In L. Meyer, C. Peck, & L. Brown (Eds.), *Critical issues in the lives of people with severe disabilities* (pp. 45–66). Baltimore: Paul H. Brookes.

Giangreco, M. F., Cloninger, C. J., & Iverson, V. S. (1993). *Choosing options and accommodations for children: A guide to planning inclusive education* (2nd ed.). Baltimore: Paul H. Brookes.

Grant, C. A., & Gomez, M. L. (1996). *Making schooling multicultural: Campus and classroom.* Englewood Cliffs, NJ: Prentice-Hall.

Hahn, H. (1995). New trends in disability studies: Implications for educational policy. *National Center on Educational Restructuring and Inclusion Bulletin,* *2*(1), 1–5.

Harry, B. (1992). Developing cultural self-awareness: The first step in values clarification for early interventionists. *Topics in Early Childhood Special Education, 12,* 333–350.

Hybels, S., & Weaver, R. L. (1986). *Communicating effectively.* New York: Random House.

Knackendoffel, E. A., Robinson, S. M., Deschler, D. D., & Schumaker, J. B. (1992). *Collaborative problem-solving: A step-by-step guide to creating educational solutions.* Lawrence, KS: Edge Enterprises.

Linehan, S. A., Brady, M. P., & Hwang, C. (1991). Ecological versus developmental assessment: Influences on instructional expectations. *The Journal of the Association for Persons with Severe Handicaps, 16,* 146–153.

Lovitt, Z. (1990). Rethinking my roots as a teacher. *Educational Leadership, 47* (6), 43–46.

Mayer, J. A. (1994, May). From rage to reform: What parents say about advocacy. *Exceptional Parent,* 49–51.

McLoughlin, J. A., & Lewis, R. B. (1994). *Assessing special students* (4th ed). Upper Saddle River, NJ: Prentice-Hall.

Messick, S. (1995). Validity of psychological assessment: Validation of inferences from persons' responses and performances as scientific inquiry into score meaning. *American Psychologist, 50,* 741–749.

Moll, L. C., Amanti, C., Neff, D., & Gonzalez, N. (1992). Funds of knowledge and teaching: Using a qualitative approach to connect homes and classrooms. *Theory Into Practice, 31,* 132–141.

Moses, K. (1987, Spring). The impact of childhood disability: The parents' struggle. *Ways,* 6–10.

Moses, K. (1991). *Shattered dreams and growth: Loss and the art of grief counseling.* Evanston: Resource Networks.

Mount, B., & Zwernik, K. (1990). *Making futures happen: A manual for facilitating personal futures planning.* St. Paul, MN: Metropolitan Council.

National Information Center for Children and Youth with Disabilities (NICHCY). (1995). L. Kupper (Ed.), *Helping students develop their IEPs.* (Technical Assistance Guide, 2). Washington, DC: Author.

Ordover, E. L., & Boundy, K. B. (1991). *Educational rights of children with disabilities: A primer for advocates.* Cambridge: Center for Law and Education.

Perl, J. (1995). Improving relationship skills for parent conferences. *Teaching Exceptional Children, 3,* 29–31.

Powers, L., & Sowers, J. (1996). Transitions to adult living: Promoting natural supports and self-determination. *Equity and Excellence, 4,* 215–247.

Pugach, M. C., & Johnson, L. J. (1995). *Collaborative practitioners: Collaborative schools.* Denver, CO: Love.

Rainforth, B., MacDonald, C., York, J., & Dunn, W. (1992). Collaborative assessment. In B. Rainforth, J. York, & C. McDonald (Eds.), *Collaborative teams for students with severe disabilities* (pp. 105–155). Baltimore: Paul H. Brookes.

Rainforth, B., York, J., & MacDonald, C. (1992). Foundations of collaborative teamwork. In B. Rainforth, J. York, & C. McDonald (Eds.), *Collaborative teams for students with severe disabilities* (pp. 9–41). Baltimore: Paul H. Brooks.

Ryndak, D. L. (1996). Education teams and collaborative teamwork in inclusive settings. In D. L. Ryndak & S. Alper (Eds.), *Curriculum content for students with moderate and severe disabilities in inclusive settings* (pp. 77–95). Needham Heights, MA: Allyn & Bacon.

Ryndak, D. L., & Alper, S. (1996). *Curriculum content for students with moderate and severe disabilities in inclusive settings.* Needham Heights, MA: Allyn & Bacon.

Ryndak, D., Downing, J., Jacqueline, L., & Morrison, A. (1995). Parents' perceptions after inclusion of their children with moderate or severe disabilities. *Journal of the Association for Persons with Severe Handicaps, 20,* 147–157.

Ryndak, D., Morrison, A., & Sommerstein, L. (1999). Literacy prior to and after inclusion in general education settings: A case study. *Journal of the Association for Persons with Severe Handicaps, 24*(1), 5–22.

Schaffner, C. B., & Buswell, B. (1996). Ten critical elements for creating inclusive and effective school communities. In S. Stainback & W. Stainback (Eds.), *Inclusion: A guide for educators* (pp. 49–65). Baltimore: Paul H. Brookes.

Schuler, A. L., & Perez, L. (1991). Assessment: Current concerns and future directions. In L. Meyer, C. Peck, & L. Brown (Eds.), *Critical issues in the lives of people with severe disabilities* (pp. 101–105). Baltimore: Paul H. Brookes.

Shepard, L. A., & Bliem, C. L. (1995). Parents' thinking about standardized tests and performance assessments. *Educational Researcher, 24*(8), 25–32.

Simpson, P. (1990). *Conferencing parents of exceptional children* (2nd ed). Austin: Pro-Ed.

Singer, G. H. S., & Powers, L. E. (1993). *Families, disability, and empowerment: Active coping skills and strategies for family interventions.* Baltimore: Paul H. Brookes.

Sommerstein, L. C. (1994, November). *Curricular adaptations/classroom modifications.* Paper presented at the Launching The Dream Conference, Rochester, New York.

Sommerstein, L. C. (1995, August). *Inclusion goes to college: Transitioning to age-appropriate settings.* Paper presented at National Down Syndrome Congress 23rd Annual Convention, Washington, DC.

Thomas, C. C., Correa, V. I., & Morsink, C. V. (1995). *Interactive teaming: Consultation and collaboration in special programs.* Englewood Cliffs, NJ: Merrill.

Turnbull, A., & Turnbull, H. R. III. (1991). Family assessment and family empowerment: An ethical analysis. *Critical issues in the lives of people with severe disabilities* (pp. 485–488). Baltimore: Paul H. Brookes.

Turnbull, A. P., Blue-Banning, M. J., Anderson, E. L., Turnbull, H. R., Seaton, K. A., & Dinas, P. A. (1996). Enhancing self-determination through group action planning: A holistic emphasis. In D. J. Sands & M. L. Wehmeyer (Eds.), *Self-determination across the life span: Theory and practice* (pp. 237–256). Baltimore: Paul H. Brookes.

Turnbull, A., Turnbull, R., Shank, M., & Leal, D. (1999). *Exceptional lives.* Columbus, OH: Merrill.

Ulrich, M. (1991). Evaluating evaluation. In L. Meyer, C. Peck, & L. Brown (Eds.), *Critical issues in the lives of people with severe disabilities* (pp. 93–100). Baltimore: Paul H. Brookes.

Utley, C. A. (1995). Culturally and linguistically diverse students with mild disabilities. In C. A. Grant (Ed.), *Educating for diversity: An anthology of mulitictural voices* (pp. 301–319). Boston: Allyn & Bacon.

Villa, R. A., & Thousand, J. S. (1996). Student collaboration: An essential for curriculum delivery in the 21st century. In S. Stainback & W. Stainback (Eds.), *Inclusion: A guide for educators* (pp. 171–191). Baltimore: Paul H. Brookes.

Villa, R. A., Udis, J., & Thousand, J. S. (1994). Responses for children experiencing behavioral and emotional challenges. In J. S. Thousand, R. A. Villa, & A. I. Nevin (Eds.), *Creativity and collaborative learning* (pp. 369–390). Baltimore: Paul H. Brookes.

Vohs, J. (1989). Vision and empowerment. *Infants and Young Children, 2*(1), 7–10.

Ward, M. J. (1988). The many facets of self-determination. *Transition Summary, 5,* 2–3.

Wood, J. W., & Lazzari, A. (1997). *Exceeding the boundaries.* New York: Harcourt Brace College Publishers.

CHAPTER 11

Assessment of Infants and Young Children With Disabilities

MAUREEN A. CONROY
University of Florida

STACY PAOLINI
University of Florida

OBJECTIVES

After reading this chapter, you will be able to

1. Identify and describe best practices for assessment of infants and toddlers in inclusive settings
2. Describe informal techniques and strategies team members may use to collect assessment information
3. Outline and describe procedures to target functional goals for infants and young children in inclusive settings
4. Discuss how to modify and adapt the assessment process to address individual differences in culture or disability

KEY TERMS

anecdotal record (p. 211)
authentic assessment (p. 208)
checklist (p. 209)
culturally sensitive assessment (p. 216)
direct observation (p. 211)
environmental (ecological) assessment (p. 212)
event sampling (p. 212)
functional goals (p. 200)
naturalistic assessment strategies (p. 201)
portfolio assessment (p. 208)
rating scale (p. 209)
running record (p. 211)
time sampling (p. 212)
transdisciplinary play-based assessment (p. 202)

Facilitating successful inclusion of young children with disabilities is a challenge often discussed by teachers in the fields of early childhood and early intervention. At the heart of facilitating successful inclusion for young children is the assessment of skills and abilities that enable these children to successfully participate within the inclusive classroom and to target for intervention in the inclusive classroom. The purpose of this chapter is to provide team members with the knowledge and skills needed to facilitate successful inclusion of infants and young children with disabilities through the use of informal, applied assessment practices that lead to the identification of **functional goals** to target for intervention. The chapter is divided into three main sections. In the first section, we will provide an overview of the development of best practices in assessment, including current trends, professional standards, and legal considerations. In the next section, we will provide information on the use of informal assessment strategies for team members to use in inclusive settings to identify target goals. Within this section, areas of assessment as well as specific assessment techniques and strategies will be presented. In the final section, we will discuss the link between informal assessment, the identification of target goals, and the development of interventions that facilitate inclusion. After studying the concepts presented in this chapter, you should have the knowledge and skills to implement informal assessment practices for the purpose of targeting functional goals and implementing instructional programming within inclusive early childhood settings.

Current Trends and Best Practices in Assessment of Young Children

The assessment of infants and young children with disabilities presents many challenges for professionals in the field of early intervention. One of the primary challenges lies in the nature of young children's characteristics and development (McLean, 1996). Consider the following scenario.

> *Alex, a three-year-old with cognitive, communication, and behavioral disabilities, needs an evaluation to determine his strengths and needs across developmental domains and his need for special education services. At the request of the school district, Alex's parents bring him to the testing center where the evaluator (a stranger to Alex) separates him from his parents. Alex and the evaluator enter a small room with a table, chairs, and several developmental assessment instruments. The evaluator places Alex at the table and begins to "test" Alex by presenting different test items and materials and instructs him to complete activities. Alex, who is scared, confused, and wants to be with his parents, does not respond. The evaluator persists at encouraging Alex to comply. Eventually, Alex begins to tantrum and cry. The evaluator eventually stops the evaluation and returns Alex to his parents, stating that "he is uncooperative."*

This scenario, an example of traditional assessment techniques commonly used with older children, often is applied inappropriately with young children. As suggested by McLean

(1996), "young children [are] poor candidates for assessments that are conducted by unfamiliar adults in unfamiliar settings and that require children to do what the adults ask them to do" (p. 13). For example, infants and young children (particularly those who have disabilities) may have limited attention spans, limited communication abilities (both receptive and expressive), and have behavioral problems that interfere with the traditional assessment process.

As a result of these unique characteristics, professionals have suggested the need for using alternative methods when assessing young children (Overton, 1996). Unlike more traditional assessment methods that typically are used with older students with disabilities and rely heavily on the use of standardized measures, early intervention professionals advocate that naturalistic and ecologically based strategies should be used to assess young children with disabilities in order to obtain an accurate measurement of children's abilities (McLean, 1996). In addition to using naturalistic strategies, professionals advocate for implementing a collaborative team approach toward the assessment of young children. This approach often is called transdisciplinary play-based assessment (Linder, 1993). Finally, there are legal and professional indicators to guide team members in the assessment of young children. These current trends and best practices—that is, naturalistic strategies, transdisciplinary play-based assessment, legal and professionally recommended practices—will be described next. It is critical that team members in inclusive settings who are assessing young children's abilities incorporate these principles into their assessment practices.

Naturalistic Assessment Practices

There is an overall emphasis within early intervention of service delivery in inclusive settings (Downing, 1996; Fox, Hanline, Vail, & Galant, 1994; Wolery & Wilbers, 1994). As suggested by Fox and her colleagues, assessment is the "cornerstone" of early intervention; through assessment, team members are able to identify children with disabilities and develop meaningful intervention plans. If young children are going to be served in inclusive settings, assessment procedures should be conducted in these settings with the emphasis placed on evaluating meaningful outcomes and developing functional goals (Peck, 1993). Assessment of young children in natural settings provides a holistic view of children's abilities and how they relate to their environment (Schwartz & Olswang, 1996).

Naturalistic assessment strategies, usually informal evaluations, may include techniques such as systematic observations, performance assessments, rating scales, checklists, portfolios, and ecobehavioral assessment (Fox et al., 1994; Overton, 1996; Wortham, 1995). When conducting naturalistic assessments in the inclusive setting, team members should have knowledge about and ability to use a variety of techniques and sources of information in order to gather data that can be used to help individual children fully participate within the classroom (Fox et al., 1994; Neisworth, 1993). One of the primary considerations and advantages in the use of naturalistic assessment strategies is the direct link of the assessment to the curriculum. Through naturalistic assessment, team members can measure children's performance in skills that are relevant to classroom activities through the use of direct or indirect measures completed across multiple occasions. The outcome of a naturalistic assessment process is the identification of functional skills for development of an Individual Family Service Plan (IFSP) or Individual Education Program (IEP) that facilitates children's needs and inclusion in the classroom.

Transdisciplinary Play-Based Assessment

In early intervention, assessment is viewed as a collaborative process between professionals and parents. Best practice suggests that multiple perspectives on the abilities of children should be obtained, including the family's views. **Transdisciplinary play-based assessment** (Linder, 1993) is one team model developed for assessment of young children and can be conducted during informal and formal play activities in an early childhood setting. Linder describes transdisciplinary play-based assessment as a functional approach to both assessment and intervention that provides meaningful information that easily translates into target goals and strategies for intervention. Therefore, it is particularly applicable for use in inclusive settings.

Transdisciplinary play-based assessment is conducted by a team of individuals that includes both professionals (e.g., occupational and physical therapists, classroom teachers, speech and language pathologists, and so on) and an individual child's parents or guardians. The team begins the assessment process by gathering background information on the child. Next, the team plans the content and process of an assessment "play" session, which provides team members opportunities to observe a child's skills across development domains (i.e., cognition, communication, social, and motor skills) that occur during naturalistic play activities. A single team member typically serves as the facilitator and encourages the child to interact with the play activities. Children are observed in both unstructured and structured play activities, play with their peers and parents, as well as a social time, such as lunch or snack. The purpose of transdisciplinary play-based assessment is to obtain information about children's level of functioning in each of the developmental domains. In addition, it provides opportunities to obtain information about children's ability to interact dynamically with their environment.

There are several advantages for using transdisciplinary play-based assessment with infants and young children. One advantage is that transdisciplinary play-based assessment occurs in the natural environment where children have rapport with the examiner and the parents are included. Second, the process is holistic in nature, evaluating all aspects of children's development and how they process information. Third, procedures used in transdisciplinary play-based assessment are flexible, allowing children to be individually evaluated. Finally, transdisciplinary play-based assessment is useful in planning relevant and effective interventions.

The transdisciplinary play-based assessment method is particularly applicable for use in inclusive settings. Infants and young children served in inclusive settings often have a variety of needs that require service from many different professionals (e.g., occupational therapists, physical therapists, speech and language pathologists, nurses) as well as early interventionists and early childhood educators. Frequently, these professionals provide consultative services to individual children, families, and the early childhood staff, and may directly serve an individual child only on a once-a-week basis or less. Because children with special needs may interact with these professionals infrequently, the child may be less likely to respond or comply during a formalized testing situation as described earlier in this chapter. The use of a transdisciplinary play-based assessment provides an opportunity for these professionals to observe and evaluate children's skills in a natural environment without the restrictions that can come from a more formalized and structured approach. In addition, this team model provides an opportunity for professionals across a variety of disciplines to meet and discuss their evaluations about children's development and progress. Because this approach includes all individuals (i.e., both professionals and parents) who are working with children and facilitates collaborative planning, it is particularly suited for use in an inclusive setting. A transdisciplinary teaming model may help to facilitate identification and integration of different skills and therapy strategies that can improve children's progress and participation in the inclusive classroom.

Legal and Professional Guidelines

The field of early childhood special education is compelled by law to conduct assessments of infants and young children with disabilities for the purposes of determining eligibility and instructional planning. Public Law 99–457, the Education of the Handicapped Amendments (1986), required that assessments focus on the children's strengths, needs, and services required to meet those needs (303.322, Federal Register, 1993). Assessments must be conducted by trained professionals using appropriate methods that include a review of history and an evaluation of current levels of developmental functioning (Overton, 1996). The assessment of the family's needs, resources, and concerns related to their child's development also is outlined as a part of the assessment process. In addition to these guidelines, assessment must follow the regulations outlined in IDEA, including nondiscriminatory assessment, parental consent, confidentiality, and due process procedural safeguards (Overton, 1996). It is critical for team members in inclusive settings to be aware of and comply with the legal components of assessment. A discussion on each of these legal factors is beyond the scope of this chapter. However, we have summarized these legal requirements in Table 11.1 and encourage you to become familiar with them (for further information, see Overton, 1996; Taylor, 1997).

TABLE 11.1 Legal Aspects of Assessment for Infants and Young Children*

- Assessment must be conducted by a multidisciplinary team and include multiple measures and sources of information.
- Assessment must include a review of the child's background and medical history as well as an evaluation of the child's current level of functioning across developmental areas related to the suspected disability.
- Assessment must be nondiscriminatory, culturally nonbiased, and conducted in the child's native language or mode of communication.
- Assessment must be conducted by a trained professional using valid and appropriate instruments.
- Assessment should not be conducted without informed consent from a child's parent or guardian.
- Assessment of the child's family should be done in order to identify resources, priorities, and concerns related to the child's development.
- Assessment should follow confidentiality guidelines and due process procedural safeguards as outlined in IDEA.
- Assessment must be conducted within a 45-day period from referral.

**Note:* For further discussion, see Overton, 1996.

In addition to the legal guidelines provided, professionals in the fields of early intervention (DEC Task Force on Recommended Practices, 1993) and early childhood (NAEYC & NAECS/SDE, 1991) have developed recommended practices for assessing infants and young children (see Table 11.2). Although these recommendations refer to assessment practices in general, several practices particularly are applicable for use in inclusive settings.

Professionals from both fields agree that assessment should be relevant to children's curriculum and is essential for planning and implementing children's educational programs. Professionals also agree that assessment is an ongoing process that includes a wide base of information on the children's development and is obtained across many sources and occasions. As outlined by Neisworth (1993), for young children with disabilities particularly it is important that assessment identify objectives that are functional, applicable to development of the IEP or IFSP, and help to improve their skills. Finally, professionals in both fields agree that another primary goal of assessment is to document ongoing progress and evaluate program effectiveness (Fox et al., 1994).

To summarize this section, team members using assessment practices with infants and young children in inclusive settings should be aware of current trends and best practices in the field. Since the beginning of early intervention, professionals have continually examined

TABLE 11.2 Summary of Recommended Assessment Practices

Early Childhood (NAEYC & NAECS/SDE, 1991)	Early Intervention (DEC, 1993)
■ Assessment is important for planning and implementing developmentally appropriate practices. ■ Assessment should be directly related to the curriculum and result in improved instruction or provide for individualized learning. ■ Assessment should be relevant to classroom activities and involve natural performance of skills. ■ Methods for assessment may include anecdotal notes, running records, specimen records, language samples, records, systematic observation, and so on. ■ Assessment is a collaborative process that involves the child, family, and community. ■ Assessment should be culturally sensitive. ■ Standardized tests should be used with caution when evaluating young children.	■ The purpose of assessment is to gather information about children, families, and environments for the purposes of identification, screening, eligibility, program planning, monitoring, and evaluation. ■ Assessment should include information from multiple sources and across multiple occasions. ■ Assessment should be a collaborative decision-making process. ■ Assessment should be culturally appropriate and nonbiased. ■ Assessment procedures should be appropriate for young children and include adaptions of materials and procedures to accommodate disabilities. ■ Assessment should include development and functional areas that facilitate intervention.

Sources: Adapted from "Guidelines for Appropriate Curriculum Content and Assessment in Programs Serving Children Ages 3 through 8," by National Association for the Education of Young Children (NAEYC) and National Association of Early Childhood Specialists in State Department of Education, 1991, *Young Children, 46,* pp. 21–38; *DEC Recommended Practices: Indicators of Quality in Programs for Infants and Young Children with Special Needs and Their Families,* by DEC Task Force on Recommended Practices, 1993, Reston, VA: Council for Exceptional Children.

new approaches to the concept of assessment for infants and young children. This inquiry has resulted in a progression from a more traditional approach to a more naturalistic approach. Included in the naturalistic approach is a trend toward assessment using a team model that observes young children in what they do best—play. Although legal requirements must be followed in the assessment of infants and young children, professionals from the fields of early childhood and early intervention have developed recommended practices that provide a framework for conducting assessments. These practices should be considered when assessing young children within inclusive settings.

Informal Strategies for Collecting Assessment Information

Assessment of young children involves more than just administering tests. Assessment is an ongoing process that provides information about children's qualities, characteristics, behaviors, and their interaction with the environment so that team members can plan appropriate instruction (Choate & Evans, 1992). The trend for assessing young children is moving toward the use of more informal methods of gathering information, rather than using formal testing procedures. Collecting information on children's development and behavior within the context that it occurs provides authentic information that can be used for program planning, developing functional learning objectives, and implementing interventions that meet individual goals and needs. This section of the chapter will provide you with knowledge about areas to assess, assessment techniques, and targeting skills for intervention in relation to assessment within inclusive settings.

Areas of Assessment

In the field of early childhood and early intervention, assessment and instruction typically occur across different development domains, including cognition, language, social, and motor skills. The development of children's skills in these domains is influenced by changes in chronological age, maturation, and experiences (Nicholson & Shipstead, 1994). The sequence of development is typically the same for all children; however, some children develop at a different rate, acquiring a variety of skills at different times (Nicholson & Shipstead, 1994). In other words, all children of the same chronological age do not necessarily acquire age-appropriate skills at the same time. One reason may be exposure to different experiences and opportunities. Another reason, however, may be that some children may demonstrate disabilities in one or more areas of development.

Children's development of age-appropriate skills across developmental domains is both a sequential and continuous process. In this process, children constantly are acquiring new skills to create more sophisticated traits (Nicholson & Shipstead, 1994). A thorough knowledge of early childhood development is important for team members so they may recognize developmental delays in young children and determine the need for more extensive assessment. In addition, knowledge of children's development can provide the teacher a framework for targeting goals for intervention. Specific areas of development relevant to the assessment of infants and young children are discussed next. It is particularly important for team members in inclusive settings to be familiar with skills across these areas of development in order to identify potential delays and examine how these delays may impact children's ability to participate in activities. For an in-depth discussion of assessment in each developmental domain, see McLean, Bailey, and Wolery (1996).

Cognitive Development. Cognitive development is described as children's ability to learn and understand their world (Wortham, 1995). It is a product of the interaction between their environment and their biological capacities (Cook, Tessier, & Klein, 1992). Because all children do not have identical environmental experiences, their cognitive development may vary. When assessing young children, it is important to understand their environments at home and in school, and examine how these environments may impact their cognitive development.

Piaget (1964) described cognitive development in terms of successive stages. Beginning at birth through approximately age 2, infants progress through the sensorimotor stage. During this stage, intellectual growth develops through children's concrete interactions with their environment. Eventually, infants are able to differentiate themselves from objects. Between the ages of 2 and 6, children progress through the preoperational stage, which consists of the symbolic and intuitive phases of development. During the symbolic phase, children are egocentric and unable to incorporate viewpoints of other people. It is during this time that language largely is developed. Through the intuitive phase, children gradually understand relationships between people but are unaware of relationships between objects, such as classification of objects. When children reach the stage of concrete operations at age 7, they are able to use logical operations, such as seriation, classification, conservation, and one-to-one correspondence. Cognitive development occurs in stages, and the nature of children's intellect changes dramatically over time (Piaget, 1964). Each stage is a major transformation in thought processes compared with the preceding stage.

Because cognition provides a foundation for children's learning and interactions with their environments, team members in inclusive settings should have an accurate measurement of children's cognitive abilities and needs. Through this assessment, team members can plan and implement intervention strategies and arrange learning environments that are appropriate for children's levels of understanding, thus facilitating interactions with their physical and social environments.

Language Development. Children's language development is closely related to their cognitive and social development. Language is the central means through which children transmit their thoughts and ideas to others and is expressed most easily by children in their natural environment with familiar people.

During the first eight years of life, children acquire a complex set of rules, including vocabulary and grammar skills, that govern their language. However, some children are unable to use speech and language skills to communicate their messages due to their developmental age level or the presence of a disability. Therefore, the mode of communication used by children may vary depending on their age or developmental skill level (Linder, 1993). Infants and young children begin communicating through various modes other than verbalizations. They may use eye gaze, gestures, physical manipulation, or vocalizations (Linder, 1993). As children grow, they begin to develop sounds and progress toward verbalizing to communicate their needs and wants. Children with disabilities who cannot talk still may use gestures (e.g., sign language) or assistive and augmentative methods to communicate their thoughts and ideas. When assessing language skills, team members should include an evaluation of children's mode of communication (i.e., verbal, motor, or augmentative). In other words, a language assessment should include information about both what and how children communicate.

An evaluation of children's communication and language development is an important component for planning successful interventions in inclusive settings. Because language and communication often build the foundation for social relationships between children and their peers, the team will need to assess children's level of communication to assist in planning peer-related social activities.

Social Development. Children's social development is interrelated with their cognitive and language abilities. The development of children's social skills depends largely on their ability to understand and communicate about and within their environment. As children interact with their environment and others, they are constantly developing their repertoire of social skill abilities, which ultimately leads to social competence—that is, the ability to implement interpersonal goals appropriately and effectively through their interactions with peers and adults (Guralnick, 1992).

Child development theorists and researchers have noted that beginning in infancy, children become social with familiar adults. During the second year of life, infants and toddlers begin to interact briefly with other young children. As children reach preschool age, their peer interactions increase in frequency and complexity. Many educators and developmental theorists have agreed that successful adult-child and child-child social interactions provide the foundation and context for acquiring and developing skills across other developmental areas, including language and cognitive abilities.

The social development domain particularly is applicable to young children in inclusive settings. Children with disabilities often demonstrate social skill deficits that can impact their ability to interact with their peers in inclusive settings (Odom, McConnell, & McEvoy, 1993). Therefore, it is critical for team members to have knowledge and understanding of children's social development in order to design effective intervention strategies to help children with delays in this area to participate successfully within the inclusive setting.

Fine and Gross Motor Development. Children learn through doing. Therefore, children's motor skills play a critical role in their development and can impact their cognitive, language, and social abilities. There are two main areas included in children's motor development: gross motor and fine motor. Gross motor skills involve children's large motor muscles. These include motor milestones such as rolling, creeping, walking, and running. Fine motor abilities involve the use of smaller motor muscles of children's arms and hands. Fine motor developmental milestones include reaching, grasping, and releasing. The assessment of motor skills provides necessary information for team members to incorporate into environmental planning in the inclusive preschool setting. It is critical for team members to have an accurate assessment of children's motor abilities in order to provide children with motor delays the necessary adaptations for them to have optimum experiences and participation in the inclusive setting.

To recap, a thorough assessment across developmental areas is essential prior to planning intervention strategies for young children with disabilities in inclusive settings. It is critical for team members to have in-depth knowledge of children's abilities in order to plan and implement accommodations and interventions that can facilitate their successful participation in the inclusive classroom. There are many techniques that can be used by team members to obtain information about children's developmental skills. Next, we will present several strategies that can be implemented easily by team members within an inclusive classroom.

Authentic Assessment Techniques

Conducting ongoing authentic assessment is critical in the area of early childhood. Because a number of young children demonstrate developmental delays, effective early childhood team members need to continually assess and monitor their children's needs and developmental progress to assist in the selection of curriculum materials and planning individualized programs that support their growth. They realize that an accurate assessment identifying children's strengths and needs is a critical part of this process; enabling them to plan a program that is developmentally appropriate for each child. Although there are many commercially available tests, many team members have begun to use informal assessment procedures that provide authentic information on children's development within a contextual framework. The use of authentic assessment strategies within children's natural settings particularly is applicable for young children served in inclusive classrooms. In order to plan for effective intervention within the inclusive setting, it is critical for team members to know how different children are functioning within that particular setting. Using informal, naturalistic assessment strategies can provide team members that information, so they can be better able to plan intervention and supports.

The concept of authentic assessment gradually is gaining popularity and support from the early childhood education community (NAEYC, 1986). **Authentic assessment** is defined as "the process of observing, recording, and otherwise documenting the work children do and how they do it, as a basis for educational decisions that affect them" (Bredenkamp & Rosegrant, 1992). Authentic assessments involve many forms that concentrate on skills within a context rather than in isolation. It provides continuous qualitative information about the children's accomplishments that can be used to plan instructional goals and interventions, as well as choose instructional materials. Authentic assessment is an effective technique; it employs a number of different types of assessment tools and strategies that require children to demonstrate behaviors in real-life contexts—meeting the realistic demands within the classroom (Choate & Evans, 1992). Next, we will discuss several different methods of conducting authentic assessments that can be implemented by early childhood teachers and transdisciplinary teams in inclusive settings.

Portfolio Assessment. A portfolio is a collection of individual children's work that illustrates efforts, progress, and achievements over a period of time. This collection can be represented by print, video, or audio recordings (McLean et al., 1996). Materials in portfolios should be sequenced to reflect children's most recent work, documenting the date of the work. Portfolios can include children's work samples, anecdotal notes, records of teacher observations and screenings, and other pertinent information. For young children, interpretations about children's achievements should be based on the range of the children's development as documented by the portfolio (Grace & Shores, 1992). **Portfolio assessment** is valuable in monitoring children's cumulative performance particularly when used in conjunction with more frequently used observations of specific skills and intervention goals. In addition, portfolios provide a historical perspective of children's progress. This type of information can be very beneficial for children served in inclusive settings. It not only helps the teacher monitor individual progress, but it also can provide information that can be used for program evaluation.

Rating Scales. One method for collecting information on specific characteristics and development of young children is through the use of a rating scale. The purpose of a **rating scale** is to identify quickly specific information about children in order to plan instruction. Although there are many commercially available rating scales evaluating particular areas of development (e.g., social skills, adaptive behavior), team members also can develop their own rating scales to measure skills and abilities that reflect success in their own classrooms. One feature of a rating scale is that the rater is able to make qualitative judgments about the extent to which a particular behavior or skill is demonstrated by children (Wortham, 1990). This allows the teacher to obtain more detailed information about a particular area of interest.

Two types of rating scales have been used primarily in the field of early childhood: graphic and numerical (Nicholson & Shipstead, 1994). The numerical rating scale lists characteristics of development and requires the rater to score the children's performance using a Likert scale (e.g., 1–4 with 1 meaning unsatisfactory and 4 meaning outstanding). The graphic rating scale requires the rater to score the children's performance with descriptors ranging from never to always.

Rating scales can be purchased or designed by the user. Teachers or team members may not be able to find an existing scale for a selected area of concern and, therefore, may need to design their own scale. Use the following guidelines when designing rating scales (Nicholson & Shipstead, 1994):

1. Select an appropriate area of development or skill area
2. Research the area of development or skills
3. Identify clear and distinct items to be rated within the area of development or skills
4. Design a recording form for the rating scale
5. Pilot test the rating scale to validate items

One nice feature about using rating scales with young children is that they do not have to be completed while the behaviors are occurring. In fact, the teacher or team member can complete them anytime. In addition, rating scales are quick and require no specific training by the user. One disadvantage, however, is that rating scales are subject to user bias, making their validity questionable. Figure 11.1 presents examples of teacher-made rating scales.

Checklists. A **checklist** is a list of items measuring skills in a particular area or areas of development. The observer or teacher marks off the item if it is demonstrated by children (Nicholson & Shipstead, 1994). The purpose of a checklist is to evaluate young children's development and record the results. Checklists are usually organized by areas of development, such as cognition, fine and gross motor, or language development. A checklist may involve one or more observations depending on the amount of information needed for the

FIGURE 11.1 Examples of numerical and graphic rating scales.

Numerical Rating Scale

Area of Development: Prosocial characteristic—takes turns with toys and activities

1	*2*	*3*	*4*
Does not take turns with toys or activities	Actively takes turns with toys or activities when asked	Actively takes turns with toys or activities with a friend	Actively takes turns with toys or activities with others

Graphic Rating Scale

❐ *Often* takes turns with toys and activities
❐ *Occasionally* takes turns with toys and activities
❐ *Never* takes turns with toys and activities

assessment. A second purpose of a checklist is to track changes in children's development over time (Nicholson & Shipstead, 1994). The teacher or team member may use a checklist, such as the one in Figure 11.2, on a daily or weekly basis to track progress in gross motor skills. In this example, the teacher is observing during free play time. The information gathered from the checklist can be used for program planning and making instructional adjustments. It is important for the checklist user to have knowledge of the sequence of development in order to differentiate typical and atypical behaviors and make appropriate instructional modifications.

Similar to rating scales, checklists can be either purchased commercially or developed by the teacher. Team members may chose to design their own checklist if they are observing a unique set of behaviors in their classroom. For instance, the checklist in Figure 11.2 is designed to measure independent classroom skills.

FIGURE 11.2 Independent classroom skills checklist.

Name: Cadena　　　Date: 9/15/97

Observer: Ms. Holly　　　Classroom: Blue Bees

Mark the skills that the child is able to complete independently.

❐ Toilet self independently
❐ Follow directions
❐ Initiate needs and wants
❐ Feed self independently
❐ Move around classroom
❐ Engage in an activity independently

Nicholson and Shipstead (1994) suggest five steps for team members to use when designing a checklist:

1. Select an appropriate area of development or skill area
2. Research the developmental or skill area
3. Identify clear, distinct items to be included in the checklist
4. Design a recording form with check boxes
5. Pilot test the instrument

Direct Observation. **Direct observation** involves watching, listening, and recording children's actions and behaviors. Typically, observation methods are used in the classroom to gather information regarding children's development or behavior in an effort to better meet their developmental needs within that setting (Wortham, 1995). Observations may occur in children's natural environments such as their homes or classrooms. The flexibility of observations makes them a particularly useful tool for use in inclusive early childhood settings. Early childhood environments offer many opportunities to observe children's functioning, including during play, interactions with others, and responses to different situations.

Before collecting observational data, the teacher or team member must identify the purpose of observing, what they intend to observe, and when the observation will take place. Observation requires the teacher or team member to have both the knowledge of developmental domains and the skills to interpret the children's interactions in order to obtain a global understanding of their abilities. Various types of strategies can be used to record data during an observation, including anecdotal records, running records, time sampling, and event sampling.

The **anecdotal record** is an objective description of when and where a specific behavior or behaviors occurred. Its purpose is to record from observation significant information regarding children's behavior that can support decisions for planning interventions, learning experiences, modifications, or further assessment. The teacher or team member should record the information in an anecdotal record as soon as possible after an event happens. Later, further comments concerning the behavior(s) observed may be added, if necessary. According to Goodwin and Driscoll (1980), the anecdotal record has five characteristics:

1. It is the result of a direct observation
2. It is a prompt, accurate account of an event
3. It includes the context of the behavior
4. Interpretations are recorded separately from the event
5. It requires the observer to focus on behavior that is unusual or typical

The **running record** is used to collect data on a specific child's development and behavior. It does not require the observation of a specific behavior at a particular moment. Rather, observation is completed over a specific time period, typically 10–30 minutes using a narrative format. Although it can be a time-consuming method and requires skill, running records can provide detailed information for team members and can document the effectiveness and appropriateness of interventions.

Time sampling is a direct observation method used to identify and measure a specific behavior or behaviors within a particular time interval. For example, a teacher may want to observe how many peer interactions a child initiates within a 20-minute period. In this case, the teacher would observe the child socially interacting and record the frequency of peer interactions. Usually, time sampling is conducted using an interval time recording method. In this method, the observer measures the presence or absence of a specific behavior at predetermined time intervals that are indicated on a chart. The outcome is a measurement of the frequency of the behavior over the specific time period. Time sampling is useful with young children, because many of their behaviors are very brief. In addition, time sampling allows the teacher or team member to observe many children at one time.

Another observation technique, **event sampling,** is used to record a behavior that happens within a particular setting. Although event sampling is a time-consuming process, it also provides detailed information for the teacher or team member. Through event sampling, the observer records the time of occurrence as well as the sequence of the antecedent, behavior, and consequence. These factors are recorded and examined to determine patterns in behavior that may be suggested by the data. The intent of event sampling is to provide information concerning the cause of children's behavior. Event sampling has been particularly useful for collecting information about the causes and effects of a particular behavior. By observing the antecedent event, the behavior, and the consequences of the behavior (the ABCs), the observer may be better able to develop an intervention strategy that appropriately addresses that behavior. For example, a teacher or team member may want to better understand the separation anxiety or behaviors some young children demonstrate when their parents drop them off at school in the morning. In order to observe this event, the observer would record the antecedent (i.e., how the parent drops the child off), the behavior (i.e., the child's reaction to the parent leaving), and the consequence (i.e., the teacher's response to the child). Figure 11.3 illustrates this example. By watching behavior in the context of antecedents and consequences, team members can gain a better understanding of their children and plan intervention strategies to meet individual needs.

Environmental Assessment

In addition to assessing development using authentic assessments, an evaluation of children's interactions with their environment is an important component of assessment for children in inclusive settings. Linder (1993) describes **environmental** (or **ecological**) **assessment** as the process of examining and evaluating the physical, social, and psychological aspects of children's development and context. Inclusive environments need to be assessed with respect to their impact on individual children and their potential for facilitating personal and social development in children. There are relatively few formal instruments team members can use to observe the impact of the environment on children. Assessments that focus on observations of children's behaviors in the context of normally occurring routines are considered to be the most representative and ecologically valid strategy for examining environmental impact (Cook et al., 1992). Natural settings and activities have the greatest potential for providing frequent opportunities for assessing children's skills and abilities to adapt through learning new behaviors or alternative responses (Bailey & McWilliam, 1990). Through the analysis of the inclusive environment, potential barriers to participation and learning can be identified and skills required to overcome barriers can be targeted for intervention.

FIGURE 11.3 Time sampling using an ABC analysis.

Name: Emily-Ann

Description of behavior: Acting out behaviors (e.g., crying, screaming, tantrum)

Date	Time	Antecedent	Behavior	Consequence	Comments
9/15/01	8:30 A.M.	Mom walks into room with Emily-Ann	Emily-Ann grabs Mom's hand and says "no"	Mom lets go of her hand and leaves	
		Teacher says, "come here" and walks over to Emily-Ann	Emily-Ann runs to the window and cries "mama"	The teacher says, "come here" and pulls Emily's hand	
		Teacher brings Emily-Ann to the breakfast table	Emily-Ann begins to kick, scream, and cry	Teacher ignores her behavior	

As discussed previously in this chapter, children and environmental factors operate together as a system to support development; thus it is important to gather information about the broader ecological context in which children learn (Munson & Odom, 1996). The Ecologically Based Model Activity Plan (EBAP) can assist in the assessment process (Haney & Cavallaro, 1996). This model, designed to be used in conjunction with additional assessments, identifies and develops opportunities for facilitating the attainment of individual goals and social inclusion in inclusive early childhood settings.

With the EBAP, teams task analyze specific activities, describe the classroom activity, and list inclusion strategies for a specific child (see Figure 11.4). The first step in the EBAP process is to identify the environments and subenvironments in which the activity occurs and curriculum areas addressed during the activity. The EABP assessment is conducted by observing individual children directly during the specified activity. Materials for use and any modifications to those materials for the individual child's use are noted on the form (see part 2.c). This is important because some children may benefit from the modification of materials, enabling them to complete the step successfully. In addition, other children are chosen to be involved in the activity, and the reason for picking those children is noted (see part 1.d). For example, the teacher may want to choose specific children that are highly social or can act as a peer mediator. Once the other children have been chosen, their roles in the activity are identified (see 2.d). Finally, adults present in the environment and the roles they are involved in are described (see 1.e and 2.e).

Following the implementation of the EBAP, the teacher or team member should complete a postactivity evaluation that addresses the following three questions: (1) Describe the target child's behavior and include examples; (2) Describe the types of interactions that took place during the activity, and (3) Describe how to modify the activity to meet

FIGURE 11.4 An ecologically based activity plan (EBAP).

Child: Emily Date: 2/1/01

Classroom: Full Day Observer: Stacey

Environment	**Subenvironment/Activity**
■ Indoor play ■ Outdoor play ■ Circle ■ Small group ■ Lunch	■ Housekeeping/Setting table

Curriculum Area(s): Fine Motor, Language, Cognitive, Social, Self-Help, Gross Motor

Part 1: Classroom Activity Analysis	**Part 2: Inclusion Strategies**
1.a. Description of children's activities (What are they doing?) The children pretend to set a table, put a dish at each place setting, put utensils at each place setting, decide who will sit in each of the four chairs, and pretend to eat.	2.a. Goal for child with special needs (What do you want the child to be able to do in this activity?) I want her to be able to interact with at least two of her peers, to help set the table, and sit down.
1.b. Skills needed for participation (task analysis) 1. Recognize appropriate roles for housekeeping areas. 2. Select items with which to set the table. 3. Find the plates and utensils in the kitchen cupboard. 4. Set the table. 5. Sit down at the table. 6. Pretend to eat.	2.b. Assessment of child's skills (Which skills can this child do?) She can physically perform items 1, 2, and 3 but has a difficult time setting the table and knowing where to put the plates and utensils (one-to-one correspondence). She needs to be prompted by her peers for this and when it is time to sit down. Once seated, she interacts with all three of her peers.
1.c. Materials: The entire housekeeping area and its contents.	2.c. Modification to materials: None
1.d. Children involved in this activity Kathy and Carol often play in the housekeeping area, and Nancy is Emily's best friend.	2.d. Peer mediators and roles: Kathy and Carol act as role models and use prompting strategies with Emily. Nancy and Emily are good friends—she will be a natural for peer socialization.
1.e. Adults present descriptions of their involvement Usually one teacher, one teacher assistant, and a parent volunteer are in the room. The volunteer usually leaves to prepare snacks. The teacher can sit in the housekeeping area to observe the children while the teacher assistant moves about the room providing assistance as needed.	2.e. Strategies for adult involvement: I will set up the housekeeping area to prompt the children to sit down to a meal. I will place their snack on the counter and prompt them to set the table so they can eat their snack. Participate in model and role play initially and fade out as the children get involved and Emily is participating.

the child's needs. The answers to these questions provide an anecdotal record of a child's behavior as well as valuable information that can be used to modify an activity or plan interventions.

Environmental assessment facilitates the inclusion of children with disabilities into early childhood classrooms. This method has potential for facilitating personal and social development by embedding individual learning activities within natural settings.

Targeting Functional Skills for Instruction

Analysis of assessment information allows teams to plan meaningful intervention programs for children within inclusive early childhood settings. Typically, assessment information is reviewed by the assessment team, including the parents. The team will develop an Individualized Family Service Plan (IFSP) or an Individualized Education Plan (IEP), stating specific instructional annual goals and short-term objectives the team will address for instruction. It is the team's responsibility to translate goals and objectives into interventions that incorporate developmentally and individually appropriate practices within inclusive settings. When selecting interventions, the team should consider three general guidelines: (a) the interventions should result in the child meeting the objectives; (b) the interventions should be able to be implemented within the inclusive setting and be teacher friendly, and (c) the interventions should be naturalistic (McLean et al.,1996).

In this section of the chapter, we explained that when evaluating assessment information to determine target goals, team members should consider both the developmental aspects of the children's abilities as well as environmental factors. There should be an emphasis placed on targeting goals that are functional for children within the inclusive classroom. Goals and interventions that maximize children's participation in naturalistic activities within familiar settings are important. It is also important for team members to target and implement goals and interventions that can be implemented practically in the inclusive setting. Finally, team members need to provide ongoing monitoring and assessment of children's attainment of goals and objectives.

Special Considerations in the Assessment Process

One of the challenges in the assessment of infants and young children is conducting a nondiscriminatory assessment to ensure an unbiased and accurate evaluation of the children's strengths and needs. As outlined in IDEA, the description of a nondiscriminatory assessment addresses several factors that may serve as bias in the assessment process. First, IDEA mandates that testing materials and procedures used in the assessment must not be racially or culturally discriminatory. In addition, testing materials must be administered in children's native language or mode of communication. Finally, testing materials must be valid and administered by trained personnel (Overton, 1996). This final section of the chapter will provide strategies for addressing these sources of assessment bias for young children who may come from culturally diverse backgrounds or have physical disabilities that impair performance during the assessment process.

Culturally Sensitive Assessment

Children's unique cultural characteristics (e.g., language) can impact greatly their successful inclusion into early childhood programs (Hanson, Gutierrez, Morgan, Brennan, & Zercher, 1997). Although legal and professional guidelines state that assessment procedures should be culturally sensitive, conducting a nonbiased assessment can be a challenge for team members. There are several cultural factors that should be considered when assessing young children, including their ethnic and cultural background, socioeconomic status/poverty, family structure and characteristics, and religion (Lynch & Hanson, 1996). It is important to consider these factors and incorporate cultural competence into the assessment process (Lynch & Hanson, 1996).

A **culturally sensitive assessment** begins with a nonbiased philosophy by professionals who are flexible and respectful of individual differences. Active family involvement in the assessment process should be encouraged and may help to minimize cultural bias. In addition to a culturally sensitive philosophy, selected assessment instruments and strategies should be free from bias (Lynch & Hanson, 1996). When evaluating instrument bias, the following factors should be considered: (a) language of the instrument, (b) child's background experiences, (c) cultural beliefs, and (d) the need for a translator (Lynch & Hanson, 1996). Finally, when implementing the assessment, team members should create an environment that considers children's cultural differences. For example, if you want to observe a child interacting with peers, it would be important to provide an opportunity for the child to interact with peers who speak the same language (e.g., Spanish). Input on the part of the family should be encouraged and strongly considered on all assessment information collected. As described earlier, transdisciplinary play-based assessment is one technique that naturally incorporates the family into the assessment process. This technique may be useful particularly with children and families from diverse backgrounds, because it provides an opportunity for direct family involvement and observation of children's abilities in a natural, play-based setting.

In conclusion, team members assessing infants and young children should be culturally competent when planning and implementing the assessment process, as well as interpreting assessment information. A culturally sensitive philosophy, selecting culturally appropriate materials, collecting assessment information in naturalistic settings using informal procedures, and including the children's family members may help facilitate an assessment that is free from cultural biases.

Assessment of Children With Communication and Physical Disabilities

Young children who have physical or communication disabilities often have difficulty being included in early childhood programs (Hanson et al., 1997). In addition, team members often find it hard to conduct valid assessments of these children's abilities. Although IDEA mandates that assessment instruments and techniques not discriminate against children with an existing disability (e.g., speech or physical impairment), providing appropriate modifications or adaptations can be a challenge.

Children with physical challenges often are unable to perform physically on assessment tasks, even though they may cognitively be able to complete the task. In addition, children with communication disabilities may not be able to use speech to answer assessment questions or communicate their understanding; thus, an accurate and valid assessment is difficult to implement. Children's physical or communication impairments must be considered and accommodated in order to complete a nondiscriminatory assessment that reflects their true abilities and potential.

There are several factors to consider when assessing children with physical or communication needs. First, using informal and naturalistic assessment strategies in natural settings and activities is particularly important when evaluating children with physical and communication needs. Providing both structured and unstructured opportunities for children to interact across different settings (e.g., home, school) will provide the most accurate representation of children's abilities. When implementing informal and naturalistic assessment strategies, team members can incorporate the use of technology, adaptive equipment, and augmentative forms of communication, as well as modify assessment materials. Incorporating these factors into the assessment process may assist the team in obtaining a more accurate and reliable picture of children's strengths and needs and provide the opportunity for children to demonstrate their full abilities. For example, when assessing children with physical disabilities, it is critical to position them correctly using adaptive equipment prior to assessment. By correctly positioning children, the team will enable them to perform at their full potential physically, as well as across the areas of development being evaluated. In addition, assessment materials should be modified to meet the physical needs of children. For example, if children have difficulty demonstrating fine motor skills (e.g., buttoning or zipping a coat), modification may be made to the buttons or zipper by enlarging them. With such modifications, children may be able to perform the task independently. Considering the impact of children's physical disabilities on their demonstration of knowledge and skills, and making appropriate modifications to address this bias, are critical components of assessing children whose physical disabilities impact assessment of their skills.

When evaluating children with communication needs, team members also should make modifications and accommodations in the assessment process. For example, if the child does not have the ability to answer questions using speech, provide visual examples of the correct responses to which children can point or gesture. In addition, the teacher may want to ask children's parents to interpret speech that is difficult to understand or use information provided by parents. When modifying or accommodating assessment items, first, team members should examine the developmental construct being assessed. For example, if the teacher wants to determine whether children can answer yes or no questions, the teacher would identify the construct to evaluate receptive language abilities to comprehend yes and no questions, rather than assessing children's ability to say yes or no. After determining the construct of the assessment task, the teacher can develop a nonbiased accommodation, such as having the children either point to the printed words yes or no, or shaking their head yes or no.

Nondiscriminatory assessment of young children with physical and communication disabilities requires team members to have a thorough knowledge base of assessment and development. In addition, team members must work collaboratively with each other to make modifications and accommodations. Implementing a transdisciplinary play-based assessment within the inclusive setting can facilitate a valid and accurate assessment.

Summary

This chapter provides an overview of issues and practices related to the assessment of young children in inclusive settings. Assessment of young children in general is a challenge. However, the assessment of young children in inclusive settings may be even more of a challenge if the appropriate supports do not exist. Team members need to have a variety of skills and abilities to conduct valid and authentic assessments. These skills include the knowledge of developmental domains, expertise in naturalistic assessment practices and environmental assessment, and skills in adapting assessments to accommodate learner needs and cultural diversity. Although assessment within the inclusive classroom may be a challenge, this setting is the most appropriate place for assessment. An accurate and valid assessment may help provide the necessary information to facilitate independence and success for young children with disabilities.

REFERENCES

Bailey, D., & McWilliam, R. A. (1990). Normalizing early intervention. *Topics in Early Childhood Special Education, 10,* 33–47.

Bredenkamp, S., & Rosegrant, T. (Eds.). (1992). *Reaching potentials: Appropriate curriculum and assessment for young children (Vol. 1).* Washington, DC: National Association for the Education of Young Children.

Bricker, D., & Cripe, J. J. (1992). *An activity-based approach to early intervention.* Baltimore: Paul H. Brookes.

Choate, J., & Evans, S. (1992). Authentic assessment of special learners: Problems and promise. *Preventing School Failure, 37,* 6–9.

Cook, R. E., Tessier, A., & Klein, M. (1992). *Adapting early childhood curricula for children with special needs.* New York: Merrill.

DEC Task Force on Recommended Practices. (1993). *DEC recommended practices: Indicators of quality in programs for infants and young children with special needs and their families.* Reston, VA: Council for Exceptional Children.

Downing, J. E. (1996). *Including students with severe and multiple disabilities in typical classrooms: Practical strategies for teachers.* Baltimore: Paul H. Brookes.

Federal Register. (1993). Washington, DC: U.S. Government Printing Office, July 30, 1993.

Fox, L., Hanline, M. F., Vail, C., & Galant, K. R. (1994). Developmentally appropriate practice: Applications for young children with disabilities. *Journal of Early Intervention, 18,* 243–257.

Goodwin, W. R., & Driscoll, L. A. (1980). *Handbook for measurement and evaluation in early childhood education.* San Francisco, CA: Jossey-Bass.

Grace, C., & Shores, E. F. (1992). *The portfolio and its use: Developmentally appropriate assessment of young children.* Little Rock, AK: Southern Early Childhood Association.

Guralnick, M. (1992). A hierarchical model for understanding children's peer-related social competence. In S. L. Odom, S. R. McConnell, & M. A. McEvoy (Eds.), *Social competence of young children with disabilities: Issues and strategies for intervention* (pp. 37–64). Baltimore: Paul H. Brookes.

Haney, M., & Cavallaro, C. C. (1996). Using ecological assessment in daily program planning for children with disabilities in typical preschool settings. *Topics in Early Childhood Special Education, 16,* 66–81.

Hanson, M. J., Gutierrez, S., Morgan, M., Brennan, E. L., & Zercher, C. (1997). Language, culture, and disability: Interacting influences on preschool inclusion. *Topics in Early Childhood Special Education, 17,* 307–336.

Linder, T. W. (1993). *Transdisciplinary play-based assessment: A functional approach to working with young children* (Rev. Ed.). Baltimore: Paul H. Brookes.

Lynch, E. W., & Hanson, M. J. (1996). In M. McLean, D. B. Bailey, & M. Wolery (Eds.), *Assessing infants and preschoolers with special needs* (2nd ed.) (pp. 69–95). Columbus, OH: Merrill.

McLean, M. (1996). Assessment and its importance in early intervention/early childhood special education. In M. McLean, D. B. Bailey, & M. Wolery (Eds.), *Assessing infants and preschoolers with special needs* (2nd ed.) (pp. 1–21). Columbus, OH: Merrill.

McLean, M., Bailey, D., & Wolery, M. (1996). *Assessing infants and preschoolers with special needs.* New York: Merrill.

Munson, L. J., & Odom, S. L. (1996). Measure parent-infant interaction. *Topics in Early Childhood Special Education, 16,* 1–25.

National Association for the Education of Young Children (NAEYC). (1986). Position statement on developmentally appropriate practice in early childhood programs serving young children from birth through age 8. *Young Children, 41,* 3–19.

National Association for the Education of Young Children (NAEYC) & National Association of Early Childhood Specialists in State Department of Education (NAECS/SDE). (1991). Guidelines for appropriate curriculum content and assessment in programs serving children ages 3 through 8. *Young Children, 46,* 21–38.

Neisworth, J. T. (1993). Assessment: DEC recommended practices. In DEC Task Force on Recommended Practices, *DEC recommended practices: Indicators of quality in programs for infants and young children with special needs and their families* (pp. 11–18). Reston, VA: Council for Exceptional Children.

Nicholson, S., & Shipstead, S. G. (1994). *Through the looking glass: Observations in the early childhood classroom.* New York: Merrill.

Odom, S. L., McConnell, S. R., & McEvoy, M. A. (Eds.). (1993). *Social competence of young children with disabilities: Issues and strategies for intervention.* Baltimore: Paul H. Brookes.

Overton, T. (1996). *Assessment in special education: An applied approach* (2nd ed.). Columbus, OH: Merrill.

Peck, C. A. (1993). Ecological perspectives on the implementation of integrated early childhood programs. In C. A. Peck, S. L. Odom, & D. D. Bricker (Eds.), *Integrating young children with disabilities into community programs: Ecological perspectives to research and implementation* (pp. 3–15). Baltimore: Paul H. Brookes.

Piaget, J. (1964). Development and learning. In R. Ripple and V. Rockcastle (Eds.), *Piaget rediscovered.* Ithaca, NY: Cornell University Press.

Schwartz, I. S., & Olswang, L. B. (1996). Evaluating child behavior change in natural settings: Exploring alternative strategies for data collection. *Topics in Early Childhood Special Education, 16,* 82–101.

Taylor, R. L. (1997). *Assessment of exceptional students: Educational and psychological procedures* (4th ed.). Boston: Allyn & Bacon.

Wolery, M., & Wilbers, J. S. (1994). *Including children with special needs in early childhood programs.* Washington, DC: NAEYC.

Wortham, S. C. (1990). *Tests and measurement in early childhood education.* New York: Merrill.

Wortham, S. C. (1995). *Measurement and evaluation in early childhood education* (2nd ed.). Columbus, OH: Merrill.

CHAPTER

12 Transition Assessment and Evaluation

Current Methods and Emerging Alternatives

BRUCE M. MENCHETTI
Florida State University

VICKY C. PILAND
Florida State University

OBJECTIVES

After reading this chapter, you will be able to

1. Discuss the transition assessment and planning requirements of the Individuals with Disabilities Education Act (IDEA)
2. Explain how the concept of transition has changed over time and how these changes have resulted in the need for a more comprehensive form of transition assessment
3. Identify several domains and outcome areas that research has suggested as the indicators of an individual's quality of life
4. Describe how the concept of quality of life can be used as a framework for transition assessment, transition service planning, and transition outcome evaluation and how this framework is compatible with the transition planning requirements found in IDEA
5. List two purposes of comprehensive transition-referenced assessment
6. Describe the traditional assessment approaches and methods that are currently used for transition assessment
7. Discuss ways to determine whether a traditional assessment method or instrument is appropriate for transition assessment of students with severe disabilities
8. Describe the methodological problems associated with using traditional methods to assess and plan transition and adult services for individuals with severe disabilities
9. Identify and describe newly emerging strategies and methods of transition assessment and outcome evaluation for students with more extensive support needs

10. List the elements or characteristics that are common to all person-centered planning methods
11. Discuss the components of the Personal Career Plan and how this method has been used to coordinate the efforts of state agencies, public schools, and local adult providers in the delivery of transition assessment services to students with more extensive support needs

KEY TERMS

adaptive behavior and quality of life rating scales (p. 232)
career interests and career decision-making ability (p. 229)
community-based assessment (p. 236)
competency analysis (p. 233)
comprehensive transition-referenced assessment (p. 227)
ecological assessment (p. 236)
interagency coordination (p. 238)
learning and study strategy assessment (p. 231)
life skills knowledge assessment (p. 232)
multiple aptitude batteries (p. 232)
personal career planning (p. 239)
person-centered planning (p. 237)
quality of life (p. 222)
situational assessments (p. 236)
statement of needed transition services (for IEP) (p. 221)
transition services (p. 222)
work sample systems (p. 232)

Since 1990, schools have been responsible for planning transition services for youth with disabilities. The Individuals with Disabilities Education Act (IDEA) of 1990 required a **statement of needed transition services** be included on the Individualized Educational Plan (IEP) for all special education students. Consequently, local education agencies must now have a formal IEP transition statement for each student by age 16, and this statement must describe needed transition services and, if appropriate, describe the linkages and responsibilities of adult and community agencies in the provision of transition services. Stodden (1998) pointed out that this IEP transition statement essentially required planning for life after school and strategies for connecting students to appropriate adult and community services and supports.

The transition requirements of IDEA have led to the need for assessment information to assist in transition planning and evaluation of transition services. Local education agencies have addressed this need in a variety of ways—utilizing many arrangements, strategies, and methods to gather transition planning and evaluation data. Many professionals have become involved in transition assessment and evaluation efforts. Special educators, general educators, vocational educators, school psychologists, guidance counselors, rehabilitation counselors, vocational evaluators, employment consultants, school-to-work coordinators, and others may be involved in assessing students and evaluating the outcomes of transition services. The specific transition assessment and evaluation methods used by local education agencies and their personnel ultimately depend on how professionals view the purpose of transition and its planning and service requirements.

The purpose of this chapter is to provide information that can assist in the selection of appropriate strategies and methods for transition assessment and evaluation of students with more severe disabilities. Conceptual models of transition will be reviewed to identify useful transition assessment and planning domains. A variety of transition assessment approaches—including formal, informal, and newly emerging alternative approaches—will be described and analyzed in this chapter to assist individuals in selecting and using the most functional approaches and methods for students with more extensive transition planning and support needs.

Identifying Transition Assessment Domains

Before we can identify specific transition assessment areas or domains, it is important to discuss the various models that have been used to conceptualize successful transition from school to adult life. As in every other assessment endeavor, transition assessment must be based on a clear and generally accepted conceptual model. Over the last 15 years, there has been much discussion about the meaning of successful transition for students with disabilities.

Early Models of Successful Transition

The transition of students with disabilities from school to work was first identified as a major priority by the Office of Special Education and Rehabilitative Services (OSERS). Madeline Will (1984), assistant secretary of OSERS at the time, defined transition as an outcome-oriented process encompassing a broad array of services and experiences that lead to employment. Recommended **transition services** were provided during high school, at the point of graduation with additional postsecondary education or adult services, and during the initial years in employment. The OSERS view of transition involved three major components: (a) the high school foundation, (b) employment opportunities, and (c) bridges between these two components. Successfully managing the transition between high school and employment involved different levels and intensities of support, ranging from no special services (e.g., family and friends) to time-limited services (e.g., short-term job training) to ongoing services (e.g., job coaching), throughout an individual's life (Will, 1984). Thus, this earliest transition model offered three levels of support to bridge the gap between the security and structure offered by the school and the opportunities and risks of adult life.

Halpern (1985) revised the OSERS model by incorporating a more holistic approach to transition. He contended that success in adult life depended on preparation and support provided in the areas of work, residential living, and social relationships. Halpern viewed these three community adjustment areas as interdependent, suggesting that problems in one area affect adjustment in other areas. Thus, in order for individuals to be successful in employment, they needed to have satisfactory living arrangements and social relationships. The focus of transition now shifted from one dimension (i.e.,work) to a multidimensional (i.e., community adjustment) perspective. Following Halpern's model, successful transition to adult life in the community was now viewed as encompassing three outcome domains—employment, independent living, and social interpersonal relationships.

Quality of Life Models

Recently, authors have suggested that successful transition be more broadly conceptualized as attainment of a personally satisfying **quality of life** (Dennis, Williams, Giangreco, &

Cloninger, 1993; Halpern, 1993; O' Brien, 1987; Rusch & Millar, 1998). Quality of life is a complex, subjective, culturally sensitive, and thereby elusive concept to define (Halpern, 1993; Hughes & Hwang, 1997; Schalock, 1994). In this chapter, quality of life will be discussed solely for the purpose of guiding the identification of specific transition assessment areas and outcome domains.

Quality of Life as the Framework for Transition Assessment. Current conceptual models of successful transition, as well as governmental transition policies, clearly support the use of quality of life as the framework for assessment. There has been much discussion among professionals about the specific quality of life areas that need to be addressed in transition assessment and planning.

Wehman (1995) suggested ten areas of life that should be addressed to plan adequately for successful transition: (a) employment, (b) vocational education, (c) postsecondary education, (d) financial/income needs, (e) independent living, (f) transportation/mobility, (g) social relationships, (h) recreation/leisure, (i) health and safety, and (j) self-advocacy. Wehman pointed out that federal legislation, such as the Individuals with Disabilities Education Act of 1990, made a direct reference to the need for planning in these areas to promote the successful transition of each student with a disability.

A large body of literature has emerged discussing quality of life concepts and measurement issues for people with and without disabilities. A full, meaningful discussion of the concepts and implications of quality of life is beyond the scope of this chapter, and you are referred to excellent treatments of the topics by Halpern (1993), Goode (1994), and Schalock (1996). In order to focus the discussion on assessment and planning issues, Table 12.1 presents legislative guidelines and a sample of those quality of life models suggested as a framework for planning and evaluating transition services and supports specifically for people with disabilities.

Legislation Supporting Quality of Life Outcomes. Federal and state policies also clearly support a quality of life approach for transition assessment, service planning, and outcome evaluation. Legislation such as the Individuals with Disabilities Education Act of 1997 (IDEA, P.L. 105-17) has continued to emphasize the importance of planning for a wide range of individualized postschool outcomes on the IEPs of adolescents with disabilities. Rusch and Millar (1998) said that IDEA "established a broad conceptualization of desired student postschool outcomes" (p. 43) and proceeded to delineate the seven federally defined transition outcomes listed in Table 12.1. IDEA also stipulated that IEP transition services shall take into account a student's preferences and interests. Storms, DeStefano, and O'Leary (1996) pointed out that IDEA is explicit in encouraging the active participation of students in the development of their IEP transition statements. Storms et al. (1996) also suggested that IEP transition statements should specifically focus on quality of life improvement.

Similar quality of life enhancement issues were expressed in the Rehabilitation Act Amendments of 1992 (P.L. 102-569). Section 7(22) (B) of this legislation encouraged use of "functional" assessment information provided by individuals that focus on their unique strengths, resources, priorities, interests, and needs. Menchetti and Bombay (1994) suggested that person-centered assessment and planning methods—which enable personal choice and self-determination, as well as highlight individual strengths—are viable strategies for complying with the Rehabilitation Act Amendments of 1992.

TABLE 12.1 QOL Domains and Outcome Areas Addressed in Select Transition Legislation and Literature

Reference	Assessment Domain/Outcome Area
IDEA (P.L. 105-17) as cited in Rusch and Millar (1998)	Postsecondary Education Vocational Training Integrated Employment (including supported employment) Continuing and Adult Education Adult Services Independent Living Community Participation
Hughes and Hwang (1996)	Social Relationships and Interaction Psychological Well-Being and Personal Satisfaction Employment Self-Determination, Autonomy, and Personal Choice Recreation and Leisure Personal Competence, Community Adjustment, and Independent Living Skills Residential Environment Community Integration Normalization Support Services Received Individual and Social Demographic Indicators Personal Development and Fulfillment Social Acceptance, Social Status, and Ecological Fit Physical and Material Well-Being Civic Responsibility
Schalock (1994)	Home and Community Living Activities of Daily Living, Choices, Possessions, Recreation/Leisure Activities, Volunteer Activities, Using Generic Services, Home Ownership, Private Telephone/Mail Box, Safety and Security, Adaptive Devices, Accommodations, Social Interaction and Supports Employment Adequate Salary and Benefits, Safe Work Environment, Performance Evaluation/Feedback, Job Support, Job Accommodations, Advancement Opportunities, Due Process, Social Interaction Health Functioning Nutritional/Health Status, Mobility, Medication Level, Health Care Access/Coverage, Exercise Opportunities
Halpern (1993)	Physical and Material Well-Being Physical and Mental Health, Food, Clothing, and Lodging, Financial Security, Safety from Harm, Performance of Adult Roles Mobility and Community Access, Vocation, Career, Employment, Leisure and Recreation, Personal Relationships and Social Networks, Educational Attainment, Spiritual Fulfillment, Citizenship (voting), Social Responsibility (doesn't break laws) Personal Fulfillment Happiness, Satisfaction, Sense of General Well-Being
O'Brien (1987)	Community Presence Choice Respect Competence Community Participation

In some areas of the country, state policies also are beginning to reflect a person-centered, quality of life assessment philosophy. For example, the Florida Developmental Disabilities Act, Chapter 393.0651, has required adult service providers to give priority to consumer choice and community-inclusive experiences. Choice, empowerment, self-advocacy, community inclusion, and the attainment of personally satisfying adult lifestyles are becoming the cornerstones of service delivery in numerous states. It seems reasonable, then, that quality of life areas should be addressed in transition assessment, support planning, and program evaluation efforts.

Federal and state policies reflect the importance of using quality of life as the framework for assessment, planning, service delivery, and outcome evaluation. These new policies require assessment methods that provide opportunities for a person with disabilities to become an equal, active partner in all transition processes. In this new policy environment, individual involvement and lifestyle enhancement become the central forces for all transition assessment, planning, support, and evaluation activities.

Quality of Life Indicators in the Literature. Recently, Hughes and Hwang (1997) reviewed the quality of life literature to empirically validate those quality of life indicators that could be used reliably for assessment, individualized planning, and program evaluation purposes. As shown in Table 12.1, these authors identified 15 areas encompassing quality of life. Hughes and Hwang suggested that these 15 areas provide a taxonomy of quality of life measures that may be used for a variety of purposes, including meeting individualized needs, program evaluation, research analysis, and policy development.

In an earlier model, Schalock (1994) suggested that quality of life for people with disabilities may be conceptualized along three domains: (a) home and community living, (b) employment, and (c) health functioning. Within each of the three domains, Schalock identified several subareas to further define quality of life. These are also shown in Table 12.1.

Schalock (1994) pointed out that while quality of life is not a new concept, what is new "is the belief in the 1990s that a person's perception of his/her quality of life is an integral part of service delivery and the evaluation of habilitation outcomes"(p. 266). He suggested that quality of life has emerged as an important issue in our time because of current policies emphasizing quality outcomes, inclusion, equity, empowerment, positive service strategies, and natural supports. Given the integral role played by quality of life concepts in contemporary service delivery, it is imperative that these same concepts guide transition assessment, service planning, and outcome evaluation.

Reflecting on the beginning of the transition initiative in the United States, Halpern (1993) concluded that the early transition models (Will, 1984; Halpern, 1985) were insufficient to guide contemporary transition assessment and measurement efforts. Halpern (1993) suggested the "full array of adult roles" and "subjective dimensions of quality of life" were "the important criteria for evaluating the impact of transition programs" (p. 497).

After reviewing the quality of life literature, Halpern (1993) synthesized the various perspectives into three content domains. As shown in Table 12.1, these were (a) physical and material well-being, (b) performance of adult roles, and (c) personal fulfillment. Within each of his three domains, Halpern identified several outcome areas (also shown in Table 12.1) to further explicate his conceptual model of quality of life.

Some authors have recognized that quality of life may become a difficult concept to define for persons with the most significant disabilities. Many of the widely accepted quality of life criteria, such as educational attainment and independent living, may challenge some of our beliefs and appear to have limited practical utility when applied to the current life situations of people with multiple and severe disabilities.

Instead of abandoning quality of life enhancement as a valid transition goal, O'Brien (1987) identified five essential criteria for conceptualizing lifestyle improvement for people with the most severe disabilities. As shown in Table 12.1, these were

1. Community Presence: Sharing ordinary places in the community (e.g., grocery stores, malls, theaters, and so on)
2. Choice: Autonomy in small, everyday matters and in large, life-defining matters (e.g., employment, food, clothing, housing, and so on)
3. Competence: Performing meaningful activities with whatever level or type of assistance necessary
4. Respect: Having a valued place within a network of friends and valued roles in community life
5. Community Participation: Having access to a growing network of relationships, including close friends

Summary of Quality of Life as an Assessment and Evaluation Framework. While there are some who view quality of life as a potentially dangerous concept for people with disabilities, especially when it is reified as a single QOL score (Taylor, 1994; Wolfensberger, 1994), Schalock (1994) said we must look at quality of life "from a positive, holistic perspective wherein it is viewed as a guiding principle for enhancing a person's development and evaluating the results of intervention/support efforts" (p. 266).

Quality of life models can be used to guide efforts to identify a student's transition preferences, abilities, and needs. Specific quality of life domains can also help teachers assess and plan community connections, acceptance, and participation. Conceptual models of quality of life assure that choice, empowerment, self-advocacy, and self-determination will be considered when assessing transition support needs and evaluating outcomes of transition services. When considering the numerous models of quality of life, however, a practical question becomes, Which quality of life dimensions and indicators should be considered in transition assessment and outcome evaluation?

Schalock (1996) helped answer this question by reducing the multidimensional constructs of quality of life to eight "core" dimensions that should be considered when planning and delivering services for persons with disabilities: (a) emotional well-being, (b) interpersonal relationships, (c) material well-being, (d) personal development, (e) physical well-being, (f) self-determination, (g) social inclusion, and (h) rights.

The eight core dimensions of quality of life identified by Schalock (1996) represent an empirically validated, comprehensive framework for assessing and planning transition services and supports. Special educators, rehabilitation counselors, and other human service providers must insist that any transition assessment instrument they utilize will promote quality of life enhancement by measuring clearly at least one of the dimensions discussed in this chapter. In addition, it is imperative that transition assessment be comprehensive; that is, that it address the breadth and depth of quality of life as represented by its core dimensions. It is important to point out, however, that critical aspects of quality of life—especially those addressing self-determination, community presence and participation, availability of options, and informed choice—often have been missing from some of the current transition assessment approaches and methods. We will now critically review some of these widely used transition assessment methods and the advantages and disadvantages of using these techniques for transition assessment and evaluation of students with more severe disabilities. As stated earlier in this chapter, our purpose is to assist individuals in selecting and using the most functional approaches and methods for students with more extensive transition planning and support needs.

Transition Assessment Approaches

Given the broad range of lifestyle areas that may need to be assessed to assist young adults in making a successful transition from school to adult life, it should not be surprising to learn that a variety of assessment approaches and methods are necessary. Clark (1996) recommended a "systematic, comprehensive transition-referenced assessment approach," which utilized "multiple types and levels of assessment" (pp. 87–88). According to experts, a variety of assessment approaches—including formal instruments, teacher-made and curriculum-based techniques, and the newly emerging person-centered alternatives—all have roles to play in a **comprehensive transition-referenced assessment** approach (Clark, 1996; Dennis et al., 1993; Hughes & Hwang, 1996). The selection of the appropriate combination of approaches and methods will depend on the overall purpose of the transition assessment.

Purposes of Comprehensive Transition-Referenced Assessment

For youth with more severe disabilities, we believe that the most useful and comprehensive transition assessment should serve two broad purposes. First, transition assessment should be used to involve and assist young adults and their families in gathering information about preferences, abilities, and goals in areas that promote quality of life enhancement. Second, transition assessment should be a process used to connect young adults to their preferred sources of formal and informal adult support. Youth with more extensive support needs will probably require both formal agency-sponsored programs and natural circles of community support in order to attain their preferred postschool outcomes and personally satisfying adult roles and lifestyles. A functional assessment approach links youth to all sources and forms of support they choose in order to pursue the postschool goals they and their families desire.

When used for these two purposes, a comprehensive transition assessment can also guide the evaluation of socially valid, consumer-oriented transition outcomes and the use of best practices for transition programming. Kohler (1993) identified transition practices and program structures, which had been substantiated in the literature as positively impacting transition outcomes. Two factors or categories of best practice that emerged from her analysis were student-focused transition planning and family involvement (Kohler, 1993; 1998).

Both categories stressed the active involvement of students and families in the selection of transition goals, services, and support strategies.

When a transition assessment is conducted for these two purposes, postschool outcomes, adult roles, and lifestyle goals will be chosen by youth and their families with guidance and support coming from professionals. This information can later be used to identify student-focused transition outcome evaluation measures. In the kind of transition assessment proposed here, students and their families are directly involved and empowered to select both the outcomes and the type of transition services and supports they receive.

Using Kohler's taxonomy as our rationale, we believe that a functional, comprehensive transition assessment should be based on a collaborative effort between professionals, youth with disabilities, their family, and their friends. This assessment or transition planning team should use a variety of approaches and methods to help adolescents and their families gather the information they need to make a successful transition. The transition planning group should use methods that help students to (a) identify their adult and career interests, preferences, and abilities; (b) generate goals for obtaining personally satisfying adult-life outcomes; (c) assist in planning transition services and supports that help them accomplish their personal career goals; (d) evaluate the success of the services and supports students receive; and (e) revise their transition plans based on successful strategies and services.

Currently, several methods are being utilized by professionals for a variety of transition assessment and evaluation purposes. These include formal and informal tests, inventories, batteries, and work samples. As these current methods are reviewed, ask yourself two questions. First, does this method appropriately assist young adults and their families in gathering information about preferences, abilities, and goals in areas that promote quality of life enhancement? Second, does the assessment method help to connect young adults to their preferred sources of transition support?

Traditional Transition Assessment: Formal and Informal Approaches

Clark (1996), citing a distinction made by Hammil (1987), differentiated between formal and informal transition assessment approaches. According to Clark (1996), formal transition assessment refers to approaches and instruments that research has shown to have some form of psychometric reliability, validity, or both. Formal approaches tend to be standardized instruments with norm-referenced scoring and interpretations. Informal transition assessment approaches, on the other hand, tend to be criterion-referenced instruments that allow one to determine whether the person being assessed can exhibit some behavioral criteria. Often, informal criterion-referenced methods are based on survey data or published theories about the behaviors needed for successful transition.

Both formal and informal instruments may have applicability in transition assessment. Determination of any instrument's applicability for transition assessment depends on the link between the skills measured by the instrument (e.g., learning and study strategies) and the enhancement of an individual student's personal life goals (e.g., educational attainment). The areas that traditionally have been associated with postschool outcomes include (a) academic skills, (b) career interests and decision-making, (c) learning and study strategies, (d) verbal knowledge of life skills, (e) life-skill and social vocational behavior checklists,

(f) multiple aptitude batteries, and finally, (g) samples of work performance. These seven approaches are included in our comprehensive transition-referenced assessment because students with severe disabilities may choose postschool goals that can be supported by an assessment of these traditional skill areas. The transition planning team assisting youth and their families should suggest a combination of assessment instruments that best aid in gathering information about preferences, abilities, and transition outcomes (e.g., educational attainment, obtaining a career). The methods suggested by professionals and other members of the team should also be useful in identifying and connecting youth to informal and formal sources of transition support (e.g., financial support for college, vocational training).

Psychoeducational Assessment of Academic Skills. Psychoeducational assessment of academic skills utilizes formal instruments to measure abilities and achievement in areas such as reading, mathematics, and written and oral language. This approach includes both standardized, norm-referenced tests and curriculum-based instruments that help teachers, psychologists, and other practitioners to determine a student's abilities and needs in these academic domains.

Psychoeducational approaches and instruments certainly have vital roles in a comprehensive transition-referenced assessment approach, especially when academic abilities and achievement are related to a student's future life goals such as attending college. The assessment of abilities and achievement in reading, mathematics, and language arts produces useful lifestyle enhancement information; and when combined with formal assessment information in related areas (e.g., learning styles, self-advocacy), they can help students and their families make plans and identify the services needed for a successful transition from school to postsecondary education and beyond.

A detailed discussion of psychoeducational assessment of academic skills is well beyond the scope of this chapter, however. For extensive treatments of formal and informal academic assessment relating specifically to students with disabilities, see McLoughlin and Lewis (1994), Taylor (1997), and Salvia and Ysseldyke (1996).

Career Interest and Decision Making. Instruments representing measurement of **career interests and career decision-making ability** have been based on different theories of career development (Harrington, 1997; Peterson, Sampson, & Reardon, 1991). Some career development theories have a strong research base and have engendered formal, standardized interest and decision-making instruments. Other approaches to measurement of career interests and decision-making ability have been based on informal models of career development.

Two well-researched models of career development provide the conceptual foundation for several widely used measures of career interests and career decision-making ability. These are (a) measures of the 12 career interest areas identified by the U.S. Department of Labor, and (b) approaches based on the person-environment theory developed by John Holland. Each of these two models has produced several popular approaches for assessing career interests and career decision-making ability.

Department of Labor Interest Areas. The U.S. Department of Labor has developed a model for organizing career interests within 12 major interest areas (JIST Works, Inc., 1995). The 12 U.S. Department of Labor career interest areas are (a) artistic, (b) scientific, (c) plants and animals, (d) protective, (e) mechanical, (f) industrial, (g) business detail, (h) selling, (i) accommodating, (j) humanitarian, (k) leading and influencing, and (l) physical performing. Each of the 12 U.S. Department of Labor interest areas has been further divided into 66 work groups, such as educational and library services, social research, and law within the leading and influencing interest area. Each of the 66 work groups is divided again into 350 specific subgroups of related jobs. For example, within the educational and library services work group, general teaching and instructing and vocational and industrial teaching are two related job subgroups. For definitions of the 12 interest areas and the U.S. Department of Labor organizational structure of interest areas, work groups, and subgroups, see the *Enhanced Guide for Occupational Exploration* (JIST Works, 1995). The *EGOE* is the current edition of the standard career reference, the *Guide for Occupational Exploration,* first published by the U.S. Department of Labor in 1979.

Career interest and decision-making instruments based on the U.S. Department of Labor career interest grouping model ask students to review descriptions of the 12 career interest areas or to read about activities corresponding to the interest areas and indicate their likes and dislikes. Based on these student self-ratings, high, moderate, and low interest areas are identified. Many instruments provide for further exploration of a student's general career interests by providing a list of relevant jobs, often organized by work group and subgroup. These jobs often are indexed numerically to the *Dictionary of Occupational Titles (DOT)* or the *EGOE*—two reference books that describe jobs, skills needed to perform the job, education required, and other useful career awareness and exploration information.

Two instruments that exemplify the U.S. Department of Labor model are (a) *The Guide for Occupational Exploration Inventory* (Farr, 1996); and (b) *The Career-Decision Making System–Revised (CDMS-R)* (Harrington & O'Shea, 1992). Both of these instruments engage students in making responses that indicate their career interests and preferences. After completing a series of exercises, students are given a profile showing their high, moderate, and low areas of interest. Students are also provided with charts showing groups of related jobs, specific job titles, and the educational and skill requirements for a cluster of jobs. Students can use this information in conjunction with standard occupational reference books such as the *DOT* and *EGOE* to learn more about their career and educational options. It is important to understand that *The Guide for Occupational Exploration Inventory* and *The Career-Decision Making System–Revised* represent only two of the many career interest and career decision-making measures based on the U.S. Department of Labor interest grouping. For information about other interest and decision-making instruments based on those categories, refer to *A Comparison of Computerized Job Matching Systems* by Karl F. Botterbusch (1983).

Holland's Person-Environment Theory. Another model of career development, which has been widely applied to measurement of career interests and career decision-making, is the person-environment theory of John Holland. Harrington (1997) described Holland's theory as "the most researched of all vocational development theories" (p. 14).

Holland theorized that people can be characterized by six personality types: (a) realistic, (b) investigative, (c) artistic, (d) social, (e) enterprising, and (f) conventional (Holland, 1985). This typology is often abbreviated using the acronym RIASEC. Further, Holland (1985) assumed that work environments can be classified according to the same six RIASEC types. Finally, Holland proposed the concept of "congruence" to suggest that people will seek out work environments that closely match their personality type. The more congruence between the person and the occupational environment, the better the fit between the person and the job. According to Holland's theory, job satisfaction, job maintenance, and career advancement can be predicted from the degree of congruence. More simply stated, the degree to which personality types and environmental types are matched will predict job satisfaction and career advancement. The elaborate and well-researched career development theory of John Holland cannot be given its due within the confines of this discussion. For a more extensive treatment of Holland's theories and concepts, consult the excellent reviews by Harrington (1997) and also by Peterson, Sampson, and Reardon (1991).

The career interest inventory that is associated most closely with Holland's model is *The Self-Directed Search,* or SDS (Holland, 1994). The SDS Form R, which is appropriate for high school students, requires students to list their occupational daydreams, indicate their preferences (likes and dislikes) for a variety of activities, state their occupational interests, and rate their occupational abilities. Using this information, students are required to score and summarize their responses using the RIASEC codes. Students who complete SDS Form R are provided with suggestions for interpreting their summary codes to further their career exploration and development. The SDS is also available in Form E for adolescents and adults with limited reading ability.

Summary of Career Interest and Career Decision-Making Assessment. Regardless of the approach taken to measure career interests and decision-making abilities, this area plays a critical role in a comprehensive transition assessment. Understanding one's career interests can promote self-awareness—one of the foundations of both career development and self-determination (Field, 1996). Opportunities for career development and increasing self-awareness are two important components of quality of life mentioned by the research reviewed earlier in this chapter. High interest areas can be targeted for career exploration through school-based (e.g., career day) and work-based learning activities (e.g., job shadowing). Finally, knowledge of career interests and preferences at an early stage of adolescence (e.g., age 14) can facilitate the systematic planning of career development services via the transition IEP.

Learning and Study Strategy Assessment. **Learning and study strategy assessment** usually involves ratings of skills such as time management, organization, note-taking, test-taking, and self-advocacy. The typical learning and study strategies instrument solicits self-ratings or requires someone who is familiar with a student's study skills (e.g., teacher, parent) to rate the student's abilities. Often, student self-ratings are compared to ratings of familiar others for counseling purposes and program planning. Information about a student's learning and study strategies can be used to plan needed transition services such as participation in a learning strategies intervention program. In addition, knowledge of effective learning and study strategies can foster self-awareness and self-advocacy by helping students understand their strengths and preferred learning styles. Students can use this self-knowledge to advocate for accommodations that match their preferred learning and study strategies.

One formal instrument that exemplifies this assessment approach is the Learning and Study Strategies Inventory (LASSI) (Weinstein & Schulte, 1987). LASSI is a diagnostic and prescriptive measurement tool. This tool takes approximately 30 minutes to complete and score. It uses a self-report format and does not require any special procedures for administration. There are 10 scales on the LASSI that address areas such as attitude, time management, anxiety, and motivation.

Life Skills Knowledge Assessment. There are two approaches to assessing student knowledge of daily living skills, personal social skills, communication skills, and other functional life skills. The first approach measures a student's written or verbal responses to multiple choice, true/false, and open-ended questions. These questions may appear in a paper-and-pencil, computerized, or spoken format. This form of **life skills knowledge assessment** involves indirect measurement of life skills because it assesses what students say they can do rather than directly observing how they actually perform life skills. Two instruments that assess life skills knowledge are the Life-Centered Career Education Competency Assessment: Knowledge Batteries (Brolin, 1992a) and the Social and Prevocational Information Battery–Revised (Halpern & Irvin, 1986). Both the LCCE Knowledge Batteries and the SPIB-R use paper-and-pencil responses to assess knowledge in a variety of life skill areas such as employability, money management, and hygiene and grooming.

The second technique for measuring knowledge of life skills involves direct observation of student performance using hypothetical situations and materials (e.g., you have $20 and purchase an item costing $18.62; use this play money to count your change). One instrument that exemplifies this approach is the Life-Centered Career Education Competency Assessment: Performance Batteries (Brolin, 1992b).

Adaptive Behavior and Quality of Life Rating Scales. The Weller-Strawser Scales of Adaptive Behavior for the Learning Disabled (Weller & Strawser, 1981) and the Quality of Life Questionnaire (Schalock & Keith, 1993) represent instruments designed to assess transition-related adaptive behavior and overall quality of life, respectively. These behavior checklists and rating scales constitute a specialized type of the familiar adaptive behavior assessment used to determine service eligibility and plan programs for students. Transition-related **adaptive behavior and quality of life rating scales** use the same self-rating interview or familiar other questionnaire administration procedures as general adaptive behavior scales. The more sophisticated instruments correct for the potential response bias of student self-ratings, such as contradictions and giving the answer the student thinks the interviewer desires. For example, the 29-item Lifestyle Satisfaction Scale (Heal, Rubin, & Park, 1995), another quality of life measure, interviews students and uses statistical techniques to adjust scores for obvious contradictions and acquiescence.

Multiple Aptitude Batteries and Work Sample Systems. Some commercial **work sample systems,** such as the Talent Assessment Program (TAP) (Talent Assessment, Inc., 1988), measure general abilities and traits. TAP includes 10 samples of gross motor ability, fine motor or finger dexterity, manual dexterity, visual discrimination, tactile discrimination, and retention of details. Because of the general abilities measured, trait-oriented work samples are highly similar to **multiple aptitude batteries,** such as *the General Aptitude Test Battery* (GATB) (U.S. Department of Labor, 1970) and the popular APTICOM System (Vocational Research Institute, 1992). Multiple aptitude batteries and trait-oriented work samples have little or no role to play in transition assessment because of technical limitations addressed elsewhere in this chapter.

The use of work-oriented samples, however, continues to be popular as a transition assessment tool (Parker & Schaller, 1996; Peterson, 1986; Menchetti & Piland, 1998). Systems such as the *Singer Vocational Evaluation System,* or VES (Singer Company Career Systems, 1982), represent the work skill assessment branch of work sampling. VES has 27 samples, including drafting, electric wiring, plumbing and pipe fitting, refrigeration and air conditioning, sales processing, masonry, sheet metal, cooking and baking, engine service, medical services, cosmetology, data collection and recording, filing, shipping and receiving, packaging and materials handling, electronics assembly, office services, and basic laboratory analysis. VES was designed to provide simulated hands-on experience in selected occupations from the *Dictionary of Occupational Titles (DOT)* specifically for populations with special needs, that is, individuals with social and educational disadvantages, mild retardation, and physical disabilities. The presentation is audiovisual, removing many demands for reading.

Peterson (1986) suggested a procedure called **competency analysis** to design a special type of work sample called a locally developed work sample. The competency analysis procedure involves gathering comprehensive information about a training program or job. This information is used to develop statements of the skills needed for success in the program or job, as well as potential curriculum adaptations or modifications that may be available in a setting. This procedure involves interviews with program teachers or work supervisors and on-site observations. Peterson (1986) recommended using locally developed work samples, designed around a competency analysis, as powerful tools for developing transition IEPs.

The Need for New Methods in Comprehensive Transition Assessment

Traditional approaches to transition assessment, like the seven formal and informal approaches just discussed, may not be sufficiently comprehensive to measure all areas that students with more severe disabilities require for quality of life enhancement. Kozloff (1994) pointed out that "quantitative change in a child's competence does not necessarily amount to qualitative change in a child's place in the world" (p. 3). Measuring competence in academic skills, career interest, career decision making, study strategies, life skills knowledge, adaptive behavior, and work aptitudes may not produce all the information needed to change a student's place in the world. Many traditional assessment methods do not address core dimensions of quality of life such as self-determination, social inclusion, and rights (Schalock, 1996). These dimensions must be addressed in any comprehensive transition-referenced assessment approach for students with more severe disabilities because these factors are important qualitative determinants of lifestyle improvement.

Special educators, general educators, vocational educators, rehabilitation professionals, employment consultants, and others who assist students and their families with planning for the future must insist that *all* aspects of quality of life be included in a comprehensive transition assessment approach. Recently, Thomas (1997) suggested that vocational evaluation professionals take on new roles that promote informed choice, self-determination, and career development. Thomas wrote that these new roles "have taken on even more importance in the current rehabilitation and transition environments" (p. 9). He concluded by stating that assessment and evaluation services must help individuals "achieve independence, financial self-sufficiency, and improved quality of life" (p. 11).

Addressing areas such as choice, self-determination, career development, and other core dimensions of quality of life in transition assessment will not be an easy task. Some have suggested that development and implementation of new, more comprehensive transition assessment will require systemic-level change (Clark, 1996; Menchetti & Piland, 1998; Parker & Schaller, 1996; Thomas, 1997). Among his recommendations for "developing and expanding current transition planning assessment systems" (p. 88), Clark (1996) suggested that transition assessment (a) have a futures orientation based on a student's preferred adult life outcomes; (b) start early (no later than age 14) and continue throughout life; (c) use a variety of assessment approaches, including quantitative, qualitative, portfolio, individual, and group methods; (d) be well organized, collaborative, and coordinated; and finally, (e) take advantage of cultural and language differences to make the information-gathering process relevant to diverse populations.

Systemic change of transition assessment will be a difficult and sometimes frustrating journey, but there are several reasons why we must embark on this path. In addition to the need for expanding the comprehensiveness of transition assessment, there are moral, legal, and methodological reasons for systemic change in the assessment of individuals with more severe disabilities.

Limitations of Traditional Transition Assessment Methods

Because the moral and legal reasons for implementing new assessment approaches have been articulately presented elsewhere (Mount, 1994; Mount & Zwernik, 1988; O'Brien & O'Brien, 1992; Wehman, 1993), this section will focus on methodological problems and social consequences of limiting transition assessment and planning to only traditional methods.

Technical Problems. The methodological problems associated with using psychoeducational tests, aptitude batteries, work samples, and other traditional methods to assess and plan transition and adult services for individuals with more severe disabilities have been discussed for three decades (Gold, 1973; Menchetti & Udvari-Solner, 1990; Murphy & Hagner, 1988; Parker & Schaller, 1996; Wolfensberger, 1967). Nevertheless, standardized tests and criterion-referenced instruments continue to be used today as the primary means of gathering transition assessment information and planning adult programs for people with severe disabilities (Hagner & Dileo, 1993; Menchetti & Piland, 1998; Peterson, 1986). Peterson (1986) suggested the most predominant methods of vocational assessment in special education were (a) trait assessment, (b) task assessment, and (c) assessment of present level of student functioning. Peterson recommended expanding assessment methods to include an environmental adaptation (i.e., natural support) approach and the assessment of effective learning and support strategies.

In a critical review of other traditional assessment approaches, Kozloff (1994) concluded that methods such as achievement tests, developmental checklists, and adaptive behavior scales were oversimplified, contrived, decontextualized, and misused. Kozloff provided the following reasons for his conclusions: (a) assessments confined to one domain do not depict the range of behavior necessary to promote true lifestyle enhancement; (b) assessments conducted using formats, people, and places unfamiliar to the student may be unreliable and invalid; (c) assessments that study the student in isolation from environmental interaction provide little or no information about needed changes in environmental supports; and (d) assessments that are used simultaneously for many purposes (e.g., eligibility, placement, program planning) may sacrifice validity for any one function.

In the vocational realm, Hagner and Dileo (1993) suggested that life skills checklists, multiple aptitude batteries, and work samples were artificial and had limited usefulness for transition planning. Some reasons given by Hagner and Dileo were that (a) these procedures captured small isolated pieces of real jobs; (b) these procedures lacked the work pressures, sights and sounds, and social interactions of the real world; and (c) many procedures did not adequately address the effects of training or natural supports on task performance.

Because of these technical limitations, many authors have called for changes in assessment practice (Menchetti & Piland, 1998; Murphy & Hagner, 1988; Parker & Schaller, 1996). According to some, because of the psychometric problems associated with traditional assessment approaches, the sole use of these instruments for transition planning with individuals with more severe disabilities "would be unprofessional, unethical, and irresponsible" (Menchetti & Udvari-Solner, 1990, p. 305).

Negative Social Consequences. In addition to having psychometric problems, the use of traditional assessment instruments and planning approaches produce unintended social consequences. Social distance—the socially created perceived differences between people—may be one outcome of using traditional methods in transition assessment (Kozloff, 1994).

Dileo (1991) indicated that formalized assessment tools often produced "the unfortunate result of stereotypes and expectations for poor performance" (p. 11). These stereotypes and low expectations usually lead to labels, self-fulfilling prophecies, and assumptions of life-long dependency for people who are labeled. Dileo (1991) said "a label can work against an individual in powerful ways. Language can stereotype a person in reducing expectations of his or her performance or potential due to preconceived notions of what labels such as 'profoundly retarded,' or 'behaviorally disordered' mean" (pp. 12–13).

Mount and Zwernik (1988) suggested an explanation for the negative consequences and limited usefulness of traditional approaches to planning for people with more severe disabilities. They said that these approaches have tended to focus on "deficit-finding" (p. 6). Mount and Zwernik (1988) identified three problems with traditional approaches: (a) the assessment process highlights deficits, (b) the process results in goals that are already part of the existing program, and (c) the process relies solely on professional judgment and decision making.

Summary of the Need for New Methods. Traditional methods such as academic achievement tests, interest inventories, learning and study strategy checklists, knowledge assessments, adaptive behavior scales, multiple aptitude batteries, and work samples have a role to play in comprehensive transition assessment. When there is a relationship between the interests or abilities measured by one of these techniques and a student's postschool or adult life goals, the technique should become one part of a comprehensive transition assessment. When this relationship exists, the information provided by traditional techniques is useful for fulfilling the two purposes of a comprehensive transition assessment proposed in this chapter. First, such information can be used to identify outcome-oriented transition goals and objectives that are based on students' interests, abilities, and needs. Second, such techniques may produce information that helps in connecting students to informal and formal transition services and supports.

However, there are at least three reasons why traditional methods must be complemented by some new transition assessment approaches. First, we have discussed how certain core dimensions of quality of life are not measured adequately with traditional approaches. Assessing choice, self-determination, inclusion, and other quality of life dimensions require new approaches. Second, the use of traditional assessments with individuals with severe disabilities, especially for planning transition and adult services, has been challenged for technical reasons. For over 30 years, professionals have questioned the psychometric reliability and validity of such approaches for planning programs for individuals with disabilities. Third, there have been negative social consequences for people with disabilities who were assessed with some of the traditional approaches. Many people have been stereotyped, the expectations for their performance of adult roles have been lowered, and the use of traditional assessment methods have often resulted in creating social distance, rather than social inclusion for people with disabilities.

New Transition Assessment Methods

For these reasons new methods must become a part of a comprehensive transition assessment approach. Two methods promise to address the problems associated with traditional transition assessment. Community-based ecological assessment and career exploration activities and person-centered planning should be considered as additions to traditional transition assessment for individuals with more severe disabilities.

Community-Based, Ecological Assessment Activities

While in use for many years, **community-based assessment** opportunities are not always available to adolescents with more severe disabilities. Transition-oriented community exploration and assessment methods, however, may be effective ways to facilitate informed choice, self-determination, and career decision making. The community-based exploration and assessment methods that have been developed for vocational assessment illustrate how such an approach can become a part of the comprehensive transition strategy.

For many years, work-based techniques such as situational assessments and on-the-job evaluations have been suggested as needed community-based additions to traditional vocational assessment methods (Botterbusch, 1989; Fry & Botterbusch, 1988; Menchetti & Rusch, 1988). **Situational assessments** and on-the-job evaluations, simply stated, involve performance of job duties in a real work situation. Botterbusch (1989) recommended this approach to assess both student skills and the degree and type of environmental support available to individuals. By assessing environmental support, work-based approaches can identify strengths and weaknesses in support systems and be used to build an effective network of natural supports around the student (Botterbusch, 1989). This type of environmental assessment has sometimes been called ecological assessment (Kozloff, 1994; Menchetti & Flynn, 1990; Parker & Schaller, 1996). Parker and Schaller (1996) defined **ecological assessment** as the process of gathering "comprehensive information about the individual, including current and potential environments, perceptions of parents and family, service providers, and employers; and interactions between the individual and the environment" (p. 158). Ecological assessment information can be used to determine the degree of congruence or fit between the individual and environmental supports and to plan environmental modifications, if needed (Botterbusch, 1989; Menchetti & Flynn, 1990; Parker & Schaller, 1996).

Community-based assessment can also be used to promote career exploration and development. Work-based exploration and assessment activities can be helpful when students do not know their career interests, or what a job entails, or what social behaviors are expected in the workplace. Community-based exploration and assessment methods ensure that students with disabilities have opportunities for exposure to, and exploration of, a wide range of careers. These assessment techniques can assist students in identifying a personally satisfying career path by providing information or experiences that may be used to determine interests and abilities in a particular field. In addition, community-based assessment activities allow us to assist students in making informed choices and developing self-determination skills—two core dimensions of quality of life.

Botterbusch (1989) presented a "holistic vocational evaluation process" that incorporated not only community-based, ecological assessment activities but also traditional assessment methods. As such, the holistic vocational evaluation model represents one of the earliest attempts at building a comprehensive transition assessment approach.

Person-Centered Career Planning

Recently, a new information-gathering and planning process has emerged as another way to facilitate transition assessment and planning. This process reflects new ways of thinking about disability and policies emphasizing personal choice and empowerment. Called lifestyle planning (O'Brien, 1987) or person-centered planning (Nisbet, 1992), this process has been used primarily with individuals who are difficult to plan for, that is, those people for whom an acceptable quality of life is difficult to imagine. These people have usually been labeled severely disabled, autistic, developmentally disabled, severely emotionally disturbed, or multiply handicapped. As discussed earlier, these labels have made transition planning even more difficult by producing stereotypes and expectations for limited adult performance (Dileo, 1991; Mount & Zwernik, 1988).

Person-centered planning refers to several strategies and techniques, including personal futures planning (Mount & Zwernik, 1988), essential lifestyles planning (Smull & Harrison, 1992), and group action planning (Turnbull & Turnbull, 1993). These person-centered methods were not designed specifically for transition planning but can be easily adapted for such purposes. Person-centered processes specifically designed for career planning were described by Dileo (1991), Hagner and Dileo (1993), Menchetti and Piland (1998), and Murphy and Rogan (1995).

Several authors have studied person-centered methods and identified the elements or characteristics that are common to all person-centered planning (Butterworth, Steere, & Whitney-Thomas, 1997; Menchetti & Sweeney, 1995; Menchetti & Piland, 1998). Menchetti and his colleagues (Menchetti & Sweeney, 1995; Menchetti & Piland, 1998) reduced the common elements of all person-centered techniques to (a) group facilitation and support,

(b) capacity-based description, (c) positive vision of the future, (d) plan of action and commitments, and (e) respect and empowerment. These characteristics make person-centered planning especially suitable as a complement to traditional transition planning approaches.

Suitability of Person-Centered Planning in Transition Assessment. While fundamentally different from traditional assessment approaches, person-centered planning is highly compatible with the transition IEP requirements of the Individuals with Disabilities Education Act. It provides a process for meeting both the letter of the law and accomplishing the lifestyle enhancement and community connection purposes of transition assessment discussed in this chapter.

Person-centered planning and IEP transition plans have the same purposes: (a) to build connections or linkages in the community, (b) to support an individual's career preferences and interests, and (c) to help the person achieve satisfying adult lifestyle outcomes.

Person-centered planning provides the structure for making transition assessment more comprehensive. During person-centered planning meetings, traditional assessment information, ecological assessment information, and the input of students, parents, family members, and service providers can be considered. Further community-based exploration can be planned, if needed or requested by the support group. Transition goals and services can be identified in a context that promotes student empowerment, choice, and self-determination. Interagency services can be coordinated. The next section of this chapter will describe our version of a comprehensive, coordinated, and person-centered transition approach.

Comprehensive Transition Assessment: Coordinating Transition Services and Supports. In addition to the use of new methods, implementation of a comprehensive transition assessment approach will require the coordination of a team of professionals representing many disciplines. Special educators alone have neither the resources nor the opportunities to assess all aspects of quality of life. They will need assistance from vocational rehabilitation or other state agencies and from local adult service providers to deliver comprehensive transition assessment and planning services. Any one discipline or agency alone should not be expected to provide traditional assessment, person-centered planning, and community-based, ecological assessments. They simply do not have enough time or resources to provide such a comprehensive assessment. Interagency collaboration utilizing a team approach is a necessary condition for implementation of the comprehensive transition assessment proposed in this chapter.

Fortunately, **interagency coordination** of transition services is required in federal legislation such as IDEA and the Rehabilitation Act Amendments. The comprehensive transition assessment approach provides a perfect opportunity for agencies to work together, share resources, and coordinate needed transition services and supports for individuals with disabilities.

Unfortunately, research has suggested that interagency coordination has not readily occurred during the transition process, however. The National Longitudinal Transition Study (NLTS) (Blackorby & Wagner, 1996) examined many aspects of the transition process, including coordination of planning and provision of services for students with disabilities. Some conclusions of the NLTS concerning interagency coordination of transition planning included findings that (a) transition planning was conducted unilaterally by secondary schools, (b) nonschool personnel were not involved in developing of individualized transition plans, and (c) secondary schools were not making contact with employers, adult service agencies, or postsecondary institutions on behalf of transition-aged students.

In the same study, Blackorby and Wagner (1996) found that parents reported a need for services for their adult-aged children who had already made the transition from special education to adulthood. Of those parents surveyed whose children had been out of special education for up to 5 years, 64% indicated their children needed some adult service, 56% indicated their children needed vocational assistance, 33% indicated their children needed life skills training, 27% indicated their children needed tutoring/reading/interpreting services, and 26% indicated their children needed personal counseling. The provision of these services to young adults obviously will require the involvement and coordination of many agencies throughout the transition process.

Interagency coordination represents another of the systemic changes that must occur if the comprehensive transition assessment approach will be implemented successfully. The next section describes a practical, field-tested method for interagency collaboration in transition assessment, planning, and service delivery.

Personal Career Planning: A Coordinated Transition Assessment Process

Personal career planning (Menchetti & Piland, 1998) illustrates how state agencies, public schools, and local adult providers may work together to deliver a comprehensive transition assessment process. This process incorporates person-centered career planning, traditional assessment, community-based exploration activities, and other techniques to match an individual's preferences, goals, and strengths to local employment opportunities.

Table 12.2 shows the roles and responsibilities of the partners in the personal career planning process. In our model, the state vocational rehabilitation agency, the local school system, and a local adult service agency (in this example, an ARC) work together to provide comprehensive, person-centered transition assessment and planning services.

TABLE 12.2 Roles and Responsibilities in a Coordinated Person-Centered Transition Process

Vocational Rehabilitation	School System	Adult Agency
Referral	Linking Students to Adult Agency	Person-Centered Planning
Eligibility	Transition IEP	Situational Assessment
Funding	Teach Self-Determination, Career Planning, and Vocational Skills	Employment Services
Adaptive Equipment	Transportation Issues	Transportation Issues
Parent Education	Parent Education	Parent Education
Advocacy	Advocacy	Advocacy
Counseling	Communication and Coordination	Social Security Issues
Communication and Coordination	Process Evaluation	Communication and Coordination
Process Evaluation		Process Evaluation

Figure 12.1 shows how teachers refer high school students to state agencies, and how a state agency (in this example VR) funds a local provider (LARC) to conduct personal career planning, or PCP. The type of interagency coordination depicted in Figure 12.1 is an effective way to deliver comprehensive transition assessment services to adolescents while they are still in high school. We recommend that the interagency coordination process depicted in Figure 12.1 begin no later than the end of the eleventh grade.

Components of the Personal Career Plan. The Personal Career Plan (PCP) developed by Menchetti and Piland (1998) had five steps: (a) assembling a support group; (b) facilitating a career planning meeting; (c) developing action plans; (d) reconvening to review efforts, resources, and changes; and finally, (e) writing a résumé. The PCP process as applied to a transition-aged student is depicted in Figure 12.2 and each step is described next. In

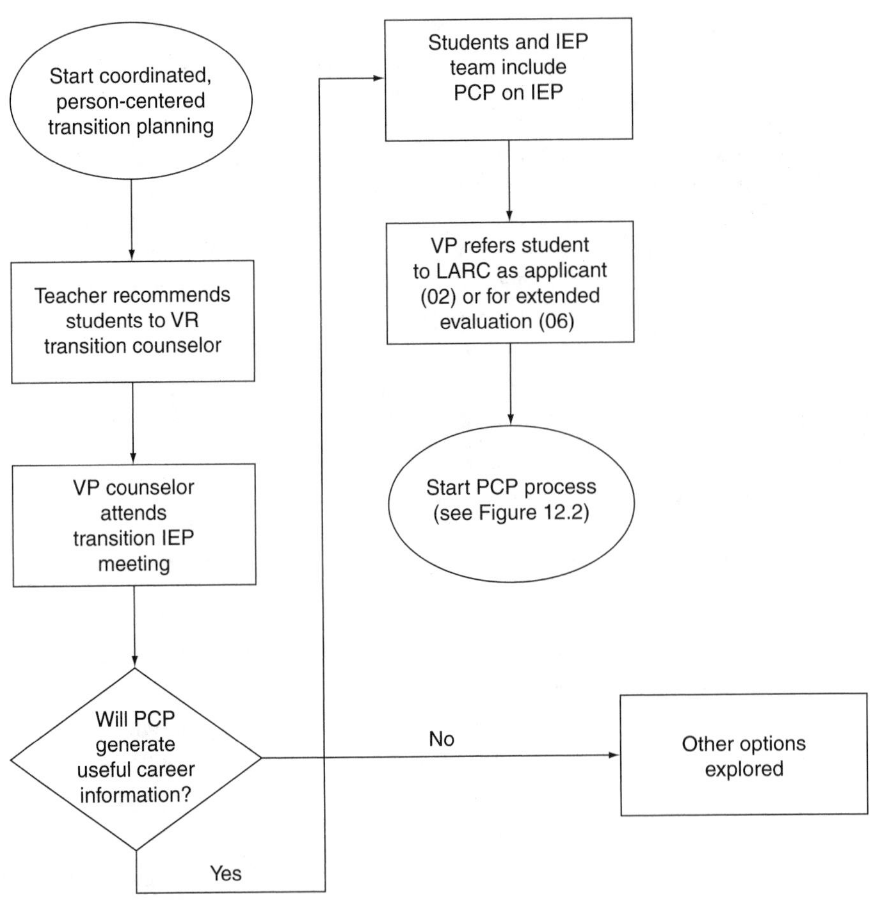

FIGURE 12.1 The coordinated transition planning process.

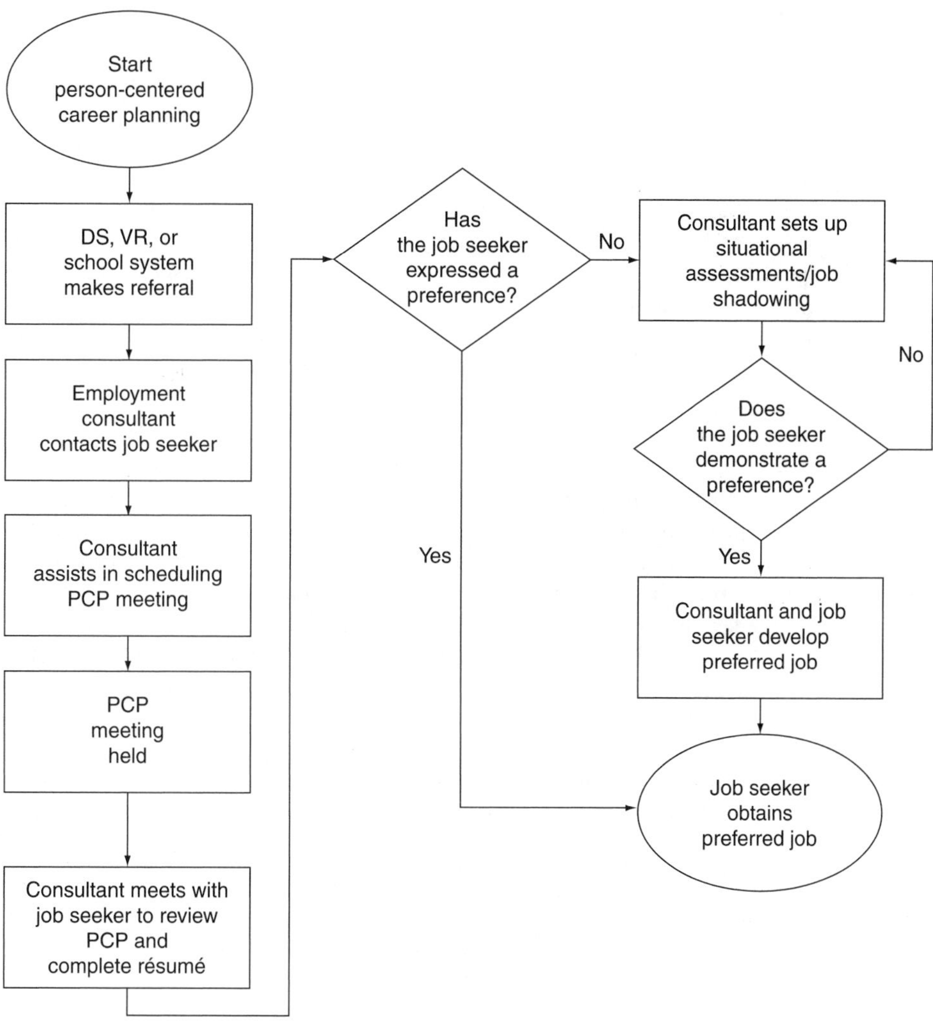

FIGURE 12.2 The person-centered career planning process.

Figure 12.2, the student is called a job seeker because the goal of personal career planning is to assist the student in obtaining his or her preferred job.

1. *Assembling a Support Group.* The Personal Career Plan process begins when a student is referred to a local agency for supported employment as part of the IEP transition planning, which occurs at the end of the eleventh grade. During the IEP meeting, a state agency representative agrees to refer the student to a local provider agency for services. An employment consultant is now available to work for the student. After the IEP has been completed, the designated employment consultant calls the student to introduce him- or herself and to notify the student that a referral has been received. After confirming that the student desires services from the agency, the employment consultant describes the career planning process and discusses possible times, places, and people for a PCP meeting. If the student agrees, invitations are mailed to potential support group members such as vocational rehabilitation counselors, developmental services support coordinators, teachers, friends, and other people that the student wishes to attend.

2. *Facilitating a Planning Meeting.* On the designated date, the support group convenes for the express purpose of developing a personal career plan with the student. The designated employment consultant, who must be trained to conduct person-centered planning meetings, acts as the group facilitator. He or she explains the purpose and format of the meeting so that everyone present understands what is about to occur. The employment consultant emphasizes the need for all group members to listen to the student, respect his or her statements, and support his or her wishes.

The employment consultant asks everyone to sign the support group page (see Appendix 12.1) and asks the student and the group for the names of other people who should be invited to future meetings. Using person-centered planning techniques, including colorful graphics and charts, the employment consultant helps the group gather information relevant for transition and career planning. The Personal Career Plan includes several forms to guide information gathering. The PCP forms included in Appendix 12.1 are (a) support group description, (b) personal data, (c) employment history and personal references, and (d) education, skills, and accomplishments. After all of the information has been collected, the employment consultant reviews the data with the student and the support group and asks for clarification and changes if needed.

3. *Developing Action Plans.* To conclude the support group meeting, participants complete the last form, called a personal career plan (see Appendix 12.1). This requires the group to assist the student to express his or her employment vision or goal and develop action steps to meet that goal. After a vision is developed in the form of an "I want . . ." statement, the group helps the student plan target dates, identify supports and barriers, and develop strategies and tactics to get a job that matches his or her vision. As shown in Figure 12.2, if the student has not expressed a career preference during the PCP meeting, the consultant may suggest a community-based exploration activity (situational assessment).

4. *Reviewing Efforts.* A few days after the support group meeting, the employment consultant calls or visits the student to review the meeting, begin implementing the career plan, and answer any questions. If necessary, or if the student requests, the employment consultant will also contact other group members or individuals the group identified as needed to implement the career plan. At this time, the employment consultant makes an appointment to visit the student and help him or her write a résumé.

5. *Writing a Résumé.* Appendix 12.2 illustrates how a résumé can be written using the Personal Career Plan. First, using information from the vision statement, the student (Jay R.) writes an employment objective. The employment consultant provides whatever support is needed to assist in writing this objective. Next, the student and the employment consultant review employment history and personal reference information to write the employment history section of the résumé. Volunteer activities and nonpaid work experiences should be presented here. Using information from the education, skills, and accomplishment section of the Personal Career Plan, the student and employment consultant together write the education and skills and accomplishment sections of the résumé. All educational experiences, training, and awards should be presented in the appropriate section. Finally, the student and employment consultant review the personal interests section of the Personal Career Plan and write the interests and hobbies section of the résumé.

Box 12.1 provides two examples of how the personal career planning process has been successfully applied to provide comprehensive, coordinated, and person-centered transition assessment to students.

Technical Adequacy of the Personal Career Plan

It is important to evaluate the technical adequacy of any assessment technique. Although relatively new, the Personal Career Plan has been evaluated for the purposes of (a) monitoring the implementation of the process, and (b) continuously improving the process to ensure quality outcomes.

Table 12.3 includes information about the first 123 individuals who completed the Personal Career Planning process. These individuals were former students who were labeled developmentally disabled and had been referred to a community agency for career planning and supported employment services.

Table 12.3 presents data examining the validity of the Personal Career Plan (Menchetti & Piland, 1998) for promoting employment outcomes. The finding that 70% of those who received person-centered career planning with the PCP-obtained employment suggests that the PCP is a valid method for promoting quality of life improvement—one of the purposes for comprehensive transition assessment stated in this chapter.

BOX 12.1
Personal Career Planning With Transition Students

Example One
Jeff is an 18-year-old transition student. He will graduate from high school in June 2001. Jeff has indicated that he would like to work but does not know what he would like to do. Jeff was referred to the Leon Advocacy and Resource Center (LARC) through the Florida Department of Vocational Rehabilitation for a personal career plan. During the personal career planning process, Jeff and his support group decided that a situational assessment would provide some useful career planning experiences. After the situational assessment, Jeff decided that he would like a job with AMC 20 Theaters. With the help of his employment consultant, Jeff gets the job!

Example Two
Nancy is a 19-year-old transition student. She will graduate from high school in June 2001. Nancy has said that she would like to work in the bakery at the Publix grocery store. Nancy was referred to the Leon Advocacy and Resource Center through the Florida Department of Vocational Rehabilitation for a personal career plan. Nancy and her LARC employment consultant developed the job. Three months later, Nancy is working in the bakery!

TABLE 12.3 Outcomes of the Personal Career Planning Process

Number Employed	
People completing process	123
People employed for first time	86 (70%)
Of those employed—number employed in preferred job	68 (79%)
Average time from referral to employment	3.5 months
Type of Employment	
Food service	29 (34%)
Retail	19 (22%)
Industrial	16 (19%)
Office	13 (15%)
Other services	09 (10%)
Length of Employment	
1–3 months	03 (03%)
4–6 months	12 (14%)
7–9 months	16 (19%)
10–12 months	23 (27%)
12+ months	32 (37%)
Wages/Hours Worked	
Average hourly wages	$5.67
Median hourly wage	$5.15
Range of hourly wages	$5.15–$7.00
Average hrs. employed/week	21.3
Median hrs. employed/week	20.0
Range of hrs. employed/week	3.0–40.0
Job Change	
People who changed job after initial employment	14 (16%)
Reasons	
Terminated	06
Resigned	08
People employed in subsequent job	08
PCP Participants	
Vocational rehabilitation	46
Parent	32
Developmental services	28
Other	17

Table 12.3 data can also be used for continuous improvement of person-centered transition assessment methods. For example, examination of the type of employment obtained by individuals receiving personal career planning indicates that most found jobs in service industries. Improvement in the variety of career opportunities produced with person-centered methods is clearly indicated by these data.

It is important that the technical adequacy of new transition assessment methods be evaluated empirically. Empirical validation will hasten the acceptance and implementation of new approaches to transition assessment. We recommend that other quality of life outcomes, including residential outcomes and community participation outcomes, also be validated and the data used for continuous improvement of new transition assessment methods and processes.

Summary

Depending on the unique local arrangements and resources, many different types of professionals may be involved in transition assessment and transition evaluation activities in schools. Special educators, general educators, vocational educators, school psychologists, guidance counselors, rehabilitation counselors, vocational evaluators, employment consultants, school-to-work coordinators, and others may be involved in assessing students and evaluating the outcomes of transition services. The transition assessment and evaluation methods these professionals select eventually comes down to making decisions about what to measure and how to measure it. The methods professionals use ultimately will depend on how they personally view the purpose of transition and its planning and service requirements.

Those who view transition as an exercise in paperwork compliance or as a "check-off procedure" (Kohler, 1998) will probably be satisfied with the information obtained from many of the traditional assessment and evaluation methods. This chapter, however, has suggested that transition assessment for youth with more severe disabilities should have two purposes. First, transition assessment should be used to assist young adults and their families in gathering information about preferences, abilities, and goals in areas that promote quality of life enhancement. Second, transition assessment should be a process used to connect youth to formal and informal sources of support that move youth toward their preferred postschool outcomes. Professionals who agree that transition assessment should be used for these two purposes will probably decide they need other types of information such as knowledge about lifestyle preferences and potential support strategies. This kind of information can be generated by emerging methods such as person-centered planning—as exemplified by the Personal Career Plan.

This chapter has reviewed current methods and emerging alternatives in transition assessment and evaluation. Conceptual models of transition were reviewed to identify appropriate transition assessment and planning domains. A variety of transition assessment approaches—including formal, informal, and newly emerging alternative approaches—were described and analyzed. Guidelines and specific techniques (i.e., the Personal Career Plan) were provided for assisting adolescents and their families in gathering information necessary to (a) identify career interests and preferences, (b) generate goals for obtaining personally satisfying adult-life outcomes, (c) assist in planning transition services and supports that help people accomplish their personal career goals, and (d) evaluate the success of the services and supports they receive. The chapter concluded with a description of a person-centered career assessment called the Personal Career Plan. The Personal Career Plan demonstrated how schools, local adult service providers, and state agencies could collaborate to provide comprehensive, person-centered transition assessment and planning support to transition-aged students with more severe disabilities.

We believe that comprehensive, coordinated, person-centered methods will become the standard for transition and career assessment in the 21st century. We urge professionals to adopt alternative transition assessment and planning methods such as those presented here and to look in new places for information to help their students attain personally satisfying adult lifestyles.

REFERENCES

Blackorby, J., & Wagner, M. (1996). Longitudinal post-school outcomes of youth with disabilities: Findings from the National Longitudinal Transition Study. *Exceptional Children, 62* , 399–413.

Botterbusch, K. F. (1983). *A Comparison of computerized job matching systems.* Menomonie, WI: Material Development Center, University of Wisconsin-Stout.

Botterbusch, K. F. (1989). A model for vocational evaluation in community-based employment. In R. R. Fry (Ed.), *Fourth national forum on issues in vocational assessment: The issue papers* (pp. 117–124). Menomonie, WI: Material Development Center, University of Wisconsin-Stout.

Brolin, D. (1992a). *Life-centered career education competency assessment: Knowledge batteries.* Reston, VA: Council for Exceptional Children.

Brolin, D. (1992b). *Life-centered career education competency assessment: Performance batteries.* Reston, VA: Council for Exceptional Children.

Butterworth, J., Steere, D. E., & Whitney-Thomas, J. (1997). Using person-centered planning to address personal quality of life. In R. L. Schalock (Ed.), *Quality of life volume II: Applications to persons with disabilities* (pp. 5–23). Washington, DC: American Association on Mental Retardation.

Clark, G. M. (1996). Transition planning assessment for secondary-level students with learning disabilities. *Journal of Learning Disabilities, 29*(1), 79–92.

Dennis, R. E., Williams, W., Giangreco, M. F., & Cloninger, C. J. (1993). Quality of life as context for planning and evaluation of services for people with disabilities. *Exceptional Children, 59*(6), 499–512.

Developmental Disabilities Act, 2 Fla. Stat. §§ 393.0651 (1995).

Dileo, D. (1991). *Reach for the dream! Developing individual service plans for persons with disabilities.* St. Augustine, FL: Training Resource Network.

Farr, J. M. (1996). *The guide for occupational exploration inventory: A self-directed guide to career, learning and lifestyle options.* Indianapolis, IN: JIST Works, Inc.

Field, S. (1996). Self-determination instructional strategies for youth with learning disabilities. *Journal of Learning Disabilities, 29*(1), 40–52.

Fry, R., & Botterbusch, K. F. (1988). *Vocational evaluation and work adjustment association glossary.* Menomonie, WI: Material Development Center, University of Wisconsin-Stout.

Gold, M. W. (1973). Research on the vocational rehabilitation of the retarded: The present, the future. In N. Ellis (Ed.), *International review of research in mental retardation: Volume 6* (pp. 97–147). New York: Academic Press.

Goode, D. (1994). *Quality of life for persons with disabilities: International perspectives and issues.* Cambridge, MA: Brookline Books.

Hagner, D., & Dileo, D. (1993). *Working together: Workplace culture, supported employment, and persons with disabilities.* Cambridge, MA: Brookline Books.

Halpern, A. S. (1985). Transition: A look at the foundations. *Exceptional Children, 51,* 479–486.

Halpern, A. S. (1993). Quality of life as a conceptual framework for evaluating transition outcomes. *Exceptional Children, 59,* 486–498.

Halpern, A. S., & Irvin, L. K. (1986). *Social and prevocational information battery–revised.* Monterey, CA: CTB Macmillian/McGraw-Hill.

Hammil, D. D. (1987). Assessing students in schools. In J. L. Wiederholt & B. R. Bryant (Eds.), *Assessing the reading abilities and instructional needs of students* (pp. 1–32). Austin, TX: Pro-Ed.

Harrington, T. F. (1997). *Handbook of career planning for students with special needs.* (2nd ed.). Austin, TX: Pro-Ed.

Harrington, T. F., & O'Shea, A. J. (1992). *The career-decision making system–revised.* Circle Pines, MN: American Guidance Service.

Heal, L. W., Rubin, S. S., & Park, W. (1995). *Lifestyle satisfaction scale.* Champaign-Urbana, IL: Transition Research Institute, University of Illinois.

Holland, J. L. (1985). *Making vocational choices: A theory of careers* (2nd ed.). Englewood Cliffs, NJ: Prentice-Hall.

Holland, J. L. (1994). *The self-directed search.* Odessa, FL: Psychological Assessment Resources.

Hughes, C., & Hwang, B. (1997). Attempts to conceptualize and measure quality of life. In R. L. Schalock (Ed.), *Quality of life volume I: Conceptualization and measurement* (pp. 51–61). Washington, DC: American Association on Mental Retardation.

JIST Works, Inc. (1995). *Enhanced guide for occupational exploration (EGOE)* (2nd ed.). Indianapolis, IN: Author.

Kohler, P. D. (1993). Best practices in transition: Substantiated or implied? *Career Development for Exceptional Individuals, 16,* 107–121.

Kohler, P. D. (1998). Implementing a transition perspective of education: A comprehensive approach to planning and delivering secondary education and transition services. In F. R. Rusch & J. Chadsey (Eds.), *Beyond high school: Transition from school to work* (pp. 179–205). Belmont, CA: Wadsworth Publishing Company.

Kozloff, M. A. (1994). *Improving educational outcomes for children with disabilities: Principles for assessment, program planning, and evaluation.* Baltimore: Paul H. Brookes.

McLoughlin, J. A., & Lewis, R. B. (1994). *Assessing special students* (4th ed.). New York: Merrill.

Menchetti, B. M., & Bombay, H. E. (1994). Facilitating community inclusion with vocational assessment portfolios. *Assessment in Rehabilitation and Exceptionality, 1*(3), 213–222.

Menchetti, B. M., & Flynn, F. R. (1990). Vocational evaluation. In F. R. Rusch (Ed.), *Supported employment: Models, methods, and issues* (pp. 111–130). Sycamore, IL: Sycamore Publishing Company.

Menchetti, B. M., & Piland, V. C. (1998). The personal career plan: A person-centered approach to vocational evaluation and career planning. In F. R. Rusch & J. Chadsey (Eds.), *Beyond high school: Transition from school to work* (pp. 319–339). Belmont, CA: Wadsworth Publishing Company.

Menchetti, B. M., & Rusch, F. R. (1988). Vocational evaluation and eligibility for rehabilitation services. In P. Wehman, & M. S. Moon (Eds.), *Vocational rehabilitation and supported employment* (pp. 79–90). Baltimore: Paul H. Brookes.

Menchetti, B. M., & Sweeney, M. A. (1995). *Person-centered planning* (Technical Assistance Packet #5.) Gainesville, FL: University of Florida, Department of Special Education, Florida Network.

Menchetti, B. M., & Udvari-Solner, A. (1990). Supported employment: New challenges for vocational evaluation. *Rehabilitation Education, 4,* 301–317.

Mount, B. (1994). Benefits and limitations of personal futures planning. In J. Bradley, J. W. Ashbaugh, & B. C. Blaney (Eds.), *Creating individual supports for people with developmental disabilities* (pp. 97–108). Baltimore: Paul H. Brookes.

Mount, B., & Zwernik, K. (1988). *It's never too early, it's never too late: A booklet about personal futures planning.* (Available from the Minnesota Governor's Planning Council on Developmental Disabilities, 300 Centennial Office Building, 658 Cedar Street, St. Paul, MN 55155.)

Murphy, S. T., & Hagner, D. (1988). Evaluation assessment settings: Ecological influences on vocational evaluation. *Journal of Rehabilitation, 53,* 53–59.

Murphy, S. T., & Rogan, P. M. (1995). *Developing natural supports in the workplace: A practitioner's guide.* St. Augustine, FL: Training Resource Network.

Nisbet, J. (1992). *Natural supports in school, at work, and in the community for people with severe disabilities.* Baltimore: Paul H. Brookes.

O'Brien, J. (1987). A guide to lifestyle planning: Using the activities catalog to integrate services and natural support systems. In B. Wilcox, & G. T. Bellamy (Eds.), *A comprehensive guide to the activities catalog: An alternative curriculum for youth and adults with severe disabilities* (pp. 175–189). Baltimore: Paul H. Brookes.

O'Brien, J., & O'Brien, C. L. (1992). Members of each other: Perspectives on social support for people with severe disabilities. In J. Nisbet (Ed.), *Natural supports in school, at work, and in the community for people with severe disabilities* (p. 17–63). Baltimore: Paul H. Brookes.

Parker, R., & Schaller, J. (1996). Issues in vocational assessment and disability. In E. Szymanski & R. Parker (Eds.), *Work and disability,* pp. 127–164. Austin, TX: Pro-Ed.

Peterson, G. W., Sampson, J. P., & Reardon, R. C. (1991). *Career development and services: A cognitive approach.* Pacific Grove, CA: Brooks/Cole Publishing.

Peterson, M. (1986). Work and performance samples for vocational assessment of special students: A critical review. *Career Development for Exceptional Individuals, 9,* 69–76.

Rusch, F. R., & Millar, D. M. (1998). Emerging transition best practices. In F. R. Rusch & J. Chadsey (Eds.), *Beyond high school: Transition from school to work* (pp. 36–59). Belmont, CA: Wadsworth Publishing Company.

Salvia, J., & Ysseldyke, J. E. (1996). *Assessment in special and remedial education* (5th ed.). Boston: Houghton Mifflin Company.

Schalock, R. L. (1994). The concept of quality of life and its current applications in the field of mental retardation/developmental disabilities. In D. Goode (Ed.), *Quality of life for persons with disabilities: International perspectives and issues* (pp. 266–284). Cambridge, MA: Brookline Books.

Schalock, R. L. (1996). *Quality of life volume I: Conceptualization and measurement.* Washington, DC: American Association on Mental Retardation.

Schalock, R. L., & Keith, K. D. (1993). *Quality of life questionnaire.* Worthington, OH: IDS Publishing Co.

Singer Company Career Systems. (1982). *Singer vocational evaluation system.* Rochester, NY: Singer Systems.

Smull, M., & Harrison, S. (1992). *Supporting people with severe reputations in the community.* (Available from the National Association of State Directors of Developmental Disabilities Services, Inc., 113 Oronoco Street, Alexandria, VA 22314.)

Stodden, R. A. (1998). School-to-work transition: Overview of disability legislation. In F. R. Rusch & J. Chadsey (Eds.), *Beyond high school: Transition from school to work* (pp. 60–76). Belmont, CA: Wadsworth Publishing Company.

Storms, J., DeStefano, L., & O'Leary, E. (1996). *Individuals with disabilities education act: Transition requirements. A guide for states, districts, schools, and families.* Stillwater, OK: Oklahoma State University, National Clearinghouse of Rehabilitation Training Materials.

Talent Assessment, Inc. (1988). *Talent assessment program.* Jacksonville, FL: Author.

Taylor, R. L. (1997). *Assessment of exceptional students: Educational and psychological procedures* (4th ed.). Boston: Allyn & Bacon.

Taylor, S. J. (1994). In support of research on quality of life, but against QOL. In D. Goode (Ed.), *Quality of life for persons with disabilities: International perspectives and issues* (pp. 260–265). Cambridge, MA: Brookline Books.

Thomas, S. W. (1997). Three roles of the vocational evaluator. *Vocational and Work Adjustment Bulletin, 30*(1), 9–12.

Turnbull, A. P., & Turnbull, H. R. (1993). Empowerment and decision making through group action planning. In *Life-long transitions: Proceedings of the third annual parent/family conference* (pp. 39–45). Washington, DC: U.S. Department of Education.

U.S. Department of Labor. (1970). *General aptitude test battery.* Washington, DC: Author.

Vocational Research Institute. (1992). *APTICOM system.* Philadelphia, PA: Author.

Wehman, P. (1993). *The ADA mandate for social change.* Baltimore: Paul H. Brookes.

Wehman, P. (1995). *Individual transition plans: The teacher's curriculum guide for helping youth with special needs.* Austin, TX: Pro-Ed.

Weinstein, C. E., & Schulte, A. C. (1987) *Learning and study strategies inventory* . Clearwater, FL: H & H Publishing Company, Inc.

Weller, C., & Strawser, S. (1981). *Weller-Strawser scales of adaptive behavior for the learning disabled.* Novato, CA: Academic Therapy Publications.

Will, M. (1984). *OSERS programming for the transition of youth with disabilities: Bridges from school to working life.* Washington, DC: Office of Special Education and Rehabilitative Services.

Wolfensberger, W. (1967). Vocational preparation and occupation. In A. A. Baumeister (Ed.), *Mental retardation* (pp. 232–273). Chicago: Aldine.

Wolfensberger, W. (1994). Let's hang up quality of life as a hopeless term. In D. Goode (Ed.), *Quality of life for persons with disabilities: International perspectives and issues* (pp. 281–321). Cambridge, MA: Brookline Books.

APPENDIX 12.1 COMPLETED PERSONAL CAREER PLAN FOR A HIGH SCHOOL STUDENT

Support Group

Name: Jay R. **Date:** 1/8/01

Who's Here Today:

Name:	**Relationship/Agency:**
Jay R.	Job seeker
Karen C.	Employment consultant
Tim B.	VR counselor
Nancy R.	Mother
Pat M.	CBI teacher
Dwight L.	Friend

Who Should Be Here:

Name:	**Relationship/Agency:**
Ben R.	Father
Sheri T.	Developmental services counselor

Personal Data

Name: Jay R. **Date:** 1/8/01 **Phone:** 555-5555

Address: 205 Stone Ave.

City: Tallahassee **State:** FL **Zip:** 32306

Social Security #: 000–00–0000 **D.O.B.:** 2/5/82

Emergency Contact: Nancy R. **Phone:** 555-5555

Benefits:

- SSI ☒ PASS ☐
- SSDI ☐ IRWE ☐

Payee: Jay R.

Referral Source:

- DS ☒ LCS ☐
- VR ☒ Other ______

DS Support Coordinator: Sheri T.

VR Counselor: Tim B.

Other: ______

Medical Concerns:

Diabetes—gives himself insulin injections
Sleep Apnea—controlled with medication

Transportation Concerns:

I will need assistance with riding Tal-Tran until I become more comfortable with the route. Specialized transportation may be an option. My parents may also provide transportation.

Employment History and Personal References

Employer: Denny's Restaurant **Address:** 738 Broad Street **Telephone:** 555-5000

Job Title: Food prep **Dates From:** 1/8/01 **To:** 3/16/01

Salary Beginning: Volunteer **Ending:** N/A

Supervisor: Pat M.—CBI teacher

Reason for Leaving: Rotation of class assignment

Employer: Healthnorth Rehab. **Address:** 164 Bond Rd. **Telephone:** 555-6000

Job Title: Transport **Dates From:** 10/3/00 **To:** 12/10/00

Salary Beginning: Volunteer **Ending:** N/A

Supervisor: Jackie Fall

Reason for Leaving: Rotation of class assignment

Employer: Dept. of Revenue **Address:** 523 Hall St. **Telephone:** 555–7000

Job Title: Clerical Aide **Dates From:** 6/18/99 **To:** 8/11/99

Salary Beginning: $4.25/hr. **Ending:** $4.25/hr.

Supervisor: Mr. Martin

Reason for Leaving: Returned to school

References

Name	Address	Phone	Occupation
Pat M.	Local H.S.	555-0121	Teacher
Jackie F.	164 Bond Rd	555-6651	Supervisor
Bill M.	523 Hall St.	555-0011	Supervisor

Education, Skills and Accomplishments

Education:

School Name: Local High School **Address:** 676 Smart St.

Dates From: August 1997 **To:** June 2001

School Name: ________ **Address:** ________

Dates From: ________ **To:** ________

School Name: ________ **Address:** ________

Dates From: ________ **To:** ________

Skills and Accomplishments:

I feel that I have worked hard at school.
I feel that I am good with people.
I am punctual.

Personal Interests:

1. **What are your hobbies/interests?**
   I am studying the driver's handbook. I hope to obtain my driver's license. I enjoy watching movies. I enjoy riding my bicycle.

2. **What volunteer/school activities have you participated in?**
   I am involved in the wrestling team at school. I participate in job training at various businesses in the community.

3. **Imagine that you could have any job in the world. Exactly what would it be?**
   I enjoy helping others and working with people. MWF are the days that I stay after school to help the wrestling team (until 5:00 or 6:00).

Personal Career Plan

Vision Statement

I want a part-time job (while I am still in school) that allows me to help others, between the hours of 12:30 and 5:00 P.M.

Target Date

During the next couple of months, I will obtain information on job openings, apply for these jobs, and go on interviews. I will obtain a part-time job before I graduate in June 2001.

Network/Support:

My Parents—Ben and Nancy R.
VR Counselor—Tim B.
CBI Teacher—Pat M.
Employment Consultant—Karen C.
Friend—Dwight L.

Barriers

I am still in school during the day, so I need to limit my employment to the hours of 12:30–5:00 P.M. I will need help with transportation.

Plan/Tactics

I will obtain information about job openings at TMRMC and TCH.
I will continue to work hard in my classes and graduate in June 2001.
I will write a résumé with my employment consultant.
I will work with my support group to look for a job helping others—after school from 12:30–5:00 P.M.
I will need additional bus training to go to work.

APPENDIX 12.2 MODEL RÉSUMÉ AND COMPLETED SAMPLE

JOHNNY JOBSEEKER

Street Address
City, State, Zip Code
Phone

Objective

The individual, together with the employment consultant, writes an employment objective. They should review and discuss the vision statement section on the Personal Career Plan form in Appendix 12.1 when writing this career objective.

Employment History

The individual and the employment consultant review information from the Employment History and Personal References form in Appendix 12.1 to develop this section of the résumé. Information in this section should be presented like a typical résumé. That is, jobs should be listed in reverse chronological order, from most recent to earliest job. Volunteer activities and nonpaid work experience should be presented here.

Education

The individual and employment consultant use the data from the Education, Skills, and Accomplishments form in Appendix 12.1 to develop this section of the résumé. All relevant education and training experience should be presented here.

Skills and Accomplishments

Referring again to the Education, Skills, and Accomplishments form, the individual and employment consultant summarize skills, talents, and accomplishments. Recognition and awards the individual may have received should be included here.

Interests and Hobbies

Finally, data from the Education, Skills, and Accomplishments form should be reviewed by the individual and employment consultant when developing this section of the résumé. Specifically, the personal interests section should be reviewed. Hobbies as well as school and community activities should be considered. Don't forget to discuss employment desires and choices here.

REFERENCES AVAILABLE UPON REQUEST

JAY R.

205 Stone Avenue
Tallahassee FL 32306
(850) 555–5555

Objective

My career goal is to work in a position helping other people.

Employment History

3/01–Present Denny's Restaurant
I am currently receiving job training that includes bussing tables and rolling silverware.

10/00–12/00 Healthnorth Rehabilitation
This volunteer position included transporting patients and providing assistance.

6/99–8/99 Department of Revenue
This volunteer position included taking phone messages, filing, and making copies of documents.

Education

Local High School
Tallahassee, FL
I will graduate in June 2001

Skills and Accomplishments

I feel that I have demonstrated that I can work well with others and that I am very punctual.

Interests and Hobbies

I am a member of the wrestling team at school.
I am in the process of obtaining my driver's license.

REFERENCES AVAILABLE UPON REQUEST

CHAPTER 13

Functional Assessment of Challenging Behaviors in School and Community

MAUREEN A. SMITH
Buffalo State College

OBJECTIVES

After reading this chapter, you will be able to

1. Identify factors that undermine the inclusion of individuals with challenging behaviors into school and community settings
2. Identify the benefits of conducting assessment and providing instruction in inclusive school and community settings
3. Define functional assessment and functional analysis and distinguish between them
4. List the purposes of assessment techniques used to measure challenging behaviors
5. Identify the steps in a functional assessment
6. Define antecedent, consequence, positive reinforcement, negative reinforcement, punishment, ABC recording, and systematic observation
7. Identify three categories of antecedents and their relationship to challenging behavior
8. Describe the relationship between three categories of consequences and their relationship to challenging behavior
9. Describe how data from a functional assessment can be used to change challenging behaviors in inclusive school and community settings

KEY TERMS

ABC recording (p. 266)
antecedents (p. 266)
behavior intervention plan (BIP) (p. 270)
consequences (p. 261)
functional analysis (p. 269)
functional assessment (p. 260)
negative reinforcement (p. 267)
positive reinforcement (p. 267)
punishment (p. 267)
topography (p. 257)

Individuals with difficult behaviors pose a unique challenge for teachers committed to conducting appropriate assessment and developing and implementing suitable interventions in school and community settings (Larson & Maag, 1998). Obviously, traditional assessment devices do not lend themselves easily to the measurement of behavior that may vary substantially in quality and quantity from what is considered acceptable in inclusive settings. In addition, while it certainly helps to know the **topography** of a behavior, that is, what behavior is being displayed and how often, intervention is more likely to be successful if the teacher understands why the individual is behaving in a particular way (Gresham, Quinn, & Restori, 1999). Specifically, an intervention program may be more effective if it addresses the purpose the inappropriate behavior serves (Gable, 1996). Fortunately, functional behavioral assessment (FBA) can assist the teacher in gaining this understanding. The purpose of this chapter is to describe and illustrate the many facets of functional behavioral assessment.

Barriers to Inclusion for Individuals With Challenging Behaviors

Statistics from the U.S. Department of Education (1994) indicate that less than 16% of children identified as seriously emotionally disturbed (SED) receive their education in general education classrooms. This figure is in contrast to the fact that 35% of students with disabilities other than SED are placed in general education settings. Six percent of students in other disability categories receive their education in segregated settings; however, this statistic increases to 20% for students with SED. Of all the students placed in residential settings, 50% are identified as seriously emotionally disturbed. These students also make up one third of the students receiving homebound instruction.

These statistics highlight the fact that children with emotional and behavior problems are most likely to be removed from inclusive settings. It is not surprising that the quality and quantity of the behavioral challenges posed by some individuals make them less welcome in inclusive settings. As students, these individuals represent the greatest challenge to the design and implementation of supported education in neighborhood schools (Meyer & Janney, 1989). There are many issues surrounding the inclusive placement for students with challenging behaviors, whether they are newly identified and hoping to stay where they are, or recently returning to inclusive settings. These issues include negative teacher attitude, low teacher tolerance for misbehavior, teachers' concerns for their own competence, and a perceived lack of collaboration and support among all those involved in serving students with SED (Martin, Lloyd, Kauffman, & Coyne, 1995). The greatest of these issues is shared by both special and general education teachers, who have identified controlling student behavior as one of their biggest challenges and an area for which they were not trained adequately during professional preparation programs (Munk & Repp, 1994).

Despite these concerns, the Individuals with Disabilities Education Act has mandated that consideration first be given to placement in the least restrictive environment, such as the general education classroom. In addition, the most recent IDEA reauthorization requires school officials to conduct a functional assessment for any student who has been suspended, whose inappropriate behavior could possibly be linked to a disability, or for whom a change in placement is being considered (McConnell, Hilvitz, & Cox, 1998). Efforts to place and maintain students with challenging behaviors in general education settings will affect both general and special educators. It will not be as easy for general education teachers to refer students for placement in special settings. Even with a referral, it can no longer be assumed that students will be removed from an inclusive setting until their behavior is under control. Nor will it be as easy for special education teachers to refer students with more severe problems to even more segregated settings. Both general and special educators will need to address the problem behaviors demonstrated by their students while still meeting the academic needs of other students in their class (Larson & Maag, 1998; Weigle, 1997).

A Rationale for Assessing Challenging Behaviors and Intervening in Inclusive Settings

Meyer and Evans (1989) emphasized the importance of typical schools and community environments to the habilitation process for learners with severe behavior problems. As you will see, challenging behaviors are generally functional; that is, they serve a purpose. Logically, the most effective intervention strategy is to teach appropriate alternatives to these behaviors. An inclusive educational or community setting is an appropriate context for this intervention. In addition, an inclusive setting offers distinct motivational and contextual advantages over segregated settings. Typical peers can model appropriate behaviors and offer support as individuals acquire and use positive behaviors. Fuchs, Fuchs, Fernstrom, and Hohn (1991) noted that students who are taught appropriate skills in segregated settings do not demonstrate competence and appropriate conduct when they move to inclusive settings. Scotti, Ujcich, Weigle, Holland, and Kirk (1996) suggested that generalization and maintenance of newly acquired behavior will be enhanced if interventions occur in the community environments in which the individual resides.

The Nature of Challenging Behaviors

Challenging behaviors generally fall into two categories: excess or externalizing behaviors and deficit or internalizing behaviors. Excess behaviors can include behaviors displayed by all people at one time or another. Young children bite, have temper tantrums, and have occasional difficulty controlling their bladders or bowels. School-aged children get into fights and don't always comply with their parents' or teachers' directives. Adults argue and swear. These behaviors become challenging when they are quantitatively different, that is, they occur at a high rate, for a long period of time, or in the wrong settings (Gelfand & Hartmann, 1984; Berdine & Meyer, 1987). For example, I knew a student named Scott who had temper tantrums that included throwing himself on the floor when his requests were denied by school or residential staff. Many students may do this, but Scott was 16 years old. In addition, these tantrums could last for up to two hours. Scott was also prone to displaying these tantrums when on field trips in the community. Given his age and the circumstances, Scott's behavior was clearly excessive. Excess behaviors can also include behaviors that are qualitatively different from what people do. Scott's tantrum behavior also included headbanging, that is, he would use his head as a weapon to hurt people or damage objects. Other individuals may bite themselves, pick at or scratch their skin until it bleeds, jab forcefully at their eyes, or constantly flap their hands. Typically, these behaviors are outside the realm of behaviors demonstrated by the average person. Meyer and Evans (1989) have organized excessive behaviors into six categories, which are presented in Table 13.1.

The second category of challenging behavior is a deficit. Individuals with deficits may not display a behavior typical for their age or the circumstances. Gelfand and Hartmann (1984) noted that the kindergartner who refuses to talk to adults or the sixth grader who still uses baby talk have behavioral deficits. In the community, an individual who hugs rather than shakes hands with someone to whom he or she has been recently introduced has a deficit. A deficit can also be a behavior that is not displayed often enough, with sufficient intensity, or in appropriate forms to meet the demands of the environment (Berdine & Meyer, 1987). In schools, children with challenging behaviors may not be turning in all of their assignments, completing them with 80% accuracy, or following guidelines specified by their teachers. In the community, an individual who does not assert himself or herself when unfairly confronted has a behavior deficit.

Behavioral excesses and deficits can go hand in hand. For example, the preschooler with autism who is engaging in self-stimulation by hand flapping (an excess) is probably not playing with peers (which will lead to social skill deficits). Of the two, however, excess behaviors are more likely to arouse concern for the individual, set him or her apart from peers, and undermine placement in inclusive settings. Students who engage in these behaviors are

TABLE 13.1 Six Categories of Excessive Behavior Problems

Category	Definition	Examples
Stereotypical Behavior	Repetitive behavior that persists for long periods of time	Body rocking, finger flapping, hand flapping, vocalizations
Self-injurious Behavior	Behaviors that could cause harm to the individual displaying them	Eye gouging, biting, headbanging, pinching
Aggression	Excess behaviors that could result in harm to the individual displaying them or others	Punching, tantruming, noncompliance, running away
Inappropriate Social Behaviors	Behaviors that result from the failure to learn skills and rules that reflect the social norm	Stealing, cursing, hugging strangers, masturbating in public
Disorders of Physical Regulation	Behaviors that result from the inability to control body functions	Drooling, enuresis, encopresis, rumination
Specific Emotional Disturbance	Problems with emotional development and psychological adjustment	Phobia, substance abuse, depression, schizophrenia

Source: Adapted from *Nonaversive intervention for behavior problems,* by L. H. Meyer and I. M. Evans, 1989, Baltimore: Paul H. Brookes.

not available to participate in educational activities. In addition, these behaviors distract teachers from their lessons and students from their tasks. Teachers may spend so much time managing aggressive and disruptive behavior that the amount of time they spend teaching is reduced, which may lead to lower rates of student learning (Weigle, 1997). In the community, excess behaviors call undue attention to the individual. Others will certainly notice these behaviors, and they are likely to avoid the individual displaying them. Access to community settings such as stores, restaurants, theaters, and public recreational facilities may be reduced.

Assessing Challenging Behaviors

Challenging behaviors arouse concern among members of educational and community settings and may undermine acceptance and participation in inclusive environments. Despite these problems, it is interesting to note that these behaviors, whether excess or deficit, may serve a function for the individuals who demonstrate them. Larson and Maag (1998) note that all behaviors are purposeful. The individual who acts is hoping to achieve a result, regardless of whether the act reflects appropriate or inappropriate behavior. This result is the intent or function of the behavior. I am familiar with a student with multiple disabilities and limited communication skills who demonstrated aggressive behavior when she was in pain. Although the form of her behavior was inappropriate (e.g., aggression), its function (e.g., communication of discomfort) was appropriate. An intervention that only focuses on this student's aggression is doomed to failure. As long as the aggression serves a powerful purpose to her, she will continue to use it.

The Office of Special Education Program identified seven strategic targets to improve the quality of educational services for students with severe and emotional behavior problems. The fifth strategic target is the promotion of appropriate assessment, including the determination of the motivation for problem behaviors before designing interventions (Wehby, Symons, & Hollo, 1997). **Functional assessment** is a process for gathering information about an individual's behavior and using it to develop effective intervention plans. Used correctly, it offers several advantages: a complete operational definition of the problem behavior, enhanced ability to predict the times and circumstances during which it will occur, a determination of the purpose of the behavior (O'Neill, Horner, Albin, Storey, & Sprague, 1990), hypothesis-driven interventions, a shift from punishment to skill building, and greater maintenance and generalization of treatment gains (Gable, 1996). A functional assessment can be conducted for each challenging behavior demonstrated by an individual. The professional uses an FBA to determine if there is any relationship between person-environmental events and the display of an inappropriate behavior (Gable, 1996). FBA enables a teacher to develop and test hypotheses about conditions that lead to or maintain a problem behavior. In addition, a functional assessment can identify a replacement skill that can serve the same function for the individual (Weigle, 1997). A teacher who identifies factors that influence or control inappropriate behavior and specifies alternative responses is well on his or her way to developing an intervention to change student misbehavior. A functional analysis occurs when environmental variables are manipulated to determine their effect on problem behavior (Dunlap et al., 1993; Wehby, Symons, & Hollo, 1997). Empirical evidence supports the use of functional assessment and functional analysis in inclusive classes (Umbreit, 1995), special education classes (Foster-Johnson & Dunlap, 1993), and community settings (Redmond, Bennett, Wiggert, & McLean, 1993); with students who are mildly disabled (Cooper, Peck, Wacker, & Millard, 1993), ADHD (Umbreit, 1995), retarded (Dadson & Horner, 1993), seriously emotionally disturbed, and autistic (Redmond, Bennett, Wiggert, & McLean, 1993).

Goals of Functional Assessment

Individuals who display serious behavior problems require comprehensive services selected and coordinated by a multidisciplinary team. To select appropriate services and develop interventions, members of this team need to gather and evaluate assessment data. One of the most valid methods for assessing challenging behaviors is to use functional assessment. Teachers conducting a functional assessment follow a multistage, multi-informant approach, incorporating a variety of assessment sources such as interviews; direct observations; and behavior checklists and ratings from significant others in the individual's environment including teachers, parents, peers, and, when appropriate, the individual (Wehby, Symons, & Hollo, 1997). Performed correctly, a functional behavioral assessment should enable the teacher to achieve several goals. First, he or she can develop a clear description of the behavior. Second, the teacher can identify factors that are contributing to the occurrence of the behavior. Third, the teacher can establish a strong link between assessment and intervention. Knowledge of contributing factors has direct implications for intervention. Manipulating a factor can be sufficient to produce the desired change in behavior. Fourth, the teacher can identify the current status of excess and deficit behaviors. The results of a functional assessment will also document the frequency, duration, and intensity of inappropriate behavior. Done correctly, the results will also allow the teacher to determine just how behavior of the individual varies from that of peers or the expectations of others in educational or community environments. This information allows the teacher to estimate future performance in the absence of treatment, thus providing a justification for the provision of services. Fifth, results from a subsequent assessment can be used to measure the effects of intervention on the behavior. Positive results indicate the program should continue; poor results suggest the need for additional modifications.

Assumptions of Functional Assessment

Foster-Johnson and Dunlap (1993) described two assumptions underlying a functional assessment. First, they noted that "challenging behavior is related to the context in which it occurs" (p. 45). As will be discussed shortly, challenging behaviors are influenced by the events or **consequences** that follow them. Specifically, inappropriate behaviors will increase if rewarded and decrease if punished. Further, challenging behavior is also influenced by the circumstances or context in which it occurs. Context can include specific instructions from authority figures; peer interactions; curricular expectations in school; and the individual's physiological and emotional status, which can be influenced by anxiety, hunger, anger, fatigue, illness, and pain. If these circumstances are changed, the behavior may change too.

The second assumption is that challenging behavior serves a function for the individual. The student uses inappropriate behavior either because he or she doesn't know what else to do (suggesting a skill deficit) or because it is easier to do than the appropriate alternative and more effective in producing desired outcomes. In either case, from the individual's perspective, the behavior is reasonable and logical. The individual may not be able to explain why the behavior works; nonetheless, he or she knows that the behavior has been successful in securing desired items or outcomes. Foster-Johnson and Dunlap (1993) hypothesized that challenging behaviors usually allow an individual to obtain something, such as adult or peer attention, an object, or sensory stimulation. I previously referred to a student named Scott who had a tantrum when his requests were denied. Although Scott never hurt himself, the tantrum was alarming to watch, particularly when it happened in community settings. It is not surprising that, at times, people gave in to Scott's requests to calm him and restore order. Similarly, challenging behaviors may enable the individual to avoid something unpleasant or difficult. Scott enjoyed mathematics activities but did not enjoy other subject matter. He would start a tantrum when it was time to move on to another item on his schedule. In the past, such tantrums would have resulted in Scott being allowed to continue working on math and postponing transitions. It is interesting to note that in both of these examples, Scott displayed temper tantrums, yet his motivation was quite different each time. The first tantrum was to obtain items; the second was to avoid unpleasant activities. The point is that the same behavior, whether demonstrated by the same individual or across different individuals, may serve a different function each time it is used.

Functional Assessment Techniques

The first step in the application of FBA is to define the target behavior. The teacher should develop an operational definition of the behavior that includes the topography and information about its frequency, duration, and intensity. It is essential to involve all interested parties in the development of this definition so that everyone understands and observes the same behavior (Larson & Maag, 1998). See Chapter 8 for information about operational definitions and Chapter 9 for information about systematic observation. Next, the teacher needs to gather information from a variety of sources to create an accurate picture of the problem (Gable, 1996). These sources can be indirect, such as checklists, rating scales, and interviews; and direct, such as anecdotal reports, ABC recording, and systematic observation. Each of these methods is discussed separately.

Checklists and Rating Scales

Of all the sources of information necessary for a functional assessment, data from checklists and rating scales are probably the most inexpensive and least time consuming to obtain. Note that checklists are indirect methods of assessment because they do not require direct contact with the individual in the setting of interest. However, they do allow the teacher to gather some tentative information regarding the nature and seriousness of the problem behavior. Some checklists and rating scales have different forms that can be completed by several people with a stake in the individual's behavior, including parents, teachers, and even the individual. Table 13.2 lists several commonly used rating scales and checklists. Of particular interest is the Motivation Assessment Scale developed by Durand (1990) which presents 16 questions about the

TABLE 13.2 Commonly Used Behavior Checklists and Rating Scales

Rating scales and checklists can be administered quickly and inexpensively. Several checklists and rating scales are available for use by professionals.

Child Behavior Problem Checklist (Achenbach, 1978)
T. M. Achenbach
University Associates in Psychiatry
1 South Prospect Street
Burlington, VT 05401

Connors Behavior Checklist (Connors, 1969)
C. K. Connors
Multi-Health System, Inc.
908 Niagara Falls Boulevard
North Tonawanda, NY 14120

The Motivation Assessment Scale (Durand, 1990)
V. Mark Durand
The Guilford Press
72 Spring Street
New York, NY 10012

Walker Problem Behavior Checklist (Walker, 1983)
Western Psychological Services
12031 Wilshire Boulevard
Los Angeles, CA 90025

circumstances under which a specific behavior occurs. People answer the questions using a Likert scale that ranges from never to always. Responses are categorized according to one of four types of motivation: sensory, escape, attention, and tangible. Sample questions from each category are presented in Table 13.3.

TABLE 13.3 Sample Questions from the Motivation Assessment Scale

Motivation	Sample Question
Sensory	Would this behavior occur continuously, over and over, if this person were left alone for long periods of time?
Escape	Does the behavior occur following a request to perform a difficult task?
Attention	Does the behavior occur in response to your talking to another person in the room?
Tangible	Does the behavior ever occur to get a toy, food, or activity that this person has been told he or she can't have?

Source: Adapted from *Severe Behavior Problems: A Functional Communication Training Approach,* by V. M. Durand, 1990, New York: Guilford Press.

Checklists and rating scales can be used during assessment and after intervention so the teacher can obtain global measures of the nature and severity of the individual's behavior as it is perceived by significant others. There are some problems in that checklists and rating scales can produce rater bias. The respondent can make an individual's behavior seem very inappropriate to justify treatment. Similarly, the rater can make the individual's behavior appear normal to avoid perceptions of deviancy. Another problem is that checklists and rating scales may not offer information regarding aspects of the context that could be contributing to the inappropriate behavior (Gross & Wixted, 1988). Third, although some of these devices include forms that can be completed by the individual with the behavior problem, he or she can lie, may not remember, or may not have the reading and language skills needed to complete it. Finally, because they are indirect measures, behavior checklists and rating scales may provide unreliable estimates of actual behavior.

Behavioral Interview

A behavioral interview is also an indirect source of data regarding the challenging behavior (O'Neill et al., 1990). It is a structured interaction between a professional and the individual or significant others (e.g., parents, siblings, other teachers, and supervisors) who are familiar with the individual's behavior in inclusive settings. The interview enables the teacher to gather information about concerns and the reasons for seeking assistance. He or she can also discuss the goals of any subsequent intervention.

Prior to the interview, the teacher should have referred to the checklists and rating scales to obtain some basic information about behavioral excesses and deficits. The interview begins with an introduction in which the teacher explains how the meeting was set up, how he or she became involved in the situation, what he or she already knows, and what the purpose of the interview is (Morganstern, 1988). Gross (1984) and Berdine and Meyer (1987) suggested using general interviewing strategies, including open-ended questions. When working with family members, the teacher can ask questions such as, "What can you tell me about Scott's behavior?", "What happens just before?", "What happens after?", "Does the behavior occur more in the morning or in the afternoon?", and "What do you want Scott to do instead?" Teachers should avoid questions that can be answered with a single word or phrase. They should ask one question at a time, using language that is understandable and being careful to use appropriate body language. Asking standard "wh" questions is appropriate, with the exception of "Why?", as it may lead to the manufacture of responses that result in inaccurate conclusions. The teacher can ask for additional background information and ideas for incentives and deterrents. If necessary, the teacher can also use the interview to obtain consent for subsequent assessment and share information about the assessment process. Finally, the teacher can get a sense of the willingness of significant others to assist in the development and implementation of any intervention.

Similar questions can be directed to other teachers or supervisory staff. In addition, one can ask about interactions with peers, how the individual functions in large and small groups, the degree of independence typically displayed, the length of attention span, and how the individual compares to peers academically and socially.

The teacher may wish to interview the individual displaying the inappropriate behavior; however, an interview may not be possible if the individual is very young or if there is a disability that precludes participation in extended conversation. If an interview is possible, bear in mind that children and youngsters will not have the poise and confidence typical of most adults. Regardless of age, some individuals with challenging behaviors may lack insight into their problems and may be unmotivated to participate in the interview or change their behavior. During the interview, the teacher is most interested in learning about the problems from the individual's perspective and in getting information about incentives and preferred activities.

Direct Observations

Whereas checklists, ratings scales, and interviews comprise indirect assessment, observations of problem behavior in the inclusive settings in which it occurs are direct methods of assessment. These observations are conducted in a natural setting while the individual is engaged in typical daily routines for an extended period of time (O'Neill et al., 1990). Direct observations offer several advantages. First, they are nonbiased because they require the development of objective definitions of behavior rather than relying on subjective impressions. Second, they can be conducted in the educational or community environment where the behavior of interest is likely to occur. Third, they link assessment to treatment by focusing directly on the behavior of concern and environmental events that immediately precede and follow this behavior. By identifying and modifying these events, an intervention program can be tailored to address the individual's problem behavior. Fourth, some direct observation techniques can be used frequently, even daily, so that the effects of the intervention are known immediately and any necessary modification can be made. Fifth, observational data are more sensitive to the types of progress individuals with challenging behaviors may display over time. Small but important improvements in behavior can be documented. Finally, they can be conducted by any teacher, parent, paraprofessional, or supervisor who is adequately trained. There are three major categories of observation within functional assessment: anecdotal, ABC recording, and systematic observations.

Anecdotal Observations. An anecdotal observation was briefly mentioned in Chapter 9. Because it is central to the FBA, it will receive more elaborate attention here. An anecdotal observation allows the teacher to become acquainted with an individual and his or her behavior in the natural environment (Gelfand & Hartmann, 1984). It can be conducted for a variety of reasons. It is useful when a professional is not sure exactly what is happening in the setting. Thus, it can verify accuracy of another person's observations. It can also be used to develop and refine all aspects of a definition of a challenging behavior. Later, a carefully structured anecdotal report can confirm both the existence of the hypothesized problem and its relationship to environmental events of behavior, which has major implications for intervention.

An anecdotal report conducted early in the assessment process can have a narrative format. A narrative report describes critical events that occurred during the observation period. It typically is used when people in educational and community settings who work closely with the individual do not have a clear idea of the exact nature of the problem. Another professional not directly participating in school or community activities is asked to observe and record events. This professional could be another teacher, school psychologist, a consultant, or anyone thoroughly familiar with FBA. The professional who is asked to conduct an anecdotal observation and produce a narrative report should have no preconceived notions about exactly what is going on; he or she is on a fishing expedition. It is a good idea to have the permission of the individual's guardian before conducting any anecdotal observation; such permission may have been obtained during interviews conducted earlier.

Once in the school or community setting, the person in charge should introduce the professional to the class or group. This person may establish a purpose for the professional's presence, suggesting that he or she is visiting and may be working with group members. It is important to keep movement to a minimum during the observation and to be as unobtrusive as possible. Clothing and jewelry should be conservative; there should be minimal interactions with the individual and his or her peers. It also helps to vary gaze so that the individual is less likely to realize he or she is being observed. During the observation, the professional should note the date, the number of people in the setting and their relationship to each other, the flow of activities and conversation, the beginning and ending times of important events, and environmental events that precede and follow each event. The professional should conduct at least two observations to verify that critical events are typical rather than unique.

The narrative report is written as soon after the observation as possible while the information is still fresh. Although a narrative anecdotal report is tedious to produce, it can confirm the suspicion that a problem is present. It can help the professional target a specific behavior in need of changing. It may suggest conditions that are contributing to the problem and factors that could be reinforcing the behavior. At this point, the professional is able to conduct a more structured anecdotal report, using ABC recording.

As mentioned previously, the information gathered during an anecdotal report can contribute substantially to the development of a definition of the inappropriate behavior. Obviously, the ease of data collection and the quality of the results are facilitated greatly by a comprehensive definition that includes all aspects of the behavior. This definition must include clear, unambiguous terms that will allow different observers across a variety of settings to record and agree on whether the behavior has occurred. It helps to include inclusionary and exclusionary behaviors. Inclusionary behaviors are examples of the target behavior; exclusionary behaviors do not reflect the target behavior. See Table 7.4 for an example of an operational definition and lists of exclusionary and inclusionary behavior. It also helps to share the definition with other people who are familiar with the individual and obtain their feedback regarding its accuracy and comprehensiveness.

ABC Recording. Antecedent Behavior Consequence recording, or **ABC recording,** was first described by Bijou, Peterson, and Ault (1968). This recording method is much more structured than the narrative format of anecdotal recording and more directly reflects the purpose of functional assessment. As previously stated, no matter how strange others may consider the inappropriate behavior, it may actually serve a purpose for the individual who displays it. The professional uses ABC recording to generate a hypothesis about the relationship between each inappropriate behavior and environmental events surrounding its occurrence. For example, the behavior may enable the individual to escape task demands, obtain attention, communicate physical status, entertain him- or herself, receive sensory stimulation, or gain access to desired objects.

Antecedents are visual, auditory, or tactile cues present in a situation that determine the occurrence and direction of a particular behavior (Berdine & Meyer, 1987). Foster-Johnson and Dunlap (1993) identified three categories of antecedents. The first category includes physiological factors, such as illness, allergies, medication, exhaustion, hunger, and thirst. The second category includes factors related to the classroom environment, such as noise, temperature, over- or understimulation, seating arrangements, and a disrupted schedule. The third class of antecedents relates to curriculum and includes the opportunity to make choices, sufficient levels of assistance from teachers or supervisors, the quality of directions, individual preference for the task, the difficulty level of the task or material, time to complete activities, the clarity of criteria, and task relevance.

An antecedent can cue appropriate behavior. For example, "Good morning" should cue a similar greeting as a response. A justified criticism should cue an apology and an explanation or the identification of an alternative behavior. Unfortunately, antecedents intended to promote the development of appropriate academic and social behaviors may in fact prompt an inappropriate response. A teacher's cue to prepare for a reading lesson may prompt an outburst from a student who can't or doesn't like to read. A librarian's request to whisper may prompt cursing. It is also possible that antecedents that typically prompt appropriate behavior are not in place. For example, Scott demonstrated headbanging when his schedule had to be adjusted due to an unforeseen circumstance.

In ABC recording, a consequence is usually staff or peer response to the individual's challenging behavior. These responses can strengthen, weaken, or maintain the behavior. Events that increase or maintain a behavior are called reinforcers. **Positive reinforcement** is an event occurring after a behavior that increases future probability because it is perceived as pleasant by the individual. Teachers who worked with Scott early in his academic career may have inadvertently reinforced his tantrums by ultimately giving in to his requests. The behavior of an obnoxious customer may be reinforced by the store manager who agrees to an unreasonable demand just to restore order and get the customer out the door more quickly.

Negative reinforcement can also increase or maintain an inappropriate behavior. It is defined as an event occurring after a behavior that increases future probability because it allows the individual to escape or avoid something unpleasant. Negative reinforcement was a primary factor contributing to Scott's tantrums. Earlier, I noted that Scott enjoyed mathematics activities but did not enjoy other subject matter. He would start a tantrum when it was time to move on to the next scheduled activity. I suspect that in the past such tantrums would have resulted in Scott being allowed to continue working on math and postponing transitions.

A third type of consequence is **punishment,** which is an event that follows a behavior and decreases the probability of future occurrences because the individual finds it unpleasant. If responses to inappropriate behavior were truly punishing, significant others in educational and community settings would not need to conduct functional assessments. One word of caution is in order. Just because the user intends for a response to punish does not mean that is how it will be perceived by the individual displaying an inappropriate behavior. A classic example is the teacher who orders a misbehaving student to leave the classroom and sit in the hall. She may think she is punishing the student. The student in fact enjoys being out of the classroom. Rather than punish, the teacher inadvertently reinforced the inappropriate behavior.

The professional can use the ABC recording form presented in Figure 9.2. The procedures for conducting ABC recording are very similar to those used to produce a narrative report. The professional reviews information from checklists, rating scales, interviews, and narrative reports. This time, however, the professional is not on a fishing expedition. He or she has a pretty clear idea of the behavior of concern; therefore, his or her attention is directed toward determining if there is a relationship between the occurrence of the behavior and the presence of specific antecedents or consequences. ABC recording should be conducted on several occasions. Observing at the same time will help the professional decide if the behavior is consistently occurring under the same set of circumstances. Observing at different times will help the professional know if the same pattern of behavior is occurring in other settings with other people.

Systematic Observation. The previous section described anecdotal recording and ABC recording as techniques suitable for use by teachers who need to describe the exact nature of the behavior in question and the circumstances under which it occurs. Having conducted anecdotal observations, particularly ABC recording, the teacher now has a better understanding of the behavior; however, he or she may need to gather more information about how often or how long the behavior happens. Thus, the next step in the assessment process involves the use of systematic observation, the most accurate and valid method for assessing behaviors. As is the case for anecdotal recording, systematic observation requires assessment of the individual in the setting of interest as the behavior is happening. As explained in Chapter 9, there are several different techniques for conducting systematic observations, including frequency recording, interval recording, and duration/latency recording. These techniques vary in purpose, complexity, and the degree of labor involved. Of course, the teacher who has as his or her sole responsibility the collection of data can use these methods with little or no difficulty. Unfortunately, most teachers are likely to be responsible for working with the individual on whom they are trying to collect data. Care must be taken to select and use those procedures that will allow teachers to collect data efficiently and consistently while doing other things. In addition, with adequate training, colleagues, parents, and supervisors can also gather systematic observation data. Chapter 9 provides a comprehensive discussion of systematic observation procedures. See Figures 9.3, 9.6, and 9.7 for sample forms.

One form of systematic observation that is particularly useful during FBA is a variation of interval recording known as a scatterplot (Touchette, MacDonald, & Langer, 1985). As illustrated in Figure 13.1, the individual's schedule is filled in along the left side of the graph. Days are plotted along the bottom of the graph. A "+" is recorded once if the behavior occurs one or more times during the activity. No mark is recorded if the target behavior did not occur. A teacher may also use a scatterplot to record frequency data by marking a "+" in the appropriate cell each time the target behavior occurs. An examination of the scatterplot can offer insights into patterns of behavior that may not be apparent with other data collection methods. For example, data from a scatterplot could indicate that inappropriate behavior consistently occurs at particular times of the day, in the presence or absence of certain people, or during specific grouping arrangements or types of activities.

Before leaving this topic, it is important to offer some general suggestions that can enhance the accuracy and usefulness of data gathered from systematic observations. First, develop a definition of the behavior of interest. The data gathered during anecdotal observations can be very useful in this effort. Second, it is essential to consider carefully the nature of the challenging behavior being measured and match these characteristics to the requirements of the systematic collection method. Third, provide adequate training so that the observers will

FIGURE 13.1 A scatterplot.

Directions: Record a "+" if the behavior occurs during the scheduled activity.

Activity	Time	Day	Day	Day	Day	Day	Day	Day	Day	Day	Day
A.M. Bus											
Homebase											
Reading											
Math											
P.E.											
Art/Music											
Lunch											
Written Language											
Library/Tech											
Science											
Social Studies											
Homebase											
P.M. Bus											

be thoroughly familiar with the definition and data collection procedures. Fourth, practice collecting data to ensure its reliability before making programmatic decisions. Fifth, conduct systematic observations on a regular basis to ensure that an accurate and comprehensive picture of the individual's behavior emerges. Foster, Bell-Dolan, and Burge (1988) noted that there are no hard and fast guidelines for how long data should be gathered; however, Farlow and Snell (1989) reported that teachers of students with severe to profound disabilities needed an average of six data points to make accurate decisions about student behavior. However, if anecdotal reports indicate that the behavior occurs in limited situations and is relatively stable, fewer observations are needed.

Functional Analysis

Having completed the functional behavioral assessment, it is now time to conduct a functional analysis. A **functional analysis** involves the manipulation of those events believed to influence the display of the inappropriate behavior and the systematic observation of their impact on the occurrence of behavior (Fox, Conroy, & Heckaman, 1998; Gresham, Quinn, & Restori, 1999). Larson and Maag (1998) provided an illustration. Data from a functional behavioral assessment may indicate that the purpose of a student's tantruming behavior is to allow him to escape from a difficult task. To test this hypothesis, the teacher can remove task demands while holding constant other behavioral and environmental variables. If the frequency and intensity of the tantrums decrease, the teacher has some evidence to support the hypothesis. She then reintroduces task demands and records behavior. An increase in tantruming behavior confirms the hypothesis. To prevent such behavior, the teacher can ensure that the student has the skills necessary to complete assignments. She can also provide a replacement behavior, such as teaching the student to request a short break during challenging work. Continuing to collect data during implementation of these ideas can verify whether intervention is effective. Larson and Maag (1998) note that at this point, functional assessment merges into intervention.

Functional analysis begins by establishing intervention priorities. An individual is probably displaying more than one challenging behavior that must be addressed. The professional must choose which to address first. Sometimes, the choice is really obvious. Meyer and Evans (1989) recommended that behaviors that pose the greatest risk to the safety of the individual and those around him or her should be addressed first. Such behaviors have serious consequences if left untreated, that is, they may be health- or life-threatening. In addition, these behaviors are likely to draw the most negative attention and undermine the potential for success in inclusive educational and community environments. The priority can come from any of the categories listed in Table 13.1, such as self-injury and extreme forms of aggression. Next, target those behaviors that interfere with learning, pose a danger to others, and are a concern for significant others.

The next step in functional analysis is to generate hypotheses. The teacher should examine the information gathered via checklists, rating scales, interviews, anecdotal reports, ABC recording, and systematic observations. He or she develops hypotheses that describe the relationship between the challenging behavior and environmental variables. These hypotheses should be specific, connected to observations, and stated so that the environmental variables can be manipulated in class or in the community to create changes in the behavior (Dunlap et al., 1993). The hypotheses can reflect different categories of variables. The first category includes functional variables in which the teacher determines what purpose the inappropriate behavior serves and identifies an appropriate alternative that will enable the student to accomplish the same goal. The second category includes contextual variables that focus on environmental manipulations of antecedent and consequences (Larson & Maag, 1998). A very specific set of contextual hypotheses includes curricular revision such as task length, task difficulty, and choice (Dunlap, Kern-Dunlap, Clarke, & Robbins, 1991; Kern, Childs, Dunlap, Clarke, & Falk, 1994).

Third, the teacher should develop and implement the intervention program, also known as the **behavior intervention plan (BIP).** The BIP should include interventions and strategies that address the individual's behavior and promote academic and behavioral success. Developing hypotheses about causes can have an enormous impact on treatment options. Now that the condition that appears to be associated with high levels of the inappropriate behavior is known, put into place the condition that is hypothesized to produce low levels of undesirable behaviors (Dunlap et al., 1993). In addition, having identified the purpose of a behavior, the teacher can select and teach an appropriate replacement skill that will allow the individual to satisfy needs and wants. The individual will no longer have to rely on the challenging behaviors to have needs and demands met.

Finally, continue to conduct evaluations of individual behavior and program effectiveness. This step is most easily addressed by conducting ABC recording as often as possible and gathering systematic observation data on a regular basis. Review and respond to the data.

They will tell the professional that an effective program must continue, an ineffective program must be identified, and a goal has been met and it is time to address other areas of concern.

Summary

This chapter made a case for assessing and addressing challenging behaviors in inclusive school and community settings. The most appropriate methods for accomplishing these tasks are functional assessment and functional analysis. Several techniques for conducting a functional assessment were described, including the use of checklists and rating scales, behavioral interviews, anecdotal reports, ABC recording, and systematic observations. Armed with the data yielded by these methods, the professional can conduct a functional analysis to determine treatment priorities, generate and test hypotheses, and develop and implement behavior intervention plans. It should be obvious that functional assessment and functional analysis will require a substantial investment of professional time and energy. Fortunately, this investment will pay off handsomely. Karweit (1984) reported that teachers spend only half of their days engaged in academic instruction, with much of the remaining time devoted to managing behavior. People in inclusive educational and community settings can either manage behavior inefficiently and ineffectively, or begin a process that will enhance their professional development, allow more time for teaching, and promote the academic and social growth of their students. Functional assessment of challenging behaviors may cause more work, but professionals will be more satisfied with their jobs and will be making fewer referrals for placement in restrictive settings.

REFERENCES

Achenbach, T. M. (1978). The child behavior profile: I. Boys aged 6–11. *Journal of Consulting and Clinical Psychology, 4,* 478–488.

Berdine, W. H., & Meyer, S. A. (1987). *Assessment in special education.* Boston: Little, Brown and Company.

Bijou, S. W., Peterson, R. F., & Ault, M. H. (1968). A method to integrate descriptive and experimental field studies at the level of data and empirical concepts. *Journal of Applied Behavior Analysis, 1,* 175–191.

Conners, C. K. (1969). A teacher rating scale for use in drug studies with children. *American Journal of Psychiatry, 126,* 884–888.

Cooper, L. J., Peck, S., Wacker, D. P., & Millard, T. (1993). Functional assessment for a student with a mild mental disability and persistent behavior problems. *Teaching Exceptional Children, 25*(3), 56–57.

Dadson, S., & Horner, R. H. (1993). Manipulating setting events to decrease problem behaviors. *Teaching Exceptional Children, 25*(3), 53–55.

Dunlap, G., Kern, L., dePerczel, M., Clarke, S., Wilson, D., Childs, K. E., White, R., & Falk, G. D. (1993). Functional analysis of classroom variables for students with emotional and behavioral disorders. *Behavioral Disorders, 18,* 275–291.

Dunlap, G., Kern-Dunlap, L., Clarke, S., & Robbins, F. R. (1991). Functional assessment, curricular revision, and severe behavior problems. *Journal of Applied Behavior Analysis, 24,* 287–397.

Durand, V. M. (1990). *Severe behavior problems: A functional communication training approach.* New York: Guilford Press.

Farlow, L. J., & Snell, M. E. (1989). Teacher use of student performance data to make instructional decisions: Practices in programs for students with moderate to profound disabilities. *Journal of the Association for Persons with Severe Handicaps, 14,* 13–22.

Foster, S. L., Bell-Dolan, D. J., & Burge, D. A. (1988). Behavioral observation. In A. S. Bellack & M. Hersen (Eds.), *Behavioral assessment: A practical handbook* (3rd ed.) (pp. 119–160). New York: Pergamon Press.

Foster-Johnson, L., & Dunlap, G. (1993). Using functional assessment to develop effective, individualized interventions for challenging behaviors. *Teaching Exceptional Children, 25*(3), 44–50.

Fox, J., Conroy, M., & Heckaman, K. (1998). Research issues in functional assessment of the challenging behaviors of students with emotional and behavioral disorders. *Behavioral Disorders, 24,* 26–33.

Fuchs, D., Fuchs, L. S., Fernstrom, P., & Hohn, M. (1991). Toward more responsible reintegration of behaviorally disordered students. *Behavioral Disorders, 16*, 133–147.

Gable, R. A. (1996). A critical analysis of functional assessment: Issues for researchers and practitioners. *Behavioral Disorders, 22,* 36–40.

Gelfand, D. M., & Hartmann, D. P. (1984). *Child behavior analysis and therapy* (2nd ed.). New York: Pergamon Press.

Gresham, F. M., Quinn, M. M., & Restori, A. (1999). Methodological issues in functional analysis: Generalizability to other disability groups. *Behavior Disorders, 24,* 180–182.

Gross, A. M. (1984). Behavioral interviewing. In T. H. Ollendick & M. Hersen (Eds.), *Child behavioral assessment: Principles and procedures* (pp. 61–81). New York: Pergamon Press.

Gross, A. M., & Wixted, J. T. (1988). Assessment of child behavior problems. In A. S. Bellack & M. Hersen (Eds.), *Behavioral assessment: A practical handbook* (3rd ed.) (pp. 578–608). New York: Pergamon Press.

Gunter, P. L., Jack, S. L., DePaepe, P., Reed, T. M., & Harrison, J. (1994). Effects of challenging behaviors of students with EBD on teacher instructional behavior. *Preventing School Failure, 38*(3), 35–39.

Karweit, N. (1984). Time on task reconsidered: Synthesis of research on time and learning. *Educational Leadership, 41,* 32–35.

Kern, L., Childs, K. E., Dunlap, G., Clarke, S., & Falk, G. D. (1994). Using assessment-based curricular intervention to improve the classroom behavior of a student with emotional and behavioral challenges. *Journal of Applied Behavior Analysis, 27,* 7–9.

Larson, P. J., & Maag, J. W. (1998). Applying functional assessment in general education classrooms: Issues and recommendations. *Remedial and Special Education, 19,* 338–349.

Martin, K. F., Lloyd, J. W., Kauffman, J. M., & Coyne, M. (1995). Teachers' perceptions of educational placement decisions for pupils with emotional or behavioral disorders. *Behavioral Disorders, 20,* 106–117.

McConnell, M. E., Hilvitz, P. B., & Cox, C. J. (1998). Functional assessment: A systematic process for assessment and intervention in general and special education classrooms. *Intervention in School and Clinic, 34,* 10–20.

Meyer, L. H., & Evans, I. M. (1989). *Nonaversive intervention for behavior problems.* Baltimore: Paul H. Brookes.

Meyer, L., & Janney, R. (1989). User-friendly measures of meaningful outcomes: Evaluating behavioral interventions. *Journal of the Association for Persons with Severe Handicaps, 14,* 263–270.

Morganstern, K. P. (1988). Behavioral interviewing. In A. S. Bellack & M. Hersen (Eds.), *Behavioral assessment: A practical handbook* (3rd ed.) (pp. 86–118). New York: Pergamon Press.

Munk, D. D., & Repp, A. C. (1994). The relationship between instructional variables and problem behavior: A review. *Exceptional Children, 60,* 390–401.

Nelson, J. R., Smith, R. K., Young, R. K., & Dodd, J. M. (1991). A review of self-management outcome research conducted with students who exhibit behavior disorders. *Behavioral Disorders, 16,* 169–179.

Nelson, R. O. (1977). Assessment and therapeutic functions of self-monitoring. In M. Hersen, R. M. Eisler, & P. M. Miller (Eds.), *Progress in behavior modification (Volume 5)* (pp. 263–308). New York: Academic Press.

O'Neill, R. E., Horner, R. H., Albin, R. W., Storey, K., & Sprague, J. R. (1990). *Functional analysis of problem behaviors: A practical assessment guide.* Sycamore, IL: Sycamore Publishing Company.

Redmond, N. B., Bennett, C., Wiggert, J., & McLean, B. (1993). Using functional assessment to support a student with severe disabilities in the community. *Teaching Exceptional Children, 25*(3), 51–52.

Scotti, J. R., Ujcich, K. J., Weigle, K. L., Holland, C. M., & Kirk, K. S. (1996). Interventions with challenging behavior of persons with developmental disabilities: A review of current research practices. *Journal of the Association for Persons with Severe Handicaps, 21,* 123–134.

Touchette, P. E., MacDonald, R. F., & Langer, S. M. (1985). A scatterplot for identifying stimulus control of problem behavior. *Journal of Applied Behavior Analysis, 18*, 343–351.

Umbreit, J. (1995). Functional assessment and intervention in a regular classroom setting for the disruptive behavior of a student with attention deficit hyperactivity disorder. *Behavioral Disorders, 20,* 267–278.

U.S. Department of Education. (1994). *Sixteenth annual report to Congress.* Washington, DC: Author.

Walker, H. (1983). *Walker problem behavior identification checklist (revised).* Los Angeles: Western Psychological Services.

Wehby, J. H., Symons, F. J., & Hollo, A. (1997). Promote appropriate assessment. *Journal of Emotional and Behavioral Disorders, 5,* 45–54.

Weigle, K. L. (1997). Positive behavior support as a model for promoting educational inclusion. *Journal of the Association for Persons with Severe Handicaps, 22,* 36–48.

White, R. B., & Koorland, M. A. (1996). Curses! What can we do about cursing? *Teaching Exceptional Children, 28*(4), 48–52.

CHAPTER 14

Assessment of Students With Physical and Special Health Needs

BARBARA P. SIRVIS
Southern Vermont College

MARY BETH DOYLE
Trinity College of Vermont

DEBRA S. ALCOULOUMRE
New Orleans Parish Schools

OBJECTIVES

After reading this chapter, you will be able to

1. Identify five representative disabilities that comprise each of the categories of physical disabilities and special health care needs
2. Define three unique aspects of and approaches to assessment adaptation for students with physical and special health care needs
3. Identify five major factors that may affect assessment performance of students with physical and special health care needs
4. Identify at least three logistical/access concerns and describe at least two adaptations for each as applied to assessment
5. Identify five skills or behaviors that might be assessed through classroom observation
6. Identify three barriers to—and interventions to resolve—communication and socialization concerns for this group of students
7. Identify and describe the six steps in the assessment and adaptation decision-making process suggested for use in inclusive settings
8. Identify and describe at least three techniques for incorporating a paraprofessional into the educational and assessment program for an entire general education class

KEY TERMS

augmentative communication (p. 280)
logistical concerns (p. 278)
physical adaptation (p. 276)
physical disabilities (p. 275)
social competence (p. 284)
special health care needs (p. 275)
transdisciplinary approach (p. 289)

Traditional assessment methods, for example, standardized achievement tests, are not considered generally a fun part of any student's school experience. Historically, students with disabilities were exempted from such experiences because they could not complete the standardized test in the method prescribed to generate normed scores. As a result, students with disabilities participated in a special event while their peers engaged in the standardized test. For example, they might go on a field trip or have extra time for recess or go for ice cream while their peers struggled with the paper-and-pencil tests.

In the context of inclusive classrooms, think about this: Although the actual scores of students with disabilities may be excluded from reported results because of modifications in the testing procedures, *all* students should take the tests! Teachers could then use the information for instructional planning, taking into consideration that the results of the students with disabilities may not be normed. If standardized tests are so important that we take a considerable amount of instructional time to engage with them, then why should students with disabilities be excused? Why not have everyone take the test and then everyone could go for ice cream together?

Examples—Adaptation and Assessment Needs of Two Students

1. Barry is a 9-year-old student who has congenital amputations of all four extremities. He has a four-inch forearm and a 6-inch forearm both without fingers. Throughout the years, he has made many adaptations and accommodations on his own. He has chosen not to wear a prosthesis to pick up and hold items. He does use both forearms to pick up medium to small items (e.g., a crayon or pencil), and he writes and colors using his cheek and forearm. He types on the computer using his right forearm. Barry uses a universal cuff with a spoon to eat; he does need assistance to attach the cuff to his arm. He is able to request assistance and to explain to peers, caregivers, and the teacher how the device is attached to his forearm. He helps to open milk cartons by holding it while a peer opens the top. He is able to carry his own lunch tray and to clean up after himself after meals. He uses an electric wheelchair for mobility and is able to roll or use a sliding motion when he is not in his wheelchair. Barry is very proud of his participation in the school band. He has played the drums with the band for the past two years. Unfortunately, because Barry rides a lift bus to school and there is no lift bus currently scheduled to take a late afternoon run, after-school transportation is very difficult for Barry and his family. (Many non-lift buses do make later runs in order to facilitate students' participation in after-school activities.) Barry is willing to attempt new challenges such as climbing down stairs by sliding backwards from stair to stair with a standby support in case of fire or other emergency. Barry is sensitive about his physical appearance, and his feelings are hurt when other children tease him or act as if they are frightened by him. How might you support Barry and his classmates in addressing this issue?

2. *Corkey is 12 years old and in the sixth grade. She has spastic quadriplegia and requires extra sitting support in her wheelchair and support to stabilize her trunk. She needs assistance to manage her clothes in the bathroom and to maintain her balance on the toilet. She has been learning to operate her electric wheelchair for mobility for the past two years and has almost mastered maneuvering around obstacles. She needs assistance to set up her meals, and her plate has to be put on nonskid material, so that the plate will not move while she is eating. Corkey uses adapted silverware and an adapted cup with a top. She is unable to write or type without assistance, but she can dictate her answers. She is unable to hold a book or to turn pages. Corkey is unable to focus her eyes on letters and words to read. She works and processes information extremely slowly. Corkey is very social and enjoys the company of her peers, and her favorite activities include hanging out with her girlfriends on the playground and at the mall—especially when there are no adults around!*

Historically, students with physical and health disabilities received educational services in segregated classes, at home, or in hospital-based settings. More recently, these students are found increasingly in inclusive settings, both in school and in the community. Assessment for most students with physical or health disabilities should focus on information to ensure maximum benefit from the instructional experience in the inclusive setting, that is, logistical concerns, adaptations, and individualized teaching and learning requirements. Although assessment methods may need to be modified, academic assessment concerns are generally those for any student in the inclusive setting. In addition, it may be necessary and appropriate to include less traditional areas in an overall assessment of a student's performance and potential.

Physical disabilities and **special health care needs** may affect development, cognition, and learning. Impact of any particular condition varies. For instance, some disabilities have no impact on cognition while others may have significant impact. Adaptation of assessment techniques and strategies provides access to performance information—strengths, interests, and abilities. This chapter will outline the general characteristics of the population, present a construct for a continuum of environmentally referenced assessment, and delineate the roles of transdisciplinary team members. Many of the assessment suggestions in this chapter have been generalized and used with students without disabilities as they interface with traditional performance-based assessments used by many general education teachers.

Overview of Student Characteristics

Categorical definition of students with physical disabilities and health care needs is virtually impossible because of the breadth of illnesses and disorders. Even the terminology to "label" this population lacks consistency, ranging from physically handicapped to physically challenged and chronically ill to special health care needs. Some would cite the federal definitions of orthopedic impairments:

> . . . a severe orthopedic impairment which adversely affects a child's educational performance. The term includes impairment caused by congenital anomaly (e.g., clubfoot, absence

> of some member, etc.), impairments caused by disease (e.g., poliomyelitis, bone tuberculosis, etc.), and impairments from other causes (e.g., cerebral palsy, amputations, and fractures or burns which cause contractures) (*Federal Register,* p. 42478)

and the parallel citation on health impairments:

> . . . limited strength, vitality, or alertness, due to chronic or acute health problems such as a heart conditions, tuberculosis, rheumatic fever, nephritis, asthma, sickle cell anemia, hemophilia, epilepsy, lead poisoning, leukemia, or diabetes, which adversely affect a child's educational performance. (*Federal Register,* p. 42478)

However, these legal definitions do not begin to describe the significant impact of many of these conditions, for example, chronic or acute medical problems that require regular medical treatments, medication, or hospitalization. Physical disabilities are more often visible and also require more frequent **physical adaptation** of the environment and activity. Included in this category are such disabilities as cerebral palsy, muscular dystrophy, osteogenesis imperfecta, spina bifida, spinal cord injury, and traumatic brain injury.

> Students with special health conditions are infants and children with chronic conditions such as asthma, those who have body deformities, those who are medically fragile, those who are supported by technology, those with infectious conditions, and those whose conditions have neurological implications. . . . Students in each of these groups have common problems resulting from their particular conditions that affect their ability to access educational services. (Caldwell, Sirvis, Todaro, & Alcouloumre, 1991, p. 3)

Included among a listing of special health care needs are such chronic or acute conditions as AIDS, asthma, cancer, diabetes, hemophilia, seizure disorders, sickle cell anemia, and ventilator assistance. The three major criteria associated with students with special health care needs are limitations in strength, vitality, or alertness that adversely affect the student's education. A final consideration encompassed within any description of these students is whether the condition is acute or chronic. An acute condition develops rather quickly and the symptoms are intense; while a chronic condition develops slowly and progresses over time.

Students who are identified as having either physical disabilities or special health care needs represent a wide variety of children and youth. Categorically, their characteristics, needs, and abilities are less similar than alike, making it challenging to provide a single approach to assessment and decision making. Therefore, in this chapter, a general overview will be presented with related suggestions and implications for practice within inclusive classrooms.

Assessment and Instructional Adaptations

Several factors may affect the ability of a student with physical or health disabilities to be successful academically or socially in an inclusive setting. Caldwell et al. (1997) identify several factors that may affect a student's ability to learn; similarly, one or more of these factors may affect a student's ability to perform to her or his fullest potential in the assessment situation:

- Lack of experience
- Frequent school absence
- Lack of concentration because of effects of the illness, including pain and fatigue
- Short- or long-term emotional/physical effects of undergoing medical treatments
- Anxiety, pain, and fatigue related to ongoing or periodic medical treatments
- Side effects of medication
- Less time for classes/studying as a result of time needed for health care procedures/therapies
- Personal concerns about health
- Acceptance and understanding of peers
- Poor self-image
- Lack of realistic expectations by program/service providers
- Specific learning disability/developmental delay/cognitive deficits (p. 5)

The impact of one or more of these factors will vary by individual; some will be short term while others may be chronic or constant. Thus, it is important for educational personnel, especially for the general education teacher, to be aware of the specific factors that play a part in an individual student's life. Knowing both what the factors are and how they affect the student's performance allows the teacher to make reasonable and appropriate accommodations. For example, if a student receives chemotherapy on a Tuesday and the teacher has observed that typically the student is tired and quiet on the following Wednesday, the teacher will be less likely to schedule a class field trip or a mid-term examination on that day. Figure 14.1 offers several suggestions matching student needs with appropriate interventions. Given the variation in characteristics and needs of students with physical and health disabilities, educators need to work with families to understand the impact of specific student characteristics to ensure that interventions and accommodations are in alignment with student needs.

FIGURE 14.1 Alignment of concerns and assessment information.

Student Characteristics	Assessment Information	Potential Adaptations
Lack of experience	Description of previous class placement	Develop a supportive transition plan.
Frequent absences	Absentee records	When developing instructional units, always develop a small packet that includes learning objectives and materials that will be ready for the student on an "as needed" basis.
Personal concerns about health	Self-reports, changes in behaviors	Work with the student and the family and school counselors to develop an emotional support plan.

Logistical Concerns

The planning process for students with physical or health disabilities should focus on the student as a participating member of the general education classroom community. The environment must be physically and socially accessible, and proper emergency procedures must be in place. **Logistical concerns** are part of the larger assessment process that facilitates ongoing success for all of the students in the inclusive classroom. Logistical concerns are best addressed by a transdisciplinary team of professionals working in concert with students and their families.

Palfrey et al. (1992) adapted the original model of the American School Health Association to define the transition process for students with special health care needs, outlining both the assessment and planning needs as well as training needs for personnel and the student in preparation for inclusion. They underscore the need for teamwork in planning and implementation and the need for families and the student to be active participants. When preparing for the transition of students with physical or health disabilities, logistical concerns include the obvious issues of physical facility as well as the establishment of student-specific emergency procedures, scheduling modifications, and safe and appropriate class placement with opportunities for the student to participate in school and after-school activities with age-appropriate peers. Assessment concerns also include preparation for necessary health care procedures and optimizing the student's ability to participate in—or at least direct—his or her own care.

Given the variety of characteristics of students with physical and heath disabilities, the classroom teacher and related services team members should take the student's specific strengths and needs into consideration when making logistical arrangements. For example, if a student uses a wheelchair, the classroom teacher would be certain to make the classroom wheelchair accessible (e.g., wide aisles, adjust height of table). After such arrangements have been made, the teacher might assess the impact and quality of the changes by sitting in a wheelchair and attempting to negotiate within the classroom. This provides a new vantage point for experiencing the general education classroom! Small details that may have been overlooked become apparent. For example, the location of the soap at the sink, the positioning of the paints at a learning center, or the height of the pencil sharpener and class displays can all be impediments. As one can see, wheelchair accessibility is more than being able to maneuver in the classroom. Similarly, the daily schedule may need to be adjusted to meet the need of a student who experiences certain side effects of medication.

Timing, Fatigue, and Absenteeism

Assessment procedures and results are only useful if they take into consideration those factors that may affect students' abilities to demonstrate their full potential. Performance may be affected indirectly by the physical effects of the actual disability.

Standardized instruments commonly used in schools and in state testing programs often have time limitations. This requirement may well create tremendous difficulties for students with physical or health disabilities. Physical limitations may affect performance on timed segments, in turn creating a potential misrepresentation of their actual ability. Thus, modification of timing requirements may yield the best information about performance. At the same time, when timing is required for normative standards, test scores of students allowed a timing modification should not be reported with the test scores of other students.

Students with chronic health impairments may tire easily and need to rest often during a regular day. Thus, in any informal or formal assessment situation, the potential effect of fatigue must be considered, recognizing that the effect of fatigue may also vary day to day, depending on medication, natural cycles of any chronic illness, activity level, and so on.

Students with physical or health disabilities also may have poorer attendance due to the nature of their chronic illness or disability. Frequent, short-term absences may be necessary for medical procedures, for example, chemotherapy, tests to adjust medication, or fitting of new equipment. At other times, there may be extended absences due to a significant medical situation, such as cancer going out of remission, sickle cell crisis, or orthopedic surgery. When absences are short-term, it is advisable to provide homework, knowing that demands for rest may preclude completing assignments. In the case of longer-term absences, plans for home or hospital instruction should be ready for immediate implementation. In all situations, it is advisable to work with the family in a proactive manner to develop transition plans to support the student's return to daily classroom activities. Given the continually changing social climates and activities within an inclusive classroom, considerations should be made to support students with and without disabilities in maintaining social contacts. For example, during a long absence, team members might want to allow students time to telephone each other, videotape or audiotape messages, and write notes. These strategies can become part of the explicit curriculum by becoming content at learning centers (e.g., computer station, writing center, reading center). The important element of such arrangements is that the adults support all of the students in maintaining healthy relationships in the inclusive classroom community. Part of this maintenance is that when one member of the community is ill, other members of the community are concerned and take action.

Physical Adaptations

Adaptation of position, instructional equipment, or both may be necessary to enhance the independent performance and comfort of students with physical disabilities. Assessment results are only as useful as the intent and appropriateness of the assessment, so adaptation should be seen as an asset to performance enhancement rather than a negative effect because it does not yield a normed score on a standardized instrument.

Adaptation of position may increase a student's performance and active participation in a wide variety of classroom activities. Because they are constant observers of students' behaviors across the entire school day, teachers can provide useful information to physical therapists who are designing adaptations for positioning or seating. Whether for assessment or instruction, students need to work in the most functional, stable, and effective position that fosters their independent functioning. For some that may mean working on the floor rather than at a traditional desk, while for others the height of the desk may simply need to be adjusted. Some students work best at a standing table that increases their body alignment and stability.

Adaptation of equipment may also enhance performance in academic as well as daily living activities. Writing implements may be more functional if the grip surface is increased. Selection of keys on the computer or pointing may be easier with a device fastened to the head or toe rather than using a finger to select objects or items on a page. Paper can be held down by a clipboard or masking tape; placing a piece of clear plastic over an assignment allows the use of a large marking pen and also protects the paper from inadvertent drooling.

Communication and Socialization

The ability to communicate with peers is an important aspect of developing meaningful relationships. Vocalized speech may be affected by some physical or health disabilities. Limited oral speech impedes development of communication skills, thus potentially impacting a student's ability to initiate and respond to questions and events in a traditional manner (i.e., speech). In inclusive settings, communication is at the center of the teaching and learning process, making it an ideal teaching and learning situation for students who have difficulty in the area of communication. Inclusive classrooms have many rich opportunities to engage in communication with peers and adults throughout the day.

Teachers need to be familiar generally with the various **augmentative communication** systems that may be used by students with physical disabilities. Team members should not lose sight of the fundamental goal of communication, that is, increased effective communication between the student and his or her peers in the inclusive educational setting and with his or her family and friends in the community. Enhanced communication will increase a student's ability to demonstrate his or her cognitive and social abilities (Bigge, 1991).

Augmentative communication systems vary from the most simple picture symbols to more complex computer-based electronic devices. As with most adaptations, there is no cookie cutter approach that applies to an entire category of students. Rather, multiple members of a transdisciplinary assessment team, including a communication disorders/speech therapist, the student, and the student's family, are involved in design and implementation of the appropriate system for any given student. Ongoing suggestions and feedback from families, teachers, and other professionals will help a communication disorders specialist/speech therapist lead the decision-making team to the best selection, keeping in mind that often as students' communication skills increase, so will their potential need for more complex (and often more expensive) systems. However, it should also be remembered that the simplest system can be the best system because it is likely to be most readily usable for interaction with students' peers. For example, a gesture/sign language-based system is only as useful as the number of people who know the gestures or signs. Electronic devices can break, leaving a student unable to communicate for long periods of time. In most situations, it is desirable to maintain a backup low-tech communication system that can be used when there is technical difficulty with the electronic device.

Communication as a Method to Gain Class Membership

Assessment for students with physical or health disabilities focuses on the same academic areas for other students. Adaptation is more likely to be accommodated to meet the student's unique physical or health needs. In addition, nonacademic areas such as communication, social skills, and self-help skills (e.g., eating, dressing, managing personal belongings, and hygiene) may be included in a comprehensive assessment in the context of the classroom environment.

Within the context of inclusive environments, the ability to interact with others in a socially appropriate manner can be the difference in whether meaningful social connections are established. The consequences of not having a rich network of personally meaningful relationships include isolation and loneliness—consequences that none of us want for children and youth. Therefore, the following sections provide an in-depth examination of assessment practices that are appropriate within inclusive situations.

Communication and Socialization

Socialization and peer interaction are fundamental to the intellectual and social development of all students. Socialization for students with physical or health impairments may be affected by their disability. Areas identified earlier in this chapter—communication; timing, fatigue, and absenteeism; and physical adaptations—may all interact with the student's ability to establish and maintain social connections with classmates.

Students learn about themselves through their daily interactions with each other. The presence of friendships and other types of peer-to-peer relationships provides students with the necessary support to develop a positive sense of self and personal identity, including the development of social skills. In many classrooms, students naturally support each other in a variety of ways. Students remind each other of upcoming activities, help each other with assignments, offer emotional support following a difficult interaction with a teacher, loan instructional materials to each other, and listen to each others' feeling about everyday occurrences. They act as acquaintances, friends, and fellow problem solvers. They learn that relationships are necessary in order to support the social, emotional, and academic growth of each of the members of the community. In order for these things to occur, students need to have physical and emotional access to each other. In classrooms where students do have access to one another, peers provide a rich source of natural support. They support each other in ways that adults cannot.

Negotiating the subtle realities of friendships and relationships can be difficult. Relationships, whether they are based on friendship (e.g., positive regard, reciprocity) or need (e.g., tutor, helper), cannot be forced. However, skilled teachers can facilitate the creation of classrooms where it is more likely that positive, reciprocal relationships will exist among students with and without disabilities. In order to begin this process, classroom personnel need to engage in a social assessment process that (a) examines the socialization patterns of all of the students in the classroom community, (b) ensures that students have physical and emotional access to each other, and (c) focuses on individual student socialization competence. Such an assessment process can begin with a variety of formal and informal observations of all of the students in the class. Eventually, the classroom personnel will focus on those students with and without disabilities who seem to be having difficulty on social dimensions.

Observe Socialization Patterns. Begin to assess the nature and quality of the relationships for each student in the classroom by formally observing them in a variety of settings. A specific focus of the observation is to determine if the students within the class have informal and formal access to one another. Are they (including the student with disabilities) ever in the same environments together without the presence of adults? Do they interact with each other in a variety of school settings? Do any of the students (i.e., with or without disabilities) appear to be socially isolated or withdrawn? Are any of the students continuously in the shadow of an adult (i.e., teacher or paraprofessional)? Watch and listen to the students during structured (e.g., instruction, learning centers) and unstructured (e.g., recess, lunch) times. Record your observations and simultaneously jot down questions that come to mind. Refer to the observation form in Figure 14.2 as an example.

The goal of this type of observation is to determine whether all of the members of the classroom community are connected with each other in positive and supportive relationships. Once connectedness is determined, then the classroom personnel can watch and listen carefully to determine degree of reciprocity within the relationships. This is especially important for students with disabilities. For example, is the student with disabilities always involved in peer-tutor relationships? Is the student always the tutee? Does the student with disabilities ever interact with students without disabilities without the facilitation of an adult? How often and under what circumstances does the student with disabilities support, encourage, and contribute to the social life of the classroom community? It is important to keep in mind that the ability to contribute to others is an important aspect of all of our lives. Some students with physical or health disabilities need to be taught how to engage in a reciprocal relationship.

Access to Relationships. In some cases, it is helpful to examine issues that surround the ability of the student with disabilities to have basic access to his or her classmates. Students with and without disabilities need basic access to each other accompanied by the least intrusive types of support, in order to have ongoing opportunities to develop and maintain friendships. To accomplish this task, examine the student's daily schedule to see if he or she is in the same places and involved in the same activities as nondisabled peers throughout the instructional day. Verify this by observing the student across several school days. Answer the questions: Does the written schedule reflect the student's actual daily activities? Is the student with disabilities in the same classes and actively participating in the same instructional and noninstructional activities as his or her peers, even if the instructional objectives are different? Within these same settings and activities, is the student with disabilities participating socially to the same degree as the other students in the classroom? If not, what seem to be the barriers?

If the student is involved in many of the same activities as his or her nondisabled peers but the nature of social involvement is different, the next step is to investigate the cause(s) of the social differences. A common cause of difference is the level and degree of involvement of adults. Unfortunately, it is not unusual for adults (e.g., instructional assistants, teachers, therapists) to accompany a student with disabilities for the majority of the school day. While the intentions may be good, as Giangreco, Edelman, Evans-Luiselli, and MacFarland (1997) found, adults often become the barrier to the student's true participation and class membership. Rather than facilitating the student's involvement in the social and programmatic aspects of instruction, they actually separate students from each other.

Instructional assistants were regularly observed separating the student with disabilities from the class group. Even when the students were basically stationary, such as seated on the rug to hear a story, the instructional assistant often physically separated the student with disabilities from the group by positioning him or her on the fringe of the group (e.g., farthest away from the teacher). Instructional assistants reported that their positioning of the student allowed them to leave the group whenever they chose (Giangreco, Edelman, Evans-Luiselli, & MacFarland, 1997, p. 6). Clearly, adults can become a significant barrier to the student's basic access to naturally occurring social and communication opportunities among students.

FIGURE 14.2 Classroom observation.

Date: 2/25/01 Observer: Mrs. Smith, fourth grade teacher

Time: 11:30–11:40 Environment: Cafeteria

1. Sketch a picture of the environment. Include initials of the students whom you are observing.

2. Does the atmosphere appear to be: positive negative neutral?
   What do you see or hear that would indicate the tone of the atmosphere?

   Children are making plans for recess activities. They are laughing and telling each other jokes.

3. List the students who are interacting together and the topic(s) of their interactions.

   Sara, Juana, and Rose are sitting together and planning what they will play during recess.

   They decide to play on the gym equipment.

   James, Melanie, and Amanda are sitting together talking about a basketball game that they will play during recess.

   Joseph is sitting in between both groups. Occasionally he looks at members of either group but does not break into either conversation. After the lunch bell rings, the two groups run to the playground. Joseph remains at the table. Slowly he moves his wheelchair toward the door. When he is on the playground, he watches the kids playing basketball.

   Question: I wonder if he chose to watch the group playing basketball because he likes those particular children or the game itself?

4. Have you seen these behaviors before, or is this an unusual occurrence? If you have seen them before, when and under what circumstances?

   It seems to me that I have seen this type of situation during other semi-structured activities like art, music, classroom projects. Joseph doesn't appear to initiate interactions with the kids.

   Question: I wonder if Joseph knows how to initiate interactions?

5. At this point, can you take immediate action? Describe the action.

   Gather additional information related to Joseph's ability to initiate and maintain interactions with others. Use the Social/Communication Opportunities form across several environments.*

   Facilitate social bridges by including Joseph in two different cooperative groups. Each group consists of children from the two lunch table groups. This may give information about whether Joseph enjoys one or the other of the two groups.

**Note:* See Figure 14.3, the Social/Communication Opportunities form adapted from Macdonald and York (1989).

To avoid the problems associated with excessive proximity, adults must examine the student's social needs and strengths in a variety of classroom and school environments and in relationship to a variety of the student's friends and classmates. Simultaneously, adults need to examine their own roles and actions in relationship to the students with and without disabilities in order to make an honest determination of whether they are facilitating or inhibiting social connections among students.

Assessment of Individual Student Social Competence. After it is determined that students with and without disabilities have social access to each other, if **social competence** still appears to be a problem, then team members should gather more specific information to answer the question, "What are the barriers that are preventing social connectedness between this particular student and other students in the classroom? Macdonald and York (1989) have developed an assessment tool that can be used to examine how students participate in social and communication opportunities (see Figure 14.3). Classroom personnel can use this observation tool to gather social assessment data in a variety of instructional and noninstructional settings and over several days.

In assessing the specific socialization strengths and needs of an individual student, classroom personnel will be in a better position to develop appropriate interventions. An intervention may involve (a) teaching the student a new skill, or (b) teaching students without disabilities how to interpret the student's communication attempts.

Communication and Behavioral Concerns

Communication and socialization issues are often interrelated with each other, as well as with a student's behavior. Students with physical or health disabilities may demonstrate unusual behaviors for a variety of reasons (e.g., inability to communicate in traditional modes, fear related to an impending medical treatment). A variety of observational assessments may help to identify if a student's communication skills or strategies are facilitators or barriers to participation in classroom activities, as well as in the establishment of friendships. For example, if a student engages in disruptive or unusual behaviors that are bothersome in an attempt to communicate with peers, it may be less likely that peers will want to work at establishing friendships unless they understand the communicative intent of the behavior(s). In such cases, it is important to assess the functional intent of the behavior so that classmates understand the student's communication attempts and members of the educational team can teach the student more acceptable means of communicating. York-Barr, Doyle, and Kronberg (1996) developed a simple tool that can be used in most school and community-based settings to examine the communicative intent of the unusual behaviors (see Figure 14.4). This type of assessment information can be used by the classroom teacher, special educator, and communication specialist to make the appropriate instructional decisions.

Inclusive settings provide hundreds of opportunities for students to communicate every day. It is important for team members, including the general education classroom teacher, to assess formally and informally a student's communication attempts at different points throughout the day. Multiple perspectives provide a rich source of contextually based information that can be used by team members when making decisions related to communication and participation.

FIGURE 14.3 Assessment of communication and socialization skills.

Social/Communication Opportunities

Student: Class: Group Format:		KEY: + Performs consistently +/– Performs inconsistently – Never or rarely No No opportunity			
		Date Initials			
1. Interacts with peers:	a. Responds to others				
	b. Initiates				
2. Interacts with adults:	a. Responds to others				
	b. Initiates				
3. Uses social greetings					
4. Uses farewells					
5. Uses expressions of politeness					
6. Participates in joking or teasing					
7. Makes choices and indicates preferences					
8. Requests help (e.g., for clarification)					
9. Asks questions (e.g., for information, for clarification)					
10. States or indicates:	a. Don't know/understand				
	b. When finished with an activity				
11. Follows directions:	a. For curricular tasks				
	b. For helping tasks/errands				
12. Follows directions:	a. Given to the student individually				
	b. Given to the students as a group				
13. Orients toward speaker					
14. Secures listener's attention before communicating					
15. Takes turns communicating in a conversation with others					
16. Gives feedback:	a. Positive				
	b. Negative (disagrees)				
17. Uses appropriate gestures and body movements when interacting					
18. Uses appropriate language for topic of conversation					
19. Is understood by listeners					
Suggestions or comments:					

Source: Adapted from "Instruction in Regular Classes for Students with Severe Disabilities: Assessment, Objectives, and Instructional Programs" (pp. 83–116), by C. Macdonald and J. York. In J. York, T. Vandercook, and S. Woll (Eds.), *Strategies for full inclusion,* 1989, Minneapolis: University of Minnesota, Institute on Community Integration.

FIGURE 14.4 Behavioral assessment form.

Student: ____________ Subject: ____________ Date: ____________

Instructional Format: ❐ Lecture ❐ Independent work
❐ Cooperative group ❐ Other, specify: ____________

Instructions: Use this form to assist in determining why students display certain behaviors that are disruptive, perplexing, or otherwise difficult to understand.

Behavior: Describe what the student is doing. How is the student acting? What do you see and hear? Be descriptive.

Cause: What might be causing the student to act in this manner?

❐ Demand or request ❐ Change in activity or location
❐ Task difficulty ❐ Interruption
❐ Lonely, no attention ❐ Illness
❐ Other, specify: ____________ ❐ Do not know

Function: What might the student be trying to communicate?

❐ Wants attention ❐ Needs help
❐ Wants to be involved ❐ Frustration
❐ Anger ❐ Pain or discomfort
❐ Other, specify: ____________ ❐ Do not know

How was the situation handled by staff, the student, and peers?

Source: Adapted from: *Creating Inclusive School Communities: A Staff Development Series for General and Special Educators: Module 3,* by J. York-Barr, M. B. Doyle, and R. Kronberg, 1995, Baltimore: Paul H. Brookes.

Curricular Adaptations

In an overview of assessment procedures and adaptations, it is impossible to identify all of the potential curricular adaptation options that might be considered for any given student. This is especially true for students who have physical or health disabilities, as there is the whole continuum of ability related to ability and participation. The process of identifying the most appropriate adaptation is a matter of problem solving. One gathers information about the student and the instructional context and combines the information to generate the most appropriate and least intrusive adaptation that will support the student's active participation in the given activity. No one adaptation works for all students with physical or health disabilities. Each student must be considered individually and requires an individualized assessment plan and appropriate adaptations. Thus, we are providing a generic overview that can be applied to each student in the inclusive setting. It is essential that teachers, parents, and related services personnel make appropriate adaptations in response to a given student's needs, strengths, and abilities, whether or not the student has a disability!

As educators, we routinely make changes in (i.e., adapt) our teaching and assessment procedures to support the daily needs of students without disabilities. For example, if a student is not feeling well on the day of an exam, it is likely that the teacher would allow the student to take the exam on another day. Or, if a student's parents are in the midst of a divorce, it is likely that the same consideration would be given relative to exams and assignments. Obviously, accommodation is necessary in unusual circumstances because the overall goal of an assessment is to gather accurate information about a student's needs and abilities under "normal" circumstances.

Similarly, considerations are necessary when students with physical and health disabilities are members of the classroom community. Classroom personnel need to be keenly aware of the individual characteristics (e.g., physical, emotional, health status) of students with disabilities, so they are able to make appropriate adjustments and modifications in short- or long-term curriculum and instruction as well as assessment techniques.

Challenges and opportunities continually emerge when working with students with physical or health disabilities in inclusive classrooms. It is helpful if the classroom-based instructional team shares one framework from which instructional decisions are made; such an approach increases the likelihood that the student's individualized educational needs will be addressed in the most appropriate and least intrusive manner. Kronberg and Filbin (1993) developed a six-step decision-making framework (see Figure 14.5) to identify the necessary adaptations to support the active participation of students with disabilities in general education classes.

The model is based on a discrepancy approach where one compares the performance of two different students given the same activity. While the framework may appear awkward or cumbersome at first, the more frequently it is used by team members, the more likely it will become a natural part of the ongoing assessment and decision-making process within the classroom. Refer to Figure 14.6 for an example of the process.

FIGURE 14.5 Curricular adaptation process.

Step 1: Identify typical daily schedule and activities

Step 2: Delineate needs, strengths, and abilities of the student with disabilities

Step 3: For each scheduled class, identify specific routines and activities

Step 4: Assess the performance of a student without disabilities

Step 5: Observe and compare the performance of the learner with disabilities

Step 6: If the discrepancies have an impact on the student's participation in the activity, brainstorm possible adaptations in areas where the learner is discrepant in performance of the routines or activities

Source: Adapted from *Ideas and Suggestions for Curriculum Adaptations at the Elementary and Secondary Level* (p. 8), by J. Filbin and R. Kronberg, 1993, Colorado Department of Education: Denver.

FIGURE 14.6 Example of the curricular adaptation process.

Step 1: *Identify typical daily schedule and activities*

Michael arrives and departs with peers on a school bus with a lift for his wheelchair. He follows the regular fifth grade schedule. Michael needs four additional breaks during the school day to attend to personal care needs. Michael participates in an after-school activity program with nondisabled peers. He is a member of a local Boy Scout group.

Step 2: *Delineate needs, strengths, and abilities of the student with disabilities*

Michael is proud of his abilities/strengths in the following areas:

- Independent use of a computer to word process his school work
- Independent use of a computer to play computer games with friends
- Increasing number of friends (from one friend to five new friends)
- Ability to respond to the initiations of others
- Ability to activate switches to utilize tape recorders, radios, some computer games
- Can use multiple strategies (e.g., manipulative, number line, and calculator) to solve addition and subtraction problems

Michael would like to work on some of the following areas:

- Independent mobility using his wheelchair
- Independent use of a personal daily schedule
- Increased knowledge and use of grade-level vocabulary across curricular areas
- Increase skills and abilities related to self-advocacy
- Remember to swallow frequently to decrease drooling and to wipe his chin when appropriate

Step 3: *For each scheduled class, identify specific routines and activities*

Michael is in a multi-age fifth/sixth grade classroom and therefore has the same two teachers for all of his academic classes. Generally speaking, the routines are similar:

- Students bring textbook, notebooks, and related materials (e.g., ruler and calculator for math)
- Students sit at round tables in groups of four
- A daily agenda is written on the chalkboard; the agenda includes the daily class and activity schedule, assignments, and reminders
- Students record assignments and reminders in assignment notebooks

Activities for math class:

- Teacher presents the new concept to the whole group, typically using an overhead projector and manipulative
- Students engage with the teacher answering questions. Students are not required to raise their hands to offer contributions
- Using manipulatives that are placed in the center of the tables, students practice the new concept with each other
- Students have an opportunity to practice the new concept independently; the teacher circulates and provides individual assistance during this time

Step 4: *Assess the performance of a student without disabilities*

Routines:

- Most of the students followed the class routine; five students arrived without materials (e.g., pencils, paper)
- Students referred to the agenda, pulled out their assignments from yesterday, and wrote down tomorrow's assignment.

Activity:

Students were actively engaged in the whole-group instruction, practicing with their table mates, and the independent practice. Four students require individual assistance during the independent practice time.

Step 5: *Observe and compare the performance of the student with disabilities*

Highlight the discrepant behaviors when compared with Step 4. Determine the impact of the discrepancies on the activity or routine, curriculum and instruction, and assessment.

1. A paraprofessional pushed Michael's wheelchair to his table. The paraprofessional pulled Michael's materials from a backpack that was attached to the back of his wheelchair and placed the materials on the wheelchair tray. The paraprofessional sat next to Michael.
2. Michael did not offer any answers during the initial phase of whole-group instruction.
3. During the small-group work, Michael did participate when a peer placed some of the materials in front of him and asked Michael to hand him five items to add to the total.
4. Michael smiled whenever a peer initiated any form of interaction. He did not initiate interactions.
5. During independent practice, the paraprofessional worked with Michael. The teacher did not approach Michael.
6. Michael seemed to drool more when he responded to the initiations by his classmates. The paraprofessional constantly wiped his chin.

Step 6: *If the discrepancies have an impact on the student's participation in the activity, brainstorm possible adaptations in areas where the learner is discrepant in performance of the routines or activities*

1. Michael and a student without disabilities can push his wheelchair.
2. Hang the backpack on the side of the wheelchair to increase Michael's ability to access the materials. If he needs help, teach him to ask a peer (rather than the paraprofessional) for assistance.
3. The paraprofessional should avoid constant physical proximity to Michael.
4. During whole-group instruction, the teacher will ask Michael questions that are within his ability range. Simultaneously develop a plan to support Michael to initiate interactions within math class and across settings.
5. During independent practice, both the teacher and paraprofessional float around the classroom offering individual assistance to any student in need. Note, specific effort should be made to ensure that the classroom teacher has opportunities to work with Michael.
6. Contact the physical therapist to conduct an assessment of Michael's physical position while he is in his wheelchair. The addition of a head rest to support his neck and head may provide the necessary stability to decrease his drooling.

Source: Adapted from *Ideas and Suggestions for Curriculum Adaptations at the Elementary and Secondary Level* (p. 8), by J. Filbin and R. Kronberg, 1993, Colorado Department of Education: Denver.

Teaming for Assessment

The **transdisciplinary approach** for the student with a physical or health disability requires a team with a large variety of potential members. Given the potential multiple disabilities and related health concerns that may be associated with an individual student who has physical or health disabilities, it is imperative that the core team members have a logical and consistent strategy to determine team membership that support the tenets and spirit of the Individuals with Disabilities Education Act (IDEA). Specifically, IDEA mandates that related services must "be required to assist a child with a disability to benefit from special education" (IDEA, 1990). Hence, related services must be educationally relevant and necessary. Ideally, members of an educational team work in a collaborative manner to meet the needs of a student within the general education classroom. However, merely assigning professionals and paraprofessionals to work with a student ensures that groups are formed but does not guarantee that a collaborative team will emerge. Collaborative teaming requires a deliberate effort. Giangreco (1996) offers a decision-making process that focuses specifically on the identification of team membership. This approach is called *VISTA: Vermont Interdependent Services Team Approach: A Guide to Coordinating Educational Support Services.* Collaboration is more than a group of professionals agreeing to work with a specific student. It requires problem solving around who is on the team and for what purpose, establishing shared beliefs and assumptions, and clarification of roles and contributions.

Given the likelihood of team membership that extends beyond the general and special educators, you should examine Giangreco's (1996) work to guide you through an intentional decision-making process. For the purposes of this chapter, we will focus solely on the potential roles of the paraprofessional.

Paraprofessionals Assist Classroom Teachers

While not considered a "specialized" support service, it is commonplace for paraprofessionals to assist general educators with the inclusion of students with disabilities in general education classes. This is supported by the substantial increase in the numbers of paraprofessionals working in public schools today. In the 1960s, there were approximately 10,000 paraprofessionals working in schools, while current estimates are 500,000 (Doyle, 1995). Unfortunately, it is uncommon for teachers to plan specifically for how the paraprofessional will provide assistance to the student with a disability and then to assess the effects of the paraprofessional's involvement in the student's active participation in both the academic and social events of the classroom.

The lack of planning around the roles and responsibilities of paraprofessionals has led to a common practice of paraprofessionals maintaining a constant physical presence to the student with disabilities. Under the federal law, this shadowing is not considered "specialized instruction." It is more likely babysitting, and, for many students with disabilities, it can be problematic. Giangreco, Edelman, Evans-Luiselli, and MacFarland (1997) identified eight problems associated with excessive proximity of paraprofessionals to students with disabilities: interference with ownership and responsibility by general educators, separation from classmates, dependence on adults, interference in peer interactions, limitations on receiving competent instruction, loss of personal control, loss of gender identity, and interference with instruction of other students. All of these negative effects can be avoided if the general educator, special educator, and paraprofessional engage in a continuous cycle of planning, assessment, and decision making.

In situations where a paraprofessional has been hired to assist a student with disabilities to access and participate in the general education classroom, the first and most important assessment question that the classroom teacher must ask is, "Whose student (i.e., the student with disabilities) is this?" If the answer is "the paraprofessional is responsible for the student with disabilities," then the possibility of supporting the student's social and academic involvement as a member of the classroom community is virtually impossible. The paraprofessional's presence is likely to result in some or all of the negative effects identified by Giangreco et al. (1997). This is particularly true if the instructional personnel have defined the paraprofessional as a "one-to-one" assistant, because the most common misinformation is that the phrase "one-to-one" means that the paraprofessional works only with the student with disabilities and the classroom teacher works with the rest of the students in the classroom. A more logical way to describe a general education classroom with both a teacher and a paraprofessional is to consider the characteristics and needs of all the students in the classroom and determine the appropriate role for each adult to maximize the overall educational experience for all of the students. It is important to include the student with disabilities in the phrase "all students."

However, if the answer to the original query (i.e., Whose student is this?) is "This is my (i.e., general educator's) student, and the paraprofessional is here to assist me in meeting the needs of all of the students in my classroom," then the possibilities are endless! An initial clarification and assessment of the roles and responsibilities associated with the classroom teacher's duties and the paraprofessional's duties as they relate to all of the students in the classroom is a perfect place to begin. Figure 14.7 lists several specific tasks that may need to be performed in a classroom where a student with physical disabilities or other health impairments is a member. As you progress through this list, you may want to add items that reflect your specific classroom situation.

After the classroom-based team (e.g., teacher, special educators, related services personnel, paraprofessional) have clarified their roles and responsibilities, the next step is to identify the areas in which individual team members require training, modeling, and feedback and determine who will provide these services. As a teacher, reexamine the items in Figure 14.7 using the following categories:

N = No training necessary
T = Need training
M = Need specific modeling
F = Need feedback

After team members have determined their training needs, they can develop and implement an action plan where training priorities are listed. As the action plan is being implemented, it will be important for members of the team to be aware of the likelihood for training to continue in a variety of areas. Given the complexities and realities of inclusive classrooms and the changing needs of students with physical or health disabilities, it is impossible to anticipate all of the training needs in advance. However, if team members are constantly engaged in a cycle of curriculum and assessment, the needs will emerge.

FIGURE 14.7 Roles and responsibility clarification.

Responsibilities	Classroom Teacher	Special Educator	Paraprofessional	Other
1. Plan instruction				
2. Implement instruction				
3. Evaluate instruction				
4. Grade student work				
5. Assign report card grades				
6. Facilitate large-group instruction				
7. Facilitate small-group instruction				
8. Implement teacher-designed instruction				
9. Contribute ideas and reinforce instructional content				
10. Participate in team meetings				
11. Identify curricular modifications				
12. Develop curricular modification				
13. Evaluate effectiveness of curricular modifications				
14. Perform clerical and organizational tasks (e.g., attendance records, lunch count)				
15. Monitor students in common areas (e.g., hallway, playground)				
16. Supervise during snacks and meals				
17. Provide specified personal care (e.g., toileting assistance, feeding assistance)				
18. Physically position student to maximize participation				
19. Administer prescribed medical procedures				

Summary

Students with physical disabilities or other health impairments represent very diverse populations, and the differences within the populations are far reaching. Assessment and decision making must be based on clear logic, established best educational practice, and the context within which the students live, work, and play. The purpose of assessment is to gather meaningful information about the needs, interests, and abilities of children and youth. Therefore, the assessment process needs to be flexible enough to allow members of the educational team to gather meaningful information in both breadth and depth. For this particular group of students, assessment is not focused on selection or design of unique assessment tools. Rather, assessment will focus on adaptation of existing instruments and techniques selected based on academic, behavioral, and social assessment needs. Assessment and curricular interventions need to accommodate the unique response modes and physical abilities and disabilities of each student.

REFERENCES

Bigge, J. L. (1991). *Teaching individuals with physical and multiple disabilities.* New York: MacMillan.

Caldwell, T. H., Sirvis, B. P., Still, J., Still, M., Schwab, N., Jones, J., Anderson, B., Blanchard, R., & Appel, S. (1997). Students who require medical technology in school. In S. Porter, M. Haynie, T. Bierle, T. H. Caldwell, & J. S. Palfrey, *Children and youth assisted by medical technology in educational settings: Guidelines for care* (2nd ed.) (pp. 3–18). Baltimore: Paul H. Brookes.

Caldwell, T. H., Sirvis, B. P., Todaro, A. W., & Alcouloumre, D. S. (1991). *Special health care in the schools.* Reston, VA: Council for Exceptional Children.

Doyle, M. B. (1995). *A qualitative inquiry into the roles and responsibilities of paraeducators who support students with severe disabilities in inclusive classrooms.* Unpublished doctoral dissertation, University of Minnesota, Minneapolis.

Federal Register. (1977, August 23). *42*(163), 42474–42518.

Filbin, J., & Kronberg, R. (1993). *Ideas and suggestions for curriculum adaptations at the elementary and secondary level,* p. 8. Colorado Department of Education: Denver , CO.

Giangreco, M. (1996). *VISTA: Vermont Independent Services Team Approach: A Guide to Coordinating Educational Support Services.* Baltimore: Paul H. Brookes.

Giangreco, M. F., Edelman, S. W., Evans-Luiselli, T., & MacFarland, S. (1997). Helping or hovering? Effects of instructional assistant proximity on students with disabilities. *Exceptional Children, 64*(1), 7–18.

Individuals with Disabilities Education Act of 1990 (IDEA), P.L. 101476. (October 30, 1990). Title 20, U.S.C. 1400 et seq: *U.S. Statutes at Large, 104,* 1103–1151.

Macdonald, C., & York, J. (1989). Instruction in regular classes for students with severe disabilities: Assessment, objectives, and instructional programs. In J. York, T. Vandercook, & S. Woll (Eds.), *Strategies for full inclusion* (pp. 83–116). Minneapolis: University of Minnesota, Institute on Community Integration.

Palfrey, J. S., Haynie, M., Porter, S., Bierle, T., Cooperman, P., & Lowcock, J. (1992). Project school care: Integrating children assisted by medical technology into educational settings. *Journal of School Health, 62*(2), 51.

York-Barr, J., Doyle, M. B., & Kronberg, R. (1996). *Creating inclusive school communities: A staff development series for general and special educators: Module 3b, Curriculum as everything students learn in school: Individualizing learning outcomes* (pp. 3b, 47b). Baltimore: Paul H. Brookes.

AUTHOR INDEX

SUBJECT INDEX